Social Consequences of Internet Use

Also by James E. Katz and Ronald E. Rice

The Internet and Health Communication (coeditors)

James E. Katz

Arms Production in Developing Countries (editor)

Congress and National Energy Policy

Connections: Social and Cultural Studies of the Telephone in American Life

Nuclear Power in Developing Countries (coeditor, with Onkar Marwah)

People in Space: Policy Perspectives for a Star Wars Century (editor)

Perpetual Contact: Mobile Communication, Private Talk, Public Performance (coeditor, with Mark Aakhus)

Presidential Politics and Science Policy

Social Science and Public Policy in the United States (with Irving Louis Horowitz)

Sowing the Serpents' Teeth: The Implications of Third World Military Industrialization (editor)

Ronald E. Rice

Accessing and Browsing Information and Communication (with Maureen McCreadie and Shan-Ju L. Chang)

Managing Organizational Innovation (with Bonnie McDaniel Johnson)

The New Media: Communication, Research, and Technology (editor)

Public Communication Campaigns, 3rd edition (coeditor, with Charles K. Atkin)

Research Methods and the New Media (with Frederick Williams and Everett M. Rogers)

Social Consequences of Internet Use

Access, Involvement, and Interaction

James E. Katz and Ronald E. Rice

The MIT Press
Cambridge, Massachusetts
London, England

This book was set in Sabon on 3B2 by Asco Typesetters, Hong Kong.
Printed and bound in the United States of America.

Library of Congress Cataloging-in-Publication Data

Katz, James E.
 Social consequences of internet use : access, involvement, and interaction/
James E. Katz and Ronald E. Rice.
  p. cm.
 Includes bibliographical references and index.
 ISBN 0-262-11269-8 (hc. : alk. paper)
 1. Internet—Social aspects—United States. 2. Digital divide—United States.
3. Telecommunication—Social aspects—United States. I. Rice, Ronald E.
II. Title.
HM851 .K38 2002
303.48′33′0973—dc21   2002022765

To Charlotte and Robert Rowe
and Gregg, Steven, and Jeff Rice

Contents

List of Boxes, Tables, and Figures   xi

Preface   xvii

    The First National Random Study of the Internet's Social
Consequences   xvii

    What Hath the Mouse Wrought?   xviii

    The Syntopia Project   xx

    Acknowledgments   xxii

1   **America and the Internet: Access, Involvement, and Social
Interaction   1**

    Making Sense of the Internet   1

    Three Central Social Issues of the Internet: Access, Civic and
Community Involvement, and Social Interaction and
Expression   4

    Major Dystopian Liabilities Claimed   6

    Major Utopian Possibilities Proclaimed   11

    Syntopian Realities   13

I   **Access**

2   **Access: Basic Issues and Prior Evidence   17**

    Conceptualization and Consequences of Access   18

    The Dystopian Perspective   20

    The Utopian Perspective   30

    Conclusion   34

3   **Access and Digital Divide: Results   35**

    Factors Influencing Awareness and Usage   35

Nonusers and Users across the Survey Years   38
A Persistent but Declining Digital Divide   39
Differences in Usage by Cohort and Survey Year across
Demographics   41
Awareness   48
Combined Influences on Usage and Awareness   50
Motivations for Internet Usage: Nonusers and Users, Recent and
Long-Term Users, 1995 and 2000   55
Results from the Pew Internet and American Life Project Survey,
March 2000   61
Conclusion   65

4   **Logging Off: Internet Dropouts**   **67**
Results   68
Discussion   80
Conclusion   81

5   **Access and Digital Divide Examples**   **83**
Perspective on the Digital Divide   83
Access: An Important Human Right   84
Access Programs to Overcome Group or Individual Isolation   86
Access for Self-Identity and Advancing Personal Interests   88
Reducing Barriers to Accessing Culture   89
Interest in Access Limited by a Lack of Perceived Usefulness   91
Recurring Problems with Attempts to Overcome the Digital
Divide   94
Barriers Are Cultural and Social, Not Technological   96
Conclusion   99

II   **Civic and Community Involvement**

6   **Civic and Community Involvement: Basic Issues and Prior
Evidence**   **103**
Civic and Political Involvement   103
Community Involvement   114
A Broader Question of Impacts   129
Conclusion   132

7 Political Involvement: Survey Results   135
Offline and Online Political Activity   135
Related Results from the Pew 2000 Surveys   146
Conclusion   149

8 Community Involvement: Survey Results   153
Involvement in Religious, Leisure, and Community
Organizations   153
Conclusion   159

9 Involvement Examples: Evidence for an "Invisible Mouse"?   161
Social-Support Networks   163
Family   166
Personal Social Networks: Maintaining, Restoring, and
Affirming   170
Involvement with Life and Death: Keeping Memory Alive   172
Sex as a Motive for Involvement with the Internet   172
Community Building: Political Involvement   174
Community Building: Ethnic, Cultural, and Historical Affiliation
and Enrichment   183
Community Building: Social and Recreational   186
Altruistic Endeavors Encourage Involvement Feelings   195
Negative Consequences of Certain Forms of Involvement   198
Conclusion   199

III Social Interaction and Expression

10 Social Interaction and Expression: Basic Issues and Prior
Evidence   203
The Dystopian Perspective   204
The Utopian Perspective   207
Potential Transformations   223
Conclusion   224

11 Social Interaction: Survey Results   227
Offline Interaction by Users and Nonusers   227
Additional Offline Analyses for 1995   235
Additional Offline Analyses for 2000   239

Online Interaction   239
Additional Online Analyses for 1995   247
Additional Online Analyses for 2000   249
Results from the Pew March 2000 Survey   254
Conclusion   261

12 **Interaction and Expression: Self, Identity, and Homepages   265**
What Self?   266
Counterexamples to the Postmodern Argument   271
The Personal Homepage as Presentation of an Integrated Self   277
Conclusion   282

13 **Interaction and Expression Examples   285**
Interaction to Form Social Ties and Relationships   285
Self-Expression: An Underestimated Aspect of the Internet   295
Self-Expression Leading to Interaction with Others   298
Political Expression   310
Self-Expression, Self-Identity, and Human Memory   315
Conclusion   317

IV Integration and Conclusion

14 **Access, Involvement, Interaction, and Social Capital on the Internet: Digital Divides and Digital Bridges   321**
Summary of Basic Issues and Survey Results   321
The Internet: Access, Involvement, Interaction, and Social Capital   327
Conclusion   352

Appendixes

A **Methodology   357**
National Telephone Surveys   357
Statistical Analyses   365
User Interviews and Site Samples   369

B **Descriptive Statistics from Surveys   371**

References   411
Index   439

Boxes, Tables, and Figures

Boxes

1.1   Superlative Praise for the Internet: Selected Comments from the Internet about the Internet   2

5.1   Local Initiatives Speed the Internet's Arrival to an Isolated County   85

5.2   How the Blind Access the Internet   87

5.3   Bringing the Internet to the Inner Cities   88

5.4   Local Rock Band Stimulates Fans' Interest via Web Site and E-mail   90

5.5   One Well-Funded Federal Effort to Close the Digital Divide Yields Tepid Results   95

5.6   Highlights of the Morino Institute Report   97

9.1   The First Eight of the Many Support Groups Listed by Yahoo!   164

9.2   Expression of Appreciation E-mailed to a Support Group   165

9.3   Reuniting Birth Families via Internet Research   167

9.4   Genealogy Resources at a University of Minnesota Web Site   168

9.5   Topics Available at ⟨www.protest.net⟩   175

9.6   Involvement Opportunities Listed on the Richard Vinroot (Republican, North Carolina) for Governor Web Site, Election 2000   179

9.7   Sample of Web Sites That Serve Communities of Interest   184

9.8   Virtual Baby Shower   188

9.9   Game-Makers' Description of Majestic   194

12.1   Limitations of Privacy on the Internet   273

12.2   Example of Anonymity on a Listserv   274

12.3   Follow-up Example of Anonymity on a Listserv   276

13.1   Student Opinions about Online Dating   286

13.2   The Value of Online Dating, from an Online Journal   287

13.3   Looking for a Spouse on the Internet   291

13.4   Comments of a Church Webmaster   297

13.5   A High School Senior's Confession   298

13.6   Examples of Blog Self-Descriptions   300

13.7   Jesse and I Met via My First WebCam Page   301

13.8   Creative Fiction on the Internet   304

13.9   "Uirapuru," by Eduardo Kac: A Multimedia Web Art
        Performance   306

13.10   Joe Arluck   316

13.11   Memorial Web Pages as Catalysts for Expressions of
        Grief   317

13.12   An Online Memorial as an Outlet for Grief and Tribute   317

13.13   Garden of Memories as an Interactive Work in
        Transition   318

Tables

1.1   The Dystopian View of the Consequences of the Internet   7

1.2   The Utopian View of the Consequences of the Internet   12

3.1   Summary Sample Size and Usage Statistics   38

3.2   Sample Sizes, Chi-Squares, and Etas for Cross-tabulations of
        Variables with Nonusers and Users by Survey Year   40

3.3   Demographic Variables for Users by Survey Year   42

3.4   Demographic Variables for Users by Start Year   44

3.5   Children, Work, and Residency, Nonusers and Users, 1995 to
        2000   46

3.6   Overload and Satisfaction, Nonusers and Users, 1995 and 2000   48

3.7   Frequencies for Some Recoded Variables, 1995 to 2000   49

3.8   Awareness of the Internet by Survey Year   51

3.9   Logistic Regressions Predicting Awareness and Usage of Internet, 1995 to 2000   52

3.10   Extended Logistic Regressions Predicting Awareness and Usage of Internet, 1995 and 2000   54

3.11   Motivations for Internet Use, from Nonusers and Users, 1995 and 2000   56

3.12   Differences in Motives and Obstacles for Recent (less than a year) and Long-Term Users (more than a year)   59

3.13   Demographic Differences between Nonusers and Users, and between Recent and Long-Term Users, from the Pew Survey, March 2000   63

3.14   Logistic Regressions Predicting Internet User Categories from Demographics, from the Pew Survey, March 2000   64

4.1   Dropouts Compared to Users, Overall and by Year, 1995 to 2000   70

4.2   Logistic Regressions Predicting Dropouts by Selected Demographics, Overall and by Year, 1995 to 2000   77

7.1   Questions about Offline and Online Political Activity and about the Political Importance of Media   137

7.2   Principal Components (Dimensions) of Offline Political Activity, Importance of Media, and Online Political Activity   139

7.3   Predicting Voting and Offline Political Activity by Demographics and Internet Use and Nonuse   141

7.4   Predicting Online and Offline Political Activity and the Political Importance of Media from Demographics and Internet Usage   143

7.5   Beliefs Regarding the Personal Impact of the Internet   144

7.6   Dimensions and Loadings of Outcomes Concerning Political Awareness, Information, and Privacy   145

7.7   Predicting Political Outcomes from Demographics, Online Political Activity, Political Importance of Media, and Internet Usage   147

8.1   Internet Usage and Community Involvement, 1995 and 2000   154

8.2   Predictors of Membership in One or More of Three Types of Organizations (Religious, Leisure, and Community) by Demographics and by Internet User and Nonuser, 1995 and 2000   156

8.3   Differences in Membership in Mean Number of Three Types of Organizations, for Internet Users and Nonusers, 1995 and 2000   158

8.4   Predicting Membership in Total of Three Types of Organizations   159

9.1   Statistics on GenConnect   169

11.1   Interactions of Internet Users, 1995 and 2000   229

11.2   Differences in Offline Media Use and Online Interactions, by Types of User and Levels of Expertise, 1995 and 2000   230

11.3   Logistic Regressions Predicting Offline Media Use and Online Interactions, by Demographics, Types of User, and Levels of Expertise, 1995 and 2000   232

11.4   Sociability and Internet Usage: Differences and Predictors, 1995   236

11.5   Additional Variables from the 2000 Survey   240

11.6   Differences between Users and Nonusers on Sociability and Media Measures, 2000   244

11.7   Predicting Internet Usage and Nonusage by Sociability and Media Measures, and Controlling for Demographics, 2000   245

11.8   Predicting Online Interaction from Sociability, Controlling for Demographics and Usage, 1995   248

11.9   Differences between Low-Belonging and High-Belonging Groups on Usage, 2000   250

11.10   Predicting Online Interaction from Sociability, Controlling for Demographics and Usage, 2000   253

11.11 Differences in Media Use and Sociability between Nonusers and Users and between Recent and Long-Term Users, from Pew March 2000 Survey   255

11.12 Online and E-mail Activities, of Various Subsets of User, from the Pew Survey, March 2000   257

11.13 Correlations between Selected Outcomes and Usage Measures, from the Pew Survey, March 2000   260

11.14 Linear Regressions Predicting Selected Outcomes from Usage Measures, from the Pew Survey, March 2000   262

13.1 Comparative Attributes of Online Dating Services   288

13.2 Selected Listing of the Largest Archives of Fan Fiction and Number of Stories, July 2001   303

14.1 Definition, Rationale, and Action Environment of Competing Theories of Social Capital   338

A.1 Sample 1995 Demographics versus U.S. Census Data   361

A.2 Sample November 1996 Demographics versus U.S. Census Data   363

B.1 Measures Occurring in at Least Two Surveys, by Survey Year   372

B.2 Descriptive Statistics for Variables Used from the Pew Survey, March 2000 ($n = 3533$)   396

Figures

3.1 Survey Respondents Who Are Users, Former Users, Aware Nonusers, and Not Aware Nonusers   39

4.1 Three User Categories (User, Dropout, and Nonuser) by Income and Age, 1995, 1996, 1997 and 2000   79

5.1 Survey of Attitudes toward the Internet from Three Access Groups   92

14.1 State 1999 Murder Rate by 2000 Putnam Social Capital Index   339

14.2 State 1999 Murder Rate by 2000 Household Internet Use   340

Preface

The First National Random Study of the Internet's Social Consequences

The diminutive computer mouse has roared. The lives of millions of people have been irrevocably changed because of the personal computer and its linkages via the Internet. This much is clear. Less clear—and in fact warmly contested—is how these lives have changed. This book explores the Internet's consequences in three domains of human communication endeavors—access to Internet technology, involvement with groups and communities through the Internet, and use of the Internet for social interaction and expression.

We believe we have the earliest comparative national survey data on the social consequences of the Internet. Our nationally representative quantitative snapshot of the American people's use (and nonuse) of the Internet has shed new light on important questions. Beginning in 1995, we have been able to create an evolving picture of the situation that has been adopted by many other social science research projects.

Our initial reports (Katz & Aspden, 1997a, 1997c) found that the Internet did not increase social isolation but was a source of civic organizational involvement and new personal friendships. A subsequent study of users in Pittsburgh responded to our findings by suggesting that heavy Internet use might lead to depression and isolation (Kraut, Lundmark, Patterson, Kiesler, Mukophadhyay & Scherlis, 1998). Kraut et al. expressed numerous reservations about our findings. The media controversy surrounding these competing views helped highlight and call attention to our earlier work, but sharp questions were raised about which view was correct. The situation became even cloudier when Nie

(2000) also concluded that the Internet harms social cohesion and inter-action. However, in 2000 UCLA (Cole, 1999) and the Pew Internet and American Life Project (Howard, Rainie & Jones, 2001) seemed to con-firm our 1995 findings. When in 2001 researchers at Carnegie-Mellon in Pittsburgh were not able to find further evidence of the so-called Internet paradox (that is, a social technology that made people lonely), our orig-inal conclusions were sustained (Kraut et al., in press). Although science and knowledge are always subject to challenge and change, our national studies appear to have been borne out by our severest critics.

We also discovered what was thought to be a virtually nonexistent group (excuse the pun)—Internet dropouts (our name for people who at one time had Internet access but currently did not have any access). When our research first uncovered this substantial group of people, it was greeted with skepticism. Critics thought that such a group would be invisibly small. We too were surprised at the size of this group, but our subsequent surveys as well as surveys by the Pew Internet and American Life project have confirmed that Internet dropouts are no *rara avis*.

This book, then, is the detailed story of what our research has found. It begins with analysis of the data we collected in the mid-1990s and continues with research done in the twenty-first century. We draw pri-marily on quantitative data to show our points in a rigorous way but also use the scholarly literature and specific qualitative examples to ex-plore the nuances and richness of what is happening.

What Hath the Mouse Wrought?

Part of the reason we have written this book is to respond to arguments that the Internet is harmful or that it is a revolutionary liberating force. We are concerned about the accuracy of these dystopian and utopian views and also about the consequences of accepting an overly negative or overly positive view of the Internet if indeed those views are wrong.

According to the dystopian view, the Internet has had bleak con-sequences, and the future trend is more dismal still. As commercial and technological forces gain control of the Internet, individual users are susceptible to misinformation, deception, and hucksters. The Internet exposes users of all ages to violence, pornography, and hate messages.

Lonely and outcast people waste their time in unreal relationships. To explore whether the Internet is indeed a case of good human intentions that have gone awry, we have looked for evidence of whether the "social technology" known as the Internet decreases interpersonal connection or leads to less real-world participation in community events. Contrary to other analysts, we found that use of the Internet in general has not led to a mass wave of despair and loneliness and has not released on the world armies of disembodied multiple selves acting apolitically. It has not destroyed ordinary social intercourse or turned us into puppets of global corporate capitalism.

According to the utopian view, the Internet provides an overwhelming potential for the development of liberating communities, for exponential increases in human and social capital, and for the achievement of each individual's full democratic participation in every policy decision. In essence, utopians maintain that the Internet's revolutionary nature frees people and groups to achieve an egalitarian, multimedia information society. Just as we do not agree in the main with the dystopian view, we do not find that the Internet has ushered in an era of Woodstock-like peace and love. It has not lifted from mankind the blight of hate, prejudice, vindictiveness, poverty, and disease—nor will it.

Our view is that neither perspective is correct. The little computer mouse—hooked to a keyboard and a central processing unit and linked with vast networks, servers, and other infrastructure—has acted to weave a rich tapestry of friendship, personal information, and community among people of all nations, orientations, ethnic groups, and economic classes. In a manner not unlike that of Adam Smith's invisible hand of the marketplace, the sum of the mouse movements and keyboard clicks (and increasingly voice and video streams) has allowed individuals and small groups to find common interests, engage in various types of exchange, and create bonds of concern, support, and affection that can unite them. The "invisible mouse tracks" have led around the world, creating electronic and emotional strands among people and their software representations. The result is an intricate tapestry of individuals engaging in what they already do in other arenas, for good or bad, while expanding possibilities for new kinds of thought, interaction, and action.

The big task of saying what *has* transpired requires, literally, a book-length response. This volume is our attempt to provide an answer. In the chapters ahead, we assess the consequences of this process for American society in three significant domains—access, civic and community involvement, and social interaction and expression. To support our arguments, we have relied on national data, much of which was collected in our own surveys. And we have reviewed the uses and abuses of the Internet in a large range of online and offline discussions, reports, publications, research studies, and commentary. As mentioned above, we have supplemented our statistics with cases and data from other researchers, including those of the Pew Internet and American Life Project. (Our thanks to Lee Rainie of the Pew Internet and American Life Project for generously sharing his data with us.) Finally, we have also included specific gleanings from the Internet to show the social forces acting on and stemming from the Internet.

One book cannot cover all aspects of the topic. In this book, we point to a few outstanding summits, offer a glimpse of a few details of those peaks, but leave unexplored the many details and lesser hilltops. Nonetheless, we believe we have provided a worthwhile guide to a perspective about the social consequences of the Internet in the area of access, involvement, social interaction and self-expression.

The Syntopia Project

We seek not only to evaluate the answers proposed by a variety of commentators, researchers, policy advocates and industry proponents but to propose our own view as well. We refer to this view as *syntopia*, and thus the name of our initiative is the Syntopia Project. The Syntopia Project team was originally headed by James E. Katz and Philip Aspden; Ronald E. Rice joined as a coprincipal in 1999 and has contributed mightily to the project since then. Our joint aim has been to create—through a series of national random telephone surveys—a multiyear program that charts the social aspects of Americans' Internet behavior. We began work in 1994, fielded our first surveys in 1995, and fielded surveys again, with variations, in 1996, 1997, and 2000. These surveys appear to have been the first to use national random telephone survey methods to track social and community aspects of Internet use, to compare users and nonusers, to identify and analyze Internet dropouts, and to identify and analyze those still unaware of the Internet.

We chose the word *syntopia* for our project for several reasons. First, we have looked at a wide array of emerging communication technologies, including the Internet, the mobile phone, and related technologies. Although we focus on the Internet, the Internet is one of many tools that people use to communicate. Our analysis also touches on technologies such as newspapers, magazines, television, and the telephone. Thus, an important aspect of the syntopia concept is that the Internet is part of a much larger fabric of communication and social interaction. Second, in this connection, focusing exclusively on the online world can be misleading. People do have a physical embodiment, and their actions online are influenced by their physical and social situation and history. Likewise, what they learn and do online spills over to their real-world experiences. Our neologism *syntopia* underscores this synergy across media and between mediated and unmediated activities.

Third, the term *syntopia* is drawn from the Greek *syn* ("together") and *topia* ("place"), so the word means literally "together place," which is how we see the Internet (and associated mobile communication) and its interaction with unmediated interpersonal and community relations. *Syntopia* invokes both utopian and dystopian visions of what the Internet does and could mean. At the same time, it brings these two visions together symbolically and alludes to the Internet's dark side in the homophone *sin*. Other nominal connections are *synthetic* and *syntheses*, all of which are appropriately evocative and fit with our project results to date. The Internet is a place for people to interact, express themselves, emote, and find new friends. It is also a place in which people seek to hurt, cheat, and exploit others. The Syntopia Project aims to identify what these activities mean for issues ranging from social and community involvement to friendship formation and webcams.

In the Syntopia Project, we have relied heavily on quantitative survey data to provide a rigorous base on which to build insights and understand the broad flow of social change. But we also draw on an array of ethnographic observations, case histories, and concrete examples to develop a nuanced and detailed understanding of peoples' uses of and reactions to the Internet.

Something as vast as the Internet cannot be covered in any detail in one volume, and we therefore have no intention of dealing with e-commerce, entertainment, personal information privacy, telecommunications convergence, or a host of other issues that do not bear directly on our interests in the social aspects of the Internet in the areas of access, civic and community involvement, and social interaction and expression. Sex is a big business on the Internet, but as we are not covering commercial issues, we also bypass commercial sex. However, romance and finding meaningful relationships (at many levels) are something we do address.

Our suggestions for how to read this book are that those who seek an in-depth treatment of prior research into the social consequences of the Internet should read chapters 2, 6, and 10. Readers who would rather focus on our findings and interpretations might want to just skim these chapters as they are designed more for the research audience. Quantitative analysis of our surveys are presented in chapters 3, 4, 7, 8, and 11. Qualitative analysis of the Internet may be found in chapters 5, 9, 12, and 13. Chapter 14 presents our overall conclusions.

The authors can be reached at the following addresses:

James E. Katz: ⟨jimkatz@scils.rutgers.edu⟩
                    ⟨www.scils.rutgers.edu/~jimkatz⟩
Ronald E. Rice: ⟨rrice@scils.rutgers.edu⟩
                    ⟨www.scils.rutgers.edu/~rrice⟩

Acknowledgments

Robert K. Merton stimulated this line of work through a series of discussions he had with Jim Katz during the early to mid-1990s. Bob shared generously of his time and thoughts. As this preface is being written, he continues to illuminate the history and traditions of the social sciences even as he carves out new areas of insight and inquiry for them.

Irving Louis Horowitz deserves special mention for his encouragement and thoughtful comments during the gestation and maturation of this research project. He inspired Jim to seek higher levels of integration and meaning in abundant data. Meanwhile, Irving fights tirelessly on behalf of quality research in all the social sciences and for the protection of human freedoms. To these towering figures, we offer our profound gratitude.

The John and Mary Markle Foundation of New York and The Robert Wood Johnson Foundation of Princeton were the kind lead sponsors of the research reported on in this book. Lee Rainie and the Pew Internet and American Life Project generously shared their data with us.

Philip Aspden was a crucial intellectual collaborator during the first several years of the project. Throughout the research process, he has been an excellent colleague and remains so today. His comprehensive planning, energetic execution, and innovative analyses helped make our early work significant and enduring. His generous sharing of his labor and insights throughout our work is deeply appreciated. Philip is an outstanding team player who has used his enormous abilities in steadfast pursuit of understanding the Internet. He was able to do whatever the task required, from the highest conceptual framing to the tedious data checking and correction. His spirit may be seen throughout this volume. We look forward to new opportunities to work with him in the future.

Our talented colleagues Eleanor Wynn and Warren Reich helped draft early versions of papers that we have released during the course of our research. Some themes and data from those earlier articles rematerialize in this volume. Internet veterans—Mary Ellen Curtin, Maxine Rockoff, and Billy Samples—have generously shared their experiences. Sheri Chaitman, Margaret DeYoung, Leora Lawton, Joseph Rotbart, and Ming Yi made important contributions to the research effort during various project cycles. Jim would like to acknowledge the lively conversations and thoughts from students—including Marissa J. Alexander, Josie Chiu, Anike Elegbe, Maggie Herbasz, Jeannie Rodriguez-Diaz, Jamie Snook, and Noe Tiangco—that have revealed engaging aspects of the Internet. Andy Stein, who also worked with Jim, has been an able researcher and participated in many productive discussions with him. Katherine Innis and Robert Prior at The MIT Press have been enormously constructive, and it has been a pleasure working with them. Deborah Cantor-Adams and Rosemary Winfield performed their usual copy editing magic. Lorrie Cranor and Andrew Blau provided much valuable counsel. We thank these fine people for all their help.

Some of this book was developed from materials that have been published or presented elsewhere, though in all cases the materials have been substantially rewritten, extended, and revised from those earlier pieces: Katz and Aspden (1997a, 1997b, 1997c, 1998), Katz, Rice, and Aspden (2001), Katz and Wynn (1997), Rice (2001b), and Wynn and Katz (1997).

Social Consequences of Internet Use

1

America and the Internet: Access, Involvement, and Social Interaction

People have been curious about how the powerful new information and communication medium known as the Internet is affecting society. Some exuberant opinions are presented in box 1.1.

In the early days of the Internet, speculation was rampant. The Internet quickly attracted scholarly interest, but good representative data about the uses of the Internet and their social consequences were scarce. We were fortunate to have been what appears to have been the first researchers to use national random sampling to investigate the social consequences of the Internet by comparing users to nonusers. We also seem to have been the first to distinguish between those who are were aware of the Internet and those who were unaware of the Internet and to have identified a substantial group we have called "Internet dropouts." Yet despite the "firsts" we can claim, our research was framed against a backdrop of theorizing about the Internet specifically and the impact of new media generally. This chapter provides an overview of contending views of how the Internet has affected U.S. society in three areas—access, involvement, and social interaction.

Making Sense of the Internet

Much has been written about the Internet and what it means for U.S. society and the world. As recently as the early 1990s, information technology experts expected the Internet to be consigned to the trash heap of history. One expert, Mark Resch of Xerox PARC, called it "the CB radio of the 1990s" (Perkins, 1996)—that is, a craze that would soon pass. Others, such as John Perry Barlow, said that it would be the "most

Box 1.1
Superlative Praise for the Internet: Selected Comments from the Internet about the Internet

---

- "The Internet is the greatest revolution since the invention of the automobile except that its growth is 40 times faster" (Anonymous, n.d.).
- "I think that Internet communication is the greatest invention since electricity" (Moses, 1996).
- "The Internet's influence on disseminating information is equal to Gutenberg's invention of the printing press, which made printing and dispersing information 1,000 times cheaper than had ever been possible before" (Goldsmith, 2000).
- "The Internet makes it possible for people like me to live the way I do now. Without it, I'd have to be in New York or some other city. With it, I have the research resources of a great city, and I'm off on a side road 30 miles from the nearest major shopping center. I think the Internet is the greatest invention in history after antibiotics" (Haddam, 1999).
- "The Internet is the greatest invention of the century, if not ever. The printing press sparked 600 years of ideology, scientific achievement, and discovery, all because it allowed for the exchange of ideas. The Internet is the printing press on souped-up steroids for superheroes" (Sterling, 2000).
- "The Internet is the greatest invention since the light bulb" (Lou Holland of Lou Holland Growth Fund, quoted in Dingle, 1999).
- "The Internet is the greatest invention since the printing press and the telephone" (Anonymous, 1998).
- "The Internet is the greatest invention since the wheel" (Dines, 1998).
- "I think the Internet is the greatest invention since chocolate" (Wanda Hennig of *Diablo Magazine*, quoted in Hennig, 1999).

---

transforming technological event since the capture of fire" (quoted in Putnam, 2000, p. 172). UCLA professor Jeffrey Cole said, "Everyone either loves or hates the Internet, but there's no question that the impact of the Internet is real and profound" (Cole, 1999). The final assessment of the Internet and its impact is yet to be made. What it is and what it does change hourly. Yet few, including ourselves, are willing to wait the intervening years necessary to form a "distant mirror" assessment. To the contrary, the history of the Internet and even the analysis of Internet assessments are themselves growing cottage industries.

The data and consequent analytical insights on what the Internet is and does are always improving, and after more than a decade of experience, society has begun to acquire a substantial foundation of understanding. Besides our own efforts, the federal government's "Falling Through the Net" surveys (⟨www.esa.doc.gov/fttn00.htm⟩) and the Pew Internet and American Life Project (⟨www.pewinternet.org⟩) have shed significant light on the topic.

Before efforts such as these, too often much of what was "known" about the social consequences of the Internet was cast in terms of pre-existing broad beliefs about human behavior. Some of this was predicated on computer-mediated communication (CMC) work that had gone before. Other work grew out of scholars' and media commentators' own predispositions and experiences. Throughout the 1990s and largely still today, researchers' interpretations of what the Internet "is" or "does to people" reflected these preexisting frameworks.

For example, Marxists, rational-choice advocates, or feminists would see the Internet reproducing (or suppressing) precisely those phenomena that they had identified in other realms of discourse. So if in the 1960s someone thought that communication technology was dominated by ex-ploitative capitalistic corporations, then his or her research in the 1990s on the Internet "found" that this trend had continued. If researchers believed that television was bad for kids, then they found that the Inter-net was bad for kids. If they once thought that people in developing countries could use communication technology to advance their material well-being and overthrow local elites, then, by gosh, the Internet would help advance those processes as well. It is not surprising that analysts apply their preexisting worldviews (*Weltanschauungen*) to the Internet. The process of extending domain perspectives to new material occurs everywhere. But when in the absence of good data people argue from preexisting views, little in the way of new perspectives can be offered.

As a result, we have not understood the actual impact and con-sequences of the Internet. There have been various assessments of how the Internet is affecting American society. And, of course, what the Internet actually has been is different from what it is and from what it will be. Despite the existence of some important variations in themes, we find it helpful for our analysis to categorize these views into three central social issues—access, involvement, and interaction—and two contradic-tory perspectives about the outcomes of Internet use for those issues—dystopian and utopian.

The book's three sections correspond to these three vital issues concerning Internet and human communication—access, civic and community involvement, and social interaction and expression. Each section reviews the theory and research to date, summarizes what our data say about the issue, and highlights some qualitative examples of Internet sites and experiences. By combining quantitative and qualitative analysis, we hope to provide mutual reinforcement for our findings. By considering these sources of information and developing an argument about how individuals interact with each other through the Internet to create both individual and collective outcomes (whether costs or benefits), we hope to present a coherent picture about the Internet's consequences for life in America.

Three Central Social Issues of the Internet: Access, Civic and Community Involvement, and Social Interaction and Expression

Before we present and discuss the data, we present our definitions of the three central social issues of the Internet—access, civic and community involvement, and social interaction and expression.

Access
We define *access* in a minimal way. If a person with (or without) effort can have access to a networked computer and is able to use that networked computer to find material (such as webpages) or to communicate with others (such as through e-mail), then that person has access to the Internet. Having knowledge of what is there with no means of obtaining it or having technology but no knowledge of how to use it does not constitute access.

Access to the Internet is important at the levels of economic activity, social interaction, awareness of current events, and political monitoring. It has been a major hallmark of federal efforts surrounding the Internet and of numerous initiatives by nonprofit organizations and foundations. Hundreds of millions of dollars are raised annually through telecommunications taxes to subsidize access via the Universal Service Fund Fee. Yet these efforts should be driven not only by a concern about the costs and penalties of a "digital divide" but also by an understanding of the contours and qualities of such a digital divide so that educational and assistance resources can be most effectively targeted.

Civic and Community Involvement

Involvement as we use it means participation in a jointly produced social, civic, or community activity. Involvement requires a person to participate and interact with others. Involvement can generate benefits and costs at two levels—the individual and the collective. At the individual level, people spend time, money, effort, and psychological commitment to acquire a wide range of benefits, from intrinsic enjoyment to extrinsic financial rewards and influence. At the collective level, organized interaction among motivated participants can generate resources and influences that would not otherwise be available to any particular individual and that may actually generate even more subsequent benefits. For example, civic involvement aimed at fostering political awareness and activity creates more informed and active citizens. This in turn makes political processes more deliberative and representative, thus helping to achieve a more democratic society. Community involvement creates a greater understanding of salient community issues and helps to create and maintain social capital. One's involvement in civic and community structures might well include many people with whom that individual might not actually meet or even communicate with directly.

Social Interaction and Expression

Social interaction includes both the exchange of information among individuals and groups online and the influences of online interaction on offline communication, both face to face and through other media (such as the telephone). Social interaction is more focused on individual relations and goals than is city and community involvement and entails interaction with specific others whom one either knows initially or eventually comes to know. This interaction is likely to involve dyadic, familial, friendship, romantic, and group relations. It speaks less directly to the interests and goals of collectivities. *Expression* refers to the material that is created by individuals or groups to reflect their views, interests, or talents. These materials are produced for the observation, interest, or response of their creators and, usually, others. Expression also represents a view, perspective, reflection, or quality of the individuals or groups that produce the material. This expression may be in any externally perceptible form, including text, sound, or image.

We distinguish at times between self-expression and other types of expression. At some level all expression is individual expression, but we use the term to mean the process of making public some internal aspect of the self. Self-expression blends ineluctably with group expression. People can express their thoughts through Web pages for others to view, listen to, and interact with; people can also work with others on joint expression, such as making music; or they can collaborate on a group project where no single contributor is identifiable in the finished product. Here we would distinguish between the act and the motive: self-expression can be thought of as designed for the gratification of the individual ("getting it out") rather than for the benefit and appreciation of the audience.

Major Dystopian Liabilities Claimed

These are three important issues, and the two opposing perspectives—dystopian and utopian—have much to say about them. (Table 1.1 summarizes the dystopian arguments.) An acerbic critic—popular author Caleb Carr (2001)—has written that information technology is

making people dumber: It is teaching them how to assemble massive amounts of information, of arcane minutia, without simultaneously teaching them how to assemble those bits of information into integrated bodies of knowledge.... what we will see is the triumph of corporate interests, the deterioration of educational, environmental, and public health programs, and increased violence in those parts of our country and our world that are left behind in the information-generated scramble for wealth and material satisfaction.

Access

The dystopian perspective says that the digital divide between sociodemographic groups is worsening and that unequal access to digital information and communication technology (and to the advantages they bring) hurts already disadvantaged minorities in both political and economic terms. The cost and complexity of the Internet limit access to information and communication resources by those most in need of

Table 1.1
The Dystopian View of the Consequences of the Internet

Access
Narrows the range of participants
Foments racial division
Limits discourse
Limits economic opportunity
Reduces self-esteem
Stifles political voice
Erodes cultural traditions
Creates cyberbalkanization
Limits benefits
Is inconvenient
Erodes political legitimacy due to lack of representativeness
Reduces individual and overall privacy

Involvement
Destroys local and indigenous cultures
Exploits people
Reduces quality of life
Reduces community involvement
Fragments community, leading to the pursuit of narrow interests and cyberbalkanization
Limits social connections (isolation and anomie)
Stimulates excessive social connections (addiction)
Leads to cyberstalking and even killings
Provokes ethnic and racial strife
Incites hatred of others

Social Interaction and Expression
Is dominated by multinational corporations
Encourages child pornography
Encourages predation on children
Invites emotional swindles
Develops multiple selves that lead to confusion
Kills creativity
Leads to rote learning
Lowers the quality of intellectual products
Allows plagiarism
Lacks artistic integrity
Propagates addictions (to sex, gambling, interaction, violent games, nonviolent games, fantasies)

them—ethnic minorities, the poor, and the elderly. These same groups will also forfeit access to governmental benefits (Cooper & Kimmelman, 1999).

Table 1.1 highlights some reasons that nonaccess and nonparticipation are viewed as socially corrosive. The reasons revolve around the loss of economic, political, and social opportunities. The bad effects of nonparticipation are also viewed as fundamental harms to the quality of life. As the economy becomes more information oriented, those who do not have access to information will be marginalized and put at a great economic disadvantage (a process that has been referred to as *cyberbalkanization*). Concomitant with economic benefits are political benefits: without access to information resources, the political voice of minorities will be stifled.

Critics also say that the Internet reinforces the power of pernicious cosmopolitan groups at the expense of virtuous local groups. A common claim is that commercial interests and multinational capitalistic enterprises will use the Internet to suppress small-group enterprise, isolate peripheral groups, and erode the hard-earned income of poor or minimally educated people. Long-time observer of cyberspace Howard Rheingold raises precisely this specter when he writes: "The odds are always good that big power and big money will find a way to control access to virtual communities; big power and big money always found ways to control new communications media when they emerged in the past. The Net is still out of control in fundamental ways, but it might not stay that way for long. What we know and do now is important because it is still possible for people around the world to make sure this new sphere of vital human discourse remains open to the citizens of the planet before the political and economic big boys seize it, censor it, meter it, and sell it back to us" (Rheingold, 1993, p. 193).

Civic and Community Involvement

Critics see Internet participation as bad for those who participate in it. Worse, the bad effects of Internet surfing do not end with the individual surfer: society itself is impoverished by the Internet.

One criticism notable for its heated and protracted character has been that the Internet erodes vigorous civic and community participation and thus social capital, which are vital to the continued well-being of society and even to the survival of democracy. Influential writers from academia, including Sherry Turkle at the Massachusetts Institute of Technology (1996) and Robert Putnam at Harvard University (2000), have expressed concerns over the declining quantity and quality of community involvement in U.S. society. Among the worrying trends they see are decreasing levels of organizational participation, declining interpersonal trust, and decreasing social contact. The culmination of these trends could lead to a breakdown of civil society, with catastrophic consequences. But even the less catastrophic consequences they predict include a drastically lowered quality of life along many continua, from public safety to elder care. Perhaps not surprisingly, television viewing and the values that many programs promote have traditionally been seen as an important cause of this worrisome trend.

But with growing intensity and anxiety, social critics have fingered the Internet as a culprit for another, possibly more profound cause of decline. They fear that time spent surfing on the Internet displaces "real-world" life, friendships, and community involvement, with consequential damage to social capital and democratic participation. This view has been advanced in several books, ranging from *Silicon Snake Oil: Second Thoughts on the Information Highway* (Stoll, 1995) to *Highway of Dreams: A Critical View along the Information Superhighway* (Noll, 1997). Noll sees the Internet as a bleak waste of time and without interest, while Stoll sees that it takes away valuable time for real life: "Every hour that you're behind the keyboard is sixty minutes that you're not doing something else" (Stoll, 1995, p. 14). There seem to be huge productivity costs as well, with corporations losing hundreds of years of their employees' time due to excessive and inappropriate use of the Internet. In one provocative example, a network traffic analysis of a popular erotic site claims to show that 300 "workyears" of time are spent every workday viewing the site. The site proprietor extrapolates that, at an employee pay rate of $24 per hour, his site is costing the world economy $8 billion annually in wasted time (Igor, 2001).

Social Interaction and Expression

Stoll (1995) is one of many who argue that a lack of authenticity in Internet relationships often leads to disastrous consequences. The media have prominently covered exploitation of the young by predators that they encountered on the Internet, and accordingly, political leaders have sought to regulate Internet-related content and behavior, both here and in foreign countries.

At another level, some have expressed concerns about the impact of the Internet on the nature of reality itself. The arguments generally are oriented around the pseudo nature of the online experience and its spill-over into real life. Here one line of attack has been the postmodern view that the Internet only temporarily shields but ultimately heightens the despair and emptiness of existence. Thus, Jean Baudrillard has cleverly compared the Internet to Disneyland. Like the theme park, he claims, cyberspace creates an imaginary effect by "concealing that reality no more exists outside than inside the bounds of the artificial perimeter" (Baudrillard, 1983, p. 26). Norman Nie of Stanford University claims that the Internet is causing "aloneness and anomie." Further, the time that users spend on the Internet comes out of the time "spent in social activities within the household and outside the household with friends and family" (Nie, 2000).

Irony is often an important element in arguments about the Internet's impact. One variation on this, which reflects a thread of Baudrillard's argument, has been the work of Kraut and colleagues (Kraut, Lundmark, Patterson, Kiesler, Mukophadhyay & Scherlis, 1998) that too much use of the Internet, a supposedly social technology, will make people iso-lated. This is the flip side of one of Stoll's arguments, which is that too much online contact will make people forget what is truly important.

A second line of attack, also with an ironic twist, has been the exami-nation of attempts at "personalization" via the Internet and other com-munication technologies. Critics hold that attempts to make the user's experience more personally meaningful are actually counterproductive, yielding instead a homogenizing sense of mass society and depersonali-zation. Thus James Beniger (1987, p. 369) argues:

The development of countless technologies with which to personalize mass com-munication has brought forth a new infrastructure for major societal change, a reversal of a centuries-old trend from organic community—based on inter-personal relationships—to impersonal association integrated by mass means. Increasingly we will experience the superficially personal relationships of pseudo-
\mmunity, a hybrid of interpersonal and mass communication—born largely of
\puter technology.

Major Utopian Possibilities Proclaimed

The Internet is also characterized by superlative claims about real and potential benefits, as highlighted above (see box 1.1). Table 1.2 lists some of the many positive effects either anticipated or claimed to have been realized by the Internet, relative to the three social issues of access, involvement, and interaction.

Access

Government programs spend several billion dollars each year in the belief that access to the Internet is good. These programs include preferential access rates for schools and hospitals and community-based hardware and training courses. The rationale for these programs is captured in the 1998 Benton Foundation report, "Losing Ground Bit by Bit": access for these groups can be improved, the rationale claims, then society will benefit from the full economic participation and political enfranchisement of its citizens. Optimists also feel that cross-culture communication is good: when different types of people interact on the Internet, all benefit by creating and sharing ideas, perceptions, and knowledge.

Civic and Community Involvement

Those who see the Internet as good point to the ease with which the Internet can link those interested in certain volunteer activities with the organizations that need them. This cost-efficient coupling will stimulate more people to volunteer since their interests will be more fulfilled. Likewise, since it will be easier to get involved, more will do so and will mobilize resources and solve problems.

Social Interaction and Expression

The Internet is seen as helping people make friends and find life partners (or short-term partners). Families can stay in touch more easily, and information about family history and events can become part of a permanent archive. Many worthwhile audio, visual, or literary works can be produced by people who would not ordinarily have a chance to pursue these activities. Audiences, in the comfort of their homes, can enjoy these various artistic endeavors.

Table 1.2
The Utopian View of the Consequences of the Internet

Access
Overcomes differences such as
  Geography
  Social class
  Race and ethnicity
  Age
  Sex
  Time zone
  Chronology (older materials are available, and contributions are less ephemeral than with other media)
  Ideology
Offers more opportunities for participation
Identifies new talent, which enriches culture
Encourages greater tolerance

Involvement
Overcomes physical and temporal constraints on community boundaries
Revives community
Increases volunteerism
Creates shared information and community views
Spurs activism beyond a local region
Enriches cultural production
Complements offline relations

Social Interaction and Expression
Is social, diverse, and frequent
Complements and strengthens offline interactions
Allows friendships to form
Maintains or restores relationships with family and friends
Helps young users to develop their identity and become socialized into adult roles
Monitors infants, baby-sitters, and classrooms
Regenerates writing and correspondence
Allows new creative arts to be expressed

Syntopian Realities

We argue that the both the dystopian nightmares and utopian day-dreams are too extreme. Although we do find some evidence that could be construed as support for just about any possible assertion about the Internet, in the main we find that its primary use by Americans is as an extension and enhancement of their daily routines. We also have found some surprising twists and unanticipated uses. Often these uses focus on self-expression and the search for social interaction. Yet these activities also result in new forms of social cooperation and integration. So just as the Internet allows us to be focused and narrow in our interests and in some sense isolates us from certain people or groups, it also intro-duces us to yet other people and groups and creates sets of integrating emotional and social bonds. It thus encourages specialization and differ-entiation while also encouraging new forms of interactions and organi-zations. This is one sense we have in mind when we refer to the "invisible mouse."

In another sense, the Internet allows us to become ever more ourselves while also creating social capital for the benefit of individuals and com-munities. It enables people to use cultural attributes to recognize them-selves and construct meaning (Skog, forthcoming). This aspect of the Internet, incidentally, is referred to by some as "an identity project." When syntopian tools become easily available, identity can more readily become multifaceted, personal, self-reflexive, and subject to innovation compared to earlier eras. In terms of information, physical mobility, and latitude of acceptable morality and forms of expression, these earlier eras were more constricted (Kellner, 1992).

The Internet is not something that exists in isolation. It is a venue where interaction occurs, yet that interaction is grounded in real people (software creators), their creations (programmed responses), and the people who interact with that software and with other people. And these others have a physical reality and place, even if widely distributed on different continents and different computer servers. The Internet also fits into larger communication environments, including mobile communica-tion, letters, phone calls, magazines, newspapers, television, radio, and face-to-face interaction with family and friends.

These three themes—access, civic and community involvement, and social interaction and new forms of expression—are not mutually exclusive definitions. For example, it is reasonable to question whether distinctions between online expressions and group involvements are meaningful. In the following chapters, we present our research findings on activities in each of these three areas and draw conclusions from them about the Internet's extension of more traditional modes of communication.

I

Access

2

Access: Basic Issues and Prior Evidence

The Internet's rapid adoption has raised some sharp social policy questions that reflect both enduring issues and some novel ones generated by the unique character of the technology. In this chapter, we grapple with questions that revolve around the first of our three primary issues—access.

The Internet is being used by many adults and children in the United States, and that usage has increased quickly. The Internet took seven years to achieve a 30 percent level of diffusion into U.S. households: it took the telephone 38 years and the television 17 years to achieve the same level of diffusion. National Science Board data indicate that by 2000, 42% of American adults had access to the World Wide Web (Miller, 2001). The mid-2000 America Online national survey (AOL, 2000) (based on a representative national telephone survey of those 18 or older who have online access in their homes) found that 76 million people (39% of the U.S. population) used the Internet, up from 45 million in 1998. A study by the University of California at Los Angeles in November of 2000 reported that 66.9% of Americans used the Internet; in the first quarter of 2000, approximately 55,000 people each day became new Internet users (UCLA, 2000). In December 2000, a Pew Institute report indicated that 56% of the U.S. population over 18, or 104 million, had access to the Internet (Yahoo!News, 2001). About 75% of students older than 12 and 29% of those under 12 had access to the Internet; 56% of all users went online every day. Just a few months later, a Nielsen/NetRatings report (2001) found 60% of U.S. citizens, or a total of 168 million, used the Internet from home, work, or both. So usage has been increasingly rapidly. But this rapid growth poses some important questions that we intend to answer in the next several chapters: Is there a digital divide between information haves and have-nots? Is it increasing or decreasing? What differences in kinds of access occur across socio-economic social groups? Why is this issue important?

To formulate our answers, we first note the basic conceptualization and implications of Internet access and then group prior research and theory into dystopian and utopian perspectives. Few of the authors whose work we categorize as falling within either of those categories would consider that their positions represent an extreme dystopian or utopian vision. We use those labels simply to represent that many authors take a primarily negative or positive perspective, and we argue for a more synthesized, or syntopian, perspective.

As chapters 6 and 10 do respectively for our themes of involvement and expression, this chapter summarizes and organizes prior work on the concept of the Internet and access and places our subsequent analyses in context. Thus, the chapter covers considerable material. For those not interested in this prior work, we suggest skimming this chapter and reading the concluding section. We return to the main themes of this material, as well as our own results, in chapter 14.

Conceptualization and Consequences of Access

The broadest concept of access examines the people who have or do not have access to the Internet, the motivations of those who use the Internet, the barriers to usage, and the people who stop using the Internet (Katz & Aspden, 1997a, 1997b, 1997c). New technologies may enhance or hinder access to information in a democracy (Deetz, 1989a, 1989b; Dervin, 1980, 1990; Lievrouw, 1994; Murdock & Golding, 1989), in the work-place (Deetz, 1990; Garson, 1988; Kraut, 1989; U.S. Congress, 1987; Zuboff, 1988), or in broader social or cultural contexts (Bourque & Warren, 1987; Dervin & Shields, 1990; Krendl, Broihier & Fleetwood, 1989; Larose & Mettler, 1989; Mulgan, 1991; Pool, 1983; U.S. Congress, 1990; Weinberg, 1987). While new communication technologies can bridge gaps between rich and poor, powerful and powerless, and haves and have-nots and can provide new ways of participating and interacting (for example, Downing, 1989; ECRL, 1999; Freire, 1969; Furlong, 1989; Greenberger & Puffer, 1989; NTIA, 1999; Pfaffenberger,

1990; Schon, Sanyal & Mitchell, 1999), they may also widen existing gaps, further blocking access to those already without access (Gillespie & Robins, 1989; Hudson, 1988; Jansen, 1989; Rubinyi, 1989; Schiller, 1996; Wresch, 1996).

Access is the major public-policy area for those who see the Internet as a universal service and a significant influence on political and economic equity (McCreadie & Rice, 1999a, 1999b; Rice, McCreadie & Chang, 2001). A popular term for this unequal access to and use of the Internet according to sex, income, race, and location is "the digital divide" (Cooper & Kimmelman, 1999; Hoffman & Novak, 1998; Hoffman, Kalsbeek & Novak, 1996; McConnaughey & Lader, 1998).

Overcoming the digital divide is a fundamental implication of the universal service tradition of U.S. telecommunications policy, which aims to ensure that information resources are available for all at affordable prices. More pragmatically, U.S. Department of Commerce statistics show that information technology in general provides significant economic benefits, such as reducing the inflation rate and increasing overall productivity, and constitutes a major section of the economy (McConnaughey, 2001). The Internet and other communication and information technologies can enhance human capital by providing increased access to education and training. Information labor markets will prefer individuals who have both current and prior access to, experience with, and skills necessary for communication networks.

Thus, those who do not have sufficient resources or experience will be further excluded from human and social capital (McNutt, 1998). New applications, software, and technologies require a good understanding of the Internet and existing communication protocols that are already in place, so even if those currently without access become users, they will still be disadvantaged (Carrier, 1998). No or delayed access over the long haul are harmful in less obvious ways, too. Bikson and Panis (1999, p. 156) discovered that employees who used computers in their jobs are paid 10% to 15% higher than noncomputer users who hold similar positions. Besides economic benefits, communication technologies have greatly increased participation in communication activities such as decision making and discussions at the workplace (Carrier, 1998). Individuals with communication and information access are generally better informed about their employers. They are aware of corporate decisions and are usually more prepared to participate in decision-making processes. So there are major social and economic rationales for investing in increased access for all citizens, such as through community networks (McNutt, 1998). For example, Neu, Anderson, and Bikson (1999) describe how e-mail can provide access and general citizen information to the elderly and governmental information to Social Security beneficiaries.

The Dystopian Perspective

An Ongoing and Consequential Digital Divide

Armando Valdez, chair of the California Telecommunications Policy Forum, a group of leaders from ethnic communities who examine the impact of telecommunications policies, has warned that "We are witnessing the fracturing of the democratic institutions that hold us together.... The possibility of an information underclass is growing" (Goslee, 1998). And results from many surveys have reinforced this concern.

Bikson and Panis (1999) summarize results from the *Current Population Survey* (CPS) conducted by the U.S. Bureau of the Census in 1993 (143,129 respondents) and 1997 (123,249 respondents). Concerning network services, in 1997, 7% of individuals over age 60 and 11% under age 20 used them, compared to 33% between ages 20 through 59, all higher than in 1993. When socioeconomic variables were controlled, the gap between the under 20 users and 20 through 59 users decreased significantly. Controlling for other characteristics, the two younger groups have similar usage levels, but usage levels of older adults are still significantly lower. Usage of network services by those in the lowest income quartile (around $20,000) rose from 3% in 1993 to 7% in 1997, while usage by those in the highest quartile (above $60,000 per year) rose from 23% to 45%. Thus the gap associated with income *rose* over those four years, even after controlling for other variables, representing approximately a two-year time lag in adoption of online services between the bottom and top quartile (Bikson & Panis, 1999, p. 12). The U.S. Department of Commerce survey (2000) of over 48,000 households reported that, nonetheless, usage by low- and middle-income groups increased the most (over 70%).

Gaps in use of network services by educational level also rose, with 1993 usage by those without high school diplomas only 1% and by college graduates 34%; these percentages rose to 5% and 56% in 1997 (these differences are statistically significant even after controlling for other factors). National Science Board reports show that while 77% of college graduates had access to the Web, only 40% of those with a high school diploma but no college degree had such access, and only 13% of adults without a high school diploma did (Miller, 2001). The U.S. Department of Commerce report notes that while about 75% of those with a college degree use the Internet, only 3.7% of the least educated do so.

Concerning differences by race and ethnicity in the Bikson and Panis (1999) report, usage between 1993 and 1997 jumped for whites (13% to 28%) and Asians (10% to 25%) but was steady for Hispanics and Native Americans, again showing a widening gap (controlling for other variables). Other studies show that minorities such as blacks and nonwhite Hispanics are less likely to possess home computers, have less access to networks than whites and Asians, and therefore miss the opportunity to participate in Internet activities (Neu et al., 1999).

Differences in network access by sex were slight (approximately 2.5% more by men) yet still remains after statistically controlling for other influences (Bikson & Panis, 1999). There are, however, sex differences within other categories. For example, use by Asian American and Pacific Islander women is 87.4% of the usage rate by Asian American and Pacific Islander men (McConnaughey, 2001).

Finally, 15% of rural people and 25% of urban people used network services in 1997, up from approximately 7% and 12% in 1993. This reveals a growing gap. These differences were significant even when socioeconomic variables were controlled. The U.S. Department of Commerce survey reported that rural areas had the fastest Internet access growth rate (75%), while central cities lag behind all other areas, though rural areas still have the lowest level of high-speed Internet access (7.3%) compared to central cities (12.2%).

Different Kinds of Nonusers
An ambitious study by the UCLA Center for Community Policy (2000) is analyzing a panel of 2,096 representative households across time,

comparing Internet users to nonusers and to nonusers who become users later on. It is part of a group of similar projects in other countries. The study found that while only 31.2% of those who had not graduated from high school used the Internet in fall of 2000, 86.3% of those with at least a college degree did; 53.1% of high school graduates and 70.2% of those with some college used the Internet. At the youngest ages (12 through 15), use of the Internet is nearly universal (91.6 percent) among American females; the only other age range where they exceed male use is 46 through 55 years (74.3% compared to 66.1%). After that, the gender gap widens considerably (at 66 and over, rates are 18.4% for females and 40.4% for males).

A study published by the nonprofit Consumer Federation of America (Cooper & Shah, 2000) collected responses from a single statistically balanced panel ($n = 1,902$) measured at two time periods (February 1999 and June 2000) drawn from respondents agreeing to participate in a large-scale lifestyles study. The overall conclusion is that "the disconnected are, in fact, disadvantaged and disenfranchised" (p. 1). In particular, they compare the *fully* connected (36% of population with Internet service providers or high-speed Internet access at home), the *partially* connected (17 percent with basic Internet or e-mail service at home), the *potentially* connected (21% with no home Internet service but with home computer or cell phone), and the *disconnected* (26% with neither Internet service, computer, nor cell phone). The disconnected earn less than half the income of the fully connected ($25,000 versus $45,000), are much less likely to have a college degree (13% versus 46%), are more likely to be black (12% versus 7%), be older (53 versus 44 years), and have smaller households (2.1 versus 2.8). Each of these significantly predicts differences across the four levels of connectedness, with income being the most powerful predictor. Overall, the study concludes that there is about a three to five-year lag in penetration between those with above-median and below-median income. Cooper and Shah (2000, p. 1) agree with the argument held by Castells and others that such differential timing in access to power and information—even if the later adopters catch up after several years—is itself a significant source of social inequality and unequal participation. (We reanalyze these data in chapter 5 to highlight another interpretation that might be given to them.)

Moreover, 40% of those who are disconnected or partially connected do not expect to be connected four years hence; of the current disconnected, about 92% feel this way. The UCLA study (2000) also notes that 58.6% of current nonusers (32.1%) are somewhat likely or very likely to not gain access within a year, and this worsens for older respondents. Further, it also reports that in mid-2000, 10.3% of nonusers are actually Internet dropouts (they formerly used the Internet at least once a month but do so no longer); Katz, Rice, and Aspden (2001) report that this 10% figure is fairly consistent in surveys they conducted in 1995, 1996, 1997, and 2000 (see chapter 3).

Widespread, full connection thus is unlikely any time soon. Income, age, and education predict intentions to connect in the future, while race does not. There are few differences between the partially and fully connected in percentage of respondents who indicate that they have engaged in various activities online (consuming, gathering information, visiting government or politician Web sites, sending e-mails to a newspaper, or discussing politics online), but there are significant dropoffs for the potentially connected and even more so for the disconnected. That is, simply having access, independent of the quality or speed of the connection, is the crucial distinction. Given these ongoing differences in the types of people who have access to, and use, the Internet, it is unlikely that the current knowledge gaps between upper and lower socioeconomic groups will diminish.

Barriers, Influences, and Consequences

Clearly, there are many physical and socioeconomic barriers to equal access. Keller (1995) expands the concept of public access to the Internet beyond technical connection to a public network to include easy-to-use connections, affordable access, and useful information resources. Barriers to using the Internet reported by the UCLA study respondents (UCLA, 2000) include no computer or terminal available (37.7%), no interest (33.3%), do not know how to use (18.9%), too expensive (9.1%), and various other factors. Within the United States in 1997, "65% of public schools had access to the Internet, but schools with richer student populations were still 25 percent more likely to be connected than schools with poorer student populations" (Tapscott, 1997,

p. 260). And even within those schools, "more than 74% of schools have computers, but only 10% of students say they have used a computer at school in the past week" (p. 266). Van Dijk (1999) identifies four general obstacles that appear to prevent people from using new media:

• Intimidation (especially of the elderly and unskilled) by new technology or a bad first experience with it,
• No or difficult access to computers or networks,
• Lack of user friendliness and unattractive usage style, and
• Lack of significant usage opportunities.

Commercialization of the Internet, Information, and Users

A perhaps more pervasive and less tangible obstacle is the growing primacy of commercial motivations for the Internet over access per se: "Calling the Internet the Great Equalizer helps to sell more computers. The metaphor masquerades as a quick fix to social inequality while ignoring the factors that lead to inequality" (Wolf, 1998, p. 26). Schiller (1996) similarly concludes that the information superhighway is little more than a new medium for corporate American to control and profit from. Indeed, he argues that the concept of the national information infrastructure was grounded in privatization and commercialization and that this mentality spread to other technology areas, such as selling off spectra to large corporations.

Gandy (2002) argues that the fundamental conceptualization of the audience as citizens who actively participate in the public sphere has been largely replaced by the audience as consumers in the new media environment. He refers to this as the "real digital divide." Access to information is no longer a central presumption of human needs essential to citizenship; rather, consumer interests have become the fundamental criterion for evaluation the performance of social systems. Sunstein (2001), in his analysis of political implications of the Internet, similarly argues that political sovereignty has become confused with consumer sovereignty. Part of this process is the reconceptualization of information as a public good into information as a private good or commodity. Thus, "social interactions become market transactions" (Gandy, 2002, p. 5), and the concept of public trusteeship gives way to commercialization.

The individual becomes removed from the collectivity, content becomes simplistic entertainment rather than social debate, text and words are replaced by images and sound, and public becomes private. Also, because of the drive toward satisfying the consumer, toward cross-ownership of the media, and toward the dumbing down of media content to meet the declining expectations of the audience, more media outlets and more forms in no way guarantee increased diversity of content and may allow individuals to retreat even more from society. The public, then, even in public broadcasting programs, is increasingly treated as a market rather than as citizens. Anything that chases away viewers (lowers ratings) is avoided, and commercial production standards, which require considerable resources to meet, become the minimal threshold for acceptance.

One consequence of this real digital divide, therefore, is that access itself is insufficient (Gandy, 2002). If the content that is accessible through the Internet serves primarily the needs and interests of a consumer class (especially a wealthy one), then low-income, low-education, and minority groups will not use the Internet even if they have access and will not be able to apply Internet information to their functional needs. Indeed, the "natural," market-driven diffusion of the Internet may well decrease the traditional digital divide by providing consumer information and services to everyone with access but may widen the citizen or public digital divide by valuing that consumer information over citizen and public needs and abilities.

Variations in Motivations for Usage and Barriers to Access

Neu et al. (1999) provide some empirical support for this position. They report that the network use gap between whites and Hispanics and blacks of similar socioeconomic status widened from 1993 to 1997, implying that some of the digital divide may be due to differences in interests and priorities. A more invisible factor in this digital divide may be embedded distinctions (Van Dijk, 1999, p. 152): "the design of new media techniques carries the imprint of the social-cultural characteristics of its producers—predominantly male, well-educated, English-speaking, and members of the ethnic majority in a particular country." This style does not appeal to most women, less-educated people, and ethnic minorities. There is also a "usage gap in which well-educated people use computers for work, private business, education, and other reasons, whereas those with less education and the young use computers for entertainment and/or computer games followed by education" (p. 153). Both the learning process and resistance to change seem important in explaining why there is such low Internet access by older age groups (Neu, Anderson & Bikson, 1999, ch. 6). Further, differences in access become more pronounced for some variables when general access and home access are compared (Corrado, 2000, p. 5). Home access is associated with regular Internet use by whites with higher education and incomes. Thus, in reality, there is no simple two-tiered digital divide: "A better representation would be a continuum or spectrum of differentiated positions across the population with the 'information elite' at the top and a group of 'excluded people' at the bottom" (Van Dijk, 1999, p. 155).

Indeed, cultural differences rather than economic, education, and racial differences are receiving increased attention from both government and commercial studies. The Cultural Access Group (2001) conducted an online marketing survey of 2,205 users (766 African Americans and 1,439 Hispanics) of ethnic Web sites and 1,294 general-market respondents, via an online banner that connected interested users to a Web-based survey. Clearly, this is an extremely biased sample: African Americans who responded to this survey were more highly educated (83% had some college) and more female (76%) than the general-market respondents (79% and 35%, respectively). African Americans and Hispanics in this sample had lower in-home access than the general-market respondents, indicated that cost was the major deterrent to in-home access, had been online for fewer years, and spent less time online than the general-market respondents. African Americans were, however, more likely than Hispanics and the general market to use the Internet to access information on family and relationship issues (34% African Americans, 25% Hispanics, 13% general market), and on health issues (44%, 40%, 31%), as well as for chatting online (26%, 26%, 12%) than Hispanics or the general market. Curiously, Hispanics were more likely than African Americans or the general market to agree that the Internet has improved society overall (73 percent Hispanics, 50 percent African Americans, 55 percent general market), created opportunities for all people (80%, 69%, 70%), and broken down racial barriers (60%, 27%,

33%) and economic barriers (48%, 29%, 29%). This may be partially explained due to the fact that African Americans, compared to Hispanics and the general market, agree that people of color have unique needs on the Internet (52%, 16%, 14%), but only 37% of African American, compared to 64% of Hispanic, respondents felt that there is adequate Internet content for their ethnic group.

Rojas, Roychowdhury, Okur, Straubhaar, and Estrada-Ortiz (in press) go further in identifying other factors contributing to the digital divide, such as the interrelations among economic capital, cultural capital, ethnicity, gender, and age. Their in-depth study of 12 families in Austin, Texas, identified a variety of dispositions toward computer technology, influenced by "practices [such as family histories of technology and media use and habits], perceptions and attitudes, technical education, awareness of technology [especially relating to economic mobility], desires for information, job requirements, social relations with community members and community organizations, and geographical location" (Rojas et al., in press, p. 11). Often, particular individuals reside in a cross-fire of competing and contrasting influences (such as family and peers, cultural and social capital, educational and consumer motivations, and early gender roles) toward computer and online technology. Similarly, Haddon (2001) argues that "social exclusion" is context-dependent (neither necessarily economically based nor equivalent across all domains of a person's life), involves not only political and civic involvement but also people's ability to occupy social roles, and may also involve rejection of or lack of interest in new technologies. So, for example, his ethnographic study of 20 single-parent and 20 elderly households, using time-budget diaries and interviews, found a wide variety of influences on interest in such new media—economic constraints, need to keep in touch with children, limited conceptualizations of how these media could be used (because of the respondents' experiences surviving in low-income situations), low priorities compared to pressing issues such as daycare, smaller or less available social networks (and thus less reason to use communication media) because of not working, lowered symbolic value of used or cheaper technologies, greater resistance by the elderly to innovations or to consumerism in general, little exposure by the elderly to new technologies in their former workplaces, a greater awareness by the elderly of how they were spending their money due to their earlier experience of austere economic times, and simply greater familiarity with more traditional media such as the telephone and the television.

More Subtle Conceptualizations of the Digital Divide

Other conceptualizations of the digital divide find even more distinct gaps among social groups. Traditional measures of the digital divide have relied on a binary measure of adoption or a simple measure of time spent using the technology (including distinctions such as new, regular, or long-time users). These do not consider the extent to which the technology is incorporated into daily life or its effect on status or upward mobility, thus avoiding the social context. Consequently, traditional measures of the digital divide based on income, education, age, gender, and ethnic groups may well mask the underlying differences that affect long-term social integration and access to resources. A media system dependency theoretical approach, along with Bourdieu's (1990) concepts of "habitus" and "cultural capital," motivated Jung, Qiu, and Kim (2001) to develop an Internet connectedness index (ICI). Their ICI measure includes years owned personal computer at home; work, school, and personal tasks conducted over the Internet; number of places the user connects to the Internet; pursuit of six media-system dependency goals; participation in Internet or Web activities; time spent on interactive online activities; effects of the Internet on personal life; computer dependency; and Internet dependency.

Their study of seven ethnically and geographically distinct communities found significant differences in the ICI, with the highest scores for caucasian and Chinese, the lowest scores for Koreans, Mexicans, and Central Americans, and African American scores in the middle. However, using the measure of average time spent online in the last week, the only significant difference was that Chinese were greater users. The ICI differed across income and education, while time spent using the Internet in the last week differed only across income. Also, the ICI increased linearly with income and education, while time online fluctuated. The ICI scores correlated with education, income, age (younger), and gender (male), and these relations persisted for all demographics except education when task scope was controlled. Time using the Internet, however, correlated only with gender (male). ICI and time correlated $r = .49$, and ICI correlated with education, income, and age even when controlling for time online.

The results suggest that the more subtle ICI measures identify more persistent sociodemographic inequalities of Internet usage, while conventional measures of "time online" reveal at most a divide based on gender (Jung, Qiu & Kim, 2001). They conclude that digital divide studies that focus only on typical time-based measures of Internet usage will not address more fundamental Internet inequality issues.

Finally, not everyone is necessarily interested in using the Internet. A survey of Internet use in 30 countries by Ipsos-Reid (Bonisteel, 2001) found that 40% of nonusers said they had "no need," and 25% said they had "no interest." A third said they had no computer, 12% indicated it was too costly, and 10% reported they had no time to use it. Thus nearly two-thirds of the reasons given were related not to access or resource issues but to a basic lack of need or interest.

Other Divides: Physical and Geographic

The digital divide occurs at the international level as well. "Young and well educated people with a high income living in rich Western countries and regions have increased their lead on elderly people, less educated people, and people with lower income and from poorer countries and regions.... There is only one exception to this increase in relative differences in access to computers and networks: the gap between males and females is decreasing, though this is happening much faster in Northern America than in Europe" (Van Dijk, 1999, p. 150). Van Dijk points out that this is a familiar pattern in the adoption of new media, similar to that of the telephone, radio, television, and video cassette recorder. Nonetheless, "the information gap between have and have-not countries is growing. According to Jupiter Communications, of the 23.4 million households connected to the Net in 1996, 66% were in North America, 16% in Europe, and 14% in the Asian Pacific. The gap is not just one of developed countries versus underdeveloped countries" (Wellman, 2000; see ⟨www.nua.ie/surveys/how_many_online/index.html⟩ for statistics on the geographic distribution of users. A recent Nielsen/NetRatings report found that as of the first quarter of 2001, 27 nations and about 429 million people had Internet access (Study, 2001). North Americans have the largest usage percentage of users, 41%, but this is declining, with Europe, the Middle East, and Africa comprising 27% of users, the Asia-Pacific region at 20%, and Latin American with 4%.

Beyond equal distribution of access across demographic and national boundaries, people who have hearing, sight, movement, and other disabilities may also be disadvantaged by limitations on their ability to access information, their contacts, and their opportunities for expression on the Internet. People with disabilities have half the access rate of non-disabled persons, and those rates vary widely by type of disability, with access rates at 42.2% for those with learning disabilities, 27.2% for those with hearing problems, and 18.6% for those with walking problems (McConnaughey, 2001).

And even those who do overcome all these access obstacles do not necessarily benefit as much as utopians have predicted. For example, low-skill information- or knowledge-worker jobs are rising as fast as higher-skill jobs, information-based jobs are frequently rationalized and fragmented, and initiatives to help overcome employment-opportunity divides often end up simply subsidizing training for organizations with low-paying computer-based jobs (Tufekcioglu, 2001).

The Utopian Perspective

Disappearing Dimensions of the Digital Divide

Recent studies (ECRL, 1999; Jupiter Communications, 2000; Katz, Rice & Aspden, 2001; and see chapter 3) have found that at least racial and gender differences in Internet use disappear after other variables are taken into account statistically. Because the CPS research was conducted before the Web and browser-based Internet usage had diffused widely, the "network services" referred to in 1993 and 1997 probably did require advanced technical resources and skills. Once browsers, modems, bandwidth, popular and commercial Internet resources, and connectivity became more user-friendly and widespread, however, various digital divides could then diminish. A Pew Institute study (Yahoo!News, 2001) found that by the end of 2000, 58% of men and 54% of women were Internet users; figures for Hispanics were 47% and for blacks 43%. According to the AOL survey (2000), more women (53%) starting

Internet use in 2000 than did men; overall, 49% of Internet users were women. By June 2001, a Nielsen/NetRatings study (Net users, 2001) reported that Internet users mirror the national distribution of women and men, with 53.33 million women and 49.83 million men using the Internet. Men use the Internet about 10.5 hours per week, women use it 9 hours per week, and men view about 31% more pages than do women (Net users, 2001) (AOL, 2000; Katz et al., 2001, found similar trends).

The AOL survey found that 33% of those starting Internet use in 2000 had high school education (the overall U.S. percentage is 51%), compared to 22% in 1999. About 24% of starters had household incomes of less than $35,000 (the overall U.S. percentage is 34%), compared to 11% in 1999. Education and income was noticeably greater as users had more years online. Also, more years online correlated with more days and hours spent online per week. Although 82% of those with incomes greater than $75,000 had access, only 3% of those with annual incomes less than $30,000 did so; and while 75% of those 18 to 29 years of age had access, only 15% of those older than 75 did (AOL, 2000).

Howard, Rainie, and Jones (2001) analyzed the Pew Internet & American Life Project surveys, collected daily from March through August in 2000, from over 12,000 respondents, with over 6,000 having access to the Internet. Over half of those with Internet access go online every day (57% males and 52% females). The heaviest and most long-time users (for example, 68% of those with more than three years' experience compared to 41% of those with less than six months) are more likely to log on daily. A third used the Internet to obtain information; 30% indicated they used it for fun things; a fifth conducted life activities (health, work or job-related); and 10% performed various financial transactions. Though users are becoming more like the general U.S. population, except for income and age, significant differences in kinds of uses remain. Women seek more information about health, religion, new jobs, and online games. Men more likely obtain news (26% vs. 15% for women), financial (18% vs. 8%), hobby (21% vs. 14%), government, and sports information, and shop (including online auctions). Major differences are due to age, too: younger users are more likely to use chat rooms and instant messaging, browse, do school or work-related research, obtain popular culture information or media products, and conduct some service activities such as travel arrangements. Finally, those with more than three years' Internet experience have done more kinds of online activities, such as job-related activities and communication, and conducted financial transactions online; they are generally better educated and earn more income. Those with less education are more likely to engage in fun online activities but seek for information and conduct online transactions less frequently.

Other results from the larger Pew data show that people spend considerably less time online on weekends than weekdays, and that people use the Internet to do both nonwork activities while at work (over 66%), and work-related activities from home (over 50%). In general, "the Internet has become a part of everyday life, rather than a separate place to be" (Howard, Rainie & Jones, 2001, p. 3).

Some Ethnic Differences in Kinds of Usage

Whites are more likely to engage in all four categories of activities—information, for life activities and financial transactions—except that in the fun category blacks and Asians seek more hobby information, in the information-utility category checking the weather, and in the economics-transaction category participating in online auctions (Howard et al., 2001).

By February 2001, 50% of all Hispanics had used the Internet, up from 40% the prior year (Spooner & Rainie, 2001, reporting on the Pew Internet and American Life Project's February survey as well as on nearly a year's worth of aggregated poll data). However, due largely to income and educational differences, Hispanics are still less likely to be Internet users than are white non-Hispanics (this does not reflect recency of adoption, however). As with the population as a whole, Hispanic newcomers are more likely to be women (52%) and younger (primarily under 34), though Hispanic users overall are at the moment evenly split between men and women. Counter to the general population trends, Hispanic users are equally divided between those with greater and those with less than $40,000 annual income. Over three-quarters of Hispanic Internet users go online at least three to five times a week. Compared to non-Hispanic whites, Hispanic users are more likely to have browsed the Web for fun, listened to music online, downloaded music, played online games, sampled audio or video clips, and looked for information about books and movies. These difference are mostly related to the younger age of Hispanic users rather than cultural differences. As with white users, about half have used the Web to access health and medical information (though Hispanic women are more likely than men to have done this) and to play online games or send instant messages.

A representative postal mail survey of 80,000 U.S. households conducted by Forrester research in January 2000 (Walsh, Gazala & Ham, 2001) found that Asian Americans have the highest Internet penetration rate, and Hispanic Americans have a higher adoption rate than non-Hispanic caucasians. Connection to the Internet grew for members of all ethnic groups who bought personal computers. There are still differences in Internet access based primarily on income but also age, education, and technology optimism; but once these are statistically controlled, there are no ethnic differences. Indeed, the survey showed that consumers of all ethnicities use the Internet for the same general reasons—to communicate with others, access information, have fun, and shop. African Americans tend to seek health and job information and play games online, while Asian Americans are slightly more likely to use search engines, browse online newspapers and magazines, download music, and engage in ecommerce.

The Debate about the Significance of the Digital Divide

Compaine (2001), in his review of research and policy issues concerning the digital divide, arrives at two main conclusions. First, in one sense, the digital divide is not new: there always have been and always will be various gaps associated with the initial stages of nearly all innovations, from farming to machinery to telephones. Second, technology gaps tend to be "relatively transient" (p. xii), and later adopters tend not to need the technical expertise or have to pay the high costs of early adopters. However, Compaine argues, policies that attempt to ameliorate these initial gaps often also increase overall costs to consumers and markets and may even slow down eventual diffusion (as Mueller, 2001, argued about the "universal service" policy applied to the telephone industry). Further, the popular use of the term *digital divide* or *information have-nots* typically ignores related issues, such as access to various print media and distinctions between educational, business, and entertainment information. Compaine does not ignore the substantial implications of differential access to and use of the Internet, but he does argue that given the broader contexts, eliminating the digital divide is not worth economic or political resource expenditure.

For less developed countries, public-access sites may facilitate more rapid diffusion. These sites include schools, cafés, libraries, and corner stores. Wireless systems, too, might help overcome the limitations of local wired telephone connections (Bonisteel, 2001; Katz & Aakhus, 2002).

Efforts are being made to overcome some of the limitations on access that are encountered by people with disabilities. In 1990, the government searched for a way to provide universal service and include persons with disabilities. In 1990, Title IV of the Americans with Disabilities Act addressed disability issues by requiring all service carriers to provide communication access for hearing-impaired American citizens (Borchert, 1998, p. 56). And "Section 255 of the Telecommunications Act requires that telecommunication services and equipment providers make their goods and services accessible to individuals with disabilities" (p. 60). A good example of this are the recent Windows operating systems that offer program and application shortcuts for people with disabilities. (Another example, concerning the blind, is presented in chapter 5.) Currently in development are communication networks with full duplex voice, data transmission, graphics, and video communication.

Conclusion

Although there are points of disagreement concerning research about the digital divide, the bulk of the evidence indicates that the digital divide is decreasing or even disappearing with respect to gender and race. Differences in income and education are still great and according to some studies are increasing. The general lag in access and use may inflict enduring social damage that lingers or appears even after later adopters achieve full access. Many of the obstacles to more equitable access may be deeply embedded in cultural contexts. In the next three chapters we offer some unique perspectives on the issue of access, both empirically and conceptually.

3

Access and Digital Divide: Results

In this chapter we build on chapter 2's discussion of the first of our three primary themes—access—by analyzing changes across time and differences across socioeconomic groupings. This is done by analyzing relevant survey questions that were asked at more than one time period and also by examining questions specific to each survey. Besides the familiar concept of a "digital divide" that refers to access or usage, our data identify three other divides—cohort, awareness, and dropouts. Within any particular year, there are cohorts of both recent and long-time adopters, each with varying sociodemographic characteristics. Distinguishing these two types of users helps us detect subtle changes in the digital divide. Although "everyone" is assumed to know about the Internet, so that nonusage represents a conscious choice, possibly in light of various obstacles, we have found that across the years a persistent percentage of the population is not aware of the Internet. Finally, a persistent percentage of the population has used the Internet but no longer does so—the Internet dropouts.

Factors Influencing Awareness and Usage

The research literature identifies three overlapping influences on awareness and usage of communication technologies: built-in bias (such as sex or ethnicity), needs gratified by the communication technology, and resource availability. We assess these influences in terms of demographics, motivations and rationales, income, and education. Our aim is to identify first the extent of any digital divide within and across the years and then the factors that influence this digital divide.

Built-in Bias

Those who believe that communication technologies have built-in biases (for example, Herring, 1994) argue that communication technologies are developed by specific societal groups (for example, white middle-income male technophiles) and that the resulting products appeal much more strongly to members of that designing group. Others, including Katz (1990a), have argued that communication technologies are potentially neutral in terms of their ability to be used by various racial and ethnic groups. However, various researchers have also shown that major gender (Rakow, 1992) and racial and ethnic (Rosen & Weil, 1995) differences are displayed in the actual usage patterns of interpersonal communication technologies. These data suggest that women tend to be extensive users of telephones, for instance, and that men tend to be extensive users of computers. This built-in bias also takes the form of the overwhelming role that males play in the development of the Internet and thus of early politically involved online communities such as those participating in the Equifax/Lotus Marketplace—Household CD-ROM protest or in the Clipper Chip protest (Gurak, 1997, ch. 7).

Uses, Needs, and Gratifications

Another perspective of communication media use has been offered by the school of thought known as uses and gratifications theory. For a general perspective on uses and gratifications theory, see Blumler and Katz (1974); for a recent application of the theory to media, see Canary and Spitzberg (1993); for applications to the telephone, see Dimmick, Sikand, and Patterson (1994); and for a general critique, see Elliott (1974). This body of research has generally been concerned with examining how audiences actively consume mass media rather than how they use computers or the Internet.

Despite ample criticism of needs and gratifications theory, we can adapt it here to possible sex and race differences in Internet usage. For example, possible differences might be explained by the fact that certain subcultures and ethnic groups find their needs better served by more social technologies and therefore tend to adopt them more readily. (This indeed seems to be the case when it comes to cellular mobile telephony; see Katz & Aspden, 1997b.) Hence, rather than looking at the nature of technology, the uses and gratifications perspective might look at the psychology of subcultural or ethnic groups and their differential needs and sources of gratifications to explain variation in their choices of exposure to various media, including the Internet.

Another plausible line of reasoning under the rubric of uses and gratifications is the notion that, within the home, people use communication technologies in social ways rather than as commercial or business tools. Networked personal computers (the Internet), like other communication technologies, were first implemented in business and research environments and then migrated to the home. Many applications of the computer (for example, financial management applications) that are highly successful in the business world have not prospered in the home. Correspondingly, social applications (for example, computer games) with no antecedent in the business world have prospered in the home (Forrester, 1996). Hence, for a technology like the Internet, home users will over time find they gravitate toward social uses of the interpersonal communication system.

Resource Availability

Finally, given the expense and complexity of a technology like online communication, we would expect to find a class difference in participation, where class is defined by socially stratified financial or intellectual resources. Resource availability has long been associated (by virtually all schools of economists, including political economists) with the early acquisition of new communication technology. This was true of the telephone, broadcast television, video cassette recorder, and cable television, all of which have become (albeit imperfectly) dispersed through America's social strata. Likewise, we would expect it to be true of the Internet (Katz & Aspden, 1997c).

Most of the foregoing discussion has focused on class, sex, and racial and ethnic differences, but we believe there are other potentially important demographic variables. Age and presence of children in the household do not seem to attract the same intensity of scholarly attention as do race, class, and sex in terms of differential awareness, use, and impact of communication technology. However, from our studies (and others, such as Rosen & Weil, 1995), these factors often appear to be important

Table 3.1
Summary Sample Size and Usage Statistics

Variable	October 1995	November 1996	November 1997	March 2000
Sample *n*	2,500	557	2,148	1,305
Users	8.1%	18.8%	30.1%	59.7%
Former users as percentage of respondents	7.8%	11.5%	9.8%	10.5%
Former users as percentage of current and former users	48.7%	37.9%	24.6%	14.9%
Nonusers	84.3%	69.9%	60.1%	29.7%
Nonusers, not aware of Internet	15.2%	10.1%	9.9%	8.3%
Nonusers, aware of Internet	69.1%	59.8%	50.2%	21.4%
Supplemental users sample[a]	—	450	153	—

a. See appendix A, Methodology.

predictors of awareness and use of communication technologies and services and so are included in our analysis. These variables can often fit into a uses and gratifications perspective when it is not entirely focused on internal psychological states (Wright, 1975), as well as a (time- and income-based) resource perspective.

Nonusers and Users across the Survey Years

Before we can analyze any digital divide, we must first establish the extent of and change in usage and nonusage over the six-year period of our surveys. We begin our examination by presenting in table 3.1 a summary of the sample size and proportions of four types of respondents —users, former users, nonusers who are aware of the Internet, and nonusers who are not aware of the Internet—in each of the 1995, 1996, 1997, and 2000 surveys.

As figure 3.1 shows graphically, the overall percentage of Internet users rose from 8.1% in October 1995 to 59.7% in March 2000. However, in each year there was a surprisingly high percentage of those who

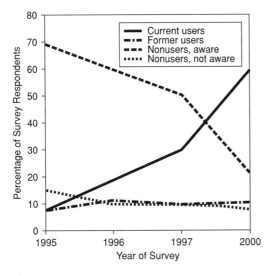

Figure 3.1
Survey Respondents Who Are Users, Former Users, Aware Nonusers, and Not Aware Nonusers

said that, as of the time of the survey, they had stopped using the Internet. Chapter 4 considers these Internet dropouts specifically. Although the overall number of nonusers has dropped dramatically over the years, one type of nonuser—those who are not aware of the Internet (or the information superhighway)—represents about a tenth of each sample (from 15.2% in 1995 to 8.3% in 2000). We also consider some aspects of this awareness divide.

A Persistent but Declining Digital Divide

Table 3.2 shows that every difference between users and nonusers across demographic comparisons in survey years is statistically significant, except for race in 1995. However, the change in demographic differences across the four survey years is statistically significant for all the demographic factors except education. Thus, the first and most common digital divide persists but is declining across all the major factors except education.

Table 3.2
Sample Sizes, χ^2's, and η's for Cross-tabulations of Variables with Nonusers and Users by Survey Year

Variables	1995	1996	1997	2000	Across Years, Users Only
Sex	2,291 (34.9***; .12)	943 (8.5**; .10)	2,091 (25.3***; .11)	1,273 (9.7**; .09)	2,404 (22.0***; .10)
Age (less than 40; vs. greater than or equal to 65)	2,238 (22.3***; .10) (26.7***; .10)	927 (39.1***; .21) (59.9***; .25)	1,955 (53.4***; .17) (121.4***; .25)	1,227 (87.3***; .27) (102.6***; .29)	2,361 (9.8*; .06) (16.2***; .08)
Income	1,844 (48.4***; .16)	596 (25.0**; .21)	1,658 (162.3***; .31)	1,033 (125.7***; .35)	1,918 (36.9***; .14)
Education	786 (78.6***; .18)	933 (81.7***; .30)	1,962 (169.7***; .29)	1,155 (63.1***; .23)	2,395 (6.2; .05)
Race (African American, white non-Hispanic)	2,058 (2.8; .04)	885 (10.1**; .11)	1,866 (18.7***; .10)	1,032 (3.4*; .06)	2,184 (10.1*; .07)

Note: Values in cells are n, χ^2, and η of the cross-tabulation.
*$p < .05$.
**$p < .01$.
***$p < .001$.

Differences in Usage by Cohort and Survey Year across Demographics

Central to the concerns about the digital divide is whether significant differences in Internet usage exist across socioeconomic groupings, such as sex, age, household income, education, and race and ethnicity. So here we compare Internet users on the major sociodemographic factors. First, however, the characteristics of the most recent Internet adopters may differ from earlier adopters (as all three factors of bias, needs, and resources would predict), yet each survey would include both those who adopted in that year as well as those who had adopted in prior years. Thus we asked users the year they started using the Internet. This enabled us to establish cohorts of Internet users based on the year they started using the Internet—those starting in 1992 or before and those starting in 1993, 1994, 1995, 1996, 1997, 1998, and 1999/2000. We report usage by demographic measures both for the survey years (1995, 1996, 1997, and 2000) and also by cohort year. Table 3.3 provides the percentages for the survey years, and table 3.4 for the cohort (start) years.

Sex

The 1995 survey year had a surprisingly large percentage of female users (63%), with a more expected rise from 46.4% in 1996 to 50.6% in 1999. Across the cohorts of users, the proportion of female users increases from 34.3% to 54.5%. Thus new Internet users are proportionally more female than overall surveys would indicate and in recent years even more frequently female than male users.

Age

The percent of over-40 users rose from 34.8% in 1995 to 44.4% in 2000. However, this proportion is still well below their proportion of the general population (approximately 55%). Again, new Internet users are proportionally older than is apparent from surveys based strictly on year of data collection, with a rise in over-40 users from 38.4% in 1992 to 48.9% in 1999. The percentage of those 65 years and older who are using the Internet is still quite small, having risen from .58% in 1995 to 5.2% in 2000.

Table 3.3
Demographic Variables for Users by Survey Year

Variables	1995	1996	1997	2000
Sex:				
Male	75	297	440	420
	(37.5%)	(53.6%)	(55.0%)	(49.4%)
Female	125	257	360	430
	(62.5%)	(46.4%)	(45.0%)	(50.6%)
Age:				
Under 40	129	339	458	460
	(65.2%)	(62.3%)	(57.8%)	(55.6%)
At least 40	69	205	334	367
	(34.8%)	(37.7%)	(42.2%)	(44.4%)
Under 65	197	528	773	784
	(99.5%)	(97.1%)	(97.6%)	(94.8%)
At least 65	1	16	19	43
	(.58%)	(2.9%)	(2.4%)	(5.2%)
Income:				
Under $35,000	51	133	145	163
	(30.7%)	(37.2%)	(21.2%)	(23.0%)
At least $35,000	115	225	540	546
	(69.3%)	(62.8%)	(78.8%)	(77.0%)
Education:				
Less than college degree	96	288	407	476
	(48.0%)	(52.4%)	(51.2%)	(56.0%)
At least college degree	104	262	388	374
	(52.0%)	(47.6%)	(48.8%)	(44.0%)
Race:				
African American	12	28	60	77
	(6.0%)	(5.1%)	(7.5%)	(9.1%)
White non-Hispanic	167	491	673	676
	(83.5%)	(88.6%)	(84.1%)	(79.5%)

Household Income

The proportion of Internet users with a household income less than $35,000 is slightly increasing across cohort years (from 23.3% in 1992 to 28.1% in 1999) but actually declining across survey years (from 30.7% in 1995 to 23.0% in 2000).

Education

For those users who started in 1992 or before, the proportion of those without college degrees was 28%, rising to 67% for the 1999 cohort. Over the survey years, the percentage rose from 48% in 1995 to 56% in 2000.

Race and Ethnicity

The proportion of African Americans using the Internet rose and then declined a bit over both the cohort (from 9.4% in 1992 to 8.9% in 1999) and survey years (from 6.0% in 1995 to 9.1% in 2000).

The Cohort Digital Divide

These results provide evidence for a second digital divide, across adoption cohorts as opposed to users responding in a particular survey year.

Additional Differences

Table 3.5 provides differences on additional comparisons between users and nonusers in each survey year. In 2000, users were more likely to have children than nonusers. In all four years, users were more likely to be full-time workers or full-time students. In 1996, users were more likely to own as opposed to rent their homes. And in 1995, 1996, and 2000, users were more likely to have been living in their homes for fewer years. Table 3.6 shows that users were less likely to feel overloaded than nonusers in both 1995 and 2000 and more likely to be satisfied with their life and communication in both 1995 and 2000. Table 3.7 provides the sample sizes and percentages and comparative census percentages of all the variables that were dichotomized for use in these analyses.

Table 3.4
Demographic Variables for Users by Start Year

Variables	1992	1993	1994	1995
Sex:				
Male	119	74	144	292
	(65.7%)	(57.8%)	(56.0%)	(49.6%)
Female	62	54	113	297
	(34.3%)	(42.2%)	(44.0%)	(50.4%)
Age:				
Under 40	109	77	178	336
	(61.6%)	(61.1%)	(69.5%)	(58.2%)
At least 40	68	49	78	241
	(38.4%)	(38.9%)	(30.5%)	(41.8%)
Income:				
Under $35,000	34	25	66	107
	(23.3%)	(23.1%)	(31.7%)	(23.5%)
At least $35,000	112	83	142	349
	(76.7%)	(76.9%)	(68.3%)	(76.5%)
Education:				
Less than college degree	54	48	121	280
	(30.2%)	(37.5%)	(47.5%)	(47.6%)
At least college degree	125	80	134	308
	(69.8%)	(62.5%)	(52.5%)	(52.4%)
Race:				
African Americans	17	3	12	33
	(9.4%)	(2.3%)	(4.7%)	(5.6%)
African Americans	152	109	218	500
	(84.0%)	(85.2%)	(84.8%)	(84.9%)

$^*p < .05.$
$^{**}p < .01.$
$^{***}p < .001.$

1996	1997	1998	1999	χ^2 and η of Variable by Start Year
266	157	88	87	
(52.7%)	(43.4%)	(48.1%)	(45.5%)	
239	205	95	104	33.1***
(47.3%)	(56.6%)	(51.9%)	(54.5%)	(.1)
282	207	99	94	
(56.7%)	(58.0%)	(55.0%)	(51.1%)	
215	150	81	90	19.6**
(43.3%)	(42.0%)	(45.0%)	(48.9%)	(.09)
106	71	39	43	
(26.9%)	(23.7%)	(26.5%)	(28.1%)	
288	229	108	110	7.5
(73.1%)	(76.3%)	(73.5%)	(71.9%)	(.6)
281	235	115	128	
(56.0%)	(65.1%)	(62.8%)	(67.0%)	
221	126	68	63	104.9***
(44.0%)	(34.9%)	(37.2%)	(33.0%)	(.21)
47	34	14	17	
(9.3%)	(9.4%)	(7.9%)	(8.9%)	
422	291	151	158	15.8*
(83.6%)	(80.4%)	(82.5%)	(82.7%)	(.09)

Table 3.5
Children, Work, and Residency, Nonusers and Users, 1995 to 2000

Variable	1995		1996	
	Nonuser	User	Nonuser	User
Children:				
None	1,079	106	189	293
	(51.7%)	(53.0%)	(49.6%)	(53.5%)
Any	1,007	94	192	255
	(48.3%)	(47.0%)	(50.4%)	(46.5%)
χ^2, η		.12		1.3
		(.01)		(.04)
Work:				
Full-time	1,125	139	198	325
	(53.9%)	(69.5%)	(51.7%)	(59.2%)
Part-time	252	20	41	71
	(12.1%)	(10%)	(10.7%)	(12.9%)
Retired	334	5	84	26
	(16.0%)	(2.5%)	(21.9%)	(4.7%)
Not paid, unemployed	251	9	38	29
	(12.0%)	(4.5%)	(9.9%)	(5.3%)
Student	124	27	22	98
	(5.9%)	(13.5%)	(5.7%)	(17.9%)
χ^2, η		56.0***		92.0***
		(.05)		(.01)
Own home?				
Rent	590	65	99	190
	(30.3%)	(36.4%)	(27.6%)	(36.4%)
Own	1,358	124	259	332
	(69.7%)	(65.6%)	(72.3%)	(63.6%)
χ^2, η		1.4		7.4*
		(.03)		(.09)
Number of years living in current house?	N = 2,069 (M = 10.5)	197 (6.4)	389 (5.2)	554 (3.5)
T-test	—	4.8***	—	2.9**

*$p < .05$.
**$p < .01$.
***$p < .001$.

1997		2000	
Nonuser	User	Nonuser	User
—	—	275	467
(—)	(—)	(65.2%)	(54.9%)
—	—	148	383
(—)	(—)	(35.0%)	(45.1%)
			11.8***
(—)	(—)		(.10)
599	530	187	533
(49.4%)	(66.3%)	(44.2%)	(62.7%)
111	88	39	113
(9.2%)	(11.0%)	(9.2%)	(13.3%)
286	37	130	67
(23.6%)	(4.6%)	(30.7%)	(7.9%)
161	39	58	62
(13.3%)	(4.9%)	(13.6%)	(7.3%)
56	105	9	75
(4.6%)	(13.3%)	(2.1%)	(8.8%)
	211.9***		147.8***
	(.10)		(.12)
—	—	—	—
(—)	(—)	(—)	(—)
—	—	—	—
(—)	(—)	(—)	(—)
(—)	(—)	(—)	(—)
—	—	414	837
(—)	(—)	(15.0)	(8.6)
—	—	—	8.9***

Table 3.6
Overload and Satisfaction, Nonusers and Users, 1995 and 2000

Scales	All	Nonusers	Users	T test
1995				
Overload	2.7 (sd = 1.1)	2.7	2.5	2.7* (df = 1,200)
Satisfaction	4.2 (.69)	4.1	4.3	−1.8 (1,200)
2000				
Overload	2.67 (.98)	2.8	2.7	1.7 (1,200)
Satisfaction	4.2 (.68)	4.1	4.3	−3.9*** (1,175)

Note: Overload is the mean of "How often do you feel rushed to do the things you have to do?" (1 = always to 5 = never) and "You feel you have more to do than you can comfortably handle" (1 = strongly agree to 5 = strongly disagree). Factor loadings were .83 for both items; alpha = .56.

Satisfaction is the mean of "Overall, how satisfied are you with the way your life is going?" and "How satisfied are you with your level of communication with friends, family, and work colleagues?" (both 1 = very dissatisfied to 5 = very satisfied). Factor loadings were .84 for both items; alpha = .57.

*$p < .05$.
***$p < .001$.

Awareness

The survey results identified a third digital divide—awareness of the Internet (here defined by the question "Have you heard of the Internet or the information superhighway?"). As table 3.8 shows, in 1995, those unaware of the Internet were more likely to be female (45.5%), at least 40 (47.9%), earning at least $35,000 a year (47.9%), college graduates (29.4%), and African American (7.2%). By 2000, those unaware of the Internet were likely to be male (46.7%), under 40 (50.2%), earning less than $35,000 (33.5%), college graduates (35.1%), and African American (10.5%). The changes in percentages across the years for those unaware of the Internet were statistically significant for each of the demographic factors. Thus, the awareness divide—not the usage divide—had pretty much disappeared between 1995 and 2000 with respect to education,

Table 3.7
Frequencies for Some Recoded Variables, 1995 to 2000

Variable and Values	Frequency	Percentage	Population
User:			
No	765	10.6	
Yes	6,477	89.4	
Start year:			
1975 to 1992	190	6.8	
1993	139	4.9	
1994	280	10.0	
1995	664	23.6	
1996	622	22.1	
1997	454	16.2	
1998	212	7.5	
1999	250	8.9	
Sex:			
Male	3,667	50.6	49
Female	3,573	49.4	51
Age:			
Under 40	3,555	50.9	49.5
At least 40	3,428	49.1	50.5
Education:			
Less than college degree	4,912	69.2	71.9
At least college degree	2,186	30.8	28.1
Race:			
African Americans	718	11.0	12.7
White non-Hispanic	5,794	89.0	82.5
Income:			
At least $35,000	2,547	45.1	44.6
Less than $35,000	3,106	54.9	55.3
Current user:			
Nonuser and former user	4,045	62.7	
Current user	2,404	37.3	

Table 3.7
(continued)
Frequencies for Some Recoded Variables, 1995 to 2000

Variable and Values	Frequency	Percentage	Population
Children:			
None	2,620	53.3	66.1
Any	2,298	46.7	33.9
Residence:			
Rent	1,055	32.2	68.9
Own	2,222	67.8	31.1

Note: Population figures taken from online *Statistical Abstracts of the United States,* 1998 counts or 2000 estimates (retrieved January 1, 2001 from ⟨www.census.gov/prod/www/statistcal-abstract-us.html⟩).

age, and race but not sex. Note that men in general were less aware of the Internet in the mid-1990s but that those who were aware were more likely than women to be users.

Combined Influences on Usage and Awareness

Because sex, age, income, education, and race are interrelated, the separate comparisons made in table 3.2 through table 3.8 may provide overestimates of actual differences. Statistical analysis can be used to separate out the unique contributions of the variables to differences in usage and nonusage or in awareness and nonawareness. An appropriate method for doing this is logistic regression. (Appendix A provides a basic explanation of the rationale and use of logistic regression.)

Summary logistic regressions were run to predict awareness and having never heard and to predict usage and nonusage (here former users and dropouts were not considered) from the same demographic variables and from a few additional variables in at least two of the surveys. Table 3.9 provides the results for each of the four survey years, and table 3.10 provides the results for the extended analyses for 1995 and 2000.

Significant predictors of being *aware* of the Internet in 1995 were younger, greater income, greater education, white American (14% of

Table 3.8
Awareness of the Internet by Survey Year

Variables	1995	1996	1997	2000	χ^2 and η of Variable by Survey Year
Sex:					
Male	1,160 (54.5%)	470 (49.4%)	1,007 (48.2%)	610 (46.7%)	
Female	968 (45.5%)	482 (50.6%)	1,081 (51.8%)	697 (53.3%)	25.8*** (.06)
Age:					
Under 40	1,085 (52.1%)	530 (56.6%)	1,026 (51.3%)	632 (49.8%)	
At least 40	996 (47.9%)	406 (43.4%)	973 (48.7%)	637 (50.2%)	10.8** (.04)
Income:					
Less than $35,000	900 (52.1%)	271 (44.5%)	635 (37.0%)	359 (33.5%)	
At least $35,000	829 (47.9%)	338 (55.5%)	1,079 (63.0%)	714 (66.5%)	122.4*** (.16)
Education:					
Less than college degree	1,502 (70.6%)	593 (62.9%)	1,330 (66.3%)	848 (64.9%)	
At least college degree	626 (29.4%)	350 (37.1%)	677 (33.7%)	459 (35.1%)	22.7*** (.06)
Race:					
African Americans	153 (7.2%)	64 (6.7%)	216 (10.3%)	137 (10.5%)	
White non-Hispanic	1,786 (83.9%)	825 (86.7%)	1,674 (80.2%)	1,029 (78.7%)	25.7*** (.07)

**p < .01.
***p < .001.

Table 3.9
Logistic Regressions Predicting Awareness and Usage of the Internet, 1995 to 2000

Variable	Awareness			
	1995	1996	1997	2000
Aware (no = 1, yes = 1)	—	—	—	—
Sex (male = 0, female = 1)	−.24	.37	.17	−.67**
Age (under 40 = 0, at least 40 = 1)	−.65***	−.89*	−.62**	−.68**
Income (under $35,000 = 0, at least $35,000 = 1)	.84***	1.4**	.92***	.76**
Education (less than college degree = 0, at least college degree = 1)	1.1***	.65	.93**	.39
Race (African American = 0, nonwhite Hispanic = 1)	1.3**	.68	.53*	.79**
−2 log likelihood	1,268	199.5	699.8	501.6
χ^2	142***	20.9***	51.2***	36.8***
Nagelkerke R^2	.14	.11	.08	.09
Correctly assigned	86%	95.5%	94.1%	92.8%
n	1,814	601	1,667	1,037

Note: Values are unstandardized beta coefficients from logistic regressions. Exp(B) (odds ratios) not shown.
*$p < .05$.
**$p < .01$.
***$p < .001$.

Usage			
1995	1996	1997	2000
6.5	8.4	7.5	10.4
.47**	−.30	−.34**	−.08
−.68***	−1.3***	−.87***	−1.5***
.76***	.67**	1.1***	1.4***
.92**	1.5**	1.1***	1.0***
.01	.71*	.38*	.46
877.5	593.7	1,660.5	787.6
124.5***	163.3***	382.5***	363.8***
.16	.34	.30	.46
90%	73.9%	69.8%	80.4%
1,651	564	1,505	922

variance explained, 86% of the 1,814 cases correctly predicted). By 2000, significant predictors of awareness of the Internet were male, younger, greater income, and white American (9% variance explained, 93% of the 1,037 cases correctly predicted). In 1995, additional predictors of awareness were having fewer children in the house and belonging to more leisure-oriented organizations (18% of variance explained, 88% of 768 cases correctly predicted). In 2000, additional predictors included being in fewer community organizations, living in one's home fewer years, and having greater satisfaction with life and

Table 3.10
Extended Logistic Regressions Predicting Awareness and Usage of Internet, 1995 and 2000

Variables	1995 Awareness	Usage	2000 Awareness	Usage
Aware	—	7.6	—	1,054
Sex	−.15	1.0***	−.61*	−.30
Age	−.57*	−.32	−.63*	−1.2***
Income	1.2***	1.4***	.67*	1.2***
Education	.74*	.98***	.16	.91***
Race	1.1***	−1.0*	.81*	.45
Children in house	−.54*	−.41	−.16	−.20
Leisure organizations	8.6**	.05	−.08	1.2
Community organizations	−.46	.24	−.9***	.94**
Years in residence	−.01	−.03	−.03**	−.03**
Overload	−.05	−.32*	−.15	−.16
Satisfaction	.14	.02	.30*	.30*
−2 log likelihood	493.8	347.4	418.9	683.6
χ^2	77.1***	98.8**	49.2***	343.2***
Nagelkerke R^2	.18	.28	.13	.47
Correctly assigned	87.6%	90.3%	93.6%	82.9%
n	768	700	983	870

Note: Values are unstandardized beta coefficients from logistic regressions. Exp(B) (odds ratios) not shown.
*p < .05.
**p < .01.
***p < .001.

communication (13% variance explained, 93.6% of 983 cases correctly predicted).

Significant predictors of being an Internet *user* in 1995 were male, younger, greater income, higher education. That is, using this model, a good statistical fit was obtained in which 91% of the 1,676 cases were correctly predicted and 16% of the variance was explained. By 2000, significant predictors of usage were younger, greater income, and greater education (45% variance explained, 80.2% of 924 cases correctly predicted). Additional predictors of usage in 1995 included only feeling more overloaded, while in 2000 only feeling more satisfied.

Note that by 2000, once awareness is achieved, the digital divide—differences between nonusers and users—on the basis of gender or race no longer appears in the multivariate analyses.

Motivations for Internet Usage: Nonusers and Users, Recent and Long-Term Users, 1995 and 2000

Now that we have a better understanding of the extent and nature of several divides, especially the most familiar one of usage, we can turn to other, more attitudinal influences on usage and nonusage and on one aspect of cohort differences.

To identify users' and nonusers' beliefs about their motivations for using the Internet, in 1995 and 2000 we asked them, "How important to you are the following reasons for becoming an Internet user? Sending and receiving email, have contact with new people, it's a good thing to do, and find information about special interests." The contact and information questions correspond well with Becker's (1979) independent "gratification" constructs (communication utility and surveillance), both of which have shown stability over time (see McDonald & Glynn, 1980). The 1995 survey also asked respondents the extent to which several factors—cost, access, and complexity associated with the Internet—were obstacles to becoming an Internet user.

Differences between Nonusers and Users

Table 3.11 provides the percentages across the choices (very good reason, good reason, not a good reason; or very much an obstacle, an obstacle, not an obstacle at all). "Send and receive email" was seen as a very good reason by proportionally nearly twice as many users (57% versus 29.5%) as nonusers in 1995 and by nearly three times as many (48.9% versus 13.8%) in 2000. "Have contact with new people" was seen as a very good reason by slightly more users than nonusers in both years (16.5% versus 14.2%; 10.1% versus 7.0%). "Find information about special interests" was seen as a very good reason by more users in than nonusers (43.5% versus 35.4%) in 1995. "It's a good thing to do"

Table 3.11
Motivations for Internet Use, from Nonusers and Users, 1995 and 2000

Reason a Person Might Be Interested in Becoming a User	1995		2000	
	Nonuser and Former User	User	Nonuser and Former User	User
Send and receive e-mail:				
Very good reason	205 (29.5%)	114 (57.0%)	63 (13.8%)	416 (48.9%)
Good reason	323 (46.5%)	62 (31.0%)	154 (33.8%)	348 (40.9%)
Not a good reason	167 (24.0%)	24 (12.0%)	238 (52.3%)	86 (10.1%)
χ^2		52.1***		315.8***
Have contact with new people:				
Very good reason	99 (14.2%)	33 (16.5%)	32 (7.0%)	86 (10.1%)
Good reason	273 (39.3%)	80 (40.0%)	129 (28.4%)	265 (31.2%)
Not a good reason	323 (46.5%)	87 (43.5%)	294 (64.6%)	499 (58.7%)
χ^2		.9		5.6
It's a good thing to do:				
Very good reason	80 (11.5%)	23 (11.5%)	35 (7.7%)	108 (12.7%)
Good reason	304 (43.7%)	87 (43.5%)	141 (31.0%)	334 (39.3%)
Not a good reason	311 (44.7%)	90 (45.0%)	279 (61.3%)	408 (48.0%)
χ^2		.01		22.4***
Find information about special interests:				
Very good reason	246 (35.4%)	87 (43.5%)		
Good reason	341 (49.1%)	86 (43.0%)		

Table 3.11
(continued)

Reason a Person Might Be Interested in Becoming a User	1995	
	Nonuser and Former User	User
Not a good reason	108 (15.5%)	27 (13.5%)
χ^2		4.4
Costs too much:		
Very much an obstacle	163 (26.1%)	22 (11.5%)
An obstacle	273 (43.7%)	77 (40.1%)
Not an obstacle at all	189 (30.2%)	93 (48.4%)
χ^2		28.4***
Access:		
Very much an obstacle	104 (15.9%)	30 (15.5%)
An obstacle	228 (34.8%)	47 (24.2%)
Not an obstacle at all	324 (49.4%)	117 (60.3%)
χ^2		8.6**
Too complicated:		
Very much an obstacle	63 (9.6%)	8 (4.1%)
An obstacle	210 (32.2%)	75 (38.1%)
Not an obstacle at all	380 (58.2%)	114 (57.9%)
χ^2		7.2*

*$p < .05$.
**$p < .01$.
***$p < .001$.

was considered a very good reason by equal percentages of users and nonusers in 1995 (11.5%), but users were more positive than nonusers (12.7% versus 7.7%) by 2000. As to obstacles rated in 1995, nonusers, compared to users, were more likely to feel that "costs too much" (26.1% for nonusers versus 11.5% for users), "access" (15.9% versus 15.5%), and "too complicated" (9.6% versus 4.1%) were very much obstacles. These differences in perceptions across users and nonusers were statistically significant for "send and receive email" in 1995 and 2000, "it's a good thing to do" in 2000, and all three obstacles (cost, access, and complexity) in 1995.

Differences between Recent and Long-Term Users

It may be that people who have been using the Internet for some time develop a different understanding and experience of the Internet and have different perceptions of relevant benefits and obstacles. That is, we again want to distinguish users on the basis of cohort. To that end we computed the number of years that a person had been using the Internet, based on the difference between the year of the survey and the year the person indicated he or she had begun using the Internet. People who had been using the Internet for a year or less were labeled "recent users," and those who had been using it for a year or more were labeled "long-term users." Then the same reasons and motivations were compared across these two kinds of users, for 1995 and 2000 (when this question was asked), as shown in table 3.12.

Differences between recent and long-term users exist for some years, motivations, and obstacles. Long-term users were significantly more likely to indicate that sending and receiving e-mail was a very good reason for becoming an Internet user, in both 1995 and 2000. However, there were no differences between types of users, for either year, in the extent to which "have contact with new people" was a motivation. While "it's a good thing to do" did not vary significantly between types of users in 1995, by 2000, long-term users were more likely to think this was a very good reason. Finally, there was no difference in perception of the "finding information about special interests" in 1995. Concerning the three obstacles, there was no significant association between type of user and extent of obstacle for either cost or access. However, long-term

Table 3.12
Differences in Motives and Obstacles for Recent (less than a year) and Long-Term Users (more than a year)

Reason a Person Might Be Interested in Becoming a User	1995		2000	
	Recent User	Long-Term User	Recent User	Long-Term User
Send and receive e-mail:				
Very good reason	52.0%	72.0%	32.8%	48.1%
Good reason	34.0%	22.0%	42.4%	40.8%
Not a good reason	14.0%	6.0%	24.8%	11.1%
n	150	50	250	750
χ^2		6.4*		34.5***
Have contact with new people:				
Very good reason	16.0%	18.0%	7.2%	10.5%
Good reason	40.7%	38.0%	35.2%	30.4%
Not a good reason	43.4%	44.0%	57.6%	59.1%
n	150	50	250	750
χ^2		.2 n.s.		3.6 n.s.
It's a good thing to do:				
Very good reason	9.3%	18.0%	7.6%	13.7%
Good reason	46.0%	36.0%	37.6%	38.1%
Not a good reason	74.4%	25.6%	54.8%	48.1%
n	150	50	250	750
χ^2		3.3 n.s.		7.5*
Find information about special interests:				
Very good reason	42.0%	48.0%		
Good reason	44.7%	38.0%		
Not a good reason	3%	4.0%		
n	150	50		
χ^2		.7 n.s.		

Table 3.12
(continued)

Reason a Person Might Be Interested in Becoming a User	1995	
	Recent User	Long-Term User
Costs too much:		
Very much an obstacle	14.0%	4.1%
An obstacle	38.5%	44.9%
Not an obstacle at all	47.6%	51.0%
n	413	49
χ^2		3.6 n.s.
Access:		
Very much an obstacle	17.2%	10.2%
An obstacle	21.4%	32.7%
Not an obstacle at all	61.4%	57.1%
n	145	50
χ^2		3.2 n.s.
Too complicated:		
Very much an obstacle	4.1%	4.0%
An obstacle	42.9%	24.0%
Not an obstacle at all	53.1%	72.0%
n	147	50
χ^2		5.8*

Note: Usage categories are computed by subtracting start year from survey year (e.g., 2000 minus 1997 equals 3). A value of 0 or 1 was categorized as "recent user," while a value of 2 or more was categorized as "long-term user." However, depending on when the survey was conducted and the person actually started using the Internet, the actual dividing line varies somewhat. For example, a person surveyed in February of one year who had started in November or in January of the prior year would be counted a "recent user," although in the first case only about three months had passed, while in the second case about 14 months had passed. We did in fact ask for both year and month of beginning Internet use but received fewer complete responses for the month question.
*$p < .05$.
**$p < .01$.
***$p < .001$.

users were marginally less likely ($p = .05$) to feel that complexity was an obstacle to using the Internet.

Motivations Summary

The findings about motivations highlight the favorable view toward potential social interaction held by many denizens, as well as nonusers, of the Internet. About half judge e-mail as a very good reason for having Internet service. Although the number itself is not high, the fact that 10% of users think "have contact with new people" is a good reason to have Internet service is an impressive number when extended to the millions of Internet users nationwide. The themes of interpersonal communication and the creation of new social relationships are central to our understanding the Internet's consequences for American society and are discussed in chapters 10 through 14.

Results from the Pew Internet and American Life Project Survey, March 2000

The coordinators of the Pew Internet and American Life Project generously shared their March 2000 survey data with us. (See appendixes A and B for an explanation of the Pew survey methodology and a summary of the survey's variables, value ranges, frequencies, and percentages.) Relevant variables include demographics, use of newspapers and television, social support and activities, a wide variety of types of uses (time spent online yesterday, recent or long-term use, various uses of the Internet yesterday or ever (such as exchanging e-mails with specific family or friends, or searching for specific kinds of information), usefulness and outcomes of e-mail with family or friends, and changes associated with Internet usage.

Demographic Differences between Nonusers and Users

Of the 2,238 responding to the question, 24.4% indicated they had never used the Internet, while 75.5% said that they had used the Internet (such as for searching for information or e-mail). Of those, 59.5% used the Internet the day before.

Table 3.13 summarizes the demographic differences between nonusers and users, between recent (less than one year) and long-term (more than one year) users, and between nonusers and recent users. Compared to nonusers, users are significantly more likely to be male, be under 40 years old, have college degrees, have incomes over $40,000, and be white non-Hispanic. Usage status does not significantly differ between full-time and other workers, between those who are married or not, or between those with children or not. All these differences (and nondifferences) persist for long-term users compared to recent users, except that long-term users are also slightly less likely to have children. Thus, in the 2000 Pew survey, the demographic differences between long-term users and recent users extends the digital divide between users and nonusers, similar to the cohort analysis of our multiple surveys.

Table 3.14 summarizes the results of a logistic regression (predicting nonuser and user and recent and long-term user) that controls for any statistical interdependencies among the demographic variables. The three main influences—younger age, more education, and more income—persist as significant components of a digital divide between nonusers and users, while sex and race disappear as factors, as in our own survey data (especially for recent cohorts). For predicting long-term versus recent usage, younger age, greater education, being white, and not having children persist as significant influences, while sex and income disappear as factors.

The analyses show that digital divides are decreasing on some major demographic variables for recent, compared to long-term, users. The third pair of columns in the table, especially the far right one (which shows the odds ratio), provides more details about this decline. The ratio of the influence of being older to being younger did increase between nonusers and recent users, compared to nonusers and users (from .45 to .56). However, the ratio decreased substantially for the influence of more to less education (from 2.6 to 1.4) and from more to less income (from 2.0 to 1.7). The opposite trend occurs for recent compared to long-term users on the other two demographic variables—race and having children. That is, while there is a greater likelihood of being a long-term user for white non-Hispanics (indicating the increasing adoption rate of African Americans, as shown in the cohort analyses) and for those no

Table 3.13

Demographic Differences between Nonusers and Users and between Recent and Long-Term Users, from the Pew Survey, March 2000

Variables	Nonusers	Users	χ^2	Recent Users	Long-Term Users	χ^2
Sex male	43.4% (548)	50.7% (1,690)	(8.8***)	46.0% (635)	53.7% (1,050)	(9.5***)
Age under 40	44.2% (539)	58.0% (1,655)	(31.5***)	54.8% (622)	60.0% (1,028)	(4.3*)
Education less than college degree	80.4% (545)	59.6% (1,680)	(77.4***)	72.7% (630)	51.6% (1,045)	(72.8*)
Income less than $40,000	46.0% (548)	30.1% (1,690)	(46.8***)	34.6% (635)	27.1% (1,050)	(10.6***)
Race black (versus white non-Hispanic)	14.1% (461)	10.2% (1,428)	(5.3*)	13.1% (534)	8.5% (889)	(7.5**)
Work full-time	70.0% (546)	66.9% (1,679)	(ns)	67.3% (630)	66.8% (1,044)	(ns)
Unmarried	45.8% (537)	43.3% (1,650)	(ns)	42.8% (612)	43.8% (1,033)	(ns)
No children	58.8% (547)	58.8% (1,685)	(ns)	55.8% (633)	60.6% (1,048)	(3.8*)

Note: To save space, the top row provides the percentages only for the listed category (of two categories) for nonusers and users, while the bottom row provides the total sample size for the two categories. The percentages for the other category for nonusers and users can be computed from these two values. The χ^2 indicates the extent of association between the two categories of the usage variable and the two categories of each other variable.

* $p < .05$.
** $p < .01$.
*** $p < .001$.

Table 3.14
Logistic Regressions Predicting Internet User Categories from Demographics, from the Pew Survey, March 2000

Variables	Nonuser (0) User (1)		Recent (0) Long-Term (1)		Nonuser (0) Recent User (1)	
	B	Exp(B)	B	Exp(B)	B	Exp(B)
Age (0 under 40, 1 at least 40)	−.80***	.45	−.40***	.67	−.58***	.56
Education (0 = no college degree, 1 = at least college degree)	.97***	2.6	.94***	2.6	.37*	1.4
Income (0 = less than $40,000, 1 = greater than $40,000)	.70***	2.0	—	—	.54***	1.7
Race (0 = African American, 1 = White non-Hispanic)	—	—	.44*	1.6	—	—
Children (0 = no, 1 = yes)	—	—	−.23*	.79	—	—
−2 log likelihood	2,276		1,774		1,556	
χ^2	164***		80.3***		43***	
Nagelkerke R^2	.11		.08		.05	
Correctly assigned	75.5%		63.4%		57.6%	
n	2,190		1,400		1,158	

Note: B values are unstandardized β coefficients, and Exp(B) are odds ratios, from logistic regression.
* $p < .05$.
** $p < .01$.
*** $p < .001$.

having children, recent users were no more likely than nonusers to have these attributes. This means that racial and parental differences were once components of the digital divide but are no longer.

Conclusion

Concerning access, on all the dimensions considered here—gender, age, household income, education, and race and ethnicity—the digital divide is shrinking. Nevertheless, all the differences within the demographic variables, based on the years of the survey, were significant. Our analyses revealed several forms of the digital divide: usage versus nonusage, cohort versus survey year, awareness versus nonawareness, and, as the next chapter discusses, continuing users versus dropouts.

For some demographic dimensions, the digital divide remains. Perhaps more crucial, however, is the level of awareness that potential users have; our results indicate that awareness is a greater, and certainly prior, divide than is usage. Public policy initiatives aimed at extending awareness of the Internet could most usefully focus on low-income families, the elderly, and African Americans. The inequities of awareness and use will become increasingly urgent as more job-related services (such as postings of job opportunities and training), government functions, and public-service information (including health, education, insurance, financial support) become available via the Internet.

4

Logging Off: Internet Dropouts

Although considerable attention has been given to questions of the adoption of new technologies, much less interest has been shown by the policy and intellectual communities in the question of people giving up or abandoning technologies. As is discussed in chapter 3, the primary access issue is the digital divide between users and nonusers and among categories of users. We also have identified and analyzed two other divides—cohorts and awareness—and introduced a fourth divide: Internet dropouts. These are people who have used the Internet for (typically) a short while and then stopped using it. This chapter probes the number of, nature of, and influences on Internet dropouts.

This group is of interest not only on its own merits but also because its size, which is substantial. Studying Internet dropouts is interesting because of its potential to reveal barriers and disincentives for Internet participation. This subject is of critical importance as policymakers and opinion leaders struggle with questions of the digital divide among the information haves and have-nots in our society (discussed in chapters 2 and 3). The existence of Internet dropouts has even been used to criticize, in a United Nations publication, the commercial nature and "exhausting pace" of the Internet (Wyatt, 2001).

It is surprising how little attention has been directed to the non-adoption or decline of technologies in general. Fischer (1992) noted that participation in the telephone system rose during the 1920s, receded in the 1930s, and increased again in the 1940s; this dip was driven by the economic conditions of the Great Depression. There has been some scholarly interest in universal access to telephone service and why some people choose not to use telephones (see, for example, Dutton, Rogers &

Jun, 1987). But generally speaking, little attention has been devoted to the rise and fall (and in some cases second rise) of communication technologies. In this regard, we note that although millions of people use citizens-band radios every day, they receive virtually no attention from scholars. Likewise, despite the rapid proliferation of cellular telephones and the millions of daily users in a plethora of situations, few articles have examined the social aspects of this technology (Katz & Aspden, 1998b). Moreover, the churn rate appears substantial for cellular telephone technologies—costing service providers $4 billion in 1997 (TR Daily, 1997). Initial adopters who stop using a technology may be "owners" of the technology but certainly cannot be considered users (Batt & Katz, 1998). The phenomenon of dropping out is different from that of not adopting a technology in the first place. (There have been a variety of interesting studies on the nonadoption of television (Edgar, 1977), video on demand (Noll, 1992; Noll & Woods, 1979), videotex (Carey & Pavlik, 1993; Pryor, 1994), and the telephone (Umble, 1996), and the time is probably ripe for a study of the nonadoption of the Internet.)

Results

Table 4.1 provides detailed percentages and cross-tabulations of dropouts and users for a variety of demographic variables for each survey year.

More Dropouts Than You Might Think

As table 3.1 showed, approximately 8% of the survey respondents were dropouts in 1995, 11% in the 1996, 10% in 1997, and 11.5% in 2000. However, across the combined four surveys, approximately one-fifth of all people *who had ever used the Internet* (that is, the total of those who were current users and of those who had dropped out) had in fact stopped using it as of the time of the survey. The specific percentages range from 48.7% in the 1995 sample, to 10.4% in 1996, 20.8% in 1997, and 15.0% in 2000. This variation across the years was statistically significant. The percentage of dropouts is larger in earlier years because there were far fewer total users, while the percentage of total respondents who were dropouts was fairly similar.

Users for Only a Short Time

Many Internet dropouts had been users only for a short time. In the 1995 survey, 38% of dropouts were users for a month or less, and the balance for two months or more; in 1996, 49% of dropouts were users for a month or less. There was no statistically significant difference between very short-term users (one month or less) and dropouts with two or more months of usage in either survey for demographic variables (age, sex, highest education level achieved, household income, race, marital status, and work status), for using a personal computer at home, or for using a computer at for work.

Across the four surveys, more than two-thirds of the 567 respondents who dropped out and who reported the year when they did so stopped using the Internet in the same year as the survey, with the other third doing so in the prior years (almost all in the preceding year). The percentage of respondents dropping out the same year as the survey ranged from 80% in 1995 to 68.4% in 1996, 79.5% in 1997, and 43.4% in 2000. Across the combined four surveys, there were no statistically significant differences in demographics (education, race, sex, work status, marital status, income) between the same-year and the prior-year dropouts, except that same-year dropouts were more likely to be under 40 (76.2%) than prior-year dropouts (66.1%) ($p < .01$). There were too few cases to analyze by separate survey year.

Dropouts Younger and Less Educated Than Users

Table 4.1 shows that across the combined four surveys, dropouts (compared to users) were

- More likely to report their Internet skill level as "novice," as opposed to average, above average, or expert,
- Not different with respect to working full time or otherwise,
- More likely to be under 40 years old,
- Less likely to have graduated from college,
- Likely to have a family income less than $35,000,
- Slightly more likely to be African American,
- More likely to have never been married or divorced/widowed/have a partner/other,

Table 4.1
Dropouts Compared to Users, Overall and by Year, 1995 to 2000

Variables	1995–2000			1995		
	User	Dropout	Total, χ^2	User	Dropout	Total, χ^2
Dropouts:						
Rate		20.3%			48.7%	
Total		614	249.5***		190	
Years used until dropout:						
Same year		68.9%	392		80.0%	
Year or more		31.3%	177		20.0%	
Total			65.7***		165	
Dropout year:						
Prior years		32.2%			20.0%	
Survey year		68.8%			80.0%	
Total		567			165	
Expertise:						
Novice	24.6%	36.7%	510	47.5%		
Average, above average, expert	75.4%	63.3%	1,490	53.5%		
Total	1,850	150	10.6***	200		
Work:						
Full-time	63.7%	61.0%	1,900	69.5%	65.8%	264
Part-time, unemployed, retired, no pay, student	36.3%	39.0%	1,109	30.5%	34.2%	126
Total	2,398	611	1.4 ns	200	190	.6 ns
Age:						
Under 40	58.7%	72.7%	1,828	65.2%	75.7%	272
At least 40	41.3%	27.4%	1,141	34.8%	24.3%	115
Total	2,351	608	40.0***	198	189	5.1*
Under 65	96.7%	98.0%	2,878	99.5%	97.9%	382
At least 65	3.3%	2.0%	91	.5%	4	5
Total	2,361	608	3.1 ns	198	189	2.0 ns
Education:						
Less than college degree	52.9%	71.0%	1,701	48.0%	65.8%	221
At least college degree	47.1%	29.0%	1,305	52.0%	34.2%	169
Total	2,395	611	65.1***	200	190	12.6***

1996			1997			2000		
User	Dropout	Total, χ^2	User	Dropout	Total, χ^2	User	Dropout	Total, χ^2
	10.4%			20.8%			15.0%	
	64			210			150	
	68.4%			79.5%			43.4%	
	31.6%			20.5%			56.6%	
	57			195			152	
	31.6%			20.5%			57.3%	
	68.4%			79.5%			42.7%	
	57			195			150	
25.8%						18.1%	36.7%	209
74.3%						81.9%	63.3%	791
800						850	150	26.5***
59.2%	50.0%	357	66.3%	63.3%	661	62.7%	56.7%	618
40.8%	50.0%	256	33.7%	36.7%	345	37.3%	43.3%	382
549	131	2.0 ns	533	85	.68 ns	850	150	2.0 ns
62.3%	74.6%	386	57.8%	73.4%	610	55.6%	67.1%	560
37.7%	25.4%	221	42.2%	26.6%	389	44.4%	32.9%	416
544	63	3.7*	792	207	16.8***	827	149	6.8**
97.1%	100%	591	97.6%	99.0%	978	94.8%	96.0%	927
2.9%	0%	16	2.4%	1.0%	21	5.2%	4.0%	49
544	63	1.9 ns	792	207	1.6 ns	827	149	.4 ns
52.4%	67.2%	331	51.2%	69.6%	551	56.0%	81.3%	598
47.6%	32.8%	283	48.8%	30.4%	451	44.0%	18.7%	402
550	64	5.1*	795	207	22.4***	850	150	34.0***

Table 4.1
(continued)

Variables	1995–2000			1995		
	User	Dropout	Total, χ^2	User	Dropout	Total, χ^2
Income:						
Under $35,000	25.7%	44.6%	715	30.7%	52.0%	130
At least $35,000	74.3%	55.4%	1,703	69.3%	48.0%	188
Total	1,918	500	68.4***	166	152	14.8***
Race:						
White non-Hispanic	83.5%	78.7%	2,490	83.5%	82.6%	324
African American	7.4%	10.3%	240	6.0%	7.9%	27
Asian	3.2%	2.3%	90	3.0%	3.7%	13
Hispanic	3.5%	6.7%	124	3.5%	4.2%	15
Other	2.5%	2.1%	74	4.0%	1.6%	11
Total	2,404	614	20.5***	200	190	2.8 ns
Race:						
White non-Hispanic	91.9%	88.5%	2,490	93.3%	91.3%	324
African American	8.1%	11.5%	240	6.7%	8.7%	27
Total	2,184	546	6.4**	179	172	.5 ns
Marital status:						
Never married	36.8%	45.5%	1,163	37.5%	47.4%	165
Married	52.2%	41.2%	1,507	51.5%	42.1%	183
Divorced, widowed, partner, other	11.1%	13.4%	348	11.0%	10.5%	42
Total	2,404	614	23.5***	200	190	4.1 ns
Sex:						
Male	51.2%	45.8%	1,513	37.5%	41.6%	154
Female	48.8%	54.2%	1,505	62.5%	58.4%	236
Total	2,404	614	5.9*	200	190	.7 ns
Reason stopped:						
Access		22.9%	510		17.4%	33
Not interesting		12.2%	510		2.1%	4
Hard, complex		14.9%	510		1.1%	2
Cost		15.7%	510		5.3%	10
Time		7.5%	510		10.5%	20

1996			1997			2000		
User	Dropout	Total, χ^2	User	Dropout	Total, χ^2	User	Dropout	Total, χ^2
37.2%	53.7%	155	21.2%	35.6%	209	23.0%	45.7%	221
62.8%	46.3%	244	78.8%	64.4%	656	77.0%	54.3%	615
358	41	4.2*	685	180	16.1***	709	127	28.5***
88.6%	76.6%	540	84.1%	78.6%	838	79.5%	74.7%	788
5.1%	9.4%	34	7.5%	10.5%	82	9.1%	13.3%	97
2.0%	3.1%	13	3.3%	1.4%	29	3.9%	1.3%	35
2.9%	6.3%	20	3.3%	8.1%	43	4.0%	8.0%	46
1.4%	4.7%	11	1.9%	1.4%	18	3.5%	2.7%	34
554	64	8.7 ns	800	210	13.7**	850	150	9.9*
94.6%	89.1%	540	91.8%	88.2%	838	89.8%	84.8%	788
5.4%	10.9%	34	8.2%	11.8%	82	10.2%	15.2%	97
519	55	2.7 ns	733	187	2.4 ns	753	132	2.8 ns
39.5%	50.0%	251	34.0%	45.7%	368	37.4%	40.7%	37.9%
52.5%	39.1%	316	55.6%	42.4%	534	48.8%	39.3%	47.4%
7.9%	10.9%	51	10.4%	11.9%	108	13.8%	20.0%	14.7%
554	64	4.2 ns	800	210	12.1**	850	150	6.2*
53.6%	42.2%	324	55.0%	51.9%	549	49.4%	44.0%	486
46.4%	57.8%	294	45.0%	48.1%	461	50.6%	56.0%	514
554	64	3.0 ns	800	210	.6 ns	850	150	1.5 ns
			14.8%		31		48.2%	52
			3.3%		7		46.4%	51
			1.0%		2		65.5%	72
			4.8%		10		54.5%	60
			4.8%		10			

Table 4.1
(continued)

Variables	1995–2000			1995		
	User	Dropout	Total, χ^2	User	Dropout	Total, χ^2
Satisfaction (life, communication):						
Less satisfied	52.9%	43.6%	616	48.2%	49.5%	101
More satisfied	47.1%	56.4%	591	51.8%	50.5%	106
Total	964	243	6.7**	114	93	.03 ns
Overload (rushed, more work):						
Less rushed	32.5%	38.3%	406	31.6%	31.2%	65
More rushed	67.5%	61.7%	801	68.4%	68.8%	142
Total	964	243	2.9 ns	114	93	.00 ns

$*p < .05.$
$**p < .01.$
$***p < .001.$

• Slightly more likely to be female,

• Slightly more likely to be satisfied in general (a scale comprising the mean of "satisfaction with your life" and "satisfaction with your communication," and

• Equally likely to feel overloaded (a scale comprising the mean of "feeling rushed" and "having more work to do than you can handle").

Both because of possible differences across the years (such as changes in demographic profiles of users) and because of smaller sample sizes, specific demographic differences within each survey year were not as pronounced. In 1995, dropouts were more likely to be younger, have not graduated from college, and have lower family income. In 1996, dropouts were slightly more likely to be younger, have not graduated from college, and have lower income. The profile for 1997 was the same as for 1996, except that dropouts were also more likely to be never married. In 2000, dropouts were much more likely to be novices, slightly more likely to be younger, much more likely to have not graduated from college, much more likely to have lower income, slightly more likely either to have never been married or to be divorced/widowed/live with a partner/

1996			1997			2000		
User	Dropout	Total, χ^2	User	Dropout	Total, χ^2	User	Dropout	Total, χ^2
						53.5%	40.0%	515
						46.5%	60.0%	485
						850	150	9.3**
						32.6%	42.7%	341
						67.4%	57.3%	659
						850	150	5.8*

other, somewhat more likely to be less satisfied with life and communication, and slightly less likely to feel overloaded.

Reasons for Dropping Out

The 1995, 1997, and 2000 surveys offered responding dropouts several reasons for their decision. The wordings and scales are not the same in 2000, so percentages are not exactly comparable. The first two surveys provided open-ended questions where respondents could offer their reasons for dropping out, and these responses were grouped into categories. The 2000 survey offered five-point Likert-style questions (from "extremely important" to "not at all important," with the first two values recoded as that reason being selected). Further, the total number of respondents providing reasons was very small except in 2000, so these are only indicative. Across the three years, the most frequent reason given was "loss of access" (22.9%), with the following less frequent reasons: "cost" (15.7%), "too hard or complex" (14.9%), "not interesting" (12.2%), and "too much time" (7.5%). "Access" was by far the most frequently named reason in 1995 (17.4%) and 1997 (14.8%). In 2000, "too hard or complex" was the most frequently named reason (65.5%), followed by "cost" (54.5%), "lost access" (48.2%), and "not interesting" (46.4%).

We appear to have been the first to detect the Internet dropout phenomenon and note that other researchers have begun following up this issue. Thus, for instance, a recent U.S. Department of Commerce report (2000) surveying some 48,000 households also reported on those who discontinued Internet usage. Extrapolating to the entire nation, it estimated there were about 4 million dropouts in both 1998 and 2000. The three primary reasons given in 2000 for discontinuing were "no longer owns a computer" (17%), "can use it elsewhere" (13%), and "cost, too expensive" (12%). Other reasons were "don't want it" (10.3%), "not enough time" (10%), "computer requires repair" (9.7%), "moved" (6.1%), "not useful" (4.2%), "problems with ISP" (2.9%), "concern with children" (2.3%), "not user friendly" (1.5%), and "computer capacity issues" (1.2%). For those with incomes of less than $25,000, "cost, too expensive" was the first or second most important reason for nonaccess at home. For those with higher incomes, "no longer owns a computer" or "can use it elsewhere" were the most important reasons. The report notes that these reasons differ from the primary reason given by nonusers for never connecting at all with the Internet, which is "don't want it."

When analyzed across the combined surveys (there were too few responses to analyze by separate years), very few of these reasons differed across the dichotomized demographic categories (age, education, race, gender, work status, marital status, income). Respondents under 40 years of age were more likely to mention each of the five reasons (all at least $p < .01$). Married respondents were more likely to mention "not interesting" ($p < .05$). And those with family income more than $35,000 were more likely to mention "hard/complex" ($p < .05$).

Combining Influences on Dropouts

Because the various demographic and other variables tend to be intercorrelated, it is useful to combine all those variables that were statistically significant across dropouts and users into a logistic regression equation, which then controls for shared variance across the predictors (again, see appendix A for a short discussion of logistic regression).

Table 4.2 provides evidence for some conceptually useful relationships between the independent variables (age, education, race, marital status,

Table 4.2
Logistic Regressions Predicting Dropouts by Selected Demographics, Overall and by Year, 1995 to 2000

Predictor	1995–2000		1995		1996		1997		2000	
	B	Exp(B)	B	Exp(B)	B	Exp(B)	B	Exp(B)	B	Exp(B)
Age (0 = under 40, 1 = at least 40)	−.51***	.60	−.54*	.58	−.32	.73	−.53**	.59	−.31	.73
Education (0 = less than college degree, 1 = at least college degree)	−.63***	.53	−.70***	.50	−.46	.63	−.58***	.56	−1.1***	.34
Race (0 = African American, 1 = white non-Hispanic)	−.23	.79	−.15	.86	−.62	.54	−.28	.75	−.30	.76
Marital (1 = no, 2 = yes)	−.15	.86	−.11	.90	−.37	.69	−.25	.78	−.06	.94
χ^2	89.0***		18.1***		9.8*		31.9***		33.3***	
Nagelkerke R^2	.05		.07		.04		.05		.07	
n	2,692		349		563		909		871	

*$p < .05$.
**$p < .01$.
***$p < .001$.

and survey year for the combined datasets), and the dichotomous dependent variable (user $= 0$, dropout $= 1$). Across the four surveys combined, dropouts are more likely to be younger and not have graduated from college. When the year of the survey is added (to test and control for any trend effect), dropouts are more likely in earlier years (again this is largely due to the dropout rate being based on the total number of users, which increases each year), and being African American becomes a slight influence on dropping out. Significant influences in the separate years are for 1995, younger and less educated; for 1996, no predictor (due to the small sample size); for 1997, younger and less educated; and for 2000, less educated.

The overall model is significant but does not yield a particularly good fit, explaining only 4% to 7% of the variance for the combined and separate years. These demographic variables are not explaining much of the variation in "dropping out," given all the other vagaries that might affect such a decision. At the same time, inefficient though it might be, the model does yield some interesting and statistically significant results. Note that in all four years the direction and magnitude of effects are approximately the same. This is a worthwhile finding, since we can think of these surveys as independent samples that confirm the hypothesized importance of variables established in 1995 that are still important in 2000. This set of results, then, increases the validity of the data and the findings. These results tend to highlight the concerns of social scientists and policymakers about the digital divide and associated social consequences of the Internet, but they do so in a different context. Rather than a digital divide being limited to the first and most common distinction (between users and nonusers), our second and third types of divides (cohort and awareness) are joined by a noticeable fourth digital divide—that between ongoing users and Internet dropouts.

Additional Analyses

The 1995 survey also asked respondents how they learned about the Internet. Looking at respondents 20 years and older only (to avoid including those still in college), there were significant differences between the routes into the Internet for dropouts and users. For dropouts, 42%

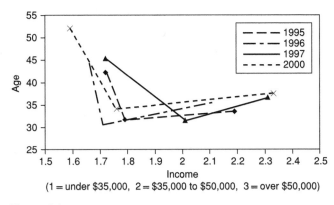

Figure 4.1
Three User Categories (User, Dropout, and Nonuser, Aware) by Income and Age,
1995, 1996, 1997, and 2000

reported being taught by a friend (19% of users), 18% learned at work
(35% of users), and 15% were self-taught (25% of users). Differences
between dropouts and users were not great for being taught by a university course (16% versus 14%) or some other course (10% versus
5%). (The overall chi square for this 2×5 cross-tabulation was 37.7,
$p < .001$.) Thus a much higher proportion of dropouts than users was
taught by family or friends, while users were more likely to be self-taught
or taught at work. This may suggest that a large percentage of dropouts
were less focused in their interest in the Internet than users were in our
survey, that they were taught in a more informal way, and that they
perhaps had a less thorough grounding in Internet techniques than users.

The analyses so far have focused on comparisons of the characteristics
of users and of dropouts of the Internet. But it is useful to relate dropouts
and users to those who are aware of the Internet but are not users (aware
nonusers), our third kind of digital divide. Across the four survey years,
these three categories differ significantly by income categories (1 = under
$35,000, 2 = $35,000 to $50,000, 3 over $50,000) (aware nonuser =
1.7, dropout = 1.85, user = 2.27; $F = 257.6$, $p < .001$), and by age
(44.2, 32.1, 36.4, $F = 258.9$, $p < .001$). (The three categories of users
significantly differ by income and by age for each separate year as well,
with all F ratios $p < .001$.) Figure 4.1 displays the relative positioning of

the three Internet experience groups—aware nonusers, dropouts, and current users—on the demographic map with mean household income measured as a ranked category and mean age as axes.

Discussion

The Dropout Digital Divide

Being a former Internet user, or dropout, is primarily associated with being younger and less educated. Other major factors appear to be lower income and not being married. These survey results do not throw any light on the specific reasons that Internet users who are younger or who have less education are more likely to become Internet dropouts. The reasons they gave when surveyed were not related to their educational level, except the response that indicated that the Internet was hard to use or too complex. Those with higher educational achievements may be more able to understand and use the Internet or better comprehend the opportunities provided by the Internet. They also may be more likely to have a job that requires the use of the Internet or simply to have interests and preferences that are satisfied through Internet use and services.

Earlier work found that users and dropouts share the same set of beliefs about the Internet's value (Katz & Aspden, 1997a, 1997b). Despite this, the fact that survey dropouts were younger, less educated, and in some years less likely to be married suggests that dropouts and users may not share the same social and economic priorities. Thus, dropouts may be more likely than users to feel that the Internet is not worthy of their attention. Our earlier finding that younger people are more likely to stop using the Internet because of lack of interest supports this view.

Reasons for Dropping Out

Our surveys identified five basic reasons for withdrawing from using the Internet—loss of physical access, lack of interest, computer being hard to use or complex, high costs, and lack of time. Those under age 40 cited these more frequently than did those age 40 or over. The most frequently cited reasons for dropping out were problems with physical access (mostly losing access) and the Internet being too hard or complex.

Loss of physical access appears more likely to affect young people, who tend to change jobs frequently or lose access when they graduate from college. Young people are more likely to have a wider range of and frequently changing demands on their time. On the other hand, older people may have more pressing business and social reasons for using the Internet. People who are not married (either never have been or once were) seem to have less time or less reason to use the Internet, while those with greater incomes were more likely to indicate that the Internet was hard or too complex to use.

Conclusion

Dropping out of, or disadopting, a new medium has not been studied to the degree that adoption of the medium has been studied. In fact, major policies, such as the Clinton administration's goal to wire all schools to the Internet by the year 2000, are predicated on a perceived inevitability about the widespread adoption and use of certain new technologies. Despite the topic's considerable relevance to both policymakers and service providers, including educators, inaction by academics has delayed its being identified as a salient question for the policy community. At the same time, the issue of dropouts may be only transient—that is, nearly all dropouts may once again become and remain users. Yet it is also possible that the Internet will indeed follow the model of the CB radio, which saw explosive growth followed by a falling back to a modest but steadily growing base of users. While the ultimate future of the Internet cannot be known, there seem at present to be millions of former Internet users. Given the substantial economic and social equity stakes, the causes and consequences of this dropout phenomenon require further investigation.

5

Access and Digital Divide Examples

We support making the Internet available to as many people as are interested in it or can be persuaded to try it, use it, and contribute to it. We want this not only for the sake of the potential users we have in mind but also in the long run for the benefit of society and ourselves. Americans will benefit from the collective social capital created through widespread participation. At a minimum, we all will benefit from network externalities—the surplus benefits that accrue to a group on a network as more people participate in that network. This is similar to a telephone network, which becomes more useful as more people have telephones—not because each new joiner can call people (an internal benefit) but because all the others can now call the new entrant, an external benefit that was not available when earlier subscribers joined the network and that is received through no effort of the subscribers (see Leibenstein, 1950; Leibowitz & Margolis, 1998). Our concerns in this chapter have a different focus—making sense of the digital divide from analytical, program, and policy viewpoints.

Perspective on the Digital Divide

Historically, individuals and groups seeking access to information have encountered numerous cultural, political, physical, and geographical barriers. Although the Internet allows many people in the United States and around the world to penetrate these historically impermeable barriers, there is continuing and legitimate frustration over difficult, costly, and inequitable access to the Internet.

In chapters 2 and 3, we discussed the ways in which a digital divide might be thought of in terms of ethnicity, social class, or gender. This chapter explores specific examples of programs that can help to overcome both these and other types of digital divides that slice and fractionate society at both the local and global levels.

Our main point is that for U.S. residents the limits to Internet access are largely psychological and cultural rather than structural and technological (though these barriers exist as well). Our evidence shows that when people see the benefits of the Internet as meaningful to them, they often activate themselves to gain access. Indeed, even the desire to have access can lead to the creation of social capital as people work together to bring local information service providers (ISPs) to their remote area (box 5.1).

The Internet may not become available or be embraced in an equitable fashion. But with tenacity some have overcome even high technical, physical, and social barriers to gain access. At the same time, many barriers cannot be overcome even with great exertions. Despite individual or group heroics, there is much to commend about systematic programs that simplify learning about and taking advantage of the enormous benefits that may be conferred by Internet access. We look at some of these programs that encourage access among communities and that lead to the individual and social benefits we discuss in chapters 9, 13, and 14.

Examining Internet use on the basis of race alone has caused some to interpret use patterns as self-evident truth of the inferiority of groups that rank low in usage. We need to be careful about attributing the explanatory sequences for the digital divide to avoid fueling arguments about cultural or ethnic superiority. In fact, racial and ethnic variables are less significant than income, education, and awareness variables.

Access: An Important Human Right

Access to information is one of the many (often conflicting) rights that are reflected in the United Nations Charter of Human Rights, in various U.S. laws, and in the U.S. Constitution. Access to information is not simply a matter of individual financial resources but is a by-product of economic systems and even social justice structures. Political and legal barriers,

Box 5.1
Local Initiatives Speed the Internet's Arrival to an Isolated County

In 1995, there were no Internet service providers (ISPs) in Garrett County, the rural, western-most county in Maryland. Few people accessed the Internet, and those who did had to pay long-distance charges to access America Online or CompuServe. The challenge facing Garrett Community College (GCC) was how to bring Internet services to the College in a way that leveraged the community's information technology expertise and benefited the wider community.

GCC decided to fund a trial community-based bulletin board service that was free and was accessed by dial-up connection. The service was a success. By early 1996, usage had grown to about 350 users accessing a pool of 25 modems, and administering the network was becoming difficult. Because the trial had demonstrated a strong demand for electronic interconnectivity in the community, GCC decided to plan a more ambitious system.

GCC put together its requirements—Intranet capability, Internet connectivity, and turnkey operation. A Chicago company was awarded the contract, and the service went live in September 1996 using seed money provided by the state. The Garrett Rural Information Cooperative (GRIC) was formed during the early stages of the bulletin board trial. To help make it a communitywide enterprise, a steering committee was set up with representatives from the college, county government, local health services, county Library, board of education, social services agencies, county economic development office, local agriculture, and Bausch & Lomb (at the time the community's largest private-sector employer but now gone from the area). In March 1996, the GRIC was formally launched. The GRIC provided oversight of Intranet and Internet service and owned the equipment, while GCC operated the service.

By early 1997, there were about 700 subscribers to the new Intranet and Internet service. Particularly important at this time were the Intranet applications, such as the family resource database and calendar of community events. Nearly 200 pages of Garrett County activities were posted on the Web site, including a page devoted to snail merchandising by a local farmer. The GRIC had put Garrett County on the telecom map.

Subscribership grew rapidly, and within two and a half years after service launch GRIC had 4,000 customers. Service was extended to customers in West Virginia, Pennsylvania, and other Maryland counties. At this point GCC decided that it no longer wanted to be in the Internet service business and spun the service off into an independent operation now referred to as GCNet.

The success of GRIC demonstrated that a market existed for Internet services in Garrett County. This stimulated other Internet service providers

Box 5.1
(continued)

> to offer service, and now about half a dozen ISPs offer service in Garrett
> County including a local start-up.
>   Don Storck, director of information technology at GCC, believes the
> local initiatives brought Internet services to Garrett County to the social
> and economic advantage of the area many years before commercial Inter-
> net services would have been available.
> *Source:* Philip Aspden, personal communication, August 8, 2001.

intentionally constructed, are important obstacles (Rice, McCreadie &
Chang, 2001; see also chapter 2). The censorship and radio transmission
blocking practices of the former Soviet Union continue to this day in
countries in Asia, Central Asia, and Africa. At the same time, political
and religious leaders in many countries have also sought to erect a variety
of barriers to cultural access to protect their populations from materials
those leaders find morally corrosive and offensive. Despite the First
Amendment, some categories of material are censored even in the United
States. Geographical distance from the physical location of the information has long been a major barrier to access, as have the health conditions of millions of people.

Access Programs to Overcome Group or Individual Isolation

The programs that have been developed to give Internet access to groups
or individuals often are framed as attempts to overcome isolation. Not
often mentioned is that many of these individuals or groups have much
to contribute to those who already use (or will use) the Internet:

• Several programs are available for the blind (see Eisenberg, 2000)
(box 5.2).

• For those with limitations on their physical mobility, the Internet offers
contact with others and vast information resources, including how to
manage their disabilities. Steve Kareau is an online digital artist from
Tennessee who has fibromyalgia and also suffers from severe spinal ar-
thritis: "My computer screen is the only contact I have with the world.

Box 5.2
How the Blind Access the Internet

The National Federation of the Blind receives thousands of phone calls, e-mails, and letters each year asking how the blind are able to "go online" and use the Internet. You may be surprised to learn that we, the blind, use much of the same technology as the sighted when going onto the Internet. However, there are some differences.

A blind person who wants access to the Internet will usually get a standard personal computer running.... But since we cannot see the video display of the computer, we need another piece of technology to recognize icons and convert the text on the screen into synthesized speech or Braille. This screen-access technology is available from a handful of specialized companies and cannot be purchased from a local computer store. It costs anywhere from $500 to $1,500....

Once screen-access technology has been purchased and installed, a blind computer user can then "go online" using pretty much the same software as someone who is sighted. For example, many of us use Microsoft's Internet Explorer to surf the Web and programs such as Eudora or Outlook Express to do our e-mail.

There are two important things that must happen if our screen-access technology is to work well with Web browsing software or e-mail programs. First, the functions available in an e-mail program or Web browser must be accessible from the keyboard; it is not yet possible for a blind person to use the mouse to "point and click." Second, the information displayed on the screen needs to be recognized and understood by the screen-access technology. This means that graphical objects (e.g., icons, buttons, and pictures) need to be labeled appropriately with a string of text and that other information is displayed using ASCII text and not bitmapped images of text.... Today, a good portion of Windows applications and the World Wide Web meets these requirements—meaning that, for the blind, the Internet is mostly accessible. However, it is still easy for an application programmer or a Web page designer to shut out the blind if careful attention is not given to issues of nonvisual access.

Source: Curtis Chong, director of Technology, National Federation of the Blind, "How the Blind Access the Internet" (retrieved August 6, 2001 from ⟨www.enabledonline.com/BackIssues/July2000/editorial6.html⟩).

Box 5.3
Bringing the Internet to the Inner Cities

Settlement houses are nonprofit, community-based organizations that provide community residents with a range of social and educational services; their goal is to help people overcome poverty. In the early 1990s, a report prepared by the United Neighborhood Houses of New York (UNH) concluded that the settlement houses in New York City needed an agencywide information system to manage more efficiently and effectively the settlement services.

In October 1994, the National Telecommunications and Information Administration (NTIA) gave the UNH a pilot grant to establish an information infrastructure for five settlement houses.

An innovative part of the pilot that was not in the original plan was to provide settlement programs and community residents with access to computers and the Internet. The computers were placed in special "family rooms" in the settlement houses.

People who are at risk for being "information have-nots" were already coming to the settlement house for ongoing programs relevant to their lives and the problems they face, and the family rooms provided a natural strategy for introducing them to the opportunities and resources of the Internet.

Source: Maxine Rockoff, personal communication, August 17, 2001.

You have no idea of the horrible battles I've fought for years to get a small bit of hope established again" (Senft, 2001).
• An innovative shelter for homeless people in New York City has taught Internet use and provided access to its clients (box 5.3).

Access for Self-Identity and Advancing Personal Interests

The Internet allows people who are isolated to interact with others who share their views and thereby to have their views reinforced and developed further. Users can progress in developing their original self-identity or can even resocialize themselves into a new identity.

This identity project has been especially noted with teenage boys who feel oriented toward homosexuality. The use and importance of the Internet in resocializing young gay boys into a homosexual identity has been described by Egan (2000). She documents how the Internet is used to make friends, explore feelings, and create a new local identity as a gay teen. She also highlights how the Internet is used as a source of sexual gratification (a use that is found across age groups and sexual preference groups).

The Internet has historically been identified with geeks who have poor social skills and a passion for computers, which may have prevented those from other social groupings from developing an interest in computing or the Internet. Yet those from all groups have found the Internet useful in fulfilling their needs. One high school football player told us that he became interested in going online to research his opponents on the teams he would playing against. With an eye for strategic advantage, he logged on and found out the nicknames, likes, and dislikes of opposing players and began playing "mind-games" with his opponents on the playing field, which he said "confused the hell out of" them. The athlete then told his teammates about this great ploy and thus persuaded several of them to go on the Internet for the first time (anonymous personal communication, April 18, 2001).

If people have a meaningful motive for going online, they will come. This is not the same as saying, "Build it, and they will come," though for a few curious individuals this will be sufficient. The cultural and political resources available on the Internet will be used by the people who are interested in them, and their purpose may not always be the same uplifting purpose advertised by Internet sponsors or various social or user groups.

Reducing Barriers to Accessing Culture

The Internet provides many with access to cultural resources they would not otherwise have a chance to see and hear—the writings of great thinkers, important works of visual and performance art, information ranging from science to religion, and even "how to" guidelines for paper folding to bomb making. Because of space limitations, we focus this discussion of cultural access provided by the Internet on music and on American Indian culture.

Musical groups have found it difficult to distribute their sound to audiences, and they have welcomed the Internet as an innovative way to

Box 5.4
Local Rock Band Stimulates Fans' Interest via Web Site and E-mail

The New Brunswick, New Jersey, rock band Boolily uses its own Web site for promotion. Boolily, a trio of students who have been friends since high school, plays at local pubs and clubs. It uses a Web site to attract prospective clients for possible dates and to encourage a fan following. The Web site includes a sample of Boolily's music along with information about band members, photos, and a schedule. A pop-up box allows visitors to sign up for e-mail about upcoming gigs. According to band member David Arnold, "Ninety percent of our audience members have received an e-mail about the show.... The growth of our fan base is directly linked to the e-mail list. Without the list, we probably would not have the turnout that we do."

Source: David Arnold, personal communication, April 7, 2001.

reach the large audiences that they feel their talent merits (box 5.4). A variety of Web sites expose new music groups to the public. Sites such as ⟨indiebiz.com⟩ ("We make a living helping bands make a living"), ⟨taxi.com⟩, and ⟨egroups.com⟩ offer a variety of services ranging from promotional tools to placement. A leader in the field, ⟨farmclub.com⟩, boasts 700,000 visitors weekly. This site not only exposes new talent to the public and tries to bring them commercial success but also has its own successful record label. Among the groups it has discovered and signed recording contracts with include Sonique (which attained "gold record" status), Fisher, Dynamite Hack, and Alley Life. ⟨Farmclub.com⟩ also connects bands with musicians and vice versa. In this way, music groups that are from geographically remote places or that play in unfamiliar genres find it easier to surmount traditional access barriers. Fledgling bands can upload their music and then be available to listeners via the Web. Listeners can vote on the groups they like and the most popular groups can then have opportunities for recording contracts and concert and television gigs. ⟨Farmclub.com⟩'s "digital jukebox" library of signed and unsigned bands can be searched, selected, listened to, and downloaded. Classical music listeners can also benefit from the Internet. Global Music Network (⟨www.gmn.com⟩) and Online Classics (⟨www.onlineclassics.net⟩) offer repeats of classical-music concerts for a period after their actual performance. Listeners are able to select programs and, in some cases, the order in which the parts of the program are presented.

Most subcultures in the United States have Web sites on the Internet to promote their continued existence and to help members and non-members understand their culture. Web sites devoted to American Indian groups, for example, provide detailed coverage of a diverse range of Indian tribes, including history, art and traditions, languages (including sign languages), and current social, civic, and legal issues. One Web site—⟨www.nativeweb.org⟩—posts news about political and cultural events and original documents and photos of Indian material. It also hosts 40 other sites. Other Web sites offer a wide range of historical references and updates about contemporary activities. These include ⟨www.csulb.edu/projects/ais/index.html#north⟩ and ⟨www.dickshovel.com/ill.html⟩. The paradox of Web site riches on the one hand and the lack of connectivity among people on the other highlights the importance of aligning resources that support the interests of the nonusers and nonawares as well as users.

Interest in Access Limited by a Lack of Perceived Usefulness

Although the Internet is extraordinarily useful to some, it is of little or no use to others. And even if it might be useful to them, many people still perceive that it is not. Such a view may be more important than any physical constraints that might limit access. We describe in chapter 2 Ipsos Reid's survey of 30 countries concerning Internet access, which found that cost was a major access factor for people in less developed countries. But the most common reason (chosen two-thirds of the time) for not accessing was "no need" for the Internet. According to the survey leader, "In the developed world, a substantial number of people who could very easily go online have decided not to. They see no compelling reason to be on the Web. The hype and the promise of the Internet clearly hasn't impressed them—not yet, at least" (Bonisteel, 2001).

A mail survey conducted by the Consumer's Union (also highlighted in chapter 2) makes the point that the Internet has no compelling interest for many people, especially in light of the physical difficulties, conceptual demands, status challenge, potential threat, and cost of the Internet. The

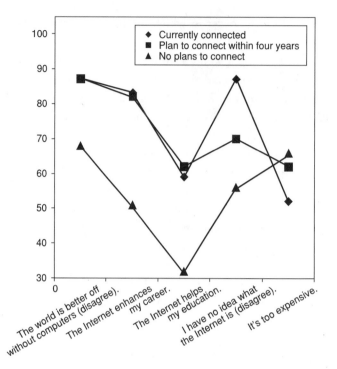

Figure 5.1
Survey of Attitudes toward the Internet from Three Access Groups
Source: Cooper and Shah (2000).

study was done by mail in two waves in February 1999 and June 2000 and yielded 1,902 respondents and claims that it is representative of the U.S. population (Cooper & Shah, 2000). Cooper and Shah divided their respondents into three groups—those currently connected to the Internet, those who plan to connect within four years, and those who have no plans to connect. As suggested in figure 5.1, those with "no plans to connect" were different from the "currently connected" for each of the five attitudinal variables. Thus, they are most likely to see the Internet as expensive and think that the world would be better off without computers. They are also least likely to see benefits from the Internet use for their professional or educational pursuits. In other words, those who have no interest in being connected also see less value in being connected. This relationship could be a form of cognitive dissonance or simply sour grapes—that is, those who cannot anticipate ever being connected might downgrade the value of what they cannot have. But those who see little value in something may rightfully not be able to justify the exertions necessary to overcome the real barriers.

Those who plan to connect with the Internet in the next four years share several attitudes with those currently connected—their attitudes toward the value of computers to the world and the potential value of the Internet to advance education or careers. The "within four years" respondents are between respondents "currently connected" and "no plans to connect" in terms of having a sense of what the Internet could do for them. They are close to "no plans to connect" respondents in terms of finding the Internet expensive. The "no plans" are most likely to think Internet access is too expensive, followed by those who plan "within four years" to be connected. Those already connected are the least likely to think that access is too expensive. This suggests that cost may be an inhibiting factor, especially since this is the one variable where the "no plans" and the "within four years" groups cluster together and both are far apart from the "currently connected."

But is it the case that the cost of access is too high for potential users? Doubtless in some cases it is, and we report in chapter 4 that cost is the second most frequently named leading factor in becoming an Internet dropout. Another aspect needs to be considered, however. Cost is almost always a dissuasive factor for most people in all areas. Yet those with below-median incomes (especially those in the second quartile) are disproportionately likely to subscribe to enhanced telephone services, the cost of which frequently exceeds $10 per month (Katz, 1999a). Lower-income people also are heavy subscribers to cable television services. There may be many reasons for these preferences, but they suggest that if low-income people valued the Internet, they would be more likely to overcome cost and technological barriers.

As we suggest below, the Internet does not have appeal for low-income and low-education people. This is compounded by the essentially passive and information-retrieval mode that too many public-access-encouragement programs emphasize. Yet interpersonal communication and entertainment are important dimensions to people's behavior patterns, which might explain the enthusiastic reception that lower-income people give to other forms of enhanced information services and communication services. This also suggests that interpersonal communication is an important rationale on which to predicate a public training program for Internet access.

Recurring Problems with Attempts to Overcome the Digital Divide

It makes little sense to undertake massive computer giveaways or wiring programs to foist Internet access on those who are not interested in it (see also Compaine, 2001). Moreover, some people fear the Internet or find their self-esteem challenged by the Internet's technological and cognitive demands. In line with our view that coercion, even if subtle, should be avoided, these approaches would be a waste of resources.

The federal program in Baltimore illustrates some of these problems (box 5.5). Good intentions and well-meaning efforts are only part of the equation. What we call the "other digital divide" is awareness. Awareness is not simply hearing a word or name. It also means being aware of what the Internet can do to serve one's own ends (and not simply to serve the ends of program administrators to have a place wired or have a certain level of Internet availability achieved for a specific population). The records of accomplishment of programs to expand access reveal several misconceptions about how best to overcome the digital divide:

• The goals of the programs are unrealistic and are defined in terms of what the program framers want to see rather than what the potential participants might want to achieve.

• Participants tend to be viewed as passive vessels who wish only to search for and retrieve information. However, our surveys and ethnographic observations suggest that both potential users and current users are interested primarily in communication as a process rather than in information as a product. Both are attractive aspects of the Internet, but emphasis on information is less meaningful to nonusers than communication.

• Many programs focus on content, which can be a useful approach when a tight link can be shown between the content (finding housing and a job) and the social situation of the individual learning about access

Box 5.5
One Well-Funded Federal Effort to Close the Digital Divide Yields Tepid Results

Since the mid-1990s, the U.S. Department of Housing and Urban Development (HUD) has established about 800 computer learning centers of varying sorts in conjunction with the private sector. Most are in privately owned apartment complexes and offer computer lessons for learning new job skills and for exploring career development. But in 1999, HUD, along with the Housing Authority of Baltimore, Maryland, initiated a major program to provide access to free computers at the Edgar Allen Poe housing complex. The complex was specially wired to provide rich capabilities in a public housing setting.

When launched two years ago, the $1.7 million program was hailed by federal and city officials who promised that the program would "close the digital divide" between rich and poor. Initially, the program was greeted with skepticism: only 75 of the 202 potential households joined the program. Jeremiah Griffith, chief operating officer of the Noah Group, a private community services organization running the program, noted that there is "typically some element of distrust and strained relations between the housing authority and the residents" in public housing. "We spent the first 10 or 11 months trying to address that, and it hasn't been an easy process."

Residents' concerns fell into three different categories. Some worried that if they took a computer that eventually malfunctioned, then they would forfeit their public housing. Others feared that if they did not take a computer, then they would not get an apartment. Finally, some simply did not want to be bothered completing 10 days of computer training, two hours per day, to qualify for a computer.

To boost the prospects of the program, officials visited residents' apartments to reassure them and solicit their participation. Christmas sharpened interest for parents who wanted to give a valuable gift to their children. In an attempt to make the program more palatable, some of its aspects were modified: training was modified to fit potential students' needs better, class hours were made more flexible and convenient, and babies were allowed in class sessions.

Despite slowly growing interest, after two years administrators still had 70 computers in unopened boxes awaiting commitments from residents.

Source: Adapted from Clines (2001).

(a homeless person). But when alignment is not made visible to program participants, there can be a mismatch between program content and the interests of the participants.

• Users often want to be creators of content, but this is not a focus of most offered activities.

• Programs often are framed by emphasizing technology rather than the social support and guidance that users want and need. This misplaced emphasis is understandable and can extend to many areas far beyond Internet access-assistance programs. Technology is cheap; training and support are expensive. Technology can be shipped in a box and installed in a day (which happens when schools are wired on annual Net days). But rapport, concentrated attention, expertise, and human communication skills are not easily attainable and certainly not fungible.

• The barriers to Internet access are primarily cultural and social, not technological. Access-enhancing programs that focus only on technology will be much more limited than those that focus on the social.

By no means do all access-enhancement programs suffer from these misperceptions, but many do. As we were preparing the manuscript of this book for publication, the Morino Institute, a noted activist organization, issued its report on how community access could best be fostered. As can be seen in box 5.6, the Morino Institute seems to have arrived independently at many of the same conclusions we have advanced above.

Barriers Are Cultural and Social, Not Technological

Katz and Wynn (1997) conducted a study for the Markle Foundation that looked at how voluntary organizations carried out member recruitment and community building on the Internet. Among the organizations they studied was the Alpha-1 Foundation, a lung disease support group that supported an online community called Alphanet. What they found was that if sufficiently motivated, individuals and groups were extremely creative at finding ways to access the Internet. They often used low-cost entry-level services in the beginning, bootstrapped their increasing expertise to expand their activities, and use their growing abilities to locate and acquire free services and technology.

Box 5.6
Highlights of the Morino Institute Report

No matter how impressive the technology or how well-intended the motives, technology initiatives imposed on a community by outsiders are often ineffective. As a result, those who hope to promote the use of technology in low-income communities should devote a great deal of time to identifying and then cultivating relationships with key local leaders and organizations.

Investments in technology must go far beyond funding for hardware, software, and wires. For most projects, no more than one-third of the funding should go to technology itself, leaving more than two-thirds for developing programs that help people and organizations understand and apply the technology.

People who are committed to narrowing social divides should not underestimate how much time and energy are required to build the case for the relevance of technology within low-income communities. Most people in low-income communities see little reason to embrace technology. Worse still, many fear or distrust it.

Source: Morino Institute, "From Access to Outcomes" (retrieved August 5, 2001 from ⟨www.morino.org/divides/⟩).

One Minnesota member of Alphanet gives the following account of his entry into the network. He was fully disabled (and thus unemployed) due to having a chronic obstructive pulmonary disease (COPD). Since he had only 12% lung function, he badly needed a lung transplant. But being disabled, where might he turn for help? Fortunately, his son used the money he had earned on his paper route to buy a computer. The disabled man started using this computer. When he was interviewed in 1996, he shared the following (Katz & Wynn, 1997, p. 14):

I started dinking around, got on the Internet surfing around looking for transplant information. I wasn't finding usable information. It was important to find a lung-specific group. I didn't know much about Alpha-1 at the time. One time I got up at 3 a.m. and decided to make a home page. I wasn't busy enough and I was freaking out. I thought about my history and I was sorry for myself. I thought I'd put the transplant information on the home page and round up other patients and make the information available to [our group].

His searches led him to the Alpha-1 Foundation in Florida (⟨www.alphaone.org⟩), a support group for those who suffer from a form of emphysema caused by a congenital deficiency of a protein known as alpha-1 antitrypsin (AAT) or alpha-1 protease inhibitor. He received from them an educational compact disk concerning Alpha-1 that had been created by the group's founder. This exchange led the Minnesota man, with volunteer assistance, to develop a local Web site, an Internet e-mail account, and Web site publishing. These efforts in Minnesota were joined with ongoing efforts in Florida to create a variety of support groups for Alpha-1 suffers, their families, and their medical providers.

The Alphanet vignette parallels the steps taken in many other Internet access cases we have encountered:

• Becoming aware of needs, interests, and desires (they may be nascent or prominent and obvious),

• Confronting the limits of a local physical setting for addressing these needs,

• Learning that the Internet exists and identifying it as a potential resource,

• Gathering tools and acquiring skills to go online to overcome local limits,

• Searching for information or help,

• Finding information or help,

• Making contact (a result of help-seeking and information searching),

• Disseminating further the information and connecting with other people with similar situations and views,

• Acquiring new skills and contacts, and

• Developing further new tools and social resources.

This is the "pull" form of access creation. It is one that millions of people have followed. Millions more have followed a different path, in which they become motivated to take formal courses in which information can be "pushed" to them in a formal setting. Under this model, information is systematically presented to the learner. Some of these courses are part of a larger social or community-service program; others are offered through public schools, libraries, and private training institutes. Both models serve different constituencies, but motive and relevance remain prominent factors for the rapid and successful assimilation of material. Simple availability and publicity will yield only modest results with those who continue to find no meaning in the Internet and in many cases see it as a threat.

As we have noted in earlier chapters, important questions that go beyond the simple questions of Internet access or intensity of use revolve around a change in behavior over time—that is, the contrast between recent users and long-term users. Another often overlooked question is that of Internet dropouts. Indeed, although academic researchers seldom attend to this question, some community programs have been started in Chicago to bridge the "summer drought" when students are cut off from the Internet access that they enjoy during the school year. Finally, the proportion of people "not aware" of the Internet continues at about 10%, and an unknown number of those people might be able to avail themselves of its benefits but have no idea of its existence or its utility.

Conclusion

To many, but by no means all, Americans the Internet fills a need created by demographic and lifestyle trends and helps expand an important area of human rights. At the same time, not all Americans want, need, or feel comfortable with Internet access. An important gap has appeared in the awareness of the Internet and its potential utility. Without appreciation for the Internet's utility, it will be difficult for well-meaning program administrators to stimulate interest among the nonadopters. Moreover, access barriers to the Internet are not primarily technical or financial, though those are real and difficult. Rather, the barriers seem to lie heavily in the realm of cultural perceptions about what is possible with the Internet and the nature of Internet activities. Once this initial barrier is pierced, individuals and groups tend to become self-organizing knowledge networks that also include an important interpersonal communication dimension.

II

Civic and Community Involvement

6

Civic and Community Involvement: Basic Issues and Prior Evidence

How will the Internet affect civic and political participation and community involvement, diversity and education, and the development of greater social capital in physical and mediated communities? This chapter reviews research on the Internet and civic and community involvement by examining both dystopian and utopian perspectives (an approach also taken in chapters 2 and 10). Chapter 14 returns to the main themes of each of our review chapters.

Civic and Political Involvement

Communication technologies embodied in media such as newspapers and television have dramatically altered the conduct of elections and the degree of citizen involvement in political affairs (Carey, 1988). The Internet is also believed to have this potential. However, whether this change will be negative or positive has been an urgent question since networked technology entered the national consciousness in the 1970s (Hiltz & Turoff, 1995). The dystopian perspective foresees a loss of privacy and an increase in voter manipulation due to governmental or corporate domination of the Internet. Slick corporate or political sites will reproduce the same limitations that have characterized prior media: unacknowledged bias in material selection and spin-doctoring that confuses and misleads the voter. Conversely, utopian predictions foresee a cornucopia of benefits, allowing instant democracy, informed public deliberations, and rapid, responsive communication with governmental officials. Interaction with candidates will make more information and perspectives available, leading to better voter decisions and greater involvement in democratic processes.

These are not futuristic or rhetorical questions. The Internet clearly is becoming a heavily used election tool and forum for political activities (Mann, 1995). Indeed, numerous case studies have highlighted how the Internet has become an extension of politics and political communication by other means (Buchanan, 1996).

The Dystopian Perspective

Narrowing the Range of Participants   Even if the Internet represents the potential for greater political involvement, the unequal access to Internet resources by various groups in society, relative to traditional outlets such as newspapers, radio, and television, could paradoxically narrow the basis of political participation and government legitimacy (White, 1997). Hill and Hughes (1998, p. 29) report that "Internet users and activists (those who use it for political reasons) are considerably younger than the general public, with Internet activists averaging a very young 32.8 years." This age may be even lower, as the survey counted only those over age 18. Males were the majority of Internet users and activists (72%). There actually seems to be a higher percentage of nonwhite Internet activists so "there is no great 'ethnic gap' in Internet activism." However, Internet users and activists do have much more education than the general public, with 53% and 56%, respectively, having college degrees. Internet activists "are not more partisan but they are more Democratic than the general public" (p. 33). On Usenet's political newsgroups, "most threads are neutral but with clear right-wing anti-government overtones," possibly because ultraconservatives may not feel represented by the media but also possibly because they are more active in posting to newsgroups (p. 73). Chatrooms are heavily conservative due to greater activity by those members and not because they have a greater number of conservative participants (p. 128). Hill and Hughes find about an equal amount of left- and right-wing Web sites, but conservative sites are more in-depth and have "higher production values."

Limiting Participants and Privacy   Others argue that the Internet could weaken the legitimacy of the governing process by encouraging the spread of small, Net-savvy special-interest communities that can pursue their own narrow agendas at the cost of the public commonweal (Starobin, 1996). The quality and validity of Internet material are also increasingly problematical, leading to concerns about the corruption or debasement of elections and a consequent reduction in political participation and legitimacy. There has been concern about a possible reduction in the objectivity of traditional media if these media were to lose their status and impact as a result of the growth of Internet usage (Symposium, 1995; Van Alstyne, 1995). Some theorists have argued that the Internet is destroying community groups and voluntary associations that are necessary for the democratic process to succeed (Putnam, 1996; Turkle, 1996). Other critics fear that the Internet will absorb and dissipate the energy of the citizenry away from traditional political processes (Carpini, 1996; Rash, 1997). Van Dijk (1999, p. 2) locates a central tension: "Some would argue that *freedom*—for example, the freedom of choice for consumers—will increase because of the interactivity offered by this technology. Others paint a more pessimistic picture and predict that freedom will be endangered by a decrease in privacy for the individual as a registered citizen, a 'transparent' employee, and a consumer screened for every personal characteristic and by the growing opportunities for central control." Darin (2000) goes further: he warns that the Internet will serve as the jackboot of political elites. Network technology will "produce a hegemonic economic order" (p. 187); the Internet will alienate, manipulate, and demean workers; and when "computer networks are to be involved in democracy at all, they are likely to be instruments of democracy at its worst" (p. 267).

Limiting Discourse According to Hill and Hughes (1998), pessimists believe that electronic voting is problematic because it doesn't involve debating or discussion and allows a voter to be more passive. Van Dijk (1999) believes that there will be so much information on the Internet that it will be hard to figure out what is valid and thus will lead to faulty decision making. The Internet also often removes the layer of filtering of political information that is done by the gatekeepers of the mainstream media. Democracy can be strengthened when citizens become politically more informed and involved in government through the Internet, but increasingly the Internet "is susceptible to control from above" (p. 2). Further, self-selection plays a large role: those who were previously politically interested are those who make up the population of Internet users who utilize the Web for political reasons (p. 183).

Free speech can be both promoted and inhibited by the Internet. Theoretically, anyone can design a Web site and post any opinion on it. However, Shapiro and Leone (1999) suggest that free speech may actually suffer with the development of the Internet, both because of exposure and access issues. First, people may have a hard time finding an audience to reach because others may not be willing to listen. People will not feel like responding to solicitations describing the opinions of others, or they may filter their information so they receive only what directly interests them. Filtering and personalization of news via software agents can lead to narrowmindedness and social fragmentation. Sunstein (2001) also feels that users' ability to personalize their online experiences and to communicate only with other members of their interest groups makes the Internet an egocentric medium that allows people to avoid opposing perspectives. Therefore, views that contradict or question particular opinions may never reach the person holding them, allowing that individual to remain ignorant of opposing perspectives. A study by Neuman (2001) indeed shows that levels of selective exposure to news is highest for Internet users, followed by newspaper readers and viewers of TV news. Further, few sites by political candidates provided any links to, or representation of, other candidates' sites. The second of Shapiro and Leone's points is that not everyone has the resources to pay for advertising or for technology and technological knowledge—thus limiting some people's right to free speech.

Having online access to government representatives does not necessarily mean interaction or deliberation. A report from the Congress Online Project (2001) noted that over 80 million e-mail messages from constituents and special-interest groups were received by U.S. lawmakers in 2000; most of them were ignored. Most messages came from advocacy groups and corporate lobbying representatives. The amount and nature of such messaging seems to frustrate Congress and increase citizen dissatisfaction rather than provide an improved dialogue between government and the populace. There is little actual discourse in the diverse informational environment of the Internet (Calhoun, 1998).

Limiting the Potential for Transformation Overall, Hill and Hughes (1998, p. 183) find little evidence supporting the claim that the "Internet changes people's minds politically.... Rather, reading Web pages seems to be an act of self-selection; people go on-line to find out more information about a subject, not to be transformed." Indeed, the UCLA study (2000) shows that while 45.6% of Internet users (versus 28.1% of non-users) feel that the Internet helps people to better understand politics, only 29.3% of users and 16.8% of nonusers feel that Internet use leads to people having greater political power. "Likewise, debate and information-based discussion in the Usenet newsgroups and political chat rooms serves to reinforce pre-existing ideological positions, not to change them" (p. 183). They also conclude that the Internet won't necessarily bring worldwide tolerance: "Simply because people can talk to each other regardless of distance does not mean they will cooperate" (p. 183). For example, 〈alt.politics.french〉 is a newsgroup that often includes "insults hurled back and forth across the English Channel between people in Britain and France" (p. 183). Rash (1997) and others note that the Internet easily supports hate groups and conspiracy theorists in the political process. Davis (2000) concludes that citizens will not take significant advantage of the Internet's potential for increasing civic involvement and that dominant political actors will be the primary beneficiaries, supporting the status quo. Calhoun (1998, p. 374) also concludes that "to only a limited extent does CMC upset rather than reinforce these hierarchies or realize dreams of cyberdemocracy and virtual community."

For example, even though governmental representatives do receive e-mail from those who wish to "express views on topics of current interest ... e-mail is rarely the medium through which individuals carry out personalized transactions with government agencies" (Neu et al., 1999, p. 3). People "may express personal opinions regarding public issues in e-mail to their congressmen, but electronic queries or filings regarding their own personal circumstances, needs, or activities are still rare" (Neu et al., 1999, p. 3). There is tremendous potential for this form of citizen-government communication for many of the usual reasons, such as decreased costs, errors, and delays. But several obstacles still have to be overcome, such as security (using a trusted intermediary and electronic signatures) and privacy issues, as well as technology implementation and personnel training. A major problem lies with knowing how to use the computer properly and being able to access specific information.

Fallows (2000) argues that most of the predicted impacts of the Internet on politics have not (yet) appeared: bypassing mass media and other gatekeeping intermediaries (Morris, 2000), circumventing centralized authority, freeing politicians from having to constantly raise money, facilitating new and diverse candidates, fostering virtual-issue constituencies, and reducing the influence of particular states or political blocs. However, two changes are already significant. The first is a reduced time for shifts in prevailing opinion and media narratives. The second is that the network economy has stimulated more and more concentrated media conglomerates using convergent bandwidth, as multinationals attempt to gain control over delivery channels of multimedia content. Fallows (2000), Hundt (2000), and McChesney (2000) all argue that this concentration of media reduces diversity in perspectives and opinions and reinforces particular kinds of coverage and programming, leading to a much more powerful effect on political knowledge, participation, and voting than any supposed consequence of extended Internet use by individuals and groups. And the inherent structural and power constraints of the political system are likely to limit the possibilities of the Internet for extensive political change (Margolis & Resnick, 2000).

The Utopian Perspective
Applying the Internet to the Political Process   Others strongly argue that the Internet may very well foster political involvement: "Life in cyberspace seems to be shaping up exactly like Thomas Jefferson would have wanted: founded on the primacy of individual liberty and a commitment to pluralism, diversity, and community" (Kapor, 1993, p. 53). Microsoft proposes that the Internet will empower citizens "to set their own political agendas, establish government priorities and help implement policies. New technology is driving the transformation of the representative democracies of today into the participatory democracies of tomorrow" (Microsoft-Europe, 2001).

Certainly the Internet has already become a powerful political tool for political parties, nongovernmental organizations, congressional campaigns, and local activist groups (Barney, 2000; Browning & Weitzner,

1996; Corrado, 2000; Davis, 2000; Lipschultz, 1999; Rash, 1997; Sarder, 1996; Selnow, 1994). It allows political actors to monitor voting records, assess campaign contributions and financing, conduct online focus groups, increase voter access, keep up with recent and distant news, obtain campaign donations more quickly and efficiently (such as through online credit-card payment), file contribution disclosure reports online, create and support mailing lists, get voters to the polling place, and more. Rash (1997), in particular, suggests that the impact of the Internet in the 1996 U.S. presidential election was comparable to the role of television in the 1960 election, and others (see Edlund, 2000) made a similar claim about the 2000 election (at least before it took place).

Gurak (1997) argues that the protests over Lotus and Equifax's MarketPlace: Households and over the Clipper Chip were the earliest instances of using the Internet for social action. Lotus and Equifax's MarketPlace: Households was a proposed direct-mail database on CD-ROM containing marketing and demographic information on 120 million Americans from 80 million households. The Clipper Chip used a federal encryption standard where the government held the encryption algorithm or key.

Gurak (1997) maintains that the online protests over Lotus and Equifax's MarketPlace: Households and over the Clipper Chip represented a new form of expression—a language that was centered around social action but that took place in a new, virtual social space at the interaction of community ethos with the new technological mode delivery, the Internet. The protests shared not only concerns about privacy but also terminology and language (including typed symbols denoting emotions or emphasis and tacit assumptions and premises) and engaged in "purposeful social action in a public arena" (p. 11). The protestors were linked by common values and discursive ethos but not limited by distance or time. Gurak notes the Greek meaning of *ethos* as "a habitual meeting place," highlighting that a shared value and language can create that sense of place necessary for a community. The shared ethos and the features of the Internet jointly allowed initially individual responses to coalesce into an online community of like-minded individuals that had access to all relevant documents, either by direct transfer, by including passages in forwarded messages, or by posting to newsgroups and replying to prior posts (p. 53). Further, these cases highlight two different initiating forces—a bottom-up movement from individual users and a top-down protest organized by an advocacy group. However, they also reveal how "self-referential and insular communities on the Internet" can be (p. 42), how online communities quickly suppress minority opinions, and how anonymous messages and reinforcing newsgroup postings can be inaccurate, incomplete, exaggerated (pp. 85 ff.), and sexist (p. 108). This raises an underlying question about whether unfettered communication (a utopian attribute of the Internet) necessarily fosters healthy and socially beneficial communities.

The response to MarketPlace: Households was dramatic: ultimately, over 30,000 people contacted Lotus to remove their names. Early messages were annotated and forwarded around the world. An online discussion group devoted to MarketPlace quickly collected nearly 300 individual postings (Gurak, 1997, p. 27). The product was cancelled within eight months after its launch. The Clipper Chip case also stimulated intense Internet debate and raised awareness, but the voluntary standard was still implemented. Thus the power of online communities to take successful social action against corporations or the government is not guaranteed. Indeed, it may be tightly circumscribed since online (and offline) civic and political action occurs within a complex network of actors, institutions, and processes. Decision making by governmental bodies at every level in the United States has to adhere to rigorous and complicated procedural requirements as well as face court challenges after the fact.

Increasing Involvement and Tolerance   Hill and Hughes (1998) summarize the perspectives of some optimists concerning the role of the Internet in citizen activism. Rheingold (1993) believes that people will become more involved in the democratic process through increased online debate, and Rash (1997) states that the Internet will open up the opportunity for new parties and ideas to develop. Because the Internet is becoming transparently integrated into existing cultural forms and provides potentially easy access to information, it can increase the democratic franchise (Sobchack, 1996). Shapiro and Leone (1999) associate the Internet with "the control revolution" that is transferring control from large institutions to individuals. Six core features of the Internet can enhance individual control. The first four already exist: (1) many-to-many interactivity, (2) digital content, making communication flexible "in terms of how it can be stored, used, and manipulated" (p. 16), (3) the design of the Internet as a distributed, packet-based network, and (4) the interoperability of the Internet, so that information can flow freely throughout a network without bottlenecks or barriers. The next two must be achieved to foster individual control: (5) broadband capacity and (6) universal access.

Recent studies show that Internet users are not necessarily social isolates who are unaware of civic and political issues. In mid-2000, 84% of the online users in the AOL survey were registered to vote, and 45% intended to go online to find presidential candidate information (39% intended to search for information about state candidates, and 32% about local candidates). In the companion AOL youth study (based on 505 young people in homes with online access), 41% of the young people (between 9 and 17 years of age) reported a greater interest in current events due to being online (55% reported no difference). And 57% feel that being online has had a much more positive influence on them than has television (39% feel that TV has been more positive). Users are more involved in information gathering and more knowledgeable about current political events than is the general public (Hill & Hughes, 1998, p. 35). In another survey, online users in 1995 were more tolerant and more in favor of free expression, such as not banning books that contain dangerous ideas (24% of users agreed with such a policy versus 45% of nonusers), even after controlling for educational level (Times Mirror, 1995). However, they were not different in terms of party affiliation in the 1992 and 1994 elections, though were slightly more likely to vote for Clinton. They were more likely, however, to vote in the 1994 election (52% versus 45% for nonusers), even controlling for age levels. One-tenth of all users (12% of men, 5% women) in the Times Mirror 1995 survey reported they had engaged in political discussions online. Consider that in 1997 over 2,800 messages were posted weekly to politically oriented Usenet newsgroups, which constitutes considerable additional political involvement (Hill & Hughes, 1997).

Users in the Times Mirror study were also more supportive of "diversity" initiatives (such as participation by women in nontraditional roles and an emphasis on independence rather than obedience in child rearing) and more apt to disagree that blacks were pushing too hard for equal rights (Robinson, 2001). Cooper (2000) reported that while nonusers are more likely to attend rallies, Internet users are more likely to engage a bit more (an additional 5% to 25%) in civic, political, and media activities than nonusers. Internet users in the UCLA study (2000), compared to nonusers, were slightly more likely to exercise and participate in clubs/organizations, were slightly less likely to socialize with household members or know neighbors by name, and were at the same levels of socializing with friends, time spent sleeping, and number of friends outside their households. Further, users held fairly similar attitudes about various personal values, having slightly higher preferences for visiting with friends but slightly lower preferences for attending religious services and contributing to efforts to protect the environment. Nonusers reported slightly higher levels of life dissatisfaction, interaction anxiety, powerlessness, and loneliness (all about .2 to .3 difference on a 1 to 5 scale). Users in the Katz et al. (2001) study were more likely to participate in community and leisure organizations but less likely to participate in religious organizations.

Increasing Opportunities for Participation   The Consumer Federation of America study (Cooper, 2000) emphasizes that comparing non-online civic activities (reading newspapers, reading news magazines, contacting local public officials, writing letters to the editor, circulating petitions, and attending a political rally), their categories of "disconnected" and "potentially connected" are fairly similar to the categories of "partially connected" and "fully connected." Further, those currently connected and those planning to gain access within four years have very similar attitudes about the importance of technology and computers. However, those *not* planning to gain access have considerably less positive attitudes about the importance of computers and Internet access. This implies that nonusers, especially those planning to become connected, are as active in political activities in physical space as are users but that users have the additional advantage of online activities and access. That is, "the problem is not that the disconnected do not participate in physical space; it is that they cannot participate in cyberspace" (p. 17). Bimber (1999, p. 413) makes a similar argument, proposing that "the Internet appears to lower barriers of time and cost and so could lead to contacting behavior [with government offices] by those with commensurately lower levels of political interest and concern." Bimber's analyses of telephone survey data gathered from 1996 and 1998 and of online surveys conducted in 1996 and 1997 found no differences in the extent to which people contacted government offices based on education or age but also found substantially more likelihood that men than women would use the Internet for government contacts (48% versus 37%). Overall, he did not find that the availability of the Internet noticeably increased contact with government offices, though it probably induced more people to become active.

Conceptualizing Realms of Political Involvement with and on the Internet
To some extent, the question of whether the Internet can foster political activism and knowledge of governance is somewhat simplistic, considering that the Internet itself interacts considerably with political, governmental, regulatory, and economic institutions and requires complex governance and even debates over what kinds of governance are appropriate and possible (Loader, 1997; Margolis & Resnick, 2000). Further, few discussions of how the Internet fosters democracy are clear about their underlying assumptions about the nature of Internet democracy. An exception is Dahlberg's (2001) distinctions among liberal individualism, communitarianism, and deliberative democracy.

Liberal individualism presumes that individuals are "rational, autonomous subjects who know and can express their own bests interests" and that the Internet makes the maximum amount and kinds of information available for individuals to use in making their political decisions, such as televoting (Dahlberg, 2001, p. 160). A classic example of a possible "electronic town meeting" is the Qube experiment in Columbus, Ohio, where from the late 1970s through the mid-1980s households could respond to televised questions. In November 1999, President Bill Clinton held the first online Presidential Town Hall Meeting. Some politicians see such individualistic online applications as a way to bypass the "distortions" of the media or interventions from Congress. Other examples include ⟨democracynet.org⟩, ⟨vote-smart.org⟩, and ⟨calvoter.org⟩. *Communitarism*, however, presumes that a well developed sense of community enables individual freedom, expression, and democracy by providing a shared identity and purpose. In achieving this goal, then, the Internet fosters community development despite individualism, commercialization, and bureaucratization (p. 163) (see also Rheingold, 1993). One paradox of conceptualizing the Internet as a forum for democracy is that online communities may just as easily involve people with shared interests who are widely dispersed geographically, thus weakening local physical communities (Doheny-Farina, 1998). Finally *deliberative democracy* presumes that rational discourse in the public sphere is required to legitimate democracy. That is, different interests and positions must be shared and debated in a free, open, reasonable, and possibly even highly procedural dialogue among stakeholders to arrive at some kind of compromise agreement based on the best information and reasons. The Internet can serve this conceptualization of online democracy through moderated Usenet groups and listserves, webforums, and procedural debate and policy sites, such as the Minnesota E-Democracy Project.

Community Involvement

The Dystopian Perspective
Online Communities Are Secondary and Controlled Relations   Simply put, some argue that cyberspace cannot be a source of real community and detracts from meaningful real-world communities (Baudrillard, 1983; Beniger, 1987; Gergen, 1991; Kiesler, Siegel & McGuire, 1984; Numes, 1995; Stoll, 1995; Turkle, 1996). Jorge Schement distinguishes two key elements of communities: primary and secondary relationships. Internet communities "are really made up of secondary relationships" in which people know each other in "a single, or only a few, dimensions" in contrast to primary relationships in which people know each other in multiple dimensions (schement, quoted in Bollier, 1995, p. 10). Calhoun (1998, p. 379) also warns that online technologies encourage indirect relationships, although they have the potential to complement relations already formed. What might appear as "online communities" are really people who share some (usually single) category, such as a special interest or an easily generalized identity, and are not people bound across multiple activities or social differences. Further, he argues, the centralized

control of online data by corporations and the use of online communications by law enforcement agencies and state regulators probably have far outweighed any of the rather fragmented and largely recreational online communities touted by the utopians. In general, "the more a particular possible use of the Internet depends on social organization and the mobilization of significant resources, the more it will tend to be controlled by those who are already organized and well-off" (p. 383).

John Seely Brown believes that "it is not always clear where accountability and responsibility reside in virtual communities" because the lack of primary relationships may induce "careless, irresponsible, and even anti-social" behavior (Brown, quoted in Bollier, 1995, p. 12). The use of online systems to communicate with more distant others may reduce the vitality and integration of physical communities (Calhoun, 1986). Shapiro and Leone (1999, p. 104) warn that careless use of the Internet may lead to three fundamental problems: (1) overpersonalization (that is, the use of information about users to target messages, products, and control) and excessive specialization (that is, the use of filters and focused discussion groups to keep us from being exposed to diverse perspectives), (2) disintermediation (that is, we may forget the value of liaisons and gatekeepers in selecting and verifying news, commerce, and politics), and (3) loss of privacy ("we may rely too much on market-based solutions to problems such as protecting privacy"). In addition, "With fewer shared experiences and information sources, citizens may feel less of a connection with, and less of an obligation toward, one another" (p. 120). Both Shapiro and Leone (1999) and Rice (1987b) point out that online ties are likely to be more ephemeral, less sustainable, and easily exitable, compared to physical community relations. Along with the increased choice that online media provide comes an increased ability to "disengage with little or no consequence" (Jones, 1999, p. 220).

Computer-mediated communication (CMC) "may yet be the clearest evidence of Beniger's (1987) 'pseudo-community,' part of the 'reversal' of a centuries-old trend from organic community based on interpersonal relationships to impersonal association integrated by mass means" (Jones, 1999, p. 369). "The new mass media have an especially characteristic ability to create an illusion of apparently intimate face-to-face communication between a presenter and individual viewer," thus creating what other researchers have called "parasocial interaction" (Jensen, 1999, p. 167). Further, differential access to and knowledge of these technologies create powerful boundaries between potential community members and reinforce certain kinds of roles, status, and social networks.

More community-oriented issues shape how identity can be formed, maintained, and adapted and how it can be accessed by others when the individuals cannot be seen; determine the social processes that are available for organizing, coordinating, and controlling online (especially deviant) behaviors in ways that promote the community; track how online communities change over time and what is necessary to maintain them; and suggest ways that online communities might support collective action and social capital (Smith & Kollock, 1998; Surratt, 1998).

Mediated Communities Detract from Social Capital   Among the most influential critics of the Internet is Robert Putnam. In his widely cited *Bowling Alone: The Collapse and Revival of American Community* (2000), he maintains that social capital—defined as informal and voluntary association, communication, and social interaction—is the glue that holds society together. Without it, he attempts to show, communities suffer, crime rates balloon, social services wither, and people become depressed, sicken, and even die. He unleashes an impressive barrage of correlations on these matters. For example, crime rates, low-birth-weight children, and poverty are all correlated with low social capital. In accounting for the decline in social capital, he points to television, suburbanization, and changing family structure as the culprits. Interpersonal communication technology, though, plays a different role. The telephone, he asserts (primarily based on Claude Fischer's work) has not had these harmful effects. This is perhaps not surprising given that unlike the "one-way" media of TV and radio, the telephone is quintessentially an interactive and personally connecting technology (Katz, 1999a).

But what is the Internet's role in affecting social capital? On the one side, he sees the Internet's potential for neighborliness without proximity—a low-cost egalitarian way of connecting people who share interests but not time or space. He also anticipates that truncation of social cues by a primarily text-based medium may lead to participation that is more egalitarian, blunter, and more participatory. In his brief survey of online activities, he notes that most kinds of social connectedness and civic engagement could be found on the Internet (Putnam, 2000, p. 170). Of particular focus is his interest in political participation. He notes the outpouring of verbiage and form e-mails to policymakers and the enormous variety of political messages and asks, "Is anybody listening?" Though he is equivocal and allows for future improvements, he concludes that CMC "inhibits interpersonal collaboration and trust" (p. 176) and that anyone who thinks the Internet could restore social capital lost through other means is a "wild-eyed optimist" (Wellman, Haase, Witte & Hampton, 2001, p. 439).

Overly Narrow Interests and Homogeneous Members   One paradox of online communities is that an "organic community" (comprised of face-to-face interactions) (Van Dijk, 1999) is made up of a relatively homogeneous group of people because they have several interests in common, whereas a virtual community is relatively heterogeneous since only one interest links them. Therefore, an organic community has a better chance of building and maintaining its own culture and identity than a virtual community does. Because virtual communities are limited, they cannot replace organic ones, but perhaps they can supplement and strengthen organic communities. Another paradox is that successful cybergovernment requires local citizens to be educated through word of mouth, newsletters, and media articles and then to provide feedback to help determine online content (Huff & Syrcek, 1997): traditional citizen participation therefore may be necessary before online participation can be successful. However, ongoing evaluation of the site through the site itself as well as through other means such as focus groups and surveys is also necessary (Patterson, 1997).

The Nature of "Real" Community
One interesting response to the possibility that richly human physical communities are threatened by new media such as the Internet is to question the very nature of communities. Wellman (2001) emphasizes that traditional communities are controlled by social class, management of labor power, access to resources, fixed capital, limited mobility, and a few powerful gatekeepers, all embedded within a primary network.

Revolutionary challenges to these community networks were associated with changes in media and transportation—horses, railroads, steamships, automobiles, and airplanes; broadsides, newspapers, and books; the telegraph, telephone, radio, and television. For example, media such as the telegraph vastly increased the speed of communicating, replacing door-to-door interaction with either place-to-place or person-to-person communication. The distance the message must travel is a much less salient constraint than the length of the message.

Thus, because community has moved inside the home or the office by means of the telephone or other media, most North Americans have little interpersonal connection with their neighborhood or the social control of a neighborhood group: "Most of the major innovations of the past hundred years have made it progressively easier to avoid contact—and particularly conversation—with people who aren't colleagues, or family, or friends; the cinema, car, telephone, and television are particularly implicated" (Johnson, 1997, p. 69). Wellman (2001) referring to Smith's (1999) research, notes that the percent of Americans regularly socializing with neighbors declined from 30% in 1974 to 20% in 1999, and the percent regularly socializing in bars from 11% to 8%. Neighborhoods or urban locales are less communities and more "enclaves of people who have made similar lifestyle choices" (Calhoun, 1998, p. 388). Putnam argues (1995, 2000) that community has been significantly declining in the United States, and Skocpol (2000) shows that interest groups with local constituencies and interaction have declined in general in the United States, creating a vacuum filled by disconnected people committed to little more than commercialism. Calhoun (1998, p. 389) laments that "this compartmentalization of community life is antithetical to the social constitution of a vital public sphere."

Putnam (2000) documents that membership in community organizations has not really declined very much but that active involvement and participation have. Further, many new voluntary organizations are lobbying and direct-mail offices with no real membership activity. People entertain less frequently in their homes, donations in terms of constant dollars has declined, voting and trust in government are low, and church attendance continues its drop.

Further, rather than finding communities of tightly interconnected groups, people tend to belong to many, weakly connected partial communities—what Wellman (2001) calls personal communities. Most physical community ties are fairly specialized, and so are most Internet community ties (Wellman & Gulia, 1999b). Further, people in physical communities rely on various media (telephone, flyers, local newspapers) to maintain relationships between face-to-face interactions. In a seminar reported by Bollier (1995, p. 7), Charles M. Firestone notes that "A lot of people have very superficial relationships with their geographic neighbors even though they see them all the time, yet have very close relationships with professional colleagues who they may only see occasionally."

Many have raised the issue of just what a "community" is, anyway. Virnoche and Marx (1997, p. 86), for example, argue that community must comprise "individual identification of and involvement in a network of particular associations." These may vary (on a dimension of shared geographic space) among ongoing, intermittent, or none and (on a dimension of shared virtual space) among shared or not. Thus, a community that shares both virtual space and ongoing geographic space is a prototypical "community network" (such as the Denver Free-Net); one that shares virtual space but no geographic space is a prototypical "virtual community" (such as a newsgroup); one that shares virtual but intermittent shared geographic space constitutes a "virtual extension" (such as an academic discipline's Web site); and one that shares no virtual space but intermittent shared geographic space is labeled an "intermittent community" (such as youth clubs). So any analysis of the relationship between new media or technologies such as the Internet and changes in the nature of and involvement in communities is naturally confounded with the changing conceptualization and reality of community itself.

The Utopian Perspective

Overcoming Physical and Temporal Constraints on Community Boundaries   Considering these alternate views of community, it can be argued that because of new communication possibilities, people are no longer forced to interact with specific, physically proximate others to participate in community. People now tend to choose physical neighborhoods for reasons of safety, schooling, and medical services (Dear, Schockman & Hise, 1996). A related consequence is that actual network ties leap over physically linked areas, so that the overall social geography corresponds much less to physical geography. We may best think of Internet communities as a supplement to physical communities rather than as complete substitutes. Figallo (1995), for example, conceptualizes the Internet as a link between regionally based electronic communities and as an information resource for those communities. The San Francisco–based WELL (Whole Earth Lectronic Link), and the New York Echo (Horn, 1998) public conferencing and e-mail systems are exemplars of this integrated online and physical community.

Cerulo (1997), somewhat rejecting Beniger's (1987) critique of the pseudocommunity created by digital mass media, argues that we need to reconceptualize community due to the rise of new communication technologies and new evidence about social interaction and social bonding (see also Rice, 1987b). First, pervasive examples of parasocial interaction with mediated personalities, call-in radio shows, and emotional support in online discussion groups argue for a wider concept of social interaction that does not presume that mediated relations are necessarily fleeting, impersonal, or deceptive. Second, although many concerns have been raised about the superficiality and isolation that are associated with online relations, new media are perhaps better characterized as "changing the nature and character of social bonds" (Cerulo, 1997, p. 53).

Mukerji and Simon (1998) (rightfully, we think) argue that traditional media, with their associated costs, stable content, and largely centralized control, serve to foster the public sphere much more successfully than they support more private and localized forms of community. Computer networks are potentially much better at providing community members improved opportunities to manage their public representations. That is, they allow members of communities—especially small or minor communities that do not have access to public media—to rehearse and negotiate their public faces "backstage" to improve the management of their public impressions. Systems such as the Internet can "sustain forms of ongoing and improvisational group life where interactions cannot easily or routinely be face-to-face—including among members of discredited groups marginalized from public spheres" (p. 261). Computer networks can proliferate versions of texts, undermine clear identity of authorship, and avoid centralized control at different levels of privacy/publicness (compare, for example, a publicly accessible Usenet discussion, a moderated listserv, and a password-protected webpage. They point out that early users of Arpanet "showed that computers could support the growth of communities, helping them to get things done and build a sense of common purpose and identity" (p. 262). Mukerji and Simon analyzed the backstage use of e-mail in scientific communities' discussion of the Alan Sokal hoax and cold fusion. They concluded that "the computer did not ... transform the dynamics of group life, destabilizing traditional identity and social networks. Instead, groups folded their social processes into the new technology, where they found new tools for doing familiar and necessary kinds of social work" (p. 260).

Cyberspace Communities Can Be Vibrant and Supportive A more forceful utopian argument is that cyberspace involvement can create alternative communities that are as valuable and useful as our familiar, physically located communities (Pool, 1983; Rheingold, 1993; Sudweeks, McLaughlin & Rafaeli, 1998). Network ties may exist in cyberspace, but they still represent places where people connect concerning shared interests, support, sociability, and identity (Wellman, 2000). Moreover the "weak ties" that online communities enable may provide better and different kinds of resources than strong, familial ties. For example, online communities of patients with various kinds of terminal or serious illnesses can supply both the anonymity and objectivity that patients cannot or may not receive from family and friends, who may try to protect the patient by not providing complete feedback or who may not feel comfortable or experienced enough to provide insights about the patient's condition.

Indeed, Turner, Grube, and Meyers (2001) surveyed participants in cancer-related listservs and found that respondents who perceived low support from face-to-face relations were more likely to participate in the online community. The authors argue that the Internet facilitates such hyperpersonal relations—what Walther (1996) called more socially desirable and in-depth relations than we can experience in traditional face-to-face interactions—especially when there is an "optimal match" between the needs and resources of online participants, such as those with serious illnesses. "The participants within online communities provide receptivity, interest, and disclosure, despite that they are strangers otherwise, because they can share a critical commonality" (Turner et al., 2001, p. 234). In effect, virtual communities may become "a counter-hegemonic movement in which socially or politically marginalized groups find expressive space on the Internet in which to locate like-minded others, speak freely, and forge solidarity" (Lindlof & Shatzer, 1998, p. 174).

The Internet's potential to support such communities is due largely to a combination of several factors—increased bandwidth, continuous access, wireless portability, anonymity globalized connectivity, and personalization (such as collaborative filtering and content associated by shared users, individual e-mail profiles and Web portals, and online communities of interests). People may use online communities to bypass constraints and inequity in unmediated interactions (Stone, 1991). Rather than being seen as disconnected from a group or a locale, these communities transcend these constraints, shifting from door-to-door relations to person-to-person and role-to-role interactions.

Easier to Create Shared Information and Community Voices   Computer-mediated communication "brings us a form of efficient social contact"; it is a "technology, medium, and engine of social relations" that allows us to move in terms of "status, class, social role[s], and character" (Jones, 1999, pp. 224–225). The vastly increased ability to share information is a crucial factor in community formation. Jones (1999) emphasizes that new media facilitate increased choice: the information highway will allow us to "forge our own places from among the many that exist, not by creating new places but by simply choosing from the menu of those available" (p. 220). Johnson (1997, p. 69) echoes this argument: "Instead of being a medium for shut-ins and introverts, the digital computer turns out to be the first major technology of the twentieth century that brings strangers closer together, rather than pushing them farther apart." For example, the ⟨soc.culture⟩ hierarchy on Usenet includes over 150 newsgroups whose memberships include nearly all of the ethnic and national cultural communities in the world. The Cultural Access Group's (2001) study of ethnic differences among online users reported that 59% of their African American and 73% of their Hispanic respondents reported that the Internet keeps them connected to their ethnic community and find that the content on African American (79%) or Hispanic (69%) Web sites is meaningful to them.

Thirty domestic informants provided Bakardjieva and Smith (2001) with five general reasons for using the Internet:

• The Internet allowed users to overcome isolation due to illness, family situation, retirement, or unemployment. "Typically commanding limited resources, and as a result deprived of mobility in the physical as well as the social sense, these users found in the Internet a handy and affordable means for being with other people without leaving their homes" (p. 73).

• The Internet provided considerable information to immigrants about the new social, physical, and economic environment and about people from their original country, thus preserving an important aspect of the users' identities.

• Users could maintain contact with globally dispersed family and social networks much more easily and spontaneously than through the telephone or letters.

• Some spent time learning and using the Internet to compensate for unchallenging, unsatisfying, or uncertain jobs.

• The Internet allowed them to belong to a dispersed community of interest, often those with similar afflictions or illnesses or similar cultural interests.

Mitra (2001) argues that the Web allows for the development of a unique form of "voice" that allows typically marginalized voices an increased participation in collective dialogue. Using the examples of Indian diasporic Web sites, she identifies these potential uses and features:

• Multiple participants make it difficult for a "specific privileged institutionalized system of expression" to emerge (p. 33).

• Discussion forums (even on corporate media sites, such as CNN's) provide a voice for minority views.

• The ability to start up new online threads allows for constant and diverse dialogs.

• Hypertextual links to unbounded circles of related topics erase the concept of a center so that being marginal becomes less salient; indeed, only one or two links are necessary to bring together sometimes extremely opposed voices.

• The general absence of identifiers of a site's geographical location remove traditional cues about the geographic distribution of power.

• Air time is neither sequential nor limited, so that anyone can present or read materials at any time as well simultaneously.

• The nature of hypertextuality precludes easy closure, thus fostering ongoing dialog.

In sum, "Dominance is no longer closely tied to ownership of the means of message production and distribution" (p. 43).

The link between online involvement and diversity may go even deeper than manifestations of particular groups of users. An analysis of the nearly 3,000 respondents to the 2000 General Social Survey data by John Robinson at the University of Maryland (Young, 2001) found that Internet users are more likely to be socially tolerant and to accept a wider diversity of opinions and social identities. The data imply, however, that Internet usage does not actually increase tolerance because higher levels of usage were not associated with higher levels of tolerance. Such results reject the arguments (such as by Sunstein, 2001) that Internet users will become more narrowminded and fragmented because they can filter their usage to interact with sites and other users who already share their perspectives.

Sherry Turkle (in Bollier, 1995, pp. 10–12) disputes the argument that Internet communities promote only secondary relationships, as suggested by Schement and Bollier. For example, she gives the example of one SeniorNet (⟨www.seniornet.com⟩) member who received dozens of calls and cards from her cyberfriends as she lay dying in the hospital. Further, Turkle claims that multiuser domains (MUDs) and multiuser domains, object-oriented (MOOs) "honor people's desires to connect and not to be lonely, and to form community" (p. 27). Paradoxically, the rapid growth of the Internet may be the single strongest indicator of people's desire for a "more connected way of living," a greater affiliation among fellow humans (Shapiro & Leone, 1999, p. 208).

Online Communities Can Spur Activism beyond Local Region   Shapiro and Leone (1999, p. 38) also reject the notion that in "cyberspace ... as elsewhere ... our actions online have ... a real impact on the lives of other human beings." They provide a good example of how the Internet helps connect those with similar political interests, activities, and goals. Htun Aung Gyaw is a Burmese dissident fighting the military government that rules his homeland Myanmar. He is currently a student at Cornell University but uses the Internet to communicate with other Burmese democracy activists around the world. Horn's (1998) account of Echo, the New York–based virtual salon, explores how online behaviors, relations, and concerns are essentially the same as those of physical communities. This case shows how online communities can reinforce and complement, even create and foster, physical communities and interest in local culture. As with the WELL in Berkeley, Echo participants get together at different New York settings for social gatherings, and conversation and relations blend together their online and offline lives.

Cherny's (1999) study of a MUD also reinforces the notion that online communities can develop cohesion, unity, shared history, and close relationships using only appropriately varied forms of online, text-based language: "If the depth of shared experience is the yardstick by which you ultimately measure your community ... then I must admit that I have a hard time imagining a better platform for community building than the traditional, text-based bulletin board system utilized by Echo and the WELL (along with many Web sites)" (Johnson, 1997, p. 70). For example, Slack and Williams (2000) studied the Craigmillar Community Information Service (CCIS), developed for a town outside of Edinburgh where many civilians are poor and underemployed. Countering positions that argue that online networks will foster isolated, inequitable, and ahistorical societies, they argue that "The growth and uptake of ICTs provide a point of contact at which the local and global intersect, wherein there is a potential for each to influence the other" (p. 321). Before the CCIS, residents of Craigmillar exhibited no sense of community feeling, were not motivated to socialize, and participated in no social or cultural activities. Through the CCIS, however, "Craigmillar has ... developed a strategy of self-presentation that counters external representations and which works by being grounded in the highly spatialized notion of a tightly knit community" (p. 322).

Online Communities Complement Offline Relations   It is misleading to represent online relationships as being mutually exclusive with offline ones; they often support and complement each other (Virnoche & Marx, 1997; Wellman, 2001; Wellman & Gulia, 1999a, 1999b). For example, Hampton and Wellman (2000) found, in their study of a leading-edge, broadband-wired suburb near Toronto called "Netville," that online users are more active neighbors (knowing about 25 neighbors) than are nonusers (who knew about eight neighbors) and that their contacts range more widely throughout the neighborhood. They also found that once the learning curve was overcome, family members helped others with the computers, shared their online discoveries, and watched less television.

Hampton (2000) found increased social network, social capital, and local community involvement associated with the Netville online infrastructure. Nearly two-thirds of the 109 homes in this suburb were connected. The study compared those who bought homes in Netville, those in the 45 homes not connected, and those in the 65 homes that were connected. After the service provider established a neighborhood e-mail list (NET-L), residents quickly used it to interact with neighbors, organize activities, perform online introductions, and increase knowledge of local events, service, and opinions; it provided common conversational topics and personalized initial interactions. Ability to recognize other community members by name was 31% among wired households but only 7% among nonwired ones. The stronger criterion of "talk with on a regular basis" revealed a density of 11% in the wired households and only 3% in the nonwired households. From a community-action perspective, the system allowed Netville members to organize quickly a great number of active residents to achieve concessions from a local housing developer.

According to Virnoche and Marx (1997), a community network focuses on local information, provides residents with the ability to access and send information, and attempts to build community in their locality.

As an example, over time the Boulder Community Network developed more dynamic online discussion groups instead of simply providing "static" local information, trained volunteers to improve access to receiving and sending information by its members, and had specific goals to involve low-income single parents in the community network. Similarly, the Big Sky Telegraph network in Montana, begun in 1988, connected the teachers, students, families, and communities of dispersed small schools throughout Montana (Uncapher, 1999). One of its guiding missions was to develop synergy among the educational, business, and civic sectors. The residents of the Jervay low-income public housing development in Wilmington, North Carolina (mostly African American women) used the Internet as a tool to support their collective action of resisting proposed demolition and reconstruction of the development by housing authority officials (Mele, 1999). They were able to overcome the constraints of their "local and exclusive pathways of information, discourse, and social action that were either controlled or influenced by the institution of the housing authority" (p. 292). Shortly after residents went online in 1995, they conducted wide-ranging online searches on housing design, rulings, and studies and then posted a request for assistance to three listservs. Within two weeks they had received offers of assistance from 23 professionals and organizational representatives, such as architects, lawyers, and development administrators. Further, the local Internet service provider helped the Jarvey residents develop their own resident-managed Web site, apparently the first in the country.

Shapiro and Leone (1999) describe the effectiveness of a supplemental community network in Blacksburg, Virginia, in which over 60% of the citizens participate. Parents and teachers communicate online, and citizens participate in surveys regarding municipal government. They also describe the development of a community network in a London neighborhood in which residents were given computers and Internet access and participated in debates over local parking rules: one participant said, "I used to know maybe five or six people on the street; now I know at least 40% of them quite well and some very closely" (p. 211). Other studies of community networks point out a variety of advantages, challenges, and developments (Gurstein, 2000; Kahin & Keller, 1995; Schon et al., 1999; Schuler, 1996; Tsagarousianou, Tambini & Bryan, 1998).

While much attention is paid to the exotic and social aspects of online communities, they also represent consequential social policy issues, such as supporting neighborhood and community relations, local school systems, and public access to government services and information (Doheny-Farina, 1998), especially health information and services (Rice & Katz, 2001).

Fostering Otherwise Suppressed Dialogue   Rheingold (1993, p. 6) says that "my direct observations of online behavior around the world over the past ten years have led me to conclude that whenever CMC technology becomes available to people anywhere, they inevitably build virtual communities with it, just as microorganisms inevitably create colonies.... I suspect that one of the explanations for this phenomenon is the hunger for community that grows in the breasts of people around the world as more and more informal public spaces disappear from our real lives. I also suspect that these new media attract colonies of enthusiasts because CMC enables people to do things with each other in new ways, and to do altogether new kinds of things—just as the telegraph, telephones, and televisions did." He concludes that the Internet, Usenet, and e-mail allow people to access and transmit information that may not be allowed to surface in other communities.

Indeed, given that online interaction can be relatively anonymous, is typically not centrally controlled, and offers many sites and interaction opportunities without charge, it seems surprising that so many people contribute so much information to the Internet and Web Kollock (1999) (as well as Connolly & Thorn, 1990; Markus, 1990; Rice, 1982, 1990; and others) argues that the extensive sharing of information in light of the lack of direct and immediate benefits is due to some of the features of online interaction and the culture of Internet participants. Kollock sees the Internet, at least the noncommercial sites, as primarily a "gift economy" involving participants in ongoing relations rather than as a site for commodity transactions among self-interested, independent actors. The intriguing aspect of the Internet, as in gift cultures, is that giving gifts (posting information online) does not necessarily generate returns from the initial recipient. Most, if not all, of the possible recipients are anonymous or unknown by the giver, and the gift is provided to a group instead of to an individual.

Online communities foster wider sharing of information than do physical communities, as it is easy to forward useful or humorous information to third parties (Wellman & Gulia, 1999a). Givers gain self-efficacy in online relationships and prestige as informed sources, the information gifts become public goods shared by all other members of the distribution list, newsgroup, or Web forum, and the economies of scale derived from having many participants typically generate positive network externalities. The cost for an individual of providing information gifts to an online community is much lower than the potential return of having access to a wide variety of information gifts provided by many (not necessarily all) of the other participants. Thus, unlike material-based gift cultures, strict dyadic reciprocity is not required and actually is not as effective. A critical mass of participants simply provides a diversity of useful information to a reasonably large group of moderately (even if unequally) active members at low cost and high convenience. Various Internet sites and applications do this quite well.

A Broader Question of Impacts

Some are skeptical that the Internet represents major change in political and community involvement (Davis, 2000; Jonscher, 1999; Stoll, 1999; Valovic, 2000; Webster, 1995). They protest that the information society and the Internet are overhyped by wildly optimistic media, corporate, and techie beneficiaries and that computers can only support, not replace, preexisting human needs for social relations.

Fischer (1997) concludes that the effects of new communication technologies on community (networks of social relations) are modest, complex, indirect, and contradictory and vary across technologies. He notes that even with the telephone, a truly discontinuous technology, only a few truly notable changes can be identified—greater ability to organize, conduct, and maintain social relations over distances, especially by women (essentially, being able to conduct normal social relations more effectively). Katz and Aspden (1997c) also note that concerns about threats to community were also raised for the telephone, automobile, radio, and television. They point out that concerns about the decline of community expressed 200 years ago (by Benjamin Franklin, Thomas Jefferson, and John Quincy Adams) often seem little different than those expressed continually since World War II (Merton, 1957, p. 356; Putnam, 1996). They note how visitors to New York in the early 1700s commented that the people there were commercially obsessed, rude, fast-paced, and fast-talking. Further, Fischer (1997) has shown that residential mobility has generally declined since World War II, local news has become increasingly more important, and telecommuting has so far had limited effects.

With respect to variations across media technologies, Fischer (1997) distinguishes between point-to-point media and broadcast media and identifies the associated differences in public and private settings. After the diffusion of cinema, there was much greater sociability before, during, and after going to the movies (especially among children and women): "It appears that movies enabled considerable social interaction, and attendance reinforced social ties" (p. 115). However, there was probably an opposite effect for television, after the social novelty wore off, as evidenced by declines in movie attendance, social visiting, and physical activity. Finally, effects are often contradictory: the use of a particular technology (simultaneously by the same user or in opposite ways by different users) may cancel out large-scale changes. For example, during its initial stages, the automobile increased sociability (especially for women and even more so for farm women), while the more modern period associates the automobile with the rise of suburban sprawl and increased distances between homes (and thus female homemakers).

Examples of other technology triggers include canals, railroads, automobiles, highways, airplanes, the telegraph, telephones, radios, televisions, and satellites (Stefik, 1999). "Technologies of connection" represent boundaries and points of resistance, often creating "conflict between global and local values" (p. 3). Legal and economic systems are not ready initially, the effects are not usually evident initially, and the form and application of the technology are not initially fixed. For example, one of the early uses of phonographs was to play recorded political speeches in public auditoriums, introducing voters to the voices of politicians. Initial goals for technologies both "limit and shape their opportunities" (p. 19). Katz (1999a) and Marvin (1990) have described how these new technologies of communication bring social and emotional transformation at the levels of trust, family hierarchy, and social relationships, and what is essentially the "moral economy."

Fischer (1997) argues that the primary source of major changes in community may be other social factors, such as family size, increased age of solitary seniors, later marriage, cross-ethnic marriages, sexual relations before marriage, social security, longevity, and so on. And although homes are more widely scattered and professions involve interaction with others across greater distances, transportation, cultural, and telecommunications facilitate increased communication across these obstacles. He concludes that, in general, we should think about "these technologies as tools people use to pursue their social ends [rather] than as forces that control people's actions" (p. 115).

Winner (1999, p. 208) also argues that we have continually transformed ourselves as a society as technology has changed. He proposes six questions to ask to see if these new technologies are creating "conditions that sustain selfhood and civic culture": "(1) Around these instruments, what kinds of bonds, attachments, and obligations are in the making? (2) To whom or to what are people connected or dependent upon? (3) Do ordinary people see themselves as having a crucial role in what is taking shape? (4) Do people see themselves as competent, able to make decisions? (5) Do they feel that their voices matter in making decisions that will affect family, workplace, community, nation? And (6) Do they feel themselves to be fairly treated?" Unlike Fischer, Winner is not sanguine about the consequences. Not only because "power over the most important decisions about how technologies were introduced was far from evenly distributed" (p. 211) but also because "during the middle decades of the twentieth century, virtues appropriate to the development of machines—productive order, efficiency, control, forward-looking dynamics—became prevailing social virtues as well." He sees a shift from those prior values to "mobility, flexibility, entrepreneurialism, expendability, and a willingness to dissolve social bonds in the pursuit of material gain."

Conclusion

Many critics are pessimistic about the impact of Internet use on civic, political, and community involvement. They fear that the Internet may influence people to use a less diverse range of media, that individuals' actions may be less private, that online activists may be more extreme, that users may have difficult assessing the vast amounts of information available, that people may basically reinforce their prior beliefs by participating only in selected interest groups, and that the greatest current threat may be the growing concentration across media industries. Some conceptualizations of the attributes of the Internet and communities reject the notion that organic communities can thrive in mediated, online form, as they constitute secondary and distant relationships. Further, individual privacy is threatened, especially by commercial interests, and online communities typically are bound only by a single shared interest. More fundamentally, the nature of current "real" communities can be debated, as some evidence (especially by Putnam) shows that various forms of social involvement have been declining for many years in the United States and that few people actually interact densely with physically proximate neighbors; rather, they participate in thin local communities and dispersed family and work networks.

On the other hand, recent studies and surveys find that Internet users tend to be more interested in current events, that campaigns and political activists have already started using the Internet for a variety of purposes, that users are more involved in civic and political activities than nonusers, and that many government offices provide e-mail and Web access. Nonetheless, real online dialogue among different interest groups is rare, and government access is typically one-way. However, many communities are strengthened through online interaction, if only because of the lower obstacles, such as time, distance, and the need to initially know others personally before communicating. It's probably more appropriate to think of online interaction as complementing physical communities. Nonetheless, there are many vibrant and long-lived mediated communities, ranging from health support groups to dispersed cultural and ethnic groups. The very growth and intensity of online communities may well speak to the perceived decline in real communities, as humans seek out social support and interaction. Indeed, many aspects of relationships, emotions, and identities are experienced as real through the Internet as they are over other media (such as the telephone) or face to face. Several case studies show that small communities have been reinvigorated through online systems. Researchers taking a more historical approach warn that there are likely few really revolutionary changes associated with new technologies and that people embed these new media within familiar social contexts.

Clearly there are strong arguments pro and con concerning the simple question of "Does the Internet change civic, political, and community involvement?" One implication of this review of pessimistic and optimistic perspectives on the nature of communities and the role of communication technologies in society in general is that this simple question is misleading. There are many aspects of civic, political, and community involvement. There are many conceptualizations of involvement and community. And there are debates about the nature and scope of social change associated with what are touted as transformational innovations. Rather, policymakers, researchers, and concerned users need to focus their questions and analyses on specific relations among specific uses and specific stakeholders.

More broadly, though, the question is simplistic because it presents the choices as mutually exclusive. Human behavior and new communication technologies can effect both positive and negative changes in civic and community involvement, as well as maintain the status quo. We would argue that all these kinds of changes are possible and that many of them occur. That is not to say that all changes are equal. Some of the more structural changes—such as creeping commercial and conglomerate control of the Internet or replacement of traditional media sources by online sources—can have pervasive ripple effects through more local and individual contexts.

Finally, the enormous range and diversity of current Internet research lead us to conclude that despite the concentration of media power in the United States and throughout the world, the preponderance of empirical evidence supports a positive evaluation. Many of the pessimistic perspectives are theoretically and ideologically grounded, while many of the positive perspectives seem supported by both broad surveys as well as in-depth, community-level case studies. The emotional and professional stakes and economic and social consequences of this debate are high.

7

Political Involvement: Survey Results

Chapter 6 highlighted two opposing views—the pessimistic and optimistic—of how the Internet is affecting civic and political involvement. In this chapter, we use our 1996 survey data to explore how the Internet was used by potential voters during a national election. In this way, we can see how a new technology (and in 1996 the Internet was quite novel) might have influenced the political involvement of citizens. The data also reflect how Internet users might have differed from nonusers in terms of using traditional mass media for political information. The answers to these questions are relevant not only to the way in which elections are conducted—and to their outcomes—but for an array of other major questions. These include the future structure and process of democracy in the United States and the likely role of traditional mass media in the electoral process. Our analyses were guided by four major questions:

· Do Internet users differ from nonusers in terms of their level of traditional forms (i.e., offline) of political activity?

· Do long-term users of the Internet differ from other Internet users?

· In what sorts of online political activities do Internet users engage, and how much is that engagement explained by demographic variables?

· How do Internet users feel that this new technology has affected their political information and activities?

Offline and Online Political Activity

The survey collected information on respondents' demographics, political activity in the period before the 1996 national election, views on the

importance of the print and television media, and perceptions of outcomes such as political awareness and political information after the
1996 election. Table 7.1 provides the specific questions and the aggregate answers.

In terms of offline political activities, only about one in 10 respondents
engaged in overt political activity, such as making phone calls on behalf
of candidates (5%) and giving money to a political cause, committee, or
campaign (14%). However, over two-thirds did either discuss the political campaign and election by phone or face to face (69%), and over half
watched the Republican or Democratic convention on television. Nearly
three-quarters of these respondents said, within a few weeks of the 1996
election, that they had voted. The actual percentage of eligible citizens
who voted was 49.1% in 1996 and 50.7% in 2000 (Calvo, 2000). There
is a perennial bias in surveys toward reporting socially approved behaviors, such as church going, contributing to charities, and voting.

The respondents tended to rate various media as either of medium
importance (campaign commercials or leaflets, 38%) or high importance
(national and local TV shows, 86%; newspapers, 81%; and television,
79%).

Table 7.1
Questions about Offline and Online Political Activity and about the Political Importance of Media

	Yes = 1	No = 2
Did you do any of the following political activities in the past year?[a]		
Attend any political rallies	10%	90%
Make phone calls on behalf of candidates	5	95
Write or fax any letters to elected officials	13	87
Give money to a political cause, committee, or campaign	14	87
Have any face-to-face or phone discussions with friends or family about the 1996 political campaign and election	69	31
Watch the Republican convention on TV	55	45
Watch the Democratic convention on TV	54	46
Vote in the November general election earlier this month	73	27

Table 7.1
(continued)

	Yes = 1	No = 2
Thinking back to the period since the beginning of October, in terms of your online activities and the 1996 election campaign, did you do any of the following?[b]		
Have any e-mail exchanges or chatroom discussions or postings with friends or family about the 1996 political campaign and election	17%	83%
Read any bulletin board postings or discussion groups about the campaign or election	22	78
Receive any e-mail about the campaign or the elections	15	85
Send or receive any e-mail from a government official, candidate for office, or political campaign committee	8	92
Send any e-mail to others about the campaign or the elections	10	90
Visit any Web sites with campaign-related information	23	77
Follow any part of the election by reading the news online	24	76
Follow the voting on election day from your computer	10	90
View information online about the election after it was over	21	79

	Highly Important	Medium Important	Low Importance	Not Important at All
In following the 1996 political campaign, how would you rate the importance to you of each of the following?[c]				
News or opinion magazines	25%	35%	17%	23%
Campaign commercials or leaflets	12	26	26	36
Newspapers	47	34	11	8
Television	46	33	11	9
National and local TV shows	40	46	8	6
TV interview shows like *Meet the Press* or *Larry King Live*	36	34	15	15

a. $n = 1,008$.
b. $n = 549$.
c. $n = 874$ to 883 for first three, 685 to 695 for second two.

Table 7.2
Principal Components (Dimensions) of Offline Political Activity, Importance of Media, and Online Political Activity

Questions	(Less) Offline Political Activity	(Less) Political Importance of Reading	(Less) Political Importance of TV
Attend political rallies[a]	.72	.08	−.02
Write letters to elected officials	.67	.02	−.06
Give money to a political cause	.66	.04	−.02
Make phone calls for candidates	.64	−.10	.11
News or opinion magazines important[a]	.09	.79	.08
Campaign commercials or leaflets	−.13	.64	.13
Newspapers important	.06	.59	.08
National and local TV shows important[b]	−.01	.07	.76
TV important in campaign	−.05	.03	.78
TV interview shows important	.08	.30	.52
Percentage variance explained	18.5%	16.6%	15.0%
Scale mean	1.89	2.35	1.77
S.D.	.20	.75	.57
Alpha reliability	.59	.57	.46

Between a tenth and a fifth of Internet users engaged in some kind of online political activity, including sending e-mail to or receiving e-mail from a government official, candidate for office, or political campaign committee (8%); reading election news online (24%); visiting campaign-related Web sites (23%); and reading bulletin board or discussion list postings about the campaign or election (22%).

Table 7.2 identifies basic underlying dimensions of each of the three sets of questions—first the offline and media variables and then the online variables (because of the different sample sizes).

The one dimension of offline political activity consisted of whether respondents attended any political rallies, wrote letters to elected officials, made phone calls on behalf of candidates, and gave money to a

Table 7.2
(continued)

	(Less) Online Political Browsing	(Less) Online Political Interaction
Read bulletin boards or disc groups[a]	.66	.10
Visit Web sites with political information	.67	.23
Follow the election online	.72	.21
Follow election day online	.64	.09
View information online after election	.62	.24
Electronic discussions	.21	.72
Receive e-mail about the election	.15	.74
Send or receive e-mail to or from the government	.12	.65
Send e-mail to others about the election	.23	.72
Variance explained	25.6%	23.9%
Scale mean	1.80	1.88
S.D.	.27	.24
Alpha reliability	.72	.70

Note: Varimax rotation.
a. 1 = yes, 2 = no.
b. 1 = high importance to 4 = no importance.

political cause. The two dimensions of traditional forms of media activity were reading (the importance of leaflets and magazines, news and opinion magazines, and newspapers in the 1996 campaign) and TV viewing (the importance of national and local TV shows, television, and TV interview shows in the 1996 campaign). Scales were computed based on the means of each set of variables.

Finally, the two dimensions of online political activity were online political browsing (reading bulletin boards and discussion groups, visiting Web sites with political information, following the election online, following the election day online, and viewing information online after the election) and online political interaction (participating in electronic discussions, receiving e-mail concerning the election, sending and receiving e-mail to and from the government, and sending e-mail to others concerning the election).

Internet Usage and the Political Importance of Media

Those who thought that the print media were important for the campaign were also slightly likely to think television was important ($r = .29$, $p < .0001$). But perceived political importance of neither print nor TV was significantly associated with being an Internet user or not or with number of hours in the past seven days spent using the Internet.

Internet Usage, Demographics, and Political Activity

Do Internet users differ from nonusers in terms of offline political activities? Table 7.3 presents the results from regression analyses treating voting and offline political activity as dependent measures, with income, education, marital status, sex, age, race, and whether one was a current Internet user or not (ignoring dropouts) as predictors. (For this analysis, all respondents under the age of 18 were deleted, as they cannot vote.)

No demographic or Internet usage variables were associated with voting in the 1996 presidential election. This is surprising. The only variable that came close to being significantly associated was marital status (single or married). When this was entered as the sole demographic variable with Internet usage in a follow-up regression (still including all users and nonusers in the sample), being never married was a statistically significant but very weak predictor of voting. For offline political activity, being married and being better educated were associated with being more politically active. Again, however, being a user or nonuser played no role in both the overall regression and a regression including only marital status and usage status. Note that none of the regressions explained more than 1% of the variance, so essentially there were no significant predictors—including user or nonuser of the Internet —of voting or offline political activity.

Critics of the Internet have argued that even if the majority of users do not change their involvement in the real world, heavy or long-time

Table 7.3

Predicting Voting and Offline Political Activity by Demographics and Internet Use and Nonuse

Independent Variables	(Did not) Vote	(Less) Offline Political Activity
Income (0 = under \$35,000, 1 = at least \$35,000)	—	—
Education (0 = less than college degree, 1 = at least college degree)	—	—
Marital status (1 = single, 2 = married)	−.47*	−.11***
Sex (0 = male, 1 = female)	—	—
Age (0 = under 40, 1 = at least 40)	—	—
Race (0 = African American, 1 = white non-Hispanic)	—	—
Current user (0 = no, 1 = yes)	−.03	.06
−2 log likelihood	711	—
χ^2 or F ratio	7.5*	4.6*
Nagelkerke R^2 or adjusted R^2	.02	.01
Correctly assigned	77.4%	—
n	672	647

Note: Excludes respondents under 18 years old. Current users exclude dropouts. Values for "(Did not) vote" are unstandardized beta coefficients from logistic regression, as dependent variable is dichotomous. Values for "(Less) political activity" are standardized beta coefficients from multiple regressions, as the dependent measure is a multi-item scale, not dichotomous variables.
*$p < .05$.
**$p < .01$.
***$p < .001$.

Internet users will tend to drop out of real-world political activities. In separate analyses of users only, neither being a long-term user (beginning usage before 1996) nor being an extensive user (spending more hours online) was associated with voting or offline political activity. Thus, all of our measures of usage were completely independent of such political behavior. In other words, for the 1996 election, two important media, print and television, were as equally important to users as nonusers, and being an Internet user did not diminish offline political behavior.

Internet Usage, Demographics, and Online Political Activity

Table 7.4 provides details on the extent to which demographics and frequency of Internet usage predict two kinds of online activities, offline political activity, and the importance of political print and TV media.

Offline political activity was only slightly more likely for males than females but was not otherwise explained by demographic or usage variables. The importance of print media for political concerns was slightly predicted by being single, but again no other factors were influential. The political importance of television was completely unexplained by the demographic and usage variables. For greater involvement in online political activities—browsing and interaction—the only predictor was, in both cases, more time spent using the Internet. Nonetheless, no more than 5% of the variance was explained.

The Personal Impact of the Internet, Demographics, and Political Activity

Finally, what do Internet users think about the way in which this new technology has affected their lives? As table 7.5 shows, the survey asked 10 questions about this topic. Principal components analysis identified three underlying dimensions, shown in table 7.6. "Political awareness" included more aware of issues in the world, following subjects of interest, participate in issues with people around the world, importance to personal growth, and improved quality of life. "Political information" included changed a political opinion, learned useful political information, and narrowed sources of information about the world. "Concern over privacy" included personal privacy is at risk and easy for government (and other organizations) to monitor online activities.

How well do the demographic factors, online political activities, offline political activities, media importance, and Internet usage variables predict the perceived impacts and reported voting in the 1996 presidential election? Table 7.7 presents the detailed results.

People engaging in greater levels of political awareness were more likely to conduct more online political browsing, perceive print media as more important for political issues, and spend more hours in the past week on the Internet (these explain 15% of the variance). People engaged in greater levels of online political information conducted more

Table 7.4
Predicting Online and Offline Political Activity and the Political Importance of Media from Demographics and Internet Usage

Independent Variables	(Less) Online Political Browsing	(Less) Online Political Interaction	(Less) Offline Political Activity	(Less) Importance of Political Reading	(Less) Importance of Political TV
Income (0 = under $35,000, 1 = at least $35,000)	.02	−.01	.07	.03	−.01
Education (0 = less than college degree, 1 = at least college degree)	−.07	−.08	−.06	−.06	−.04
Marital (1 = single, 2 = married)	.05	−.02	−.18	.11*	−.03
Sex (0 = male, 1 = female)	.07	.08	.05***	.00	.01
Age (0 = under 40, 1 = at least 40)	−.01	−.09	.02	.07	.07
Race (0 = African American, 1 = white non-Hispanic)	−.08	−.02	−.08	−.03	.03
Hours used Internet in last week	−.15***	−.20***	−.05	.01	.01
Adj. R^2	.03	.05	.03	.00	.00
F ratio	2.5*	3.7***	2.9**	.9	.3

Note: Values are standardized beta coefficients from multiple regressions, as the dependent measures are multi-item scales, not dichotomous variables. Analyses exclude respondents under 18 years old. $n = 405$.

*$p < .05$.
**$p < .01$.
***$p < .001$.

Table 7.5
Beliefs Regarding the Personal Impact of the Internet

What is your opinion about the way your online activities have affected you?	Strongly Agree	Somewhat Agree	Somewhat Disagree	Strongly Disagree	n
Information I have found or received online has changed my political opinion.	5%	12%	18%	65%	521
I have learned useful information about politics online.	19	16	18	47	527
Being online has made me more aware of issues in the world.	33	22	15	30	534
When online I can follow subjects that interest me in great depth.	61	23	7	9	537
My sources of information about the world have narrowed.	11	12	23	54	522
When online I can participate in issues with people around world.	46	26	12	16	484
Online participation has been important to my personal growth.	27	24	19	30	490
Online activities have improved my quality of life.	30	32	10	27	482
When I go online, my personal privacy is at risk.	34	26	18	22	531
It is easy for the government or business to monitor the activities of people online.	5	12	18	65	500

Table 7.6
Dimensions and Loadings of Outcomes Concerning Political Awareness, Information, and Privacy

Questions About Outcomes	n	Mean	S.D.	Political Awareness[a]	Political Information[a]	Concern over Privacy[b]
Information online has changed my political opinions.	521	3.43	.89	.16	.77	.07
I have learned useful information about politics online.	527	2.92	1.18	.37	.61	-.06
Being online made me more aware of issues in the world.	534	2.41	1.23	.60	.42	.06
I can follow subjects that interest me in great depth.	537	1.65	.96	.74	-.05	.04
My sources of information about the world have narrowed.	522	2.19	1.04	-.06	.71	-.02
When online I can participate in issues with people around world.	532	1.97	1.11	.65	.04	.07
Online participation has been important to my personal growth.	538	2.49	1.18	.72	.28	-.05
Online activities have improved my quality of life.	530	2.35	1.17	.71	.12	.03
Online my personal privacy is at risk.	531	2.27	1.15	.10	-.03	.84
It is easy for governments or businesses to monitor the activities of online people.	500	1.95	1.05	-.01	.07	.85
Variance explained				25.1%	17.5%	14.4%
Scale:						
n				511	498	495
Mean				2.17	2.38	2.10
S.D.				.80	.56	.94
Alpha reliability				.75	.54	.63

Note: Varimax rotation.
a. 1 = strongly agree to 4 = strongly disagree.
b. 1 = high importance to 4 = no importance.

online political browsing, more online political interaction, and less off-line political activity (these explain 13% of the variance). None of the variables explained one's concern over privacy. Finally, those more likely to report having voted in the 1996 election were more likely to be married and conduct more offline political activity (these explained only 3% of the variance). Thus greater time spent on the Internet in the past week was associated with increased online political awareness but was unassociated with engagement in online political information, concerns about privacy, or actually voting. Those with lower levels of offline political activity were more likely to be engaged in obtaining online political information.

Related Results from the Pew 2000 Surveys

The Pew Internet and American Life Project and the Pew Research Center surveyed 4,186 online users in October and November 2000 to provide a snapshot of the relationships between Internet use and political activity (Pew Reports, 2001). These users reported that they went online for news about the presidential campaign at a rate of 18% in 2000 (up from 10% in 1996). Usage was higher (28%) among those who voted in 2000. On the day of the election, 12% of Americans used the Internet for political news. 18% used it on the day after.

While these percentages reflect significant overall growth, the most likely users are still younger (25% by those 18 to 29 years versus 10% by those over 50), more educated (33% by those with a college degree versus 8% by those with a high school degree or less), and wealthier (30% by those earning over $50,000 a year versus 10% by those earning less than $30,000). Male Internet users (37%) are more likely than female Internet users (29%) to get some news about the election online. And those who had been online for at least three years (45%) were more likely to obtain online election information than those who started using the Internet in the prior six months (17%).

Comparing Pew 1996 results with Pew 2000 results, users went online for election news because they found that Internet information is more convenient (45% to 56%), other media don't provide enough news (53% to 29%), they could find information not available elsewhere (26% to 12%), and Internet news sources reflect their personal interests

Table 7.7
Predicting Political Outcomes from Demographics, Online Political Activity,
Political Importance of Media, and Internet Usage

Independent Variables	(Less) Online Political Awareness	(Less) Online Political Information	(Less) Concern over Privacy	(Did not) Vote in 96 Federal Election
Marital (1S, 2M)	.07	.05	−.10	−.11*
Gender (0M, 1F)	−.05	−.01	−.04	.02
(Less) Online political browsing	.19***	.25***	−.04	−.02
(Less) Online political interaction	.11	.15*	.06	−.03
(Less) Offline political activity	−.09	−.12**	.04	.18***
(Less) Importance of political reading	.10*	.15**	.05	.01
(Less) Importance of political TV	.09	.02	.00	−.03*
Hours used Internet in last week	−.21**	−.07	−.02	.07
Adj R^2	.15	.13	.00	.03
F ratio	7.9***	6.8***	.7	2.3*
N	322	321	316	341

Note: Values are standardized β coefficients; analyses exclude respondents under 18 years old.
*$p < .05$.
**$p < .01$.
***$p < .001$.

(24% to 6%). Fully 69% of election news consumers sought information about the candidates' positions on the issues, and 33% sought background on candidates' voting records. For those who advocate the Internet as a way to foster political activism, 45% of all Internet users (but more so for experienced Internet users) say they encounter election news inadvertently, when they have gone online for other purposes.

Over a third (35%) of those who went online for election news registered their views in Internet political polls, while 22% used e-mail to contact candidates, and 5% made campaign contributions over the Internet. Only 8% joined a political chat forum during the 2000 campaign, compared to 31% during the 1996 campaign. Whites and minorities got news about the elections online in similar proportions, and they cite the same reasons, primarily convenience. Men are slightly less likely than women to cite convenience and are more motivated by a desire for more news than the newspapers or television can provide. There are a few differences across race and ethnicity: 23% of blacks and 36% of Hispanics, compared to 15% of whites, who go online for election news say they sought information about when and where to vote, and almost a quarter of black and 12% of Hispanic online news users took part in chat groups, compared to only 6% of whites.

This online election information had a substantial impact: 43% of election news consumers reported it affected their voting decisions (compared to 31% in a 1996 Pew survey), while half of those under age 30 reported such an effect. However, there is no evidence from the Pew surveys that the Internet is drawing more people of any age into the political process. Other demographic groupings indicating greater influence of online information on their voting decisions include younger men and users with more than three years' experience (49% compared to 38% of those with only six months' experience). However, taking into consideration the larger picture, as with our primary 1996 results, controlling for other factors related to participation, Internet users in the Pew 2000 study are no more likely to be engaged in the political process and show no greater propensity to vote than are nonusers.

Conclusion

The Internet appears to have had a very small but positive impact on political activity during the 1996 election. Neither usage/nonusage nor frequency of usage was associated with voting, offline political activities, or perceptions of the importance of print media or TV for political issues. However, from a tenth to a quarter of Internet users did participate in some kind of online political activity. Further, more frequent use of the Internet was associated with increased involvement in online political browsing and online political interaction. Finally, frequency of

Internet usage was associated with increased online political awareness. Thus, while not diminishing traditional forms of political activity, the Internet has also provided a platform for a significant amount of additional forms of political activity.

These observations should be tempered by a number of cautionary remarks. First, the 1996 election was the first "Internet" presidential election. Second, it might be that Internet users (in 1996) as a group were more active, politically or otherwise, controlling for demographics, than the rest of the population. Certainly there was a greater percentage of respondents who said they were voters in the sample than in the population. For whatever reasons besides demographic ones, users are more likely to get involved in new areas, from politics to communication technologies (and perhaps other spheres as well). While it would suggest a different theoretical explanation, there is still a positive association between Internet usage and online political activity and awareness. Third, Internet users may have systematically overstated their political activity on the Internet compared to their nonsurfing counterparts (asking people if they have voted provokes a well-known "social desirability bias") (Fisher & Katz, 2000). Fourth, these data must be viewed as preliminary: as the public's familiarity with the Internet grows and technical capabilities expand, it is reasonable to assume that uses and impacts will also change. However, the Pew 2000 surveys show substantial increases in almost all areas.

These data reflect an innovative information and communication medium and an audience that had been, at least in 1996, relatively recently recruited. This suggests that our findings are likely to be superseded as both familiarity of users with the new medium and the power of applications increase. All our conclusions must therefore be viewed as tentative. Still, the pessimistic predictions about how the Internet will affect political participation and communication, at this point, are not sustained. Rather, the Internet appears, at least based on our 1996 survey and the Pew 2000 survey, both conducted around the time of the presidential elections, to be one way to expand political involvement without sacrificing current modes.

This would seem to be good news for traditional media, since they were reported to expect that readers and viewers would defect in 1996 and that 2000 would be a watershed change from "old economy" media to the Internet. Yet the "Year of the Internet" scenario materialized neither in 1996 nor in 2000, despite many elaborate and expensive attempts to draw potential voters. Why was this so, and will the case be any different in future elections? Will the assertion of the University of Michigan's W. Russell Neuman in January 2001 be proved true—that by 2004 "the Internet will replace newspapers as the way people get political information" (O'Neill, 2001)?

Our view is probably not. The most important reason that the Internet will not sweep all before it in the next few election cycles is that Internet-like technology, no matter how rich, will be only one portion of how people learn about the political world. Even with higher bandwidth and richer formats, this mode does not fit well with the way people get politically socialized. Rather, it is our view that the Internet is a form of syntopia—an extension of but still heavily integrated with other face-to-face and mediated channels and processes. As such, it will be influential, as it apparently was in some degree as early as 1996. But it will not become heavily dominant as a form of political socialization (but will continue growing as a source of instant news). Hence, we again underscore the usefulness of a syntopian view of human processes than either a dystopian or an utopian Internet-fixated view. The quick demise of candidate Malcolm "Steve" Forbes in 2000, who predicated his heavily bankrolled campaign on an Internet presence, remains by now mute testimony to the severe limitations of the Internet to be transformative.

A second important reason that the Internet will not dominate the next few election cycles is that the information on the Internet is not packaged in a way that would be optimally persuasive or useful. Katz (1999b) has presented an analysis of candidate Web sites during the 1999 election in New Jersey, which also included candidates who were competing in presidential primaries. He argued that most nonpresidential candidates did not have good Web sites in terms of content and that even for national contestants the content was poor. His major criticism was that the Web sites were candidate-centered and appeared to address the internal organizational needs of the candidate rather than the interests of a potential supporter. That is, the content seemed oriented toward pleasing the candidate and political party official rather than the undecided voter or even the casual visitor (Katz, 1999b). This criticism appears sustained by later research from ⟨netelections.org⟩ and the Annenberg School at Penn (⟨netelections.org⟩, 2001). The chances of great improvement over the next election cycles are limited.

Given the great expectations from both the utopians and dystopians about the dramatic impact of the Internet on elections, the 1996 and 2000 elections must be viewed as disappointments. Perhaps the least predicted outcome is the most surprising—that the Internet has had only modest consequences, especially in light of the financial and emotional investments in the technology. It facilitates greater online political activity and information exchange but does not seem to influence voting, other offline political activities, or perceptions of the importance of traditional media for the political process. We expect the situation to change only incrementally as the syntopian integration continues of various communication technologies with facets of real life.

8

Community Involvement: Survey Results

Chapter 6 reviewed prior research on the Internet and community involvement, including a wide variety of uses for online communities. This chapter looks in detail at the 1995 and 2000 data (from our surveys and from the surveys conducted by the Pew Internet and American Life Project) to see whether the Internet inhibits social capital in the form of community involvement. This is a central component of Putnam's (2000) argument that social and technological forces reduce participation in local social activities and institutions, thus decreasing individual and collective capital at the community and national levels. The following analyses are a limited treatment but do rigorously address the vital issue of community involvement. Chapter 9 provides a wide variety of examples of Internet sites supporting political and community involvement.

Involvement in Religious, Leisure, and Community Organizations

Table 8.1 provides the number, percentage, and statistical associations for membership in religious organizations (such as churches or synagogues), leisure organizations (such as hiking, biking, bowling, or tennis clubs), and community organizations (such as Lions Clubs or political campaigns). Membership was grouped into two categories—(1) none and (2) one or more. Between 1995 and 2000, membership in religious organizations decreased slightly, in leisure organizations increased greatly, and in community organizations decreased noticeably. With respect to declining local involvement and thus less social capital, Putnam therefore appears correct. The question is whether evidence shows that this decline in community involvement is associated with Internet use.

Table 8.1
Internet Usage and Community Involvement, 1995 and 2000

Variables	1995		2000	
	Never Used	Current User	Never Used	Current User
Religious organizations:				
None	687 (35.2%)	67 (37.9)%	176 (41.6%)	393 (46.2%)
At least 1	1,247 (64.8%)	110 (62.1%)	245 (58.4%)	457 (53.8%)
χ^2, η, nonusers versus users		.5, .02		2.4, .04
Leisure organizations:				
None	1,141 (62.8%)	88 (49.4%)	400 (94.6%)	794 (93.4%)
At least 1	675 (37.5%)	90 (50.6%)	23 (5.4%)	56 (6.6%)
χ^2, η, nonusers versus users		12.3***, .08		.6, .02
Community organizations:				
None	1,172 (65.4%)	103 (59.2%)	363 (85.8%)	612 (72.0%)
At least 1	644 (35.5%)	71 (40.8%)	60 (14.2%)	238 (28.0%)
χ^2, η, nonusers versus users		1.97, .03		30.1***, .15

$*p < .05.$
$**p < .01.$
$***p < .001.$

Organizational Membership Differences between Internet Users and Nonusers

No statistically significant difference was found between Internet users and nonusers in membership in at least one religious organization in either 1995 (62.1% users and 64.8% nonusers belonged) or 2000 (53.8% versus 58.4%). Users were significantly more likely to belong to at least one leisure organization than were nonusers (50.6% versus 37.5%) in 1995 but not in 2000 (6.6% versus 5.4%). Users were significantly more likely than nonusers to belong to at least one community organization in 2000 (28.0% versus 14.2%).

In 2000, users who spent more hours online per week were slightly more likely than nonusers to belong to more religious organizations ($r = .07$, $p < .01$), but there was no significant correlation between frequency of usage and membership in leisure or community organizations ($r = .01$ for both).

Based on this limited analysis, we can conclude that usage of the Internet is not associated with a decline in involvement in community-level organizations and that it is actually associated with greater participation.

Predicting Membership in One or More of the Three Organizations

Table 8.2 provides results from logistic regressions predicting 1995 and 2000 membership in religious, leisure, and community organizations. These analyses test for the influence of being an Internet user or nonuser after controlling for differences in sex, age, income, education, race, and having children (because of interdependencies among these variables, all demographic variables were entered as an initial block, followed by nonuser or user as a second block).

For religious organizations for 1995 and 2000, membership was greater for those who were older and had children. For leisure organizations for 1995, membership was predicted by being younger, having more income, and having more education. No variables predicted membership in leisure organizations in 2000. For community organizations for 1995, membership was predicted by being older, having higher income, and having more education; for 2000, membership was predicted by being older, having more education, and being an Internet user.

Essentially, after controlling for significant demographic factors, the significant association between using the Internet and membership in leisure organizations in 1995 disappeared, but the greater tendency of Internet users to belong to community organizations in 2000 persisted. Again, we see slight but robust evidence of a positive association between Internet usage and one indicator of social capital. This finding is important in grasping the social consequences of the Internet from 1995 to 2000. It certainly flies in the face of hitherto empirically based pessimistic views (Kraut et al., 1998; Nie, 2000; Putnam, 2000).

Table 8.2
Predictors of Membership in At Least One of Three Types of Organizations (Religious, Leisure, and Community) by Demographics and by Internet User and Nonuser, 1995 and 2000

	1995					
	Religious Organizations		Leisure Organizations		Community Organizations	
	B	Exp(B)	B	Exp(B)	B	Exp(B)
Sex (male, female)	—	—	—	—	—	—
Age (under 40, at least 40)	.54***	1.72	−.23*	.79	.36***	1.4
Income (under $35,000, at least $35,000)	—	—	.44***	1.6	.31*	1.4
Education (less than college degree, at least college degree)	—	—	.29*	1.3	.71***	2.0
Race (African American, white non-Hispanic)	—	—	—	—	—	—
Children (none, any)	.60***	1.8	—	—	—	—
Internet user	−.01	1.0	.16	1.2	.06	1.07
Model χ^2	45.7***	—	31.5***	—	65.9***	—
−2 log likelihood	2,181	—	1,812	—	1,720	—
Nagelkerke R^2	.04	—	.03	—	.07	—
Correctly assigned	64%	—	58.8%	—	64.4%	—
N	1,705	—	1,360	—	1,352	—

Note: B values are unstandardized coefficients from logistic regression. Exp(B) values are odd-ratios from logistic regression.
*$p < .05$.
**$p < .01$.
***$p < .001$.

2000					
Religious Organizations		Leisure Organizations		Community Organizations	
B	Exp(B)	B	Exp(B)	B	Exp(B)
—	—	—	—	—	—
.54***	1.7	—	—	.72***	2.1
—	—	—	—		
—	—	—	—	.28*	1.3
—	—	—	—	—	—
.34**	1.4	—	—	—	—
−.07	.94	—	—	1.0***	2.7
21.5***	—	n.s.	—	54***	—
1,515	—	—	—	1,193	—
.03	—	—	—	.07	—
58.8%	—	—	—	75.4%	—
1,118	—	—	—	1,118	—

Table 8.3
Differences in Membership in Mean Number of Three Types of Organizations, for Internet Users and Nonusers, 1995 and 2000

Group	1995	2000
Nonuser	1.32 (.99)	.81 (.73)
User	1.47 (1.05)	.88 (.81)
T ratio	−1.9*	−1.5 n.s.
n	1,586	1,155

*$p < .05$.

Predicting Membership in Total Number of the Three Types of Organizations

Although clear differences emerge in how Internet usage is reflected in membership in at least one of the three types of organizations, the general social capital argument (and Putnam's in particular) does not identify the kinds of organization membership that might be more likely to foster social capital. Further, although the correlations are weak, membership in at least one organization is significantly associated with membership in at least one of the other two types of organizations, across the combined 1995 and 2000 data (religious and leisure, $r = .14$; religious and community, $r = .20$; leisure and community, $r = .28$, all $p < .001$; these were strong in 1995 and weaker in 2000). Therefore, we also tested for differences between users and nonusers on a "membership" index.

This index is the sum of how many organizations (religious, leisure, and community) users and nonusers reported belonging to in 1995 and 2000. Of the 3,511 respondents in 1995 and 2000 who answered these questions, 29.2% indicated no membership in any of the three, 40.0% belonged to one, 21.1% belonged to two of the types, and 9.7% belonged to at least one of each of the types of organizations.

In 1995 users belonged to significantly more organizations, while there was no statistical difference between users and nonusers in 2000 (table 8.3 provides the means and t-test results).

Taking into account the demographic variables again, table 8.4 shows that in 1995, being a user or nonuser had no significant influence on number of types of organizations; greater membership was predicted,

Table 8.4
Predicting Membership in Three Types of Organizations

Independent Variables	1995	2000
Sex	−.03	.05
Age	.09**	.15***
Income	.12***	.08*
Education	.15***	.07*
Race	−.04	.00
Children	.07**	.06
Internet user	.02	.05
Adjusted R square	.06	.04
F ratio	11.0***	5.4***
n	1,183	847

Note: Linear regression used to predict total number of different types of organizations (0 to 3). Values are standardized beta coefficients.
*$p < .05$.
**$p < .01$.
***$p < .001$.

however, by being older and by having more income, education, and children. In 2000, user status was again not a significant predictor, while membership in more types of organizations was predicted by being older and having more income and more education. So the slight but robust association between Internet usage and involvement in local organizations seems specific to community organizations in 2000.

Conclusion

At least concerning the very specific issue of local organizational membership and its implied relation to social capital, we have evidence that being an Internet user was positively associated with being a member of at least one of the three kinds of organizations in both 1995 (leisure organizations) and 2000 (community organizations) and with being a member of more total kinds of organizations in 1995. However, controlling for basic demographic variables, only the relationship to membership in community organizations (in 2000) persisted. Note that the positive influence of usage on leisure organization membership in 1995 is relatively small (about a .6 odds ratio), while the positive influence on community organization membership is quite strong (a 2.7 odds ratio). Fundamentally, then, involvement in religious organizations seems unaffected by people's Internet usage across the years, leisure membership was somewhat associated with usage in 1995, and recently Internet users are substantially more likely to belong to community organizations, even controlling for demographic variables.

These results seem to call into question arguments that Internet usage will detract from community involvement in general. The main influences were, and remain, the basic demographic issues of age, education, and income. Further, a novelty effect of Internet usage appeared early on, with usage associated with more leisure involvement. With more widespread and familiar experience with the Internet, users tend to participate in more community organizations.

9

Involvement Examples: Evidence for an "Invisible Mouse"?

Involvement in Internet activities is embedded within social interaction and expression, which in our analytical framework are two different aspects of a related, multifaceted reality. In chapter 9, we discuss topics such as joining groups, building families and relationships, and searching for personal identity and support. In chapter 13, we explore topics that emphasize the expressive aspects, including maintainance of distant ties, artistic expressions, and efforts by immigrants or diaspora groups to maintain contact with their culture. Our main interest in both chapters is on participation in various forms of community, religious, and recreational life. This focus mirrors our reviews of research on religious, civic, and leisure organization membership in chapter 6 and our own analyses in chapters 7 and 8.

As was shown in chapters 1 and 6, some say that the Internet substantially reduces the social capital that addresses the needs of social-support networks and meaningful involvement. In this chapter, we seek to present bountiful evidence to show the positive case for Internet involvement rather than demonstrate an answer via formal hypothesis testing, which we do in chapters 3, 7, 8, and 11. Despite the harmful effects of Internet use on involvement and expression, we believe the evidence strongly favors the positive.

This chapter complements earlier chapters by providing an array of concrete examples of activities that can take place only in cyberspace or at least in computer-assisted environments. and that put into perspective the enormous richness and diversity of activities that are taking place in cyberspace. An important aspect of our argument is that the Internet can enrich lives. However, we also note that these activities take place because they fulfill the wishes and needs of the participants. Among the areas we look at are community involvement and cultural heritage. We also explore religious interests, hobbies and avocations, and identity projects. We have chosen these examples to represent the traditional forms of social capital as formulated by Putnam (2000) and by the social psychological issues raised by Bourdieu (1993). They also address our own view of syntopian social capital—that is, the rich resources made available through human agency applied through the Internet.

The examples here support the case that the Internet embodies a strong form of individualistic pursuit of self-interest combined with a modest degree of altruism. Although large numbers of people have had heavily individualistic (and hedonistic) motives when using the Internet, Internet structures still can serve the common good. Hence, when individuals pursue their self-interest (within boundaries that are discussed in chapter 14), they create new structures that transcend the individual. Further, individualistic goals are not inimical to collective goals. With acknowledgments to Adam Smith, whose "invisible hand" of enlightened self-interest generated positive benefits for society as a whole (notwithstanding negative externalities of free markets), we refer to this process as the "invisible mouse." We see the "invisible mouse" working to create individual identity, individual social capital, and collective social capital at many levels, from the local to the international.

The mouse is invisible in the sense that billions of mouse clicks and hours spent surfing the Internet do not seem directly connected to the structure of society. Social integration, psychic well-being, and increased knowledge residing within the brain—all of which we believe have been stemming from recent Internet usage among the American population—are not directly observable. The workings of the mouse are also difficult to discern in the changes in institutional arrangements of recreational, social, religious, and social action organizations. Yet communication and data flows can be observed. Social programs and institutional arrangements can be monitored and characterized. National random attitude and behavioral surveys can be conducted.

In the balance of this chapter, we present an analysis of how the Internet is helping to create new forms (and reinforcing old forms) of social involvement. We also identify some areas where Internet activities seem to harm social involvement. The list below highlights areas where we see the impact of the Internet as being most prominent. (The list also also provides a topical guide for the balance of the chapter.)

• Social support networks
• Family involvement
• Personal social networks
• Involvement with life, death, and sex
• Political involvement
• Cultural community building
• Social community building
• Altruistic endeavors
• Negative consequences

Social-Support Networks

Help Communities
A 2000 study (Davison, Pennebaker & Dickerson, 2000) estimated that nearly 3% of the U.S. population, or about 9 million people, participate in online and offline self-help groups each year. The study was based on a city sampling of online and offline support-group participation for sufferers of 20 illnesses. Based on the survey, self-help members are on average 43 years old and tend to be male. African Americans seem to participate at a rate that is one-third that of European Americans. Those diagnosed with alcoholism, cancer (all types), diabetes, AIDS, depression, and chronic fatigue syndrome are the most likely to join a support group. The least likely to seek support are sufferers of ulcers, emphysema, chronic pain, and migraines, in that order. Looking solely at the offline world, alcoholics are the most likely of all illness-sufferers to seek out in-person contact—293 times more likely than hypertension and migraine patients, who are the least likely to do so. AIDS, anorexia, and breast cancer patients also rank high on participation in face-to-face support groups.

For online support, however, multiple sclerosis patients have the highest activity level, and those suffering from chronic fatigue syndrome,

Box 9.1
The First Eight of the Many Support Groups Listed by Yahoo!

• **A Common Bond, San Francisco Chapter** Support group for gay and lesbian former Jehovah's Witnesses
• **Ageless Love** Support site for people in older-woman, younger-man relationships, with forums, newsletters, profiles, advice, and articles
• **AirCraft Casualty Emotional Support Services** A nonprofit organization offering peer grief support network for those who have survived or lost loved ones in an air disaster
• **All Things British** Various services for British expatriates
• **America's Doctor Communities** Covering a number of health ailments
• **Anonymous One** Searchable database of more than 50,000 12-step meetings and 15,000 sober clubs, hospitals, and treatment centers
• **Beyond Fear Self-help: Dental Phobia** Site aimed at overcoming dental fear, anxiety, and phobias through discussion boards, chat, and a virtual support group
• **Christian Recovery International** Site dedicated to helping Christians recover from abuse, addiction, and trauma

---

breast cancer, and anorexia are also heavy participators. According to Davison et al. (2000, p. 207), "The online domain may be particularly useful in bringing together those who suffer from rare and debilitating conditions, in which getting together physically would present a number of practical barriers. Virtual support can be very attractive to those whose disability impairs mobility, and the online community allows for anonymity." The study also concludes that suffering from embarrassing, socially stigmatized, or disfiguring illnesses is associated with higher levels of participation in all social support venues. Embarrassment was given as the primary motive for seeking support. Box 9.1 shows just the first eight online support groups listed by Yahoo! Box 9.2 provides an example of the kind of response that is typical of these support Web sites.

Mentoring
Because e-mail is easy to use at any location, organizations interested in mentoring have been looking for innovative ways to harness the Internet's capability to provide better mentoring. ⟨Tutormentorexchange.net⟩

Box 9.2
Expression of Appreciation E-mailed to a Support Group

> Just a note to tell you that I love you all and couldn't face this new year with optimism if it weren't for the support of you guys. Since finding the board in August, I have laughed, cried, and celebrated with all of you and wouldn't have missed it for the world. There is lots of love and support here and the best people I've ever met.
>
> *Source:* Anonymous (Case, 1998).

helps align tutors with students in the Chicago area and has a base at the Cabrini-Green housing project. Two other mentoring organizations— ⟨imentor.org⟩ and ⟨netmentors.org⟩—use e-mail to foster career-development relationships between professionals at the workplace and students in high schools and middle schools. Established mentoring groups—such as the National Mentoring Partnership (⟨www.mentoring.org⟩)—have begun their own online mentoring services as well.

Although career guidance is a primary rationale for students who begin a mentoring relationship, they frequently gain various broader benefits from it. For example, a youth development specialist in Minnesota who initially did not think e-mail mentoring held much promise has changed her view: "Having participated in a few programs, I do think the possibility exists that some people will be able to form emotional connections online, and sometimes they can be even stronger than those conducted face to face" (Greenman, 2000).

Programs probably cannot rely exclusively on e-mail for a long-term, meaningful monitoring program; face-to-face meetings do contribute to the program's success. However, they clearly do make it feasible for a larger group of students (and mentors) to participate than would otherwise be the case.

Tutoring
⟨Tutor.com⟩ and ⟨tutornet.com⟩ offer interactive live assistance in dozens of subjects. There's also help for senior citizens who are making their way into cyberspace, via sites such as ⟨seniornet.org⟩ and ⟨thirdage.com⟩.

Family

Sustaining Long-Distance Relationships

E-mail has long been a convenient and fulfilling way for family members and friends to remain in touch over distance (see survey results in chapter 11). An even richer technology than e-mail is the webcamera or webcam. Stokley (2001) recounts the story of Erika and Prentice, who had been dating since high school. In college, Erika spent a year in Costa Rica while Prentice stayed behind in California, and when Erika returned to California, Prentice moved to Beijing. They maintained their long-distance relationship by e-mail, live chat, and especially WebCam: "They used webcameras to be able to see each other every day. After several years of this long-distance relationship, Erika moved to Beijing, and they had their first child in October" (Stokley, 2001).

Creating New Families: Foster Children, Adoption, and Reunion

The Internet is being used to address the needs of the 120,000 foster care children in the United States waiting to be adopted. Only five of the 52 states have not established Web sites for foster children. According to Carolyn Johnson, executive director of the National Adoption Center in Philadelphia, "We have really found the Internet is an incredible way to shrink some of the barriers to adoption. We have had amazing success in finding homes for some of the most difficult children we've seen in 28 years by using the Internet, and I think it's because the reach is so broad and families can return to the site again and again" (Sink, 2000b). ⟨Adoptablekids.com⟩ allows potential adopters to look at photos of children and sort the available choices by criteria such as age, sex, race, and disability.

Other Web sites, such as ⟨adoptiononline.com⟩, reverse the search by providing those wishing to place foster children with information about prospective parents. This includes potential parental background statements and photos. Among the searchable features of potential adopters are hobby interests, area, and religion. There appear to have been 55 matches in the four years from 1996 to 2000 (Sink, 2000a).

The Internet is also useful in bringing separated families together again. For example, ⟨reunion.com⟩ has an online tool, Adoption Re-

Box 9.3
Reuniting Birth Families via Internet Research

I was adopted in 1971 when I was seven years old through Catholic Social Services. While I remember being involved in every aspect of the adoption, I have come to realize that I was missing one vital piece of information, one that I would not even notice was absent until much later in life—the identity of my birth parents. Adoption in those days was done almost secretly; there was a stigma of shame to it that, unwittingly, transferred to the child. This stigma, which is fully supported by the laws, greatly hinders adult adoptees from finding their birth parents. I have recently decided to start searching for my birth parents. My first step was to subscribe to the Adoptee Internet Mailing List, which deals with the issues surrounding adoption. This simple ideal has grown to form a group of people whose only connection is their computer and their participation in the adoption triad, which is the adoptee, the birth parents, and the adoptive parents. The issues of adoption and the rights of the adoptee are not new; they have been around as long as adoption itself. Adoption has always had attached to it a stigma of secrecy and shame; adoptees are treated as second-class citizens their entire lives. The perfect example of this is the topic of identifying information. The California Public Records Act states, among other things, that any person may request copies of their birth certificate, except persons who are adopted. It even states in the statute that the reason for this law is to protect the anonymity of the birth parents. This is fine if all birth parents want to remain anonymous, but they don't. The laws are starting to change, and what is helping that change is the abundance of information that is available through the Internet and the exchange of that information between people that ordinarily would have no contact with each other.

Source: Douglas (n.d.).

triever, which is a free search of 14 different reunion registries. The searches are performed simultaneously, and results are combined on one page. Another site providing this service is ⟨reunite.com⟩.

The Internet can exacerbate preexisting questions, such as the rights to privacy and anonymity of both birth parents and their adopted children. Another question is the sale of babies online, a practice that made headlines in 2000. These are not new issues, but they are thrown into sharp relief by the novelty of Internet technology. Clever uses of the Internet make the issues more problematical, pressing, and prominent. The poignant plea of one middle-aged adopt is presented in box 9.3.

Box 9.4
Genealogy Resources at a University of Minnesota Web Site

Associations and societies
Books, periodicals, software, and supplies
Cemeteries and obituaries
Dictionaries and translation services
Geographical information
German resources
German-Bohemian resources
Getting started
Libraries and archives
Midwest resources
Minnesota resources
Miscellaneous
Morrison County GenWeb
Nicollet County GenWeb
Online directories, subject catalogs, search engines
Religious resources
Searchable databases
Swedish resources
United States resources

Source: "Genealogy Resources" (retrieved July 31, 2001 from ⟨www.tc. umn.edu/~pmg/genealogy.html⟩).

Family History and Current Events
Genealogy   Genealogy is an extremely popular Internet activity. The Web site ⟨genhomepage.com⟩ lists more than 600 Web sites for North American genealogical research alone. Its topics range from Arcadian/ Cajun and African American to Wyoming and the Yukon. Box 9.4 shows a listing of headings for genealogy research available at a University of Minnesota Web site that specializes in Minnesota genealogy (⟨www.tc.umn.edu/~pmg/genealogy.html⟩). The oldest and largest free genealogy search service is GenConnect, which offers a suite of services and numerous bulletin boards (⟨http://genconnect.rootsweb.com⟩). Data are organized into categories that include Bibles, Biographies, Deeds, Obits, Queries, Pensions, and Wills. GenConnect has created special genealogical software, called GenBBS, that systematically collects information for the Internet genealogy community (see table 9.1).

Table 9.1
Statistics on GenConnect

	n
Countries using this system	147
Bulletin # boards	138,951
Files	4,904,711
Space used	198,930,432 bytes
Messages posted (total)	3,021,657
Messages posted (last 30 days)	115,375

Source: "GenConnect Fun Facts" (retrieved July 31, 2001 from ⟨http://genconnect.rootsweb.com/stat.html⟩).

Documenting Childhood   Two generations ago, a baby had its arrival and progress recorded in a baby book and perhaps in photographs or home movies. A generation ago, the home movie camera was replaced by a videotape recorder. All of these techniques required labor-intensive efforts to share and preserve the events. With the Internet, documentation has been transformed into a digital process. Today's newborn may even have a baby page instead of a baby book, and some hospitals set up Web pages and e-mail addresses for new arrivals. Various commercial sites have been set up (such as ⟨www.welcomenewborn.com⟩ and ⟨www.thatsmybaby.net⟩). But many parents establish their own Web sites for their newborns and e-mail their birth announcements.

WebCams: Surveillance and Monitoring of Children via the Internet
Surveillance WebCams introduce a different connotation to our concept of the "invisible mouse." Their ability to surreptitiously observe people can pose a threat to privacy. They also can be used for multitasking to allow people to be in two (or more places) at once and perform multiple roles. Parents at work or home can be involved in their young children's lives at their daycare facility. KinderView says they "put technology to good use by allowing parents to see their children even when they can't be with them! Our innovative Internet Viewing System allows parents, and other authorized users (such as grandparents), to safely and easily

view real-time images of their children from a childcare center equipped with a KinderView viewing system" (retrieved August 6, 2001 from ⟨www.kinderview.com⟩).

Personal Social Networks: Maintaining, Restoring, and Affirming

Numerous Web sites have cropped up with the purpose of reconnecting people with old friends and keeping currently existing social groups connected. The October 2000 Roper Starch Cyberstudy found that 41% of online Americans had used the Internet to find or reconnect with people they had lost touch with, and the mean number of years since contact was 12 (AOL, 2000, p. 30). The situation parallels France's Minitel, a small computer terminal connected to the phone network. Shortly after Minitel was deployed in 1982, people began using its national directory assistance capability to locate long-lost friends and relatives.

Class Reunions

⟨Classmates.com⟩ is a free portal for people who organize class reunions as well as a guide to the pop culture of earlier eras. It provides an opportunity for users to "reconnect with the past and build friendships for the future" through its reunion updates and message boards. More than 40,000 schools are listed, along with 10 million registered individuals.

Army Brats

Millions of today's adults grew up on military bases, and the frequent moves required of military families fractured many childhood friendships. The Internet has a specialized site (⟨armybrats.com⟩) to restore these friendships. In one story, a 13-year-old girl spent only one year at an army base in Pennsylvania. She made a close friend there but lost contact when she moved to another base. After almost 40 years, she found her long-lost friend through an online registry for military brats like herself. "I saw her name there in the registry list, and I said, 'That's Jeanie!' And wonder of all wonders, she remembered me, too" (Sink, 2000a).

Former Employees

⟨Everfound.com⟩ offers a convenient way for people to stay in touch, including former employees of organizations. It is access controlled so that only authorized members of a group can see its postings and offers an auto-updating address book, a feature that automatically synchronizes users with cell phone, a personal digital assistant (PDA), and a PC-based contact management system.

Affirmation Groups

Affirmation groups encompass a wide range of experiences—such as UFO abductions, eugenics advocacy, child raising, and retirement management. One notable group is American war veterans. On July 31, 2001, Yahoo! listed nearly 150 Web ring topics devoted to veterans, each containing from one to 60 Web sites. (Web rings are Web sites interrfracally linked to each other, focusing on a particular topic.) These sites allow veterans to express their views, find information, advice, and assistance, and share memories. One example of how the Internet can be used is Gunny's Links, which includes scores of site links, including one for Doc Bronson, who "is looking to connect with other Vietnam combat medics and corpsmen in hopes of starting a service organization of their own." Another of Gunny's links describes the Operation: God Bless America Web site, which is organized by "a group of volunteers from all walks of life with two things in common: respect and honor for those who have served our country and for motorcycling" (retrieved July 31, 2001 from ⟨www.ojc.org/gunny/links/vn.htm⟩).

Despite a proportionally low number of seniors on the Internet, World War II has a prominent place in Internet Web site-based relationships and contact maintenance. A great deal of historical preservation is also taking place on the Internet. ⟨Private-art.com⟩ is managed by a World War II veteran. His well-regarded site contains memoirs and photos from his war experience. The Internet is also becoming a resource for social contact for WWII veterans. One Web site is supervised by the survivors of the U.S. battleship *Houston*, which was sunk by the Japanese shortly after midnight on March 1, 1942. Survivors were put to brutal forced labor to build a railroad in Burma, which was dramatically recalled in the Hollywood film *Bridge over the River Kwai*. Survivors of these twin tragedies are represented by a lively Web site (⟨www.usshouston. org⟩) through which additional survivors are located and reunions are organized.

Involvement with Life and Death: Keeping Memory Alive

The Internet also allows people to find comfort by maintaining the memories of loved ones who have died. Numerous commercial sites even offer to webcast funeral services. ⟨Forevernetwork.com⟩ includes more than 4,500 biographies and has available movies, photos, and audio files. Given his base in Hollywood, says owner Tyler Cassity, "a high proportion of the people here have content-rich afterlives" (Leibowitz, 2001, p. 21). Many cancer and other disease support sites also offer obituary tributes. A "garden of memories" may include remembrances, original poetry, photos, and prayers. One example among many is the National Ovarian Cancer Coalition (⟨www.ovarian.org⟩). Eulogies for pets are also possible at, for instance, ⟨www.vetmed.iastate.edu⟩, where a pet "garden of memories" is maintained. More is said about the topic of death memorial sites in general in chapter 13.

Sex as a Motive for Involvement with the Internet

Although systematic evidence does not appear available, the Internet is often used in the noncommercial search for sex partners. One non-random survey of gay men in London gyms found that 80% of the 750 men interviewed had Internet access and almost 35% of those with access had gone online seeking a sexual partner. The majority of those who had ever looked for a partner said they had done so more than once. The research team, reporting results in the journal *AIDS*, found that ethnicity, employment, education, and whether a man had ever been paid for sex were not predictive of this online behavior (Reuters Health, 2001). (There is no way to generalize to any groups beyond this convenience sample, which seems unusual in other aspects, such as high interest in physical activity.)

Some have asserted that seeking sexual partners online, whether for men or women, does lead to a sad and lonely existence. Others claim that the pursuit of casual sex via the Internet allows consenting adults to do what they want, provided that minors are not involved. Children's access to the Internet and the predatory practice of many users are serious problems. At the same time, casual liaisons among adults can lead to meaningful long-term relationships. In the words of one anonymous individual, "I joined the [online community] to get laid, and ended up staying for the great friendships" (Anonymous personal communication, April 17, 2001).

The Internet is a cheap and easy way to make propositions, and online sexual intrigue and harassment flourish in every gender permutation. People in the limelight are particularly apt to receive sexual solicitations. One college football player has received "numerous emails" from women "telling me what they would do to me if they found me alone. One particular day, I received 45 e-mails from different males and females after scoring a touchdown in a home game." At one point he decided to accept one of the proposals and met a female fan following a game. "After a night of terrible conversation, I decided I did not want to see her again." Soon this woman began sending him e-mails threatening him and also "spreading false stories with e-mail to other females." She claimed that he had "a sexually transmitted virus." Because of his campus celebrity and the assiduousness with which the female propagated the rumors, he contended with her mischief for the balance of his college career and felt that whenever he was on campus, "I could never walk down a street without someone knowing who I was and what the rumors were" (Anonymous personal communication, May 3, 2001).

A second college football player has received "a healthy amount of fan email" that consists "mainly of females" sending him "nude pictures, explicit writings, and graphic depictions." The more he e-mails back to these women saying that he is not interested, the more e-mail responses he gets from them. He finally did agree to meet one of his female fans, who turned out to be a professional model. They enjoyed each other's company and plan to marry (Anonymous personal communication, April 12, 2001).

Community Building: Political Involvement

In this section, we review how the Internet fosters involvement for political action and community building—through organizing, policy monitoring, and exchanging ideas.

Political Action

Getting involved in political activities via the Internet includes monitoring political issues, organizing for civic action, and pursuing cultural interests. Some of the leading political action sites are ⟨webwhiteblue.org⟩, ⟨policy.com⟩, ⟨voter.com⟩, ⟨speakout.com⟩, ⟨vote.com⟩, ⟨grassroots.com⟩, and ⟨votenet.com⟩. Many are designed to stimulate involvement. ⟨Serviceleader.org⟩, for example, offers guidelines on how to involve volunteers through virtual activities. Some Web sites inform potential voters about the candidates, political party, or political philosophy that best fits their preferences. Another Web site, ⟨selectsmart.com⟩, has an interactive test asks visitors to respond to questions that determine which political party and which national candidates for an election best align with their preferences. It even has quizzes for some candidates for state offices.

But beyond these organized guides, a vast sea of Web sites and discussion groups encourage people to involve themselves in discussion. All shades of the political spectrum seem to have their views represented on the Internet. For those already committed to a cause, the Internet provides easy opportunities for communication, mobilization, and learning about news or upcoming events. Both cyberspace and real physical participation opportunities are made available through Internet Web sites. This hyperlinking of many different kinds of media and information allows those interested in a cause to find many ways to influence policy.

A good example of this principle in action is ⟨protest.net⟩, which, as its name implies, represents a wide variety of left-wing causes and organizes upcoming protest events by date and subject (box 9.5). One event listed at ⟨protest.net⟩ is "Borderhack," a three-day youth activist festival scheduled for August 2001 in Tijuana, Mexico, directly in front of the border fence between Mexico and the United States. The camp was to offer photographic exhibits, border cinema, Integrated Services

Box 9.5
Activist Topics Available at ⟨www.protest.net⟩

Animal rights
Children and education
Civil rights
Death penalty
Drugs
Elections and democracy
Environment
Fascism and the right wing
Feminism and reproductive rights
Food and agriculture
Globalization and imperialism
Human rights
Immigration and refugees
Iraq
Labor and unions
Media
Peace
Poverty and hunger
Prisons, police, and repression
Race and class
Religion and spirituality
Sexuality, gender, and GLBT
Third world

Source: "Topics" (retrieved August 10, 2001 from ⟨www.protest.net⟩).

Digital Network (ISDN) connections, activists' workshops, Net art, and something for "global hacktivists." Its goal was to unite politically mobilized artists and computer users from both sides of the border (retrieved August 10, 2001 from ⟨www.protest.net⟩).

In the 2000 election, the Democratic Congressional Campaign Committee (DCCC), which supports Democratic candidates for the U.S. House of Representatives, established more than 3,000 e-precincts around the country. E-precinct leaders were asked to forward e-mails from the committee to at least 10 of their friends. As part of its campaign effort during the election season, the Democratic National Committee, via its ⟨freedem.com⟩ Web site, offered free Internet access and e-mail accounts to anyone who signed up for the service and viewed party literature (Zeller, 2000).

The mobile aspects of the Internet are increasingly important. In 1999, the Democratic National Committee prepared special English and Spanish editions of its Web sites for easy downloading on mobile devices. During the 2000 presidential election, Vice President Al Gore's campaign site allowed users to download his position papers to their hand-held devices. The site also collected instant messaging addresses so that Gore supporters could assemble in online chatrooms to round up volunteers and mobilize get-out-the-vote efforts. Mobile communication will clearly be increasingly influential in the future.

Hill and Hughes (1998) claim that online discussion is dominated by conservative voices. Whether that is true today is difficult to say. Certainly, though, Web sites of every political stripe are commonly available on the Internet. The American Conservative Union (ACU) (⟨www.conservative.org⟩) says it is "the nation's oldest and largest grassroots conservative organization. Founded in 1964, ACU's purpose is to effectively communicate and advance the goals and principles of conservatism through one multi-issue, umbrella organization" (retrieved August 11, 2001 from ⟨www.conservative.org⟩). The Web site contains voting records and conservative ratings of members of Congress, allows visitors to help the ACU to block appointments of liberals to government posts, markets fragrance candles, alarm clocks, records, and household goods (such as an "AstroTurf Hitting Mat" so that golfers can "practice anytime, anywhere"), collects revelatory articles about alleged misdeeds of liberals, and facilitates computer-supported e-mail messaging to members of Congress. It also operates an ACU "Infonet" from which "We'll keep you up to date by e-mail on what's new and significant in conservative politics, and alert you when your help is needed to lobby Congress on important issues" (retrieved August 11, 2001 from ⟨www.conservative.org⟩).

An ultraconservative organization with an Internet presence is the John Birch Society (⟨www.jbs.org⟩), which includes online petitions and order forms for its American Opinion Book Services. Among its causes is helping to restore American control of the Panama Canal: "The transfer of our canal in Panama does not change the nullity of the Carter-Torrijos treaties. Americans continue to be outraged when they learn that one of our most important military assets has been illegally transferred to a foreign power. Find out how you can still help to Reclaim Our Canal! (retrieved August 11, 2001 from ⟨www.jbs.org⟩).

It is of course impossible to know the precise ratio of liberal to conservative Web sites on the Internet, or even if one or the other ideology predominates. Claims that one group has a more substantial presence cannot be verified. Although we presented several examples of conservative groups above, liberal and radical groups are also quite active on the Internet, and our examples should by no means be construed as a belief that such predominance exists. We can of course cite many examples of liberal and radical groups using the Internet to foster their causes.

For instance, one such group, Action LA, aims to serve what it terms "progressive" causes in Los Angeles, California. Their Web site, ⟨www.d2kla.org⟩, includes links and pages for its calendar of events, media contact desk, legal rights referral service, and inspirational poetry. The group spearheaded demonstrations at the Democratic National Convention in August 2000; among the issues were excessive use of cars, abusive overseas sweatshops, the North American Free Trade Agreement (NAFTA), and limits on immigration. Working with the American Civil Liberties Union Foundation and the National Lawyers Guild, Action LA used its Web site to help collect information about "any type of police misconduct" that may have occurred in response to protests during the Democratic National Convention. Their Web site provided an online forum for visitors to register their observation, complaints, and allegations about police misconduct.

Hate groups use the Internet as a tool for self-organizing and for recruiting new members. Debra Guzman, of the United States–based Human Rights Information Network, has said that the Internet is "a utopia for all kinds of hate groups, from neo-Nazis to anarchists" and that hate groups are "targeting teen-age males" (Olson, 1997). For instance, the Imperial Klans of America uses its Web site (⟨www.k-k-k.com⟩) to promote racism and an annual Nordic Fest: "The Nordic Fest–2001 was Great! We had 350 people in all here.... It was white people working together and having a good time with other white people.... That is GREAT!!! Start making your plans now to be at next years Nordic Fest–2002. Next years will be great!!!" (retrieved August 11, 2001 from ⟨www.k-k-k.com⟩). Part of the attraction of the

Internet is that it offers a free market of ideas—from democratic to demonic.

The Limits of Internet Political Mobilization

The Internet has been shown to be an effective method for people to learn more about an issue that they are interested in. However, the Internet has not been successful at transforming politics at the level of either informed discussion or electoral effectiveness. In terms of political discussion, a set of empirical reports analyzing online discussion boards was not encouraging.

In terms of electoral politics, the early assessments were positive. AOL's founder and chair, Steve Case, expressed a positive view when he said that the Internet offered "an unprecedented opportunity to reconnect people to the political process" (Edlund, 2000). Certainly, there was optimism about the role the Internet would play in the 2000 U.S. election: "The 'net in 2000 will be the equivalent of TV in 1960," declared Larry Purpuro, who headed the Republican National Committee's online effort (Johnson, 2000). This view was echoed in January 2000, when Phil Nobel of ⟨politicsonline.com⟩ asserted that "everyone will agree that the Internet in politics in 2000 is what TV was to politics in 1960.... Y2K marks the adult start of the New Politics" (Edlund, 2000). These prophecies seemed likely to be fulfilled early in the 2000 presidential contest when Republican candidate Malcolm "Steve" Forbes announced that he would be running an Internet-based campaign. Another candidate, Senator John McCain (Republican, Arizona) collected hundreds of thousands of dollars via contributions made through his Web site. In the end, however, these hopes were not realized. Neither the technology nor the content seemed to draw the levels of involvement that had been anticipated.

It is easy to find hyperbole about the potential difference the Internet might make. For example, one Web site makes this claim: "TalkToGov makes it simple and easy for you to take control and win back the government representation you deserve. With TalkToGov, not only can you discover and learn about issues that are of interest or importance to you, but you can actually write to the correct officials in Washington about them, getting yourself heard and effecting change" (retrieved August 10,

Box 9.6
Involvement Opportunities Listed on the Richard Vinroot (Republican, North Carolina) for Governor Web Site, Election 2000

How often would you like to hear from us via e-mail?

- Anytime
- No more than daily
- No more than weekly

I am willing to

- Make a financial contribution
- Volunteer locally
- Hand out literature at local events
- Distribute literature door to door
- Make telephone calls
- Place a bumper sticker on my car
- Attend rallies and speaking engagements
- Host a reception
- Make calls to talk radio programs
- Write letters to the editor
- E-mail messages to editors and opinion leaders
- Send fundraising e-mails to friends and family
- E-mail postcards
- Place a banner on my Web site

Source: "Involvement Opportunities" (retrieved August 11, 2001 from ⟨www.procatalog.com/vinroot/join.asp⟩).

2001 from ⟨www.talktogov.com/tour.htm⟩). The tools that TalkToGov offers, though, seem to be not vastly different from those offered by its competitor sites, which also offer information about issues and directions on how to send targeted e-mails to officials.

Web sites of tech-savvy campaigns encourage every possible form of involvement, both physical and virtual. A good example of this is the Web site of North Carolina gubernatorial candidate Richard Vinroot. As shown in box 9.6, it invites many possible forms of involvement. Perhaps the biggest unanswered question with regard to Internet political action is the extent to which the effects of Internet involvement are supplemental rather than cannibalistic of other forms of involvement.

In her study of the U.S. 1998 midterm elections, Norris (1998) found, as we had earlier in the 1996 presidential elections (Katz, Aspden &

Reich, 1997) and as we report in chapter 7, that Internet usage can fall into two categories—Internet users who are information seeking (such as news) and Internet users who wish to be active in discussions or in contacting officials. Her evidence, based on 1998 Pew Research Center data, finds that unlike the utopian predictions, the Internet is not (at least immediately) going to fulfill the democratic ideas of deliberative, informed discussion and full and equitable participation. She concludes, as have we, that the general consequences of the Internet are to reinforce and empower those who are already activists and influentials. In other words, the rich get richer in that the most motivated informed and engaged individuals are able to leverage further their influence via the Internet. She found no evidence of an independent Net effect that activates disinterested people to become more enthusiastic about politics.

Although Kamarck and Nye (2000) consider the 1998 election as the first one in which the Internet played a major campaign role, we are skeptical. In fact, we are dubious that even the 2000 election was markedly influenced by the Internet (but with only a few hundred votes giving George Bush the victory, anything could have influenced the election, including the Monica Lewinsky escapade). Information or discussion on the Internet did influence some people (as our surveys indicate in chapter 7), but this influence fell far short of what had been anticipated. Kamarck and Nye's analysis of campaign Web sites determined that the sites generally were simple electronic brochures containing information about the candidates' general views and background. Rare were sites that linked to other sites, gave voter registration information, or regularly updated content.

Technology can accomplish any number of impressive feats. For instance, ⟨pseudopolitics.com⟩, a unit of ⟨pseudo.com⟩, provided intense coverage the 2000 Republican National Convention. Web site visitors could select any of six real-time cameras to allow a 360-degree view of the proceedings at all times. Several dignitaries, including then-Governor Tom Ridge of Pennsylvania, were interviewed in a Skybox overlooking the convention center floor. Their video streaming interviews included e-mail interactions with visitors to a special chatroom. Jeanne Meyer, a ⟨pseudo.com⟩ senior vice president, said, "The governor was able to enter into a serious dialogue with his critics. It was really cool" (Glass,

2000). However, the audience for these activities was miniscule. It appears that, cool or not, the site found very few people who were interested in these capabilities. ⟨Pseudo.com⟩ shut down a few weeks after this experiment. So while technology can do much, if the content is not interesting to the audiences, they will not come.

The Democrats claimed they would do better with their Web activities. "The whole idea of the Web site is to draw people in with some content they can't find anywhere else," said Naz Nageer, director of technology for the Democratic National Convention (Meckler, 2000). Among the innovations available on the DNC site were:

- post-speech online chats with dignitaries;
- user-controlled cameras that would allow 360-degree panning of the convention floor;
- streaming videos, "Dems Uncut," provided by students who roamed the convention with digital video cameras in search of gritty, reality-based content;
- transcripts of speeches, after they are delivered, translated into several languages;
- streaming of panels featuring prominent Democrats discussing issues of moment.

But true interactivity was as elusive for the Democrats as for the Republicans. ⟨Speakout.com⟩, which instantaneously tracked viewer reaction to key speeches, had but a few hundred participants during an entire night (similar to their experience with the Republican convention). The post-speech chats disappointed many: big-name convention speakers declined the opportunity to go online after their speeches. Unlike the Republicans, the Democratic speechmakers who did go online took questions from surfers, but then they were highly selective in which ones they would address. Chat participants were not allowed interact among themselves. According to one observer, "It didn't seem to live up to the billing" (Associated Press, August 13, 2001). The example of the Democrats' experience shows that even when one can recognize a problem, it can be structurally difficult to do anything about it. Technology can be an important adjunct to communication, but it can also highlight vapid processes and vacuous content.

We agree with Davis (2000) that the Internet can be enormously effective in helping traditional activists to coordinate committed associates and generate publicity and in encouraging single-issue advocacy groups that have a small popular base or limited financial and intellectual resources. However, despite this, we (and Davis) think that traditional political elites can also adapt to the Internet. The Internet incrementally strengthens small groups and increases the efficiency of single-issue advocates, but it also increases the efficiency and reach of traditional well-entrenched and high-visibility groups (Katz, 1983).

The limits of the Internet can be seen in the many attempts by relatively small groups to leverage their impact by use of the Internet. One example is the Democrats who sought to use the power of the Internet to influence the post-electoral outcome of the 2000 presidential election.

Their attempt revolved around the struggle over recounting the Florida ballots. It appeared to many (both Democrats and Republicans) that there was fraud and abuse of power during the election in Florida. The popular vote in the United States gave a clear popular majority to Al Gore. However, there were large numbers of disputed ballots in Florida, where Mr. Bush's margin of victory fluctuated in the range of hundreds out of many millions of votes cast.

Conflict over the election took place in many venues, including on the promenades in front of governmental office buildings. Another was on the Internet. As victory for Bush loomed, the Democrats sought to harness the power of the Internet in a vigorous battle to reverse the Secretary of State's decision in Florida, which was, in essence, giving the national election victory to Mr. Bush.

As part of this attempt, flurries of e-mails were dispatched throughout friendship networks in Florida and the United States. One example drawn from many instances was a vigorous e-mail campaign underwritten by the liberal organization Working Assets from its site, ⟨WorkingAssets.com⟩. Using e-mails sent from friend to friend, and at times even sent to entire address book listings, people were urged to visit the organization's Web site. From there, visitors could complete a brief form that would automatically send an e-mail to the director of Florida's division of elections. The e-mail message implored the director to order a recount in contested counties (Abramson, 2000).

Numerous Web sites were also established in support of the challenge to the election's outcome. One of these, ⟨www.trustthepeople.com⟩, offered Wet site visitors the opportunity to take a "Counter-Inaugural Oath" and sign a petition to Congress. The oath included the statements: "George W. Bush Is NOT a Legitimate President.... By stealing the Presidency [he] has already violated his solemn oath to 'preserve, protect, and defend the Constitution of the United States.' I therefore solemnly affirm that I will faithfully oppose George W. Bush's illegitimate policies and work tirelessly to restore true Democracy in America." (⟨http://207.228.234.134/elandslide/petition.cfm?campaign=trustthepeople⟩, retrieved on January 10, 2002)

Communication does not mean that people will be galvanized to action, however. The whole world watched the Chinese army violently crush protesters in Tiananmen Square, but the world did not interefere. There were plenty of online reports about the Hutu government's slaughter of minority Tutsis in Rwanda, but Internet coverage and mobilization did not alter the disastrous results. Because the rules of politics tend to be more rigid than those of social community and artistic expression, the potential of Internet being transformative is lessened.

Community Building: Ethnic, Cultural, and Historical Affiliation and Enrichment

Thousands of Web sites claim to be based on ethnic or cultural affiliation. To reflect in thumbnail fashion on the way in which the Internet is able to provide communities of interest based on demographic or cultural attributes, we have compiled a list of some major sites in box 9.7. Many of these sites have been selected by ⟨zdnet.com⟩ as outstanding. They suggest the kind of specific appeals to community that the Internet allows and show how directed information and explicit socialization guidance can be delivered to self-selected individuals who wish to see themselves as part of a community of interest. Groups that are generally considered marginal are often the most assiduous in exploiting the Internet. Those whose needs are not served by current arrangements can find a wide array of service on the Internet, such as hiring a priest at hourly rates to perform ceremonies not necessarily sanctioned by the Roman Catholic Church

Box 9.7
Sample of Web Sites That Serve Communities of Interest

Teens

A popular teen Web site is ⟨katrillion.com⟩, which combines news and music reviews with advice, especially concerning relationships. But the site also has a good sense of what teenagers need to know and addresses those needs. The message board is full of discussions of topics that interest teens, such as music groups and relationships. A typical posting is "Help Me!!! I Really Want a Boyfriend."

Gays

⟨Gay.com⟩ and ⟨planetout.com⟩ are frequently visited Web sites that have community features. ⟨Gay.com⟩ has a message board that engages priority questions such as being gay and disabled or interacting with parents and vice versa.

Disabled

⟨Wemedia.com⟩ is a Web site aimed at the 54 million disabled Americans as well as their family and friends. It includes message boards, support groups, and advice about surmounting life's challenges and getting the most of daily activities. It also has information and links on assistive technology, accessible homes, sports, and career resources. There is even a political Access the Vote initiative that helps users to register online and arrange transportation to the polls.

Women

⟨Oxygen.com⟩ and ⟨ivillage.com⟩ provide a rich assortment of chat, message boards, member homepages, and advice columns. Under the topic "relationships," ⟨ivillage.com⟩ lists (presumably in chronological order) "sex," "weddings," and "divorce."

African Americans

⟨Bet.com⟩ and ⟨netnoir.com⟩ offer news, information, and chat oriented toward the African American community. The spotlight is on issues such as affirmative action, black teen suicide rates, and racial profiling. Famous people such as attorney Johnnie Cochran do guest spots.

Box 9.7
(continued)

Hispanic Americans

For Hispanic Americans, ⟨elsitio.com⟩, "Your place on the Internet," offers chat, relationship advice, and fan clubs, among many other services.

Asian Americans

⟨Aonline.com⟩ claims to be the leading global Asian Internet marketing company, with a special focus of Korean Americans and Koreans living in the United States. Among its features are chat, matchmaking and dating, messaging, and clubs. In late June 2001, the Club of the Week (the Rant Room) pronounced that "Therapy is expensive. But ranting online is free. So feel free to air your rants, raves, and general misgivings about life in this community of complaints. There, don't you feel better already?" The site also trolls for member input, asking, "Do you have an unforgettably horrible or wonderful date story?" with the plea to put it online for comments (Aonline, 2001).

Religion

Many religious groups, houses of worship, evangelical crusades, ministries, and religious clubs exist online. There are 11,000 Christian clubs, and hundreds each of atheist, Islamic, Jewish, pantheistic, and satanist clubs. ⟨Christianitytoday.com⟩, for example, provides chatrooms for fellowship among Christians and for discussion relating to personal issues of Christian faith and living. The site expresses the "hope you find information, inspiration, and encouragement as you connect with other Christians here." The 10 largest Yahoo! religious clubs combined have about 50,000 members (retrieved on June 19, 2001 from ⟨http://dir.clubs.yahoo.com/Religion_Beliefs⟩). A Pew survey done in 2000 shows that numerous houses of worship use the Internet to organize their members, send out messages, and even give "virtual tours" of their facilities. The Pew group surveyed 1,309 wired congregations, with 83% of respondents saying that Internet use bolstered the congregational life of the church. Project director Lee Rainie asserted that conventional wisdom is that the Internet caters to "young, libertarian technophiles." Hence, he was surprised when the survey found "found the exact opposite. These traditional faith-based organizations were embracing modern technologies for their own purposes. For these people, there was a quite joyous level of communication" (Associated Press, 2000).

(⟨http://www.nytimes.com/2001/06/07/technology/07PRIE.html⟩). These virtual communities do not duplicate the physical experience of face-to-face gatherings, but they do facilitate gatherings and resource networks. In other words, they offer a fair representation of what we have called syntopia.

Community Building: Social and Recreational

Hobbies as Serious Leisure

People take their leisure seriously. Stebbins (2001), who coined the term "serious leisure," has shown how involved people are in hobbies and recreation. This seems to be as true of online commitment to leisure as it is in the real world, where vast sums are spent in the United States on sporting and recreational events.

A quick search at Yahoo! in June 2001 found more than 25,000 sites that appeared related to hobbies; more than 1,400 were oriented to various types of collecting, and 177 were dedicated to rock collecting and mineralogy hobbies alone. Every hobby that exists in the real world seems represented in the online world. Indeed, the Internet, by providing an audience and a potential for interaction, seems to allow individualistic hobbies to flourish. For instance, there are hobby sites for those with an interest in snowflakes and their documentation (⟨www.snowflakebentley.com⟩ and ⟨www.its.caltech.edu/~atomic/snowcrystals⟩), in perceiving images in clouds (⟨www.cloudgazing.com/faces.htm⟩ and ⟨www.cloudman.com⟩), and in bubble-blowing (⟨www.bubbles.org⟩ and ⟨www.makestuff.com/soap_bubbles.html⟩).

Although some hobby sites are clearly meant to be ironic, most have what appear to be bona fide communities that congregate around such shared interests. The density of concentration and the enormous and variegated interests represented by hobby sites suggest that both differentiation and integration phenomena are encouraged by the Internet. That is, people are able to pursue more specialized and individually tailored interests, while at the same time they find and connect with those who share that ever-more specialized interest.

Emotional Involvement and Its Exploitation

People work together to create communities online. One example of this process is described in box 9.8, which presents the story of an online baby shower.

Another aspect of the process of emergent social organization on the level of personal commitment to group outcomes may be seen in the world of online games. In many cases, these communities modify ("mod") the original games, creating enhancements. They are called "mod" communities, which is not to be confused with MUD (multiuser domains) or MOO (multiuser, object-oriented) communities.

Players can also become emotionally involved in each other's lives. This has led, as it has elsewhere, exploitation. On November 12, 2000, the members of the EverQuest community were informed that a member, "Sheyla," a 19-year-old member, had killed herself. Sheyla had told other members via online conversation that her life had been filled with tragedy: her mother died in a car accident while looking for Sheyla when she skipped school to have sex with her boyfriend, and when she was 16, Sheyla suffered a miscarriage when her father stabbed her in the abdomen. Despite a sometimes irritating personality, some EverQuest members cared for her, and one spent several hours trying to persuade her not to commit suicide. After the death announcement, Sheyla's stepmother went online desperately seeking information about the girl. Concerned members were saddened by the tragedy and wanted more information and documentation to understand what had happened. These inquiries eventually uncovered a hoax in which one EverQuest player played the roles of both Sheyla and her stepmother (Brundage, 2001).

Hoaxes such as this have happened repeatedly on the Internet and doubtless will continue. What is significant is not that the hoax happened but that the hoax could happen (e.g., Senft, 2001). The ability of people to perpetrate hoaxes demonstrates not so much that the Internet is full of fakes and manipulators but that the Internet can be a place of concern and emotional involvement. Without a sense of caring and commitment, a sense of shared fate, the heart-rending stories that populate the Internet would have no audience and no interest.

Box 9.8
Virtual Baby Shower

The place I call "home" on the Internet is the Usenet group ⟨alt.startrek. creative.erotica.moderated⟩ (ASCEM). In the fall of 1999 one active ASCEM poster, known as "Pam," announced that she would probably be cutting back on her participation because she was expecting a baby in early 2000. Pam had been dubbed "the Feedback Queen" by other ASCEMites; she was in the habit of posting substantial comments on all kinds of stories several times a week. This made her enormously popular, and we knew we'd miss her a lot.

A few weeks before the baby was due, one ASCEMite sent an e-mail cc'ed to 24 active ASCEM posters suggesting that we throw Pam a "virtual baby shower." One person donated Web space and began putting together a page. Another person started a mailing list at ⟨egroups.com⟩ (the most popular public mailing list site at the time) so we could talk about the party where Pam couldn't "overhear." All the known members (as with other Usenet groups, there's no way of knowing all the people who read ASCEM regularly) were told about it in private e-mail, and we began working on our presents.

Most of the presents were Star Trek stories or poems with a "baby" theme. There were stories with the android Data babysitting the new baby, Doctor McCoy teaching Spock to change a diaper, a visit to a daycare center in which the original *Enterprise* crew had been regressed to tod-dlerhood, and a picture of Captain Kirk looking for the new baby under a pile of tribbles.

As people finished their gifts, the Web site designer put them up on the site, added baby-themed animations and sound files, and gave everything baby shower trimmings. Then it was a matter of waiting for Pam to an-nounce that her baby had been born so we could make the official public unveiling of the baby shower Web site.

A few days later, Pam publicly posted her enthusiastic thanks, writing, "Oh, you guys are too much!! I've seen it now, and it's a work of art!" signing herself, "feedback queen, typing with one hand, holding the baby with the other."

Source: Mary Ellen Curtin, personal communication, August 7, 2001.

Reenactment

Is the Internet able to effect time travel? People with a love of historic events or earlier times can organize and even participate in them. The Internet has shown itself to be a valuable tool for organizing historically realistic reenactments. Popular reenacting periods are the middle ages, the American Revolutionary War, World War II, and the American Civil War. In these cases, the online world helps enrich the real world, both for those interested in keeping alive the traditions and worlds of earlier eras and for those who wish to see and hear what life used to be like.

Fan Groups

A huge appeal of the Internet to contemporary music fans, and especially teens, is that it helps them search efficiently for what they want. These searches can lead to friendships and allow them to build friendships that transcend local geography and conceptual orientations. For instance, one surfer reports that, "I don't have many friends who are big into literature and the type of music I'm into. But I've found a lot of people on the Internet who share my interests.... I was surprised to see how many people built Web sites dedicated to my favorite singer, Ani DiFranco. Well, the designers' e-mail address is on the site, so I've e-mailed several of them, and there's a few I consider real friends of mine" (Anonymous personal communication, April 10, 2001).

Fantasy Sports Teams

"Every major online sports site ... offers fantasy games for nearly every sport, from football to cricket to bass fishing. Fantasy sports are now estimated to be generating over $600 million in advertising and subscription fee revenues and is one of the few business-to-consumer Web industries that actually makes money" (Berentson, 2000). Estimates of the number of people playing online fantasy sports team games vary widely. But according to one survey, at least 10 million and perhaps as many as 30 million Americans play fantasy sports, 25% of whom are women (Kilborn, 2000). (Most estimates, especially of the percentage of women who play fantasy sports, are usually much lower).

Over 100 Web sites support online sports fantasy teams. There are Web sites that help people create fantasy teams (Triple Double Computer service at ⟨www.tdcs.com⟩) and even a nonprofit Fantasy Sports Players Assocation with more than 45 supporting fantasy sports companies and institutions. According to one enthusiast who has been involved for more than five years, some people belong to "a division with their friends and check their team everyday. They actively participate, and some even keep in contact with people they have met through the game." Numerous denizens have reported that the leagues have "created a great friendship among them, even though they have never met" (Nikki Wunderlich, personal communication, April 29, 2001). ⟨Smallworld.com⟩ has over 10,000 players from around the world and allows players to exchange messages.

Many Web sites (such as ⟨rotonews.com⟩, which currently hosts about 50,000 fantasy sports leagues) are capable of performing all the calculations necessary for fantasy sports. The camaraderie is a strong appeal. Said one student: "I currently am also participating in a non-money fantasy baseball league run by ⟨CNNSI.com⟩. In this league, I compete with 48 others that I didn't know a couple of weeks ago but that I'm getting to know better by the day. We email each other and make frequent use of the message board at the Web site. It's very similar to going off to college for the first time. You don't know the people in your dorm at first, but the sense of community develops steadily over time" (Matthew Voorhees, personal communication, April 30, 2001).

This rationale was supported by a survey of Indiana University business school of students and executives aged 25 to 35 in the sports and entertainment industry. The 2000 study found that about 90% of respondents participated in fantasy sports leagues because they promoted "camaraderie and friendship, such as sharing time and experiences with friends and having something to talk about with friends and co-workers," according to study codirector Thomas Bowers. He noted that maintaining prior friendships as people separate from the fantasy league was also a high priority. (This activity may detract from workplace productivity since about 53% of respondents said they play with coworkers or friends at work) (retrieved on June 25, 2001 from ⟨www.iuinfo.indiana.edu/ocm/releases/fantasy.htm⟩).

Online Fantasy Games

The most popular Internet games are now attracting millions of users daily. Our 2000 survey data show that 22.0% of the 486 responding men and 8.9% of the 514 responding women had played a real-time interactive online game (chi square $= 32.9$, $p < .001$). Many of these games are built around a passionate and helpful support community, such as Chron X, a turn-based card game that has numerous fan sites built around the game. It has a global registration and ranking system, and its makers offer tournaments. Some are role-playing games (RPGs), which require interaction with other players. Verant Interactive's Ever-Quest has thousands of people playing at any given time. The terrain of play has an environment equivalent to 50 square miles, and it also includes dim and bright diurnal cycles. To be successful, players must cooperate within an evolving socioeconomic and ecological setting.

Clearly, this is an example of an Internet activity grounded in collective-benefit social capital rather than purely individual-benefit social capital. An intriguing interplay can occur between the two, and sometimes pure appeals for online social-capital creation seem to work, provided they are predicated on the enjoyment of the individual actor. Perhaps there is no clearer instance of this than the Sims Online game. This popular game involves players in social situations with other participants, beginning with their living environment. Players link up with compatible virtual roommates to share a house. Animated figures join in the play, and "conversation bubbles" illustrate interaction. Members can form their own online social clubs or play poker at a local virtual casino.

In other fantasy worlds, denizens elect legislatures that pass laws and prescribe penalties. Not surprisingly, politician-players, like their real-life counterparts, get themselves into nasty political spats. The play world of planet Mars, known as "the Republic of Mars," has registered more than 700 members, some of whom run its legislative and judicial branches (retrieved July 24, 2001 from ⟨www.marsgov.net⟩). Thousands of similar fantasy worlds populate the Internet.

A popular form of computer games is the action genre that depicts close-quarter battles, known collectively as first-person shooters. Players increase their chances of winning by networking among others players.

While many game formats allow teams to be arbitrarily chosen, organized teams, known as clans, can also be organized. Clans can be formed in many ways—by holding tryouts to let hopefuls compete for a spot, by organizing local or virtual friends, or by drawing from preexisting groups that share a common trait (such as all-women clans or U.S. Department of Defense–member clans). Some highly dedicated clans even have spotters who watch public play areas anonymously, looking for talented individuals to recruit. Conventions and tournaments are held where clan members gather to play one another online and in a real-world physical setting. Thus clans allow players to have teammates, identified opponents, and familiar approaches and techniques, much like professional sports teams.

The president of Gaming Leagues (⟨www.gleagues.com⟩), a company that runs online tournaments, estimates that there are at least 10,000 clans, with clan size ranging from five to 60 (PC Gamer, 2001, p. 43). Day of Defeat is an amateur modification of Half-Life, a popular on-line military game. A Day of Defeat mod forum was established by popular request "to give clans the chance to issue challenges to each other and increase clan interactions" (retrieved August 10, 2001 from ⟨www.dayofdefeatmod.com⟩). According to avid Day of Defeat player Stephen Iwanyk, a member of the (unofficial) 101st airborne clan (⟨http://bunkers.dayofdefeatmod.com/101st/⟩), "The camaraderie that goes with clans is fantastic; clan matches are much better than public games in terms of intensity and game play" (PC Gamer, 2001, p. 43).

Fantasy Migrates to Real Life

Some fantasy relationships migrate to real-life involvement. In fact, it is not uncommon for people to find significant others when playing online games. This has happened, for instance, with the Internet role-playing game (RPG) Ultima Online, which is set in medieval times and whose more than 160,000 players pay a monthly fee and take on character roles. Players use the special skills of the character, chase rewards, kill monsters, and gain points. In some cases, they participate in online marriages and adoptions.

RPGs such as Ultima Online engage the dramatic imagination and immerse people in the details of the game and interaction, according to

Billy Pidgeon, an analyst with Jupiter Communications. He said that participants in multiplayer online games average more than 22 hours a week of playing time and that the games have led to real-life marriages among the players. "Ultima is a very social and ethical world, so people tend to believe that who they are online is similar to who they are offline," he said (Bannan, 2000). Another researcher, Doug Davis of Haverford College, told the *New York Times* that "Ultima has this tremendous involvement that gives players the feeling that they get an immediate glimpse into who people are.... People quickly feel that they are learning something important about each other as they play the game" (Bannan, 2000).

Online games and their accompanying chat processes have generated a great deal of criticism, though. For example, Robert Kraut has asserted that long-term online chatting is a pale substitute for live communication (Stringer, 2000). Psychologist David Greenfield, author of *Virtual Addiction*, sees them as causing addiction and isolation: "Some of these games are so addictive they should have a warning on them ... it's very socially isolating" (Stringer, 2000). This may be the view of experts, but people continue to have high levels of involvement with these games and find them useful for making friends and socializing. Some even arrange to meet with a group of friends online for games, including poker as well as various group-based events.

This interesting tension between online and offline worlds reminds us not to focus too exclusively on analyzing the online world without reference to activities and consequences in the real world.

Mysterious Spillovers between Online and Physical Games: Playing with Reality

Majestic is a novel game that tweaks the traditional psychological barrier between the Internet and all other forms of communication. It is a puzzle game whose presentation differs vastly from earlier computer games (⟨www.game-revolution.com/previews/screens/pc/majestic/majestic.htm⟩). Expanding on the concepts in popular science fiction movies such as *Total Recall* and *The Game*, the premise of Majestic is that the player is suddenly thrust into the middle of an *X-Files*-style mystery complete with shadow governments, extraterrestrial alien cover-ups, and duplicitous

Box 9.9
Game-Makers' Description of Majestic

Electronic Arts Fact Sheet
Publisher: ⟨EA.com⟩
Developer: ⟨Synthetic.ea.com/Anim-X⟩
Ship Date: Spring 2001
Category: Adventure/online

Product Description

You use only 12% of your brain. Mind if we play with the rest?

Majestic™ is an exclusive online entertainment experience that places players in the center of a grand, sinister conspiracy, an unfolding mystery-adventure where the line between reality and fantasy is quickly blurred.

Majestic combines Internet applications, powerful content, and ground-breaking server technology to redefine online gaming. Unlike any other form of entertainment, Majestic actively pursues and interacts with the player in real time, based on events developing within the fiction, creating a unique and suspenseful entertainment experience.

Majestic delivers its engrossing, cutting-edge experience through familiar devices such as the user's Web browser, AOL's Instant Messenger service, e-mail, the telephone, and fax. Using these tools the player is placed at the center of his or her own intricate mystery suspense thriller. The Majestic player assumes the leading role, interacting with other characters, uncovering clues, solving puzzles, searching for answers, resolving challenges—all of which engages the player and drives the plot forward.

At its core, Majestic is an adventure game, complete with puzzles and proven game mechanics to draw players deeper into the experience. Many of the game elements in Majestic are made possible by digital objects—interactive virtual items that the user discovers and archives for use later in the adventure.

Majestic does not require a PC CD-ROM or large download; it uses the best capabilities of the Internet to enable a smooth and completely unique online entertainment experience.

Initiating a milestone in the evolution of interactive entertainment, Majestic is an episodic experience that will roll out monthly. The first season is planned to feature a total of nine episodes, including a free pilot episode available to anyone who has an Internet connection. Majestic will be part of the EA Platinum Service, exclusively available on ⟨EA.com⟩. Registration on the site is free, but players will subscribe to the $9.99 per month service to play the full Majestic episodes.

Source: "Majestic Fact Sheet" (retrieved August 6, 2001 from ⟨www. game-revolution.com/previews/screens/pc/majestic/majestic.htm⟩).

officials and friends. What would otherwise remain "just a game" contained on the Internet expands to suddenly become "real." The player must use certain tools—AOL Instant Messenger, a Web browser, and Real Player (for video and audio)—to solve the mysteries.

Majestic interacts with players in an unorthodox way. The free pilot introduction announces that the Majestic Web site appears to be broken, an instant message (IM) from a game character states that the server is down, and a mysterious e-mail contains a news blurb that the developer's office (Anim-X) was burned down (was it arson?). So even the way the game is to be played is a mystery that requires solving.

Via IM, e-mail, and even facsimile transmissions, the player is made aware that an underground Web site that went up after the "official" Web site's server failed must be found. A video chat recording between two characters is sent to the player and reveals that their voicemails hold the URL for the new server. To solve the puzzle, the player must go to the developer's Web site, find a phone number, dial up, enter the characters' code for the mailbox, and then enter the URL into the browser. After that, another character sends congratulations via artificial IM, and a phone call threatens danger if the player continues investigating. In addition to using telephones, instant messaging, faxes, and e-mail to interact with the story line and the various characters, the player also has a list of 20 other people online who are subscribed to the game (players can add more). A player messages these people to compare notes and solve puzzles, but it is hinted that some may be sinister characters (possibly played by actors). In sum, this intriguing melange of motifs and technologies is a full interplay between the real and online worlds and replete with various forms of interaction with "artificial intelligence" software and though many mediated channels. Most intriguing, it requires players to deal with the riddle of personalities as well.

Altruistic Endeavors Encourage Involvement Feelings

It may be the case that people can feel better by doing something altruistic to help others, an obvious case of collective social capital. If so, the Internet offers bountiful opportunities to boost self-esteem by helping worthy causes. One medical doctor who got involved offering advice to an online support group (Katz & Wynn, 1997, p. 24): "I fell in with this respiratory group. People have gotten to love each other. It's weird the way things can develop. I've been with the group two and a half years. I've never gotten tired of it. In between our weekly chat groups we talk to each other or ask about the others. We exchange personal information. That's where I switch hats and become one of them.... It's different from a regular doctor-patient relationship. I answer all their questions. There's no prescribing. It's educational, referral, descriptions of the state of a certain kind of surgery. I learn a lot from this. They turn me on to new things. Within the realm of standard medical practice, people are very aware of their illness. They hunt through the Internet and find stuff. When you're practicing, you don't always have time to do this. If they ask me something, I can look it up and interpret it."

The Internet offers some ways to support socially important projects and to do so at a vanishingly small cost to the donor. A few ways involving research are described below and are followed by a case of a simple charitable activity.

The Search for Extraterrestrial Intelligence (SETI)
More than two million personal computers have been linked to a central location that distributes data scanned from the Arecibo radio telescope in Puerto Rico for mathematical patterns that might merit further investigation into whether these patterns are evidence of extraterrestrial transmissions. This linking provides about 10 teraflops of capacity or the equivalent of the fastest supercomputers as of 2001. Internet commentator Howard Rheingold, for example, participates in this search for extraterrestrial intelligence (SETI) and finds it emotionally fulfilling (Howard Rheingold, personal communication, June 25, 2001).

Protein Folding Research at Home
The SETI approach is being duplicated by other researchers. An even more computationally intensive project is Stanford University's protein folding experiment (⟨www.stanford.edu/group/pandegroup/Cosm/using.html#goals⟩). This project, "folding@home," has enlisted about 20,000 users to help solve the question of how proteins self-assemble ("protein folding"), which has been described as "a Holy Grail of modern molecular biophysics" (retrieved June 19, 2001 from ⟨www.economist.com/displayStory.cfm?Story_ID=442975⟩).

Cheating

These community contributions have been successful, but even so cheating occurs. Ephemeral fame is offered to the top 10 contributors, whose information is posted much like the high scores on video pinball machines, and some of those anxious to win a posting have short-circuited the program to show falsely vast hours computed, thus winning undeserved recognition. Despite the potentially ruinous consequences (for the SETI project) of cheating, its existence demonstrates the difficulty of maintaining communal expectations from among heterogeneous populations. The public goods of collective social capital always run the risk of being overconsumed or exploited by individuals, and this "free-riding" leads to the "tragedy of the commons." The cases mentioned in this section are not in danger of "overconsuming" because the rewards for participation are psychic rather than material. The costs of individual participation are extremely low, but their benefits are enormous in the aggregate. Site managers at ⟨folding@home.com⟩ have written software routines to detect cheating, but this form of social control obviously has financial as well as psychological costs attached to it.

Cancer Research via Background Processing

More than a third of a million people are lending some of their computers' background processing to help find a cure for cancer. The Intel–United Devices Cancer Research Project coordinates volunteers' computers during periods of nonuse to analyze proteins that might be helpful in the fight against cancer and sends the data to Oxford University. Through a process called "virtual screening," special analysis software can identify molecules that have a potential for being developed into a drug. The sponsors compare the process to looking among hundreds of millions of keys to find the right one to open a special lock (⟨http://members.ud.com/download/gold/⟩).

Impacting Research on Martian Craters

The public can also become involved in scientific research that contributes to the understanding of the evolution of the solar system. A National Aeronautics and Space Administration (NASA) program, called "clickworkers," uses the Internet to recruit volunteers to identify craters on Mars and classify them by age. By midsummer 2001, over 1.5 million craters had been classified by volunteers. (Unlike the SETI program, the Mars crater project averages the results of many volunteers, practically eliminating the incentive for cheating.) This project has also shown that dedicated volunteers can be trained to do work that would ordinarily be done by specialists. By recruiting these volunteers, the efforts of research assistants can now be dedicated to more difficult problems that require higher skill levels (⟨http://clickworkers.arc.nasa.gov⟩).

Making Charitable Contributions by Visiting Web-sites

Some Web sites earn contributions every time someone visits them. They also present visitors with information about various charities, which can lead to further activism. A prominent example of this genre is ⟨freedonation.com⟩. Logging in (and exposing oneself to ads) generates a small donation to one of various charities. For example, when the environment sector is selected, donations go to the Alaska Conservation Alliance, which is dedicated to strengthening environmental organizations and empowering individuals to protect Alaska's environment through public education, training, advocacy, communication, and strategy development, all with respect for communities and human dignity (retrieved June 13, 2001 from ⟨www.freedonation.com/distribution.php3⟩). Saving rainforests, however, not Alaska, is the topic discussed on the webpage. This disconnection reflects the difficulties encountered by those who look to increase individual fulfillment and social capital on the Internet. It is often difficult to tell if promises will be kept and to coordinate and update all the various versions, operations, and text.

Negative Consequences of Certain Forms of Involvement

There are many ways that the Internet can be used for negative involvement. For instance, using Internet-capable mobile phones, fans can update each other concerning the whereabouts of their favorite stars. A member of the group who spots a celebrity of interest will enter the location information in the mobile phone network. Woody Allen, for instance, might be reported driving west on 57th Street, crossing Madison Avenue. As more information flows in, his fans will know that he is dining at the Sherry Netherland Hotel and that they can peer at him through the window. When he leaves for another locale, fans can continue tracking him, finding him at his next stop. Here's a case where one form of collective social capital can detract from other individuals' benefits, a form of negative network externality.

The Internet also has been used for purposes that are malicious, including tracking, stalking, and severe psychological harassment. It has proven to be a convenient way to spread malicious and hurtful stories about other people. The list of sins is long. Like any technology, the Internet can be used for evil as well as good. Although we do not wish to minimize the terror, fear, and even death that has been propagated by people using the Internet, we do argue—using both quantitative and qualitative data—that on balance the consequences of Internet use have been strongly positive.

Conclusion

The Internet neither directly creates nor diminishes social capital. Certainly, the Internet allows easy access to all the forms of social capital highlighted by Putnam, including neighborhood and family relationships, voluntary community civic, social, and religious organizations, and political mobilization. Activism and volunteering for causes can be automated and targeted. Users create their own social capital (defined as networks of contacts and organizational participation) motivated by individual interests and a desire to express themselves. They also create collective social capital motivated by altruism (the awareness that public goods benefit more people than strictly individual benefits) and by the simplicity of the process of developing and maintaining online communities. This process is more fully discussed in chapter 14.

Further, typical conceptualizations of social capital tend to emphasize the positive, inclusive aspects of social capital, ignoring the negative, socially excluding and destructive aspects of social connectivity. We see that in many ways the Internet

• Is reproductive of prior existence (that is, preexisting real-world behaviors are mapped directly onto the Internet),

• Is additive (it allows these prior activities to take place in more effective ways),

• Is novel (previously unknown activities are able to take place, and many of these are self-organizing—that is, new processes and structures are called into existence), and

• Has subtractive consequences (real-life negative consequences include lying, cheating, misrepresentation, theft, and conspiracy).

Clearly, the Internet offers new ways and means to carry out malicious activities. So spam and pyramid marketing can be seen as computer-enhanced extensions of ongoing activities in everyday life. Some uniquely cybercrimes include viruses, worms, and Web site "denial of service" assaults such as has happened when the White House's Web site is flooded by meaningless incoming messages that prevent legitimate traffic from getting through. In our judgment, these negatives, while at times destructive and even occasionally life imperiling, have been infrequent and atypical. Of course, people protect their identity and camouflage their viewpoints when in a strange public place, including the Internet. This is natural and necessary protective behavior, whether on the Internet or in a bar, on a beach, or on a bus. We find that relatively few examples of new, previously unknown forms of socially destructive activity are taking place in the realm of access, involvement, or social interaction and expression.

In sum, we have provided counterevidence to the social scientific literature theme of "Internet destroys social capital." The second and more difficult part of our argument is that the Internet does not directly foster or harm social capital but that social capital is created as a by-product when people use it for their own interests. This "invisible hand" equivalent, which we call the "invisible mouse" quality of the Internet, makes the Internet a "together place"—a syntopia where people can pursue these interests. New forms of creativity and connections are thereby created—largely by individuals pursuing their individual interests to create individual-level social capital and partially by individuals intentionally creating collective-level social capital.

III

Social Interaction and Expression

10

Social Interaction and Expression: Basic Issues and Prior Evidence

The purpose of the actual architecture of the Internet (originally the Arpanet) was to connect computers, but it quickly became a complex medium of communication that was neither completely interpersonal nor mass. Sproull and Faraj (1995) note that although people are individual information processors who contribute and benefit from information found on the Net, they are more fundamentally social beings who need to affiliate. Information seekers use the Internet as an electronic highway or a digital library, emphasizing tools such as downloading, file transfer, browsing, and retrieving. Social communicators see the Internet more as coffee houses, bowling teams, and dinner parties, emphasizing tools such as chats, instant messaging, newsgroups, organizational portals, and listservs. That is, the Internet facilitates social capital through collective interaction more than it fosters introversion through individual information seeking.

Does the Internet hinder or foster social interaction, expression, and new forms of identity (Baron, 1984; Gergen, 1991; Gackenbach, 1998; Hiltz & Turoff, 1995; Parks & Floyd, 1996; Turkle, 1996; Wynn & Katz, 1997)? Can online social activity and creativity translate into meaningful friendships and relationships? This chapter reviews Internet social interaction and new forms of expression by grouping relevant research into dystopian and utopian perspectives. The approach here summarizes and groups a wide array of materials, so browsing for relevant and interesting topics and reviewing the conclusion might be a reasonable first approach.

The Dystopian Perspective

Computer-Mediated Communication Too Impersonal and Isolating

One perspective holds that computer-mediated communication (CMC) technology is inherently antithetical to the nature of human life and is too limited technologically for meaningful relationships to form (Stoll, 1995). Thus, cyberspace cannot be a source of meaningful friendships (Baudrillard, 1983; Beniger, 1987; Numes, 1995). Many have argued that Internet use is socially isolating and psychologically depressing (Heim, 1993; Kraut et al., 1998; Kroker & Weinstein, 1994; Nie & Erbring, 2000; Stoll, 1995; Turkle, 1996). Online relationships may involve lower interdependence, commitment, and permanence than offline relationships (Parks & Roberts, 1998; Rice, 1987b).

The debate concerning whether the Internet fosters isolation, depression, and loneliness has grown in the past few years (McKenna & Bargh, 1998; Moody, 2001; Rierdan, 1999; Sanders, Field, Diego & Kaplan, 2000; Shapiro, 1999; Wastlund, Norlander & Archer, 2001). Kraut et al.'s (1998) HomeNet study analyzed 73 households during their first one to two years online. They used a panel design to improve the validity of causal claims and included reliable measures of psychological states, social involvement (social network, social support, loneliness, stress, depression), and objective system usage data (average hours per week spent online, number of e-mail messages, and Web sites accessed per week). Greater social extroversion and more extended social networks predicted less Internet use, and conversely, greater Internet use predicted decreased local and distant social networks. Neither social support nor stress was unrelated to Internet use. However, while neither loneliness nor depression predicted greater subsequent Internet use, greater use did predict increased loneliness and depression (though McKenna and Bargh, 2000, did find that users who were more lonely were more likely to develop online relationships). Kraut et al. (1998) concluded that Internet users experienced reduced communication among household members, reduced personal network size, and increased depression and loneliness. Their explanation for these results is that online activity replaces strong social ties in the unmediated world with weak online ties that cannot resolve loneliness and depression because Net correspondents are not as physically available and may not understand the contexts of particular situations. Kraut et al. note that their sample may not be representative so that the results may not be generalizable.

Their recent three-year follow-up study (Kraut, Kiesler, Boneva, Cummings, Helgeson & Crawford, in press) indeed rejects these conclusions, finding that the "negative effects dissipated," implying that their earlier results were valid but disappeared as users became more experienced. As is discussed later, several researchers argue that Kraut et al.'s original results were likely based on a biased sample.

Shapiro and Leone (1999) similarly feel that "the more time we spend online, the less time we will have to interact directly with our families, our neighbors, and other community members" (p. 118). For example, Nie and Erbring (2000) found that Web TV users spent less unmediated time with others. They argue that Internet use focuses on the individual, whereas watching TV may at least provide "some sort of shared experience." We may develop relationships online but let our relationships with those around us suffer. The same tremendous ease with which users can "personalize" the presentation, results, and use of the Internet also facilitates a narrowing of focus and exposure to diverse perspectives. Further, it helps advertisers and other information providers target their services, products, and opinions to users identified by their online preferences and usage patterns (Schroeder & Ledger, 1998; Shapiro & Leone, 1999).

Degrading Students' Academic Performance

One specific focus of this general concern is whether extensive, Internet usage harms students' academic performance. Possibly 5% to 10% of college students "may suffer harmful effect from craving, sleep disturbance, depression, and even withdrawal symptoms in association with excessive time online" (Kubey, Lavin & Barrows, 2001, p. 367). Studies have reported that half of those dismissed from college for academic failure indicated that excessive Internet usage was one of the factors (OnLine, 1996) and that synchronous communication (chatrooms, MUDS, and instant messaging) is particularly associated with Internet dependency (Scherer, 1997; Young, 1996). However, Scherer's survey of college students showed no difference in sociability between those who

ernet dependencies and regular users, even though they use
amunication more and had fewer face-to-face social inter-

Kube, et al. (2001) surveyed 572 undergraduate students to pursue
this question. Almost 10% reported that they might have become a little
psychologically dependent on the Internet. These students were more
likely to say that they were tired the next day after late-night Internet
use, they should spend less time on the Internet, they don't always have
really good control over their Internet use, and others have suggested
they spend too much time on the Internet. In addition, 14% indicated
that their schoolwork had been hurt because of extensive Internet use,
and 20% of those said they had missed class because of such use. In
reference to social interaction, the dependent students were more likely
to feel more alone than other students, to use the Internet to meet
new people, to use more synchronous communication applications, and
to communicate more with family and friends from high school. The
authors conclude that excessive Internet use is associated with weaker
academic performance and that the Internet may offer a "ready and
convenient haven" for the college students living away from home and
experiencing little control over their lives (p. 379).

Misleading and Illusory Identities

One person's freedom of expression on the Internet is another's predation and indecency, especially when the users are children (Schroeder
& Ledger, 1998). Tapscott (1997) identifies some possible disadvantages
of the increased individuality and interactivity provided to young users
by the Internet, such as disconnection from formal institutions, misleading and dangerous representations of information and identities, flaming,
overload, lack of evaluation by informed gatekeepers, and emphasis on
short-term objectives. Indeed, 70% of a Markle Foundation survey in
mid-2001 questioned the truthfulness of most things they read on the
Internet (Krim, 2001). A few critics of virtual communities (reviewed by
Bollier, 1995) feel that they and other forms of Internet communication
allow users to make superficial types of friendships instead of developing
multidimensional relationships with those around them. Issues of the
digital divide and expression intermingle, such as online representations
of racial identity and offline representations of the racial makeup of

cyberspace (Kolko, Nakamura & Rodman, 1999; Smith & Kollock, 1998).

Computer-mediated communication can foster misrepresentation and experimentation about identity and qualities (Cornwell & Lundgren, 2001; Donath, 1999; Feldman, 2000). Such an atmosphere can be dominated by trickery, lechery, manipulation, and emotional swindles. So much posturing, gender switching, and faking of identities can take place that real relationships tend to be difficult to create and maintain (Turkle, 1996). For example, online chatroom discussions often remind Johnson (1997, p. 70) of graffiti of the worst kind: "isolated declarations of selfhood, failed conversations, slogans, and tag lines. You don't see a community in these exchanges; you see a group of individuals all talking past one another, and talking in an abbreviated, almost unintelligible code."

Other Negative Uses and Consequences for Interaction
Certainly there are other negative forms of Internet interaction, such as the following, selected from ⟨http://construct.haifa.ac.il/~azy/refbehav.htm⟩:

• Addiction and dependency (Chen, Chen & Paul, 2001; Eppright, Allwood, Stern & Theiss, 1999; Greenberg, Lewis & Dodd, 1999; Greenfield, 1999; Griffiths, 1998, 2000; Griffiths & Wood, 2000; King, 1999; King & Barak, 1999; Lavin, Marvin, McLarney, Nola & Scott, 1999; Leon & Rotunda, 2000; Mitchell, 2000; Pratarelli, Browne & Johnson, 1999; Shapira, Goldsmith, Keck, Khosla & McElroy, 2000; Stern, 1999; Tsai & Lin, 2001);

• Online violence, hate, deviance, and pornography (Cunneen & Stubbs, 2000; Evans, 2001; Hamburger & BenArtzi, 2000; King, 1999; Leets, 2001; McCabe, 2000; Podlas, 2000; Suler & Phillips, 2000); and

• Stalking and victimization (Deirmenjian, 1999; Finn & Bannach, 2000).

The Utopian Perspective

Social Interaction
The positive perspective increasingly sees the Internet as a medium for social interaction (Rice, 1987b). Further, as the number of people using

eases, the number and range of possible relationships
ry Irving, former assistant secretary of the U.S. Com-
, has pointed out this dynamic social value of the
think how powerful the Internet is. Then remind yourself that
fewer than 2% of people are actually connected.... The power of the
Web increases exponentially with every person who goes online. Imagine
what we're missing" (Black, 1999). Jordan (1999) proposes that Internet
power occurs at the individual level (even at the simple level of reinforcing our sense of identity each time we log on), the community level
(determined by some extent by the capabilities and constraints of technology and virtual communities), and the collective imagination level
(contrasting, for example, online immortality and constant surveillance).

Numerous case studies of computer-mediated communication (CMC)
have shown that "the social" is an important glue that binds together the
task-oriented aspects of CMC and in some cases even supplants them
(Rice, 1987a). This work has been complemented by research on the
functioning of medical discussion lists and newsgroups, health and
psychological support groups, Internet relay chats, multiuser dungeons
(MUDs), MUDS object-oriented (MOOs), and even online dating services, all of which are essentially social- and affect- as opposed to task-
oriented (Rice, 2001a). A good proportion of those searching and
participating in health information sites and discussion groups do so as
third-party intermediaries who seek information and support for their
significant others, for themselves to help them deal with illnesses of significant others, or for stimulating, challenging, or engaging their health-
care providers (Aspden & Katz, 2001). The growth and persistence of
Web-based chatrooms and instant messaging seem to provide additional
evidence refuting claims of the nonsocial nature of CMC.

Baym (1995, p. 160) summarizes a decade of research as revealing that
"the ways in which people have appropriated the commercial and noncommercial networks demonstrate that CMC not only lends itself to
social uses but is, in fact, a site for an unusual amount of social creativity." Rice (1987b) argues that fundamental aspects of social groups and
communities may well be supported, even extended, through online communities, though the boundaries and permanence of such groups might
be quite different. Turkle (1997) wrote a classic ethnographic study of

the inhabitants of the computer community, both online, at work, and at home. Porter's (1997) edited book provides a variety of additional perspectives, including the problem of interacting with virtual bodies.

Van Dijk (1999, pp. 201–212, 239–240) summarizes some of the benefits of CMC: people can compensate for missing cues in images, sounds, texts, and data by using available textual cues; people can focus more on the content of the text by reading e-mails; people can engage in more informal conversations and settings; and electronic group conversations often encourage normally quiet people and women to participate more. Unmediated communication is highly constrained by the need for geographic and temporal proximity, limited processing and storage potential. It does, however, tend to foster greater communication quality and more explicit sequencing of contributions (Rice, 1987a; Van Dijk, 1999). Walther (1996) shows that mediated interaction is usually personal, especially when participants have time and interest, and mediated interaction may even be "hyperpersonal," managing interaction and impressions in ways that are not possible through face-to-face communication. Straus (1997) similarly found that CMC is not necessarily less personalized than face-to-face communication.

Complementing and Strengthening Offline Interactions

Hamman's (1999) ethnographic study concludes that Internet communication complements real-world relations, and Wellman and Gulia's (1999b) review of research on Internet communities argues that offline relationships may be strengthened as well as weakened. Surveys by Parks and colleagues have found evidence that intimate and well-developed online relationships often lead to real-world interactions, even though the frequency and duration of online relationships tend to be short (Parks & Roberts, 1998) and to involve issues extending beyond the Internet communities (Parks & Floyd, 1996). A Pew Research Center poll (2000) reports that e-mail improved the social and kinship connections of users, especially long-time users. Indeed, the poll found that users included fewer social isolates, had a greater number of recent social contacts, and had more access to social support. Riphagen and Kanfer (1997) showed that e-mail users and nonusers had similar numbers of relationships but that users had greater distant relationships, suggesting that e-mail reduced local interactions. Katz et al. (2001) found similar results, except that users had more offline relationships in general.

Frequency and Diversity of Uses of the Internet for Social Interaction

Survey results show diverse, extensive, and growing use of the Internet for social interaction. In 2000, AOL (2000) respondents were doing research (91%), communicating with friends and family (90%), getting information about products to buy (80%), getting news (76%), getting health information (70%), and many other activities. The percentage reporting these activities, especially for doing research and getting health information, were high for several years. Stafford, Kline, and Dimmick (1999) analyzed responses from 881 randomly selected adults who completed a monthly Ohio poll. At that time, 40.6% of respondents had a home computer, and 12.7% used e-mail from home. Of the reasons that respondents gave for using e-mail at home, 61% mentioned maintaining interpersonal relationships (keeping in touch with family, siblings, friends, and relatives who lived out of state or the country); 31% indicated having greater opportunities for satisfying personal needs than those provided by the telephone, postal mail, or even face-to-face interaction (such as time, cost, and convenience); 30% mentioned pursuing personal activities (accessing the library, acquiring consumer and travel information, keeping up with sports, exchanging information); and 25% noted having business reasons (working from home, operating home businesses). Relevant to digital divide concerns, home computer owners who used home e-mail were more likely than nonusers to be male, married or cohabiting, more educated, and richer. However, the four general categories cited above for home e-mail use were not significantly predicted by sex, relationship status, education, income, or age. That is, by far the most frequent purpose of home e-mail is to foster relationships, but home e-mail purposes are generalized and not related to demographics. Stafford et al. (1999) conclude that meaningful relationships can be maintained online and that basic motivations for using home e-mail are shared throughout the user community.

Of 12 new activities mentioned by the AOL (2000) respondents, the greatest interest was for sending and receiving pictures from family and friends (92%). AOL respondents also reported that they are more in touch with brothers and sisters (44%), more in touch with aunts, uncles, and cousins (40%), more in touch with parents (23%), more in with grandparents (12%), and more in touch with other relatives (38%). In fact, 41% reported that they have reconnected with people they had lost touch with for an average of 12 years. Instant messaging was used by 48%, especially to connect with friends (82%) but also to connect with family and relatives. And these percentages were somewhat greater for those who had been online for more years. Women were more likely to include family members on their instant messaging contact list (for 40% of female siblings compared to 26% of male siblings, 35% of mothers compared to 24% of fathers). People also spent time together online: 80% with a child, and 68% with a spouse. In the AOL survey, overall, people still preferred the telephone over the Internet to communicate with friends (57% versus 35%) and family (71% versus 24%), but these differences decreased for those people who had been online more years.

The Times Mirror (1995) national representative survey of 4,005 respondents was conducted in 1995, when access to e-mail and information was available primarily through commercial information services (America Online, Prodigy, CompuServe), and nearly three-quarters of those who had computers and modems were not yet online. Yet even then 59% (women more than men, 65% to 56%) of those who used e-mail for personal purposes ($n = 411$) said that they communicated more often with family and friends because of e-mail (1% said less often, 40% said no difference). Nearly a quarter (23%) of the online users said they had an "online buddy" that they had never met in person. There were few other differences in social interaction between users and non-users in the Times Mirror survey. On the day before the survey, 57% of users and 56% of nonusers called a friend or relative just to talk, and 72% of users visited with family or friends compared to 68% for non-users. However, users were much more likely to go to the movies (49% at least once a month versus 28% for nonusers) and felt less overloaded with information (16% versus 24%).

Contacts with Friends and Family
In Howard et al.'s (2001) analysis of the 2000 Pew survey data, about 60% of those who used e-mail to communicate with their families and with friends said that they now communicate more often with their

primary family or with their primary friend contact. And almost a third of those who email family members indicated they have begun communicating with a family member that they had not much contacted before. A logistic regression showed that users were 24% more likely than non-users to say they can turn to many people for support and 40% less likely to say they can turn to hardly anyone for support. Users were 46% more likely to have telephoned a relative or friend the prior day. And users for over three years were substantially more likely than those with less than six months' experience to say that Internet use had improved various aspects of their lives.

The online activities most frequently mentioned by those nine to 17 years of age in the AOL youth study were write letters or notes to friends and relatives (61%), use instant messages (55%), and play games (53%) (another dozen or so activities were reported by fewer than 40% of respondents). The activities reported noticeably more by young women were writing letters or notes, using instant messaging, getting information about rock stars or music groups, visiting chatrooms, and writing to a pen pal in another state or country. Young users had an average of 35 people on their instant messaging contact list, with those 15 to 17 years old reporting an average of 43.3 others. These contacts are primarily friends but also include various relatives, and 3% reported that people they met online are on their instant messaging contact lists. The National Geographic Society's Web site survey in fall 1998 received responses from 35,000 Americans, 5,000 Canadians, and 15,000 others. It showed that (1) high e-mail contact does not reduce other forms of interaction, (2) younger people used e-mail more for friends, near and far, (3) older people used it more for kin, near and far, (4) women used e-mail more with kin at a distance, and (5) overall communication frequencies for men and women were basically the same for all media. In a two-year study that complemented their earlier three-year HomeNet study, Kraut et al. (in press) found that new computer users reported positive effects of using the Internet on communication, social involvement, and well-being.

In the UCLA study (2000), more people reported feeling ignored because of others' television use (36.5%) than because of their Internet use (24.7%). Overall, 91.8% indicated no change in the time that members of the household spent together since becoming connected to the

Internet. On average, Internet users felt that the Internet had slightly increased (3.3 on a scale of 1 to 5, from greatly decreased to greatly increased) the number of people regularly contacted and increased the extent of their communicating with family and friends. As many as 26.2% reported having online friends (on average, almost 13 friends) that they had never met, and 12.4% had met in person someone they first met online (on average 5.6 such new friendships).

An Internet Generation

Tapscott (1997) discusses more than just access by, or representation of, different demographic groups on the Internet. He describes the generation that is growing up with the Internet—what he calls N-Gen (the Net generation), consisting of those aged two to 27 in 1997. This generation watches less TV and is able to communicate through e-mail, develop webpages, and start businesses. He emphasizes that young users take advantage of the Internet to play, explore their world, try out different identities, express themselves through personal webpages, develop relationships with both friends and family, and become socialized. Unlike the more passive traditional mass media, Internet activities are centered in the interactive use of the medium to communicate with others and yet are centered in a text-based medium, which promotes written literacy (see also Cherny, 1999): "Lacking facial expression, body language, tone of voice, clothing, physical surroundings, and other contextual information, the N-Gen has had to innovate within the limitations of the ASCII keyboard. As a result of this, a new script is emerging with new contextual information, subtleties, and emotion to communications" (Tapscott, 1997, p. 64). "Almost all of the adults we encountered who work with N-Geners commented on how articulate they are as a group, and that the youngsters had views on subjects that seemed advanced for their age. While this is to be expected from the Net-savvy elite demographic group, we can expect that the interactive environment will strengthen verbal ability and the expression of ideas in every group" (p. 70). He gives as just one example the rise of youth e-zines, which "provide a portrait of the culture of interaction—the antithesis of broadcast culture" (p. 84). Tapscott suggests that early online communication will foster greater collaborative skills based on "peer-oriented relationships rather than hierarchies within families and companies" (p. 212).

Tapscott (1997) summarizes one teacher's experience in a community computing center in New Haven, Connecticut. The class with the computer-savvy teacher became more computer literate than the other classes who had teachers who knew little about computers. The teacher also invited people who worked in New Haven to talk about their jobs to her students. When students sent e-mails to these visiting guests, "It broke down the power dynamic that exists between a kid and an adult" (p. 149). A third of the respondents in the AOL youth study (2000) felt that going online made them a better student, 31% said it improved their language skills, and 56% preferred going online for help with their homework (compared to 27% who preferred the library and other resources). Critics are divided about whether familial relationships are affected by increased Internet use.

It should be noted that concerns about computer and video games may be derived from earlier patterns of usage that are no longer accurate. It is not only young, social isolates who spend much time in these pursuits. Rather, 60% of Americans play computer and video games, 50% of online gamers are female, the average age of gamers is 28 years, and 72% of all gamers are over 18, with 42% over 35 years old (Grossman, 2001).

Young Users' Communication with Family and Friends

Tapscott (1997, p. 252) argues that families may become closer as a result of Internet use in the household: "The new media hold the promise of strengthening the family by moving many family activities (such as working, learning, shopping ...) dispersed by industrial society back into the home." Since children today frequently know more about computers than their parents do, the children often rise in status within the family hierarchy: "Open families adopt the interactive model.... The traditional authoritarian model is changing due to the generational lag in that, for the first time, children know more than their parents about something really important" (p. 251). For example, in the AOL youth survey (2000), 61% reported going online at least once with their parents, 44% (52% for those 15 to 17 years old) said they had some influence in getting their parents or family members to go online, and 66% said that they helped their parents get online or use the Internet.

Respondents to the UCLA study (2000) indicated that their use of the Internet helps to create and maintain friendships as well as communicate with the family. Indeed, the two most popular Internet activities reported by users were Web surfing and browsing (81.7%) and using e-mail (81.6%)—that is, general information seeking and communicating with others. Concerning the attributes of the Internet, respondents were most satisfied with their "ability to communicate with other people"—more so than with relevant information, goods and services, ease of finding information, and connection speed.

Most (89.0%) of the parents in UCLA study (2000) reported that their children spent about the same time with their friends since they started using the Internet; 4.0% indicated more time, and 7.0% less time. While 27.5% reported spending no time on the Internet together with other household members, 47.1% reported doing so at least some time each week.

Young Users' Identity Development

Tapscott (1997, p. 56) states that for the first time ever, children are taking control of critical elements of a technological revolution: "Net-based communication usually starts around 11 for girls and 13 for boys —basically during adolescence. At these ages, children seek autonomy and the creation of an identity. The Net seems to provide a vehicle to explore the self and for children to establish themselves as independent, self-governing individuals.... Of the potential 28% of American children who had potential Net access at the end of 1997, between 6.7 and 7 million individual N-Geners are characterized as active users; 85% to 90% of this population ... were participating in live chat on a regular basis." On the one hand, these media foster increased openness, but they also reduce the consequences or judgments associated with unmediated interactions. Tapscott reports some beneficial aspects of what are usually seen as harmful uses of the Internet. For example, youth see cybersex as safe, experimental, and mutual; they "can always disconnect if disinterested or harassed.... They seem more interested in developing both the emotional and the physical side of real relationships, with the Internet as just one more 'safe' mode of communication" (pp. 172–173).

Associations with Other Media Use

Kayany and Yelsma (2000) argue that households comprise both social and technological dimensions so that the addition of new elements such as online media affects the organization of roles, relationships, and functions. Their study of 185 people in 84 households showed that online use affects time spent in TV viewing, telephone use, newspaper reading, and family conversations, with greater declines reported by children. Both informational and entertainment functions of media were rated as more important by more frequent online users. The authors concluded that online media seem to be displacing TV's informational functions but not the entertainment functions for either TV or newspaper.

James, Wotring, and Forrest (1995) studied home-based media via an online questionnaire, finding that computer bulletin board use reduced time spent using TV, books, the telephone, and letters. Robinson, Barth, and Kohut (1997), analyzing data from a national probability telephone survey (1994, 1995), found that print media and computer-mediated communication seem to reinforce each other but that there was no relationship to radio or TV use. Thus, displacement effects are most likely among functionally equivalent media and among media that depend on the same limited resources and provide similar resources uses, and gratifications. Other studies find that the use of computers and the Internet decreases some other media use. Reagan (1987) reported that young computer users are less likely to use radio, newspapers, local, and network TV. The Pew Research Center (1997) found that online news consumers viewed news less, and the Graphics, Visualization, and Usabilities Center (GVU) (1997) online surveys reported that Web surfing replaces weekly TV viewing. Coffey and Stipp (1997) analyzed home media diaries, finding that only a very small percentage of respondents used their computers during prime time, few people had a computer in the same room as television (Media Metrix, 1997), heavy computer users were not heavy TV viewers (Crispell, 1997), and greater computer use was associated with greater use of print media (Perse & Dunn, 1998).

A European survey reported that from 50% to 60% of British, German, Swedish, and French Internet users said they were watching less television since going online and that 29% reporting reading fewer magazines and newspapers. However, 90% indicated that online usage did not interfere with their normal social life (Internetnews, 2000). Jessel (1995) and Miller and Clemente (1997) also show that nearly a third of online users reported spending less time watching television than before their online usage. AOL's representative national Internet users' survey (2000) also found declines in other media use but fewer declines than the European study found. Users reporting watching less television (24%, compared to 16% in 1999), reading fewer print newspapers (19% versus 13%), and reading fewer print magazines (18% versus 11%), and those percentages generally increased as users have been online more years.

Internet users report that they use more media overall than nonusers (UCLA, 2000), especially books, video games, recorded music, and radio. However, users report watching about 28% less television per week than do nonusers. More (67.3%) also rate the Internet as an "important" or "extremely important" information source, compared to 53.1% for television and 46.8% for radio.

One study applied the uses and gratifications approach (Ferguson & Perse, 2000) and analyzed data from an online survey and a three-day media-use diary from over 200 college students at two universities that had extensive Internet access. Entertainment was the most salient motivation for Web use, after required school activities. The most frequently visited sites were search engines followed by entertainment and sports. Thus, the play component of the Web may displace TV viewing, as entertainment is a primary gratification obtained from TV viewing. However, little Web surfing seems motivated by the need to pass time. The second most important motivation for watching TV is relaxation, but Web use was not much motivated by this, probably because it requires active choice and cognition. Finally, companionship motivations were not salient for Web use: "There was little evidence that the World Wide Web can substitute for personal interaction" (p. 170) or even for parasocial interaction, but this may change with greater bandwidth, which would allow for streaming video and responsive Internet telephony.

Flanagin and Metzger (2001) argue that the three primary Internet functions (conversation capabilities, information retrieval, and information giving) compare very strongly with functions of mediated interpersonal (telephone and e-mail) and mass-media (newspapers, television, books, and magazines) channels. They analyze responses from 684 individuals concerning how well 21 different needs (based on several theories of social presence, social influence, task orientation, and uses and gratifications) are met by a variety of media. Their analysis shows that the needs fulfilled by these various media cluster in ways found by prior research, regardless of the technology. Face-to-face communication was the primary cluster of needs that were met by various media (unmediated interpersonal), and it was grouped with no other media. The conversational form of the Internet clustered with the telephone and electronic mail (mediated interpersonal). And Internet information retrieval and information giving cluster with television, books, magazines, and newspapers (mass media). Face-to-face communication was rated as being better at fulfilling all needs except entertainment, staying in touch, and passing time when bored, but mediated interpersonal communication (Internet conversation, telephone, e-mail) was rated significantly better than mass media for a wide variety of needs (such as negotiate or bargain, learn about myself and others, have something to do with others, provide others with information, get someone to do something for me, solve problems, play, stay in touch, contribute to a pool of information, feel less lonely, and feel important). Note, then, that the mediated interpersonal channels (which include the conversational aspects of the Internet) meet those needs characterized as interacting with others much better than do traditional mass media.

Tapscott (1997) claims that children sacrifice TV time, not social time, to use their family's computer. He also maintains that video games are often intended for multiple users: The "average AOL homes spend almost 15% less time watching TV than the U.S. average.... More than 40% of respondents in a recent survey conducted by Jupiter Communications and the KidsCom Company said that they watch less TV because of their Internet use.... In a study conducted by Odyssey, respondents were asked, 'What activities are you typically taking time from to go online?' The number one answer, at 30%, was television" (p. 30). Kids who are part of this generation are not wasting time on the Net: "Time spent on the Net is not passive time, it's active time" (pp. 8–10). They read, investigate, learn how to solve problems, and compose their thoughts. Of the respondents to the AOL (2000) youth survey, 62% (but 73% of young men) reported that they would rather go online than watch television, though young women (54%) would prefer the telephone.

Internet Users Are Not Less Trusting

Uslaner (2000) counters Putnam's (2000) suggestion that the Internet may, as Putnam strongly argued for television, reduce and inhibit social capital. In particular, Uslaner tests Putnam's causal chain that increased trust generates civic engagement, which fosters more trust, and that media such as the television and possibly the Internet reduce that initial trust. Uslaner does agree with Putnam that Americans' overall level of trust has declined precipitously—from 58% in 1960 to just over a third in the 1990s. His analyses of 1998 survey data from the Pew Center for the People and the Press show that people with stronger offline social-support networks do not avoid the Web, that Internet users had wider social networks, and that Internet users are not less trusting. Indeed, he finds few significant associations between trust, sociability, and Internet or e-mail use. Those who believe the Internet helps keep them in touch with others are more likely to use e-mail, go online more frequently, visit chatrooms, get health and sports information, and buy goods. The only notable exception is that chatroom users, or those who report making friends online, are less trusting than others. Robinson's (2001) analysis of the 2000 General Social Survey (GSS) dataset found that users were more trusting in their fellow citizens and were more literate in their survey responses.

Uslaner's analyses of the 2000 survey by the Pew Internet and American Life Project show that those who have low trust overall (you can't be too careful in dealing with people) perceive the Internet as a threatening, untrustworthy place. Those with high levels of mistrust in general are particularly concerned about the privacy and security aspects of the Internet. Those who have made new friends online, used chatrooms, and have used online dating services are much more likely to have used a fake online identity. Overall, Uslaner (2000) rejects the romantic notion that participating in community activities such as choral societies or card-playing clubs creates more trusting attitudes. He argues that even in online groups we are probably much more likely to meet others like ourselves anyway, so trust in strangers is not increased that way. On balance, Uslaner concludes, the Internet essentially neither creates nor inhibits social relations or trust (p. 22).

No Increase in Isolation and Depression

Applying a uses and gratifications perspective to survey responses from 279 students, Papacharissi and Rubin (2000, p. 188) found that the Internet was used as a "functional alternative to face-to-face communication for those who are anxious about face-to-face communication and who did not find face-to-face communication to be rewarding." Those who rated the Internet as providing more social presence were more likely to say that they used the Internet for passing time, for convenience, and for entertainment. They note that interpersonal utilities and information seeking are distinct types of uses. For those with satisfying interpersonal relations, the Internet was used more for information seeking; for those with unrewarding or anxiety-inducing interpersonal relations, the Internet was used as an alternative medium for social interaction, and such users had a greater affinity for the Internet. This set of results reverses the causality of the Kraut et al. (1998) study: in this interpretation, the Internet provides greater freedom of expression, less visible requirements for interaction, and less stressful personal interactions: "These findings highlight the potential of the Internet as a social medium that can augment our socializing capabilities" (Papacharissi & Rubin, 2000, p. 193).

LaRose, Eastin, and Gregg (2001) also challenge Kraut et al.'s (1998, 1999) results, which indicated that Internet use by new adopters was associated with increased loneliness, depression, and stress over a one- to two-year period. LaRose et al. argue that one factor explaining these differences may be experience with the Internet; many of the studies finding a negative association between sociability and Internet use involve novice users. Experienced users would tend to have greater facility in managing social cues online, would have less stress about learning the technology, and may have been less likely to have recently moved, which would reduce their access to social networks. Also, the HomeNet respondents studied by Kraut et al. reported overall low levels of depression, so they may have not had a great need for social support. Kraut et al.'s results might have been a by-product of the selective nature of the project's participants (which included new users and community activists but almost no people between the ages of 22 and 40). Their participants were directly trained on how to use the Internet and had special 24-hour, seven-days-a-week hotline support. Numerous scholars, such as Donna Hoffman of Vanderbilt University, have raised provocative questions about the research (Bunn, 2000). Perhaps most problematical are that no one (including the Kraut et al. research team) has been able to replicate the original findings and their most recent study refutes them.

So LaRose and his colleagues (2001) analyzed a new set of respondents, 171 students. They found that Internet use influenced depression through two paths. Prior Internet experience and Internet usage increased self-efficacy, which reduced online stress and decreased depression. Second, Internet use led to more e-mail sent to known others, which increased social support and decreased depression. However, Internet use also created Internet stress, leading to more depression, which could be mediated by Internet self-efficacy. Also, they found reduced depression in Internet users among these college students, as "they may have used the Internet to obtain social support rather than to replace it" (p. 12). There was, essentially, no relation between Internet use and depression, but general stress (hassles) and Internet stress were found to be significantly related to depression. Thus, novice users may not have enough expertise to develop the self-efficacy necessary to moderate the new Internet stresses. So while the central point in the Kraut et al. studies is that Internet usage displaces strong (face-to-face) social ties with weak (online) ties, it may be more accurate to say that some people turn to the Internet to obtain strong social support, especially when it is unavailable in their unmediated situation, and do so because of online advantages (such as anonymity for sensitive topics, specialized expertise, and group norms).

Franzen (2000) also critiques the Kraut et al. (1998) results by analyzing differences between responses to an online survey from 15,842 Internet users (20% response) and a mailed survey to a control group of 1,196 nonusers (50% response). He points out that the HomeNet study used no control group and so could not test for maturation or local history (such as participants concentrating on Internet use early in the study because of the novelty) effects. Franzen's study found few differences in network size (in fact, nonusers reported 10 while users reported 12) or time spent with friends between users and nonusers (though users had 23% more friends), controlling for a variety of demographic, social, and media factors. Network size was not affected by the number of months since first starting to use the Internet on network size. Consequentially, however, he shows that the number of people contacted online via e-mail increased the number of close friends but that longer or more intensive time spent on the Internet did not affect that number, did not affect time spent socializing with others, but did slightly reduce overall network size. So the ability to contact others via the Internet leads to the associated increase in social networks. Respondents also reported many positive effects of e-mail usage on social networks: over half of Hispanic Internet users as of February 2001 said that using e-mail had improved their connection to friends (58%) or to family (52%) (Spooner & Rainie, 2001). He concludes that "Internet users are, on average, not socially isolated but quite to the contrary a relatively socially active group" (p. 13) and also suggests that larger social networks lead to greater e-mail contacts, which in turn generates larger networks.

Increasing Diversity of Voices
The Internet can be a great communication tool for those who have difficulty meeting new friends due to physical handicaps, diseases, or even poor social skills (Wallace, 1999). These people can easily find others like them throughout the country and around the world, providing support and a chance to decrease loneliness or increase self-esteem. Jones (1997) emphasizes that online communities can especially support otherwise marginalized cultures. For example, the 7,800 older SeniorNet members from the United States and Canada said that the network helps them ease their loneliness: "It hosts welcoming events, celebrates anniversary parties, and mourns when one of its members dies" (Bollier, 1995, p. 3). The WELL is another example of an Internet community; WELL members live in the San Francisco Bay Area and often meet face to face (Rheingold, 1993). Other online communities include health support groups for people with illnesses that are not common enough to foster local physical communities (Rice, 2001a).

Certainly the Internet has provided possibilities for viable communicative spaces for feminist networking and interaction (see Harcourt, 1999; Terry & Calvert, 1997). Harcourt, in particular, considers how the Internet might be used to support women's empowerment in developing countries, to bridge cultures both local and global, and to coordinate women's issues at international conferences and working groups.

Tolerance for Diversity

Internet users may increase their tolerance for a greater diversity of views because the content of the message, not the physical appearance of the messenger or writer, is emphasized. However, as Hill and Hughes (1998, p. 184) point out, people who have the opportunity to build friendships will not necessarily be amiable. New forms of online expression also include virtual sex, alternate cyber identities, and electronic stalking (Civin, 1999; Odzer, 1997). Odzer argues that while the interaction occurs in virtual and fantasy environments, the psychological and emotional relations are real in both experience and consequence. Indeed, she puts forth online eroticism as a valid form of emotional relationship and self-growth. For others, however, online sex is a manifestation of loneliness, isolation, and depression.

In examining another aspect of social relations, Cobb (1998) discusses how online technology and spirituality are reinforcing and convergent. Consider, for instance, the experience of cyberspace, which is largely nonmaterial and in some ways the antithesis of materialism. Moreover, its transcendent nature is a manifestation of the human collectivity. And what might it mean about human nature when artificial intelligence does satisfactorily mirror human actions, intentions, and communication? Certainly, many online religious communities and Web sites (from traditional to unorthodox) have been established to support people's needs for and expressions of spirituality. On the other hand, online communities in general are no substitute for the individual's own spiritual experiences and real-world relationships with other people.

Potential Transformations

Levy (1997) suggests that a social transformation is occurring that will lead us from a material economy to an information economy and into a social economy, where a collective intelligence is mediated through information and communication technology and where interactions, relationships, and communication become the central resource and social infrastructure. This viewpoint claims that the Internet is developing social capital and that the value-added and public-good aspects of shared knowledge, collaboration, and social networks cannot be captured, processed, and mass-produced. This rise of the role of social interactions— now unimpeded by physical, cultural, language, and temporal boundaries —will bring great challenges to traditional notions of countries, nationalities, and economies.

Others, such as Robertson (1998), argue that because our analytic abilities, now augmented and even superseded in some cases by computing power, can generate cumulative as well as discontinuous change, the current transformation is clearly revolutionary. Indeed, he argues that the computer and information revolution will be more transcendent than language, writing, and printing, in terms of consequences for knowledge, culture, education, entertainment, and ordinary life. Johnson (1997) makes a similar claim, equating the rise of various computer interfaces (the hardware, software, and usage patterns) with the development of literacy. In constructing this argument, he rejects the dichotomy between technology and art to be able to consider artifacts such as Gothic cathedrals and hypertext as both instances of interfaces.

Levy (1998) goes further in conceptualizing the possibilities of online identity. Rather than oppose *virtual* with *real*, he places both in a larger typology that also includes *possibility* and *actuality*. For Levy, virtualization has been occurring in many social domains because it is an inherent aspect of a human mind for which cognition and action are both social processes. Therefore, this virtualization does not replace or destroy personal identity but, rather, augments and transforms it.

Conclusion

Dystopian perspectives claim that mediated communication impoverishes the nature of interactions and that online interactions can be deceiving, simplistic, hateful, and transient. Some conclude that high or extended Internet use leads to isolation and depression, as weak mediated relations in the real world replace strong unmediated ones and as narrowly focused relations replace more diverse ones.

However, surveys and ethnographic studies show that rich, fertile, diverse, and expanded interactions are possible through the Internet. Impassioned members of many online groups provide emotional and other resources to each other, and users regularly rate communicating with others—family, friends, and new people they have met online—as their favorite and most important Internet activity. Some studies show that interactive Internet usage replaces passive television watching but that overall Internet users are greater media participants. Members of the Net generation may well be more literate, creative, and socially skilled than earlier generations because of their early familiarity with the Internet, including trying out various aspects of their developing identities online. Interacting with teachers and other students is easier when supported by the Internet, and both students and patients are more likely to talk about sensitive issues online, possibly because of the protection of anonymity. Users meet new people they come to call friends online, and some go on to meet these people in person. Several studies have specifically countered some prior research linking Internet use with isolation or depression, showing that experienced Internet users may find greater support online, become more satisfied with their interactions and communication, and generate new relationships through the ability to contact others more easily than they can offline. Indeed, some speculate that the Internet can also foster greater tolerance through exposure to a wider diversity of voices and even support spiritual growth. All these possibilities may lead to a major expansion of our concepts of identity, groups, and society.

While the uses and effects of many major communication technologies —such as the pen, telegraph, telephone, photocopier, and fax machine— have been studied retrospectively, if at all, the rapid growth of the Internet affords communication researchers a unique opportunity to describe, assess, predict, and evaluate both short-term changes as well as long-term developments. If the current speculation and research seem to indicate diverse, contradictory, and simultaneous consequences, at several levels of analysis, this may be the fundamental nature of social change. However, it is far more useful to ground this understanding of the complexity of this major phenomenon in research than in speculation and assertion.

11

Social Interaction: Survey Results

The analyses in this chapter substantially extend prior research reviewed in chapter 10 by considering the relationship of Internet usage with offline interaction, online social interaction, and online expression. Chapters 12 and 13 provide cases and overviews of personal and collective interaction and expression on the Internet.

Offline Interaction by Users and Nonusers

Indicators of Sociability

As we have noted, a central question is whether Internet usage decreases involvement in various forms of traditional social interaction. One way to empirically assess that question is to compare the extent to which users and nonusers engage in offline interaction or are otherwise sociable. Possible indicators of home and social offline activity include having any children, work situation (full-time, part-time, retired, unemployed, or student), owning one's home, number of years living in the same home, feeling satisfied with life and communication, not feeling overloaded, having a sense of belonging, using media (such as letters, telephone, and traveling), getting together or communicating recently with friends, being innovative, and knowledge of 10 neighbors.

Chapter 2 noted that in 1995 users were more likely than nonusers to work full-time (users 69.5% versus nonusers 54%) or be a student (13.5% versus 5.9%) and have lived for fewer years in their current house (6.4 years versus 10.5). The same differences existed in 1996, except that users were also more likely to own their own home. In 2000, users were significantly more likely than nonusers to have children, work full-time (62.7% versus 44.2%), or be a student (8.8% versus 2.1%) and have lived for fewer years in their current house. Finally, respondents' sense of overload (rushed, too much to do) was significantly higher for users than for nonusers in 1995 but not in 2000, and reported satisfaction (overall and with communication with friends, family, and work colleagues) was significantly greater for users than for nonusers in 2000 but not in 1995.

Table 11.1 summarizes the extent of offline media and online interaction in 1995 and 2000. Table 11.2 provides the mean percentages of offline media use and online interaction (by category of nonuser or user, recent or long-term user, and novice or more experienced user) and results of chi-square tests of association. Table 11.3 provides logistic regressions predicting offline media and online interaction, showing any significant influences from demographics or the overload or satisfaction measures, as well as the appropriate kinds of usage measures (nonuser or user, recent or long-term, novice or more expert). Influences of the usage variables are included in the final model whether or not they are significant.

Communication by Letter and Telephone

Respondents were asked how often in the week prior to the interview they communicated with other people by letter or telephone. These were dichotomized at no letters versus any letters and at fewer than 10 phone calls versus at least 10 calls.

In 1995, about equal percentages of users (45.7%) and nonusers (47.7%) sent no letters or at least one letter (54.3% versus 52.3%). There were also no significant differences between recent (began in last year) and long-term users and between novices and those with at least average Internet expertise. Users made more telephone calls than nonusers (82.9% versus 72.8% made at least 10 calls per week), as did long-term versus recent users (92.0% versus 79.9%), but there was no difference between novice and expert users.

In the overall model, letter writing was again not significantly predicted by usage status, after controlling for the significant influences of greater education and being male. Making more phone calls was no longer predicted by usage once the significant influences of greater

Table 11.1
Interactions of Internet Users, 1995 and 2000

Variables	1995	2000
Letters written weekly?		
None	1,214	667
	(45.7%)	(66.8%)
At least one	1,286	333
	(51.4%)	(33.3%)
Phone calls weekly?		
Fewer than 10	700	393
	(28.0%)	(39.3%)
At least 10	1,797	607
	(72.0%)	(60.7%)
Made online friend?		
No	177	733
	(88.5%)	(86.2%)
At least one	23	117
	(11.5%)	(13.8%)
Met a person (not necessarily friend) you first knew online?		
No	166	764
	(83%)	(89.9%)
At least one	34	86
	(17%)	(10.1%)
Member of online community?		
No	149	762
	(74.5%)	(89.6)
At least one	51	88
	(25.5%)	(10.4%)
Contacted family members online?		
Yes		
Once or twice	16	—
	(8%)	
Several times per year	18	27
	(9%)	(3.2%)
Several times per month	29	46
	(14.5%)	(5.4%)
Several times per week	21	119
	(10.5%)	(14.0%)
No	116	658
	(58%)	(77.4%)

Note: For users only, the nonparametric correlation of hours using the Internet in past week with letters written in last week (dichotomized) was $r = .03$. Phone calls in the last week (dichotomized) was $r = .05$, $p < .05$.

Table 11.2
Differences in Offline Media Use and Online Interactions, by Types of User and Levels of Expertise, 1995 and 2000

Variables	1995					
	Non-user	User	Recent User	Long-Term User	Novice	More Expert
A. Nonusers and users						
Letters per week						
None	47.7%	45.7%				
Any	52.3%	54.3%				
χ^2		N.S.		N.S.		N.S.
Phone calls per week						
Under 10	27.2%	17.1%	20.1%	8.0%		
At least 10	72.8%	82.9%	79.9%	92.0%		
χ^2		9.5**		3.9*		N.S.
n	1,710	199	149	50	94	105
B. Users only						
Contact family online						
Never	N.A.	66.0%	73.3%	44.0%		
Yes	N.A.	34.0%	26.7%	56.0%		
χ^2			14.4***			N.S.
Member of an Internet community						
No	N.A.	74.5%	82.0%	52.0%	83.2%	66.7%
Yes	N.A.	25.5%	18.0%	48.0%	16.8%	33.3%
χ^2			17.8***			7.1**
Internet friends						
No	N.A.	88.5%				
Yes	N.A.	11.5%				
χ^2	N.A.			N.S.		N.S.
Met from Internet[a]						
No	N.A.	83.8%				
Yes	N.A.	17.0%				
χ^2			N.S.			N.S.
n	N.A.	200	150	50	95	105

Note: N.A. = data not available; N.S. = not significant; blank = no value.
a. In 1995, this asked about meeting, in person, someone who had been an on-line friend. In 2000, this asked only about meeting, in person, any person one had first met online.
*$p < .05$.
**$p < .01$.
***$p < .001$.

2000					
Non-user	User	Recent User	Long-Term User	Novice	More Expert
N.A.	66.8%				
N.A.	33.2%				
N.A.	N.A.		N.S.		N.S.
N.A.	39.6%				
N.A.	60.4%				
	N.A.		N.S.		N.S.
N.A.	850	191	659	303	896
N.A.	79.5%				
N.A.	20.5%				
N.A.			N.S.		N.S.
N.A.	89.6%	94.2%	88.3%	96.1%	88.2%
N.A.	10.4%	5.8%	11.7%	3.9%	11.8%
N.A.			5.6*		8.5*
N.A.	86.2%			94.8%	84.3%
N.A.	13.8%			5.2%	15.7%
N.A.			N.S.		11.6***
N.A.	89.9%	94.2%	88.6%	96.8%	88.4%
N.A.	10.1%	5.8%	11.4	3.2%	11.6%
N.A.			5.1*		9.8**
N.A.	850	191	695	154	696

Table 11.3
Logistic Regressions Predicting Offline Media Use and Online Interactions, by Demographics, Types of User, Levels of Expertise, 1995 and 2000

| | Users and Nonusers | | | | Users Only | | | | | |
| | Letters Weekly | | Phone Calls Weekly | | Contact Family Members Online | | Member of Internet Community | | Know Internet-Only Friends | |
	B	Exp(B)	B	Exp(B)	B	Exp(B)	B	Exp(B)	B	Exp(B)
A. 1995										
Education	.43***	1.5								
Income	−.36***	.70	.49**	1.6	1.3**	3.6				
Sex (0 = male, 1 = female)										
Age (0 = under 40, 1 = at least 40)			−.55***	.58						
Race (0 = African American, 1 = white non-Hispanic)									−1.5*	.22
Overloaded (0 = less, 1 = more)			−.29***	.75						
Satisfied (0 = less, 1 = more)			−.48**	.62						
Usage (0 = nonuse, 1 = user)	.04	1.0	.45	1.6	N.A.	N.A.	N.A.	N.A.	N.A.	N.A.

Usage (0 = recent user, 1 = long-term user)	N.A.	N.A.	1.3*** (3.6)	1.4*** (4.2)	-.20 (.82)
Skill (0 = novice, 1 = more expert)	N.A.	N.A.			
χ^2	30.8***	44.8***	23.9***	16.5***	4.7***
-2 log likelihood	2,609	1,679	191	210	121
Nagelkerke R^2	.02	.08	.19	.12	.05
Correctly assigned	56%	76%	71%	75%	89%
n	1,908	1,706	166	200	179
B. 2000					
Education (0 = male, 1 = female)	.39** (1.48)	-.84*** (.43)			-.54** (.59)
Age (0 = under 40, 1 = at least 40)					
Work (1 = full time, 2 = other)	.34* (1.4)				
Children (0 = none, 1 = any)			.46* (1.6)		
Overloaded (0 = less, 1 = more)		-.28*** (.76)	.25* (1.3)		
Satisfied (0 = less, 1 = more)		-.50*** (.63)			

Table 11.3
(continued)

| | Users and Nonusers | | | | Users Only | | | | | |
| | Letters Weekly | | Phone Calls Weekly | | Contact Family Members Online | | Member of Internet Community | | Know Internet-Only Friends | |
	B	Exp(B)	B	Exp(B)	B	Exp(B)	B	Exp(B)	B	Exp(B)
Usage (0 = recent user, 1 = long-term user)										
Skill (0 = novice, 1 = more expert)					N.S.		1.2**	3.2	1.3***	3.6
χ^2	16.4***		60.0***				17.8***		20.8***	
−2 log likelihood	1,256		1,226				547		660	
Nagelkerke R^2	.02		.08				.04		.04	
Correctly assigned	66.7%		62.9%				89.6%		86.2%	
n	1,000		976				800		850	

Note: N.A. = data not available; blank = no value.
*$p < .05$.
**$p < .01$.
***$p < .001$.

income, younger age, being less overloaded, and being less satisfied by one's communication were taken into account.

In 2000, nonusers were not asked about letter or telephone usage. A third of Internet users had written at least one letter in the prior week, while 60.4% had made at least 10 telephone calls.

In the overall model, there were no significant differences between recent and long-term users or between novice and greater experts on letter writing after the significant influences of begin female and not working full-time were controlled. And there were no significant differences between kinds of users and levels of expertise on telephone calls after controlling for the significant influences of younger age, being less overloaded, and being less satisfied with one's communication.

Additional Offline Analyses for 1995

The 1995 survey contained several questions indicating aspects of respondents' sociability: the number of 10 closest neighbors known, innovativeness, and number of times in the past week they got together with friends. Table 11.4 shows differences between nonusers and users on these measures and shows results from two logistic regressions predicting Internet usage first from just the sociability variables and then controlling for any significant demographic measures.

Knowledge of Ten Closest Neighbors

We asked participants in the survey how many of the 10 people living closest to their home they knew. Of nonusers who had not heard of the Internet, 37% reported knowing the 10 closest people, and 31% reported knowing four to nine of the 10 closest people. Similarly, of nonusers who had heard of the Internet, 33% reported knowing the 10 closest people, and 36% reported knowing four to nine of the 10 closest people. Former users reported knowing slightly fewer neighbors: 28% reported knowing the 10 closest people, and 42% reported knowing four to nine of the 10 closest people. Of long-time users, 28% reported knowing the 10 closest people, and 37% reported knowing four to nine of the 10 closest people. Recent users reported knowing the fewest neighbors: 21% reported knowing the 10 closest people, and 43%

Table 11.4
Sociability and Internet Usage, Differences and Predictors, 1995

A. Cross-tabulations and χ^2

Sociability Variables	Never Used	Current User
Know 10 closest neighbors		
Low (0–5)	48.0%	56.0%
High (6–10)	52.0%	44.0%
χ^2		4.6*
Innovative		
Low (1–2.5)	49.7%	32.5%
High (3–5)	50.3%	67.5%
χ^2		21.2***
Number of times in the past week met with friends		
Low (0–2)	41.5%	29.0%
High (3 or more 3)	58.5%	71.0%
χ^2		11.7***
n	1,713	200

B. Predicting never or current usage from sociability

Sociability Variables	B	Exp(B)
Know 10 closest neighbors	−.40*	.67
Innovative	.67***	1.96
Number of times in week get together with friends	.54***	1.7
χ^2	37.5***	
−2 log likelihood	1,243	
Nagelkerke R^2	.04	
Correctly assigned	89.5%	
n	1,912	

Table 11.4
(continued)

C. Predicting never or current usage from sociability controlling for all demographics (only significant demographic variables included in this final model)

Sociability Variables	B	Exp(B)
Education	.94***	2.6
Income	.77***	2.2
Know 10 closest neighbors	−.31+	.73
Innovative	.62***	1.9
Number of times in week get together with friends	.46**	1.6
χ^2	86.7***	
−2 log likelihood	970	
Nagelkerke R^2	.11	
Correctly assigned	89.3%	
n	1,557	

Note: Blank = no value.
+$p < .1$.
*$p < .05$.
**$p < .01$.
***$p < .001$.

reported knowing four to nine of the 10 closest people. So there is evidence that long-term and recent Internet users are more likely to know fewer of their 10 closest neighbors. This implies that users' social communities are more physically dispersed than nonusers'.

The simplified comparison in table 11.4 (collapsing the measure of knowledge of closest neighbors at the mean and collapsing respondents into never-used and current users) again shows that those who are currently using the Internet know fewer of their 10 closest neighbors than do those who have never used the Internet. Further, this measure of sociability was a significant predictor of nonusage in the logistic regression that included just the sociability measures but became marginally nonsignificant ($p = .07$) when the significant influences of education and income were controlled, implying that the use of the Internet is not associated with different levels of awareness of one's neighbors.

Innovativeness

Two items on the 1995 survey represented innovativeness: "like to do things that are a little dangerous" and "first among friends to go out and try a new thing." These loaded highly on a single principal component, and the mean scale of these two items had an alpha reliability of .65. For the cross-tabulations and logistic regressions, we dichotomized this mean scale at the mean (low = 1 to 2.5, high = 3 to 5). Over two-thirds of current users (67.5%), nearly three-quarters of former users (72.1%), and around half of aware nonusers (50.3%) and nonaware nonusers (47.6%) were more innovative. Table 11.4 shows that those who are innovative are more likely to be current users (67.5%) than nonusers (50.3%). This influence persisted in both overall models.

Meeting with Friends

The 1995 survey also explored the number of times in the past week that respondents had met with friends. In the week prior to the 1995 survey, 38% of long-time users met one to three times with friends, and 54% met four or more times. Of recent users, 40% met one to three times with friends, and 48% met four or more times. Former users (dropouts) met with friends a broadly similar amount of time: 48% met one to three times with friends, and 44% met four or more times. Of nonusers who had heard of the Internet, 48% met one to three times with friends, and 40% met four or more times. However, nonusers who had not heard of the Internet reported meeting with friends less often: 43% reported meeting one to three times with friends, and 39% meeting four or more times in the week prior to the survey. In other words, those who had been using the Internet the longest also were the most likely to have met with four or more friends, while those who were not even aware of the Internet were least likely to have met with four or more friends in the prior week. Clearly, long-term Internet usage is associated with more, not less, frequent sociability.

Table 11.4 shows that the dichotomized measure of friendship sociability (no times through times versus three or more times) was positively associated with being a current user: 71% of current users had met with friends more than three times in the past week, compared to 58.5% for those who had never used the Internet. This positive influence on usage persisted in the overall model that included all four measures of sociability, as well as in the overall model that controlled for significant demographic influences.

Additional Offline Analyses for 2000

The 2000 survey contained measures that were not included in the 1995 survey. Table 11.5 provides those questions, their choices, and descriptive statistics.

Non-Internet measures included a measure of sociability, "belonging" (the mean of "there are people you feel close to" and "you feel part of a group of friends"). There were two separate items indicating introversion or shyness. Several questions asked about the extent to which respondents liked listening to the radio, liked watching TV, and liked reading the newspaper "to find out what is going on" and "for entertainment."

Cross-tabulations (provided in table 11.6) indicated that current Internet users were more likely to have a greater sense of "belonging," liked watching TV less, and liked listening to the radio more. When controlling for the significant demographic influences of age, education, and income, the greater sense of belonging and liking radio (just over significance) persisted as predictors of being a current Internet user (see table 11.7).

Online Interaction

Respondents in the 1995 and 2000 surveys were also asked the extent to which they contacted family members through the Internet (dichotomized at none or once or twice versus at least several times a year), belonged to Internet communities (none versus any), had established relationships with people online that they would call friends (none versus any), and had met anyone offline that they had met online (not necessarily one of those friends) (none versus any).

Contacting Family Members Online
In the 1995 survey, 34% of users reported contacting family members through the Internet at least several times year. Longer-term users were

Table 11.5
Additional Variables from the 2000 Survey

Variable or Scale	*n*
Belonging (the mean of "there are people you feel close to" and "you feel part of a group of friends") (alpha .56) (1 S.D. to 5 S.A.)	1,094
After meeting many new people you feel worn out (1 S.A. to 5 S.D.)	1,094
At parties you prefer to interact with a few friends rather than with many you don't know too well (1 S.A. to 5 S.D.)	1,094
Where do you primarily access the Internet?	
Home	
School	
Work	
Library	
Both home and work	
Both home and school	861
Total hours you accessed the Internet at home in the last week	848
Total hours you accessed the Internet at work in the last week	848
Total hours you were online at home and work in the last week	
Under 1	
1 to 2	
3 to 5	
6 to 10	
More than 10	788
You participated in real-time chat in the last week	1,000
Within the last day	
Within the last week	
Within the last month	
More than a month ago	362
You participated in real-time interactive games in last week	1,000
Within the last day	
Within the last week	
Within the last month	
More than a month ago	153

Percentage	Mean	Standard Deviation	Median
	4.3	.67	
	3.5	1.0	
	2.5	1.1	
62.4%			
2.8%			
20.6%			
2.1%			
9.5%			
2.7%			
81% at least once	7.6	0.0	
39.9% at least once	4.2	0.0	
10.6%			
21.2%			
22.1%			
19.6%			
26.5%	3.3	1.3	
36.2%			
14.6%			
16.6%			
18.8%			
50.0%			
13.5%			
15.3%			
17.0%			
28.1%			
41.2%			

Table 11.5
(continued)

Variable or Scale	n
You have a personal Web page	841
Your reason for having Web page:	
Better communication with friends and family	
Very important reason	249
Somewhat important reason	
Not important reason	
Make information available to new people	
Very important reason	
Somewhat important reason	
Not important reason	229
Times you used Internet in the past week to search for information	897
Times you used Internet in the past week to communicate with one or two specific people (as e-mail to friend)	897
Times you used Internet in the past week to communicate with a group (listserv or chat)	897
Your experience of the last meeting you had with a person you met online was positive (1 S.D. to 5 S.A.)	67
You like listening to radio (1 S.D. to 5 S.A.)	1,095
You like watching TV (1 S.D. to 5 S.A.)	1,095
Newspaper (mean of "you like reading newspaper" "to find out what is going on" and "for entertainment") (1 S.D. to 5 S.A.)	1,095
You like surfing the Internet (1 S.D. to 5 S.A.)	766
You like interacting with others on the Internet (1 S.D. to 5 S.A.)	766
You like reading material on the Internet about what's going on (1 S.D. to 5 S.A.)	766
You like reading material on the Internet for entertainment (1 S.D. to 5 S.A.)	766

Note: S.A. = strongly agree; S.D. = strongly disagree; blank = no value.

Percentage	Mean	Standard Deviation	Median
11.8%			
21.8%	2.18	.77	
38.4%			
39.7%			
32.8%			
38.4%			
28.8%	1.96	.79	
88.1% at least once	23.5	31.1	10.0
85.3% at least once	33.4	36.1	20.0
23.6% at least once	4.5	16.3	0.0
	4.24	.92	
	3.84	1.0	
	4.10	.91	
	3.7	.91	
	3.49	1.10	
	2.75	1.15	
	3.61	1.05	
	3.31	1.12	

Table 11.6
Differences between Users and Nonuses on Sociability and Media Measures, 2000

Sociability and Media Variables	Nonuser	User	*n*
Belonging			
Low	30.7%	69.3%	423
High	23.3%	76.7%	473
χ^2			6.4*
Worn out			
Low	26.4%	73.6%	569
High	27.8%	72.2%	327
χ^2			N.S.
Few at party			
Low	26.3%	73.7%	569
High	27.1%	72.9%	327
χ^2			N.S.
Like watching TV			
Low	24.7%	75.3%	673
High	33.5%	66.5%	224
χ^2			6.6*
Like listening to radio			
Low	42.0	58.0	131
High	24.3%	75.7%	766
χ^2			17.8***
Like reading newspaper for entertainment and information			
Low	28.1%	71.9%	413
High	25.8%	74.2%	484
χ^2			N.S.

Note: N.S. = data not significant; blank = no value.
*$p < .05$.
**$p < .01$.
***$p < .001$.

Table 11.7
Predicting Internet Usage and Nonusage by Sociability and Media Measures and Controlling for Demographics, 2000

Sociability and Media Variables	Sociability and Media Only		With Demographics	
	B	Exp(B)	B	Exp(B)
Age	N.A.	N.A.	−1.3***	.27
Education	N.A.	N.A.	1.1***	2.9
Income	N.A.	N.A.	1.2***	3.4
Belonging	.40*	1.5	.46*	1.6
Like TV	−.51**	.6	−.22	.8
Like radio	.78***	2.2	.49+	1.6
χ^2		29.7***		150***
−2 log likelihood		1,011		686
Nagelkerke R^2		.05		.27
Correctly assigned		73.3%		78.1%
n		896		729

Note: N.A. = data not available; blank = no value.
$^+p = .06.$
$^*p < .05.$
$^{**}p < .01.$
$^{***}p < .001.$

much more likely than recent users (56.0% versus 26.7%) to do so, but level of expertise made no difference. In the overall model, the influence of being a long-term user persisted after controlling for the significant influence of greater income.

In the 2000 survey, 20.5% of the users reported contacting family members online at least several times a year, but there were no differences by recent or long-term status or level of expertise. The overall model was not significant.

Membership in Online Communities
In the 1995 survey, 25.5% of users reported being a member of at least one Internet community. This percentage rose significantly to 48.0% by

long-term users (versus 18.0% of recent users) and 33.3% for those with at least average expertise (versus 16.8% for novices). This difference persisted in the overall model.

In 2000, 10.4% reported being a member of at least one online community. There were significantly more long-term users (11.7% versus 5.8% for recent users) and those with greater expertise (11.8% versus 3.9%). In the overall model, only being more expert persisted as an influence on belonging to more online communities.

Establishing Friendships on the Internet

In 1995, 11.5% of users who responded to the question had established friendships via the Internet. There were no significant differences between recent and long-term users and between novices and those with more expertise. In the overall model, the only significant influence was being African American. In 2000, 13.8% of user-respondents had established friendships via the Internet. Those with greater expertise were significantly more likely to have developed at least one online friendship (15.7% versus 5.2% for novices), and this difference persisted in the overall model after controlling for the significant influence of having lower education.

It seems consequential that about 10% of the users in 1995 and 2000 said that had met *at least* one new person online whom they now considered to be a friend. Consider the numbers of potential new friends involved: assuming that around 200 million adults lived in the United States in this time period, 11.5% of the 8.1% of users corresponds to approximately 1.9 million new friends in 1995, while 13.8% of the 59.7% users corresponds to approximately 33 million new friends in 2000, met solely through the Internet. That's a lot of social capital.

Those reporting a higher number of Internet friends in 1995 were more likely to have met at least one of them. In 1995, 17% of users who responded to the question reported that they had met face to face at least one of these friends they had first met online, with no significant differences by level of usage or experience. In 2000, 10.1% of users met an Internet acquaintance (in 2000, not online friends but simply anyone they had met first online) and were more likely to do so if they were a long-term user (11.4% versus 5.8%) or more expert (11.6% versus 3.2%). Of the 67 people responding to the question asking about whether the most recent meeting with someone they had first met online was a positive experience, 47.8% strongly agreed, 35.8% agreed, 10.4% were neutral, 4.5% disagreed, and 1.5% strongly disagreed; thus nearly 85% felt it was a positive experience. The sample sizes were too small to assess overall influences on meeting Internet acquaintances.

Additional Online Analyses for 1995

Sociability and Online Interaction
We tested to see if the three indicators of sociability in 1995 (number of 10 closest neighbors known, innovativeness, and number of times people got together with friends in the prior week) influenced our three measures of online interaction—contacting family members online, membership in online communities, and developing friendships with people met only on the Internet. Table 11.8 summarizes the three logistic regressions. It turns out that none of these indicators of sociability was significantly associated with any of the forms of online interaction, after controlling for any significant demographic influences and after including the two usage measures (recent versus long-term user, and novice versus more expert user).

Effect of Online Interaction on Communication with Friends and Family
In 1995, for the vast majority of both long-time and recent users, use of the Internet did not have much impact on the time spent with friends and family. The two groups' views were not statistically different: 88% of users reported that the time spent with friends and family face to face or by phone had not changed since they started using Internet. The same proportion of users (6%) reported they spent more time with friends and family face to face or by phone as reported that they spent less time. Given the limited variance in this variable and the lack of difference between types of users, we did not test for multiple influences on this outcome.

Table 11.8
Predicting Online Interaction from Sociability, Controlling for Demographics and Usage, 1995

Sociability Variables	Contact Family Members Online		Member of an Internet Community		Know Internet-Only Friends	
	B	Exp(B)	B	Exp(B)	B	Exp(B)
Education	N.A.	N.A.	N.A.	N.A.	−.16**	.20
Income	1.5***	4.3	N.A.	N.A.	−1.4*	.25
Know 10 closest neighbors	−.28	.75	−.14	.87	.35	1.4
Innovative	.13	1.1	.01	1.0	−.61	.55
Number of times in a week get together with friends	.48	1.6	.16	1.2	.92	2.5
Usage						
Recent (0), long-time (1)	1.0***	2.8	.65+	1.9	.16	1.2
Novice (0), more expert (1)	.01	1.1	.70*	2.0	.07	1.1
χ^2		24.4***		11.0*		14.7*
−2 log likelihood		190		216		110
Nagelkerke R^2		.19		.08		.16
Correctly assigned		70.5%		74.5%		89.9
n		166		200		179

Note: N.A. = data not available; blank = no value.
+$p < .1$.
*$p < .05$.
**$p < .01$.
***$p < .001$.

Additional Online Analyses for 2000

Questions on the 2000 survey also asked respondents where they primarily accessed the Internet, how many total hours in the past week they used it at home, at work, or overall, whether they had participated in a real-time chat session or real-time interactive games, whether they had a personal Web page (and the importance of having it for better communication with friends and family or to make information available to new people), how much time they used the Internet in the past week to search for information, to communicate with one or two specific people, or to communication with a group, and how much they liked surfing, interacting with others, reading material about what's going on, or reading material for entertainment on the Internet. Table 11.5 describes those questions and the responses.

Sociability and Online Interaction

We wanted to see if greater sociability (here, feeling close to people and feeling part of a group of friends) was related to how and how much people used the Internet. (The two introversion items were not significantly related to any of our variables of interest and so are not further considered.) Table 11.9 shows differences between "low" and "high" belongers.

Those who reported a greater sense of belonging were more likely to access the Internet at home and at work, while those with a lower sense were more likely to access the Internet at school, the library, and both at home and school. There was no difference by levels of combined hours of usage or whether users participated in chat groups, played real-time interactive games, or had a personal webpage. However, those with a greater sense of belonging did like surfing the Internet more and liked interacting with others on the Internet more. Those with a greater sense of belonging were more likely to both strongly agree and strongly disagree with these two questions, though on the whole they were more positive. Those with a greater sense of belonging were more likely to be long-term users instead of recent users but were not more likely to be more expert than novice users.

Table 11.9
Differences between Low-Belonging and High-Belonging Groups on Usage, 2000

Usage Variables	Low Belonging	High Belonging	n
Where access			
Home	44.9%	55.1%	414
School	60.0%	40.0%	15
Work	35.7%	64.3%	129
Library	71.4%	28.6%	14
Both home and work	49.2%	50.8%	65
Both home and school	58.8%	41.2%	17
χ^2			11.6*
Hours used at home and work in last week			
Under 1	47.3%	52.7%	74
1 to 2	51.8%	48.2%	141
3 to 5	46.2%	53.8%	143
6 to 10	38.3%	61.7%	128
More than 10	41.7%	58.3%	168
χ^2			N.S.
Participate in chat groups			
Yes	42.8%	57.2%	276
No	48.4%	51.6%	490
χ^2			N.S.
Participate in real-time interactive games			
Yes	43.5%	56.5%	115
No	46.9%	53.1%	651
χ^2			N.S.
Have a personal page			
Yes	46.7%	53.3%	75
High	44.6%	55.4%	579
χ^2			N.S.

Table 11.9
(continued)

Usage Variables	Low Belonging	High Belonging	n
Like surfing Internet			
S.D.	31.6%	68.4%	38
Disagree	51.5%	48.5%	134
Neutral	47.3%	52.7%	129
Agree	53.0%	47.0%	347
S.A.	24.6%	75.4%	118
χ^2			33.5*
Like interacting with others on Internet			
S.D.	38.5%	61.5%	107
Disagree	53.0%	47.0%	200
Neutral	41.9%	58.1%	148
Agree	50.0%	50.0%	200
S.A.	22.7%	77.3%	44
χ^2			19.5***
User			
Recent	54.5%	45.5%	191
Long-term	43.7%	56.3%	575
χ^2			6.7*
Expert			
Novice	48.4%	51.6%	157
More expert	45.8%	54.2%	609
χ^2			N.S.

Note: S.A. = strongly agree; S.D. = strongly disagree; N.S. = data not significant; blank = no value.
*$p < .05$.
**$p < .01$.
***$p < .001$.

Contacting Family Members Online, Joining Online Communities, and Establishing Friendships on the Internet

Controlling for demographic and usage variables, the sense of belonging scale was not a significant predictor of these forms of online social interaction. Using correlations, the belonging scale (not dichotomized) was not significantly associated with hours of use at home or at work, searching for information, communicating with other specific people, communicating with a group, liking interacting with others, liking reading on the Internet to find out what's going on, or using it for entertainment. As table 11.10 shows, however, several Internet activities were associated with online social interaction. Those who contacted family members online were more likely to participate in real-time chat sessions and less likely to like reading material on the Internet for entertainment. Those who were members of at least one Internet community were more likely to communicate in the past week with groups of other users (such as on a listserv or in a chat group) and more likely to have some Internet expertise. Finally, having developed one or more friends online was associated with communicating in the past week with groups of other users and with liking to interact with others on the Internet.

Relationship of Cellular Telephone Ownership with Telephone and Internet Use

The cellular telephone is another recent and rapidly diffusing communication medium (Katz & Aakhus, 2002). We compared cell phone non-users to users on their use of the regular telephone and several Internet variables to see if the cell phone was a completely different phenomenon or related to the broader diffusion of the Internet and thus part of a growing trend toward more mediated interaction. Over half (54.4%) of the 2000 survey respondents owned a cellular phone.

There was no significant association between cell-phone usage and categories of the number of times in the last week one contacted people by telephone (0, 1 to 4, 5 to 9, 10 to 19, at least 20) or ever engaging in online chat. There was a marginally significant ($p < .1$) association between cell-phone ownership and contacting people by e-mail more frequently in the last week (for example, 17.5% of cell-phone users contacted others at least 20 times compared to 15.1% of non-cell-phone

Table 11.10
Predicting Online Interaction from Sociability, Controlling for Demographics and Usage, 2000

Sociability Variables	Contact Family Members Online		Member of an Internet Community		Know Internet-Only Friends	
	B	Exp(B)	B	Exp(B)	B	Exp(B)
Participate in real-time chat (0 = no, 1 = yes)	1.4***	4.1	N.A.	N.A.	N.A.	N.A.
Times used Internet in past week to communicate with a group (listserv or chat) (at least once)	N.A.	N.A.	.69**	1.9	.86***	2.4
Like interacting with others on the Internet (0 = low, 1 = high)	N.A.	N.A.	N.A.	N.A.	1.6***	5.0
Like reading material on the Internet for entertainment (0 = low, 1 = high)	−.91*	.4	N.A.	N.A.	N.A.	N.A.
Expert (0 = novice, 1 = more expert)	N.A.	N.A.	1.2**	3.3	N.A.	N.A.
χ^2	12.6**		21.8***		68.0***	
−2 log likelihood	194		576		484	
Nagelkerke R^2	.07		.05		.17	
Correctly assigned	97.0%		89.6		85.4%	
n	766		897		662	

Note: No demographic or sociability variables were significant predictors of these three online interaction activities. N.A. = no data available; blank = no value.

*p < .05.
**p < .01.
***p < .001.

owners). Cell-phone owners were also marginally less likely to have a personal webpage (10.3% compared to 14.3% by nonowners, $p < .1$). However, cell-phone owners were more likely to have heard of the Internet (94.7% compared to 92.1%, $p < .05$), and vastly more likely to be a current Internet user (88.6% versus 65.0%, $p < .001$). This strong association with Internet usage persisted after major demographic influences of education, age, sex, and income were controlled (only income was a significant influence) in a logistic regression. So general Internet use (though not specific features such as chat or webpages) and cell-phone ownership are highly related, indicating a broader environment of mediated sociability.

Results from the Pew March 2000 Survey

Offline Interaction

We can look at somewhat similar questions using the several measures of media use and sociability in the Pew March 2000 survey. Table 11.11 summarizes the sociability and media differences between nonusers and users and between recent users and long-term users (less than one year versus at least one year). Users are more likely to be satisfied with the way things are going in the United States, have few or many (as opposed to no) people to turn to for help, and have visited family or friends yesterday and are not more likely to have called a friend or relative yesterday. Users are also more likely to have read the newspaper yesterday and are not more likely to have watched television news programs yesterday. The only difference that persisted when comparing recent to long-term users was greater satisfaction with the way things are going in the United States for long-term users. Thus, users are significantly more sociable and greater consumers of the newspaper than are nonusers. But more experienced Internet users are not more sociable or greater media users than recent users.

The only one of these media and sociability influences that persisted when controlling for significant demographic variables (age, education, and income) was the greater likelihood of users than nonusers to have visited friends yesterday. Even the satisfaction variable disappeared as an influence on recent versus long-term usage once age, education, race, and having children were controlled for (see table 3.14 in chapter 3). Thus being more sociable, at least in terms of having visited family or friends yesterday, is associated with being an Internet user instead of being a nonuser, but there were no other differences in sociability or media usage between nonusers and users or between recent users and long-term users. In the Pew data, as with our data, Internet users are no less sociable and are in some ways more sociable than nonusers.

Online Interaction

As table 11.12 shows, Internet users are engaging in a wide variety of online interaction. Over three-quarters of all responding users send e-mail to friends and family members, and over half have an e-mail group list for those recipients. As of March 2000, less than 5% had their own Web page, though nearly 15% reported that a family member had a Web page.

Of all online activities, e-mail is the most popular, as 87.4% indicated they sent or read e-mail the prior day, while 82.7% of those who did not go online yesterday said they had ever done so. And to whom do these respondents send e-mail? From three-quarters to half sent e-mail the prior day to friends who live far away or close by, to brothers or sisters, to people they work with, or to extended family.

Other online activities done by more than half of responding users included looking for information about a hobby (71.4%), going online just for fun or to pass time (59.7%), doing research for school or training (55.6%), checking weather information (52.3%), getting news (50.1%), and looking for health or medical information (50.0%). Over 40% looked for government information, almost 30% reported looking for political news, and 17.2% looked for religious or spiritual information online.

It seems, then, that the primary online activity is sending and receiving e-mail, especially to friends and family; indeed, over half of the users have established a group e-mail list for friends or family. The two next most frequent activities ever done online are individually oriented, involving hobbies, just having fun, or seeking health information. However, half of the users have checked for online news, and over 30% of users have looked for government information or for political news.

Table 11.11
Differences in Media Use and Sociability between Nonusers and Users and between Recent and Long-Term Users, Pew Survey, March 2000

Variables	Nonusers	Users
Read newspaper yesterday (no versus yes)	61.7% (548)	56.6% (1,690)
Watched TV news yesterday (no versus yes)	44.8% (55.2%)	43.9% (56.1%)
Satisfaction with way things going in U.S. (dissatisfied versus satisfied)	47.2% (498)	38.5% (1,598)
Can turn to people for help		
None	13.5%	8.2%
Few	41.3%	42.8%
Many	45.2% (542)	49.0% (1,669)
Can turn to people for help (none versus few or many)	12.5% (542)	8.2% (1,669)
Visited family or friends yesterday (no versus yes)	33.5% (547)	28.2% (1,686)
Called friend or relative yesterday (no versus yes)	38.6% (547)	38.3% (1,682)

Note: To save space, the top row provides the percentages only for the listed category (of two categories) for nonusers and users, while the bottom row provides the total sample size for the two categories. The percentages for the other category for nonusers and users can be computed from these two values. The χ^2 indicates extent of association between the two categories of the usage variable and the two categories of each other variable. N.S. = not significant; blank = no value.
$*p < .05.$
$**p < .01.$
$***p < .001.$

Table 11.11
(continued)

χ^2	Recent Users	Long-Term Users	χ^2
	58.7%	55.2%	
(4.4*)	(635)	(1,050)	(N.S.)
	42.0%	44.9%	
(N.S.)	(634)	(1,046)	(N.S.)
	43.7%	35.6%	
(11.8***)	(591)	(1,002)	(10.0***)
	8.3%	8.2%	
	45.9%	40.8%	
	45.9%	51.0%	
(13.4***)	(628)	(1,036)	(N.S.)
	8.3%	8.2%	
(13.2***)	(628)	(1,036)	(N.S.)
	28.6%	28.1%	
(5.5**)	(633)	(1,048)	(N.S.)
	37.8%	38.6%	
(N.S.)	(632)	(1,046)	(N.S.)

So Internet users are highly social, individualistic, and somewhat active users of civic (government and political) information.

Outcomes Associated with Online Activities and Their Relation to Different Forms of Use

We prepared a few simple scales representing several kinds of outcomes. The scales include improved family relations, improved friend relations, improved connections to family and friends, improved information, and got online news, weather, or politics information ever and yesterday (the note to table 11.13 provides the details). These represent some aspects of social relations and civic information. Then we tested for associations between these scales and several measures of usage—amount of time online yesterday, recent user versus long-term user, ever engaged in

Table 11.12
Online and E-mail Activities of Various Subsets of User, Pew Survey, March 2000

General E-mail and Web Usage		Yes
Ever send e-mail to friends		79.4%
Ever send e-mail to family members		76.7
Have an e-mail group list for friends and family		53.8
Family member has Web page		14.4
Have own Web page		4.4

Online Activities	Ever	Yesterday
Sent or read e-mail	82.7%	87.4%
Looked for information about a hobby	71.4	31.2
Went online just for fun or to pass time	59.7	34.8
Did research for school or training	55.6	18.0
Checked weather information	52.3	26.0
Got news	50.1	38.0
Looked for health or medical information	50.0	10.9
Did research for job besides e-mail	43.0	26.7
Sent instant messages	40.3	20.6
Checked sports information	32.3	13.5
Looked for news about politics	29.1	16.4
Looked for information from government Web sites	42.5%	12.0%
Looked for information about a job	31.5	8.1
Took part in chatroom	21.4	8.1
Looked for religious or spiritual information	17.2	4.6

online chat, and ever send e-mail to family members. Table 11.13 shows the correlations among the outcome and usage variables.

Basically, all the kinds of usage are significantly correlated with the outcomes, except that improved family relations are not related to amount of time online or whether one is a recent user or a long-term user. However, improved relations with friends are associated with greater time spent online yesterday, being an earlier adopter, and engaging in online chat and e-mail. Respondents who used the Internet more in

Table 11.12
(continued)

Send e-mail to:	Ever (If Didn't Yesterday)	Yesterday
Friends who live far away	64.0	74.3
Friends who live close by	56.4	66.1
Brother or sister	48.6	59.7
People you work with	46.2	58.6
Extended family	43.4	52.9
Parent or grandparent	27.0	34.8
Child not living at home	22.6	20.7
Spouse or partner you live with	20.2	27.4
Romantic partner you don't live with	10.6	16.3
Child who lives at home	9.6	9.5
Roommate	7.5	6.4

Note: "Yesterday" responses are from those who indicated they had gone online yesterday. "Ever" responses are from those who indicated they had not gone online yesterday but had gone online. All percentages are of those who answered yes to the question. Frequencies vary widely. Further, some questions were asked of one set of respondents, and others from another set (such as the question about having a webpage) to reduce overall survey time. So the "yesterday" and "ever" percentages are not from the same samples, and percentages within "yesterday" or "ever" are not necessarily from the same subsamples. Items asking about commercial or buying activities are not included here. Other items and sample sizes for all questions from the Pew survey appear in appendix B.

all these ways (but especially those who spent more time online yesterday, thus being the most ardent of users) generally felt that their connections to family and friends were improved. People were more likely to have ever obtained news, weather, or politics information online if they were longer-term users or if they were engaged in online communication (chat and e-mail). The correlations for getting such information yesterday were weaker, as smaller proportions of users actually obtained such information the prior day as opposed to ever.

These forms of usage are generally intercorrelated, so multiple linear regressions were used to assess the unique contributions of the usage

Table 11.13
Correlations between Selected Outcomes and Usage Measures, Pew Survey, March 2000

Outcomes	Amount of Time Online Yesterday	Recent versus Long-Time User	Ever Engaged in Online Chat	Ever Send E-mail to Family Members
Improved family relations[a]	.05	.01	.14***	.17***
Improved friend relations[a]	.16***	.08*	.16***	.15***
Improved connections to family and friends[b]	.30***	.16***	.18***	.18***
Improved information[c]	.18***	.15***	.18***	.41***
Got online news, weather, or politics information ever[d]	N.A.	.22***	.11***	.16***
Got online news, weather, or politics information yesterday[e]	.24***	.10***	.06*	.07**
Range of n	273 to 1,002	273 to 1,002	426 to 1,211	425 to 1,207

Note: Values are Spearman nonparametric correlations because some variables are dichotomous. All scales were unidimensional, based on principal components analysis. Cronbach α reliabilities are reported with each scale.

a. Mean of "e-mail brought me closer to family and friends," "have learned more about family and friends since using e-mail," and "e-mail has improved relationships in family and with friends" (for family, M = .35, S.D. = .39, α = .78; for friends, M = .46, S.D. = .43; α = .82).

b. Mean of "Internet improved connections to family members" and "improved connections to friends" (M = 2.72, S.D. = 1.0, α = .66).

c. Mean of "Internet improved ability to shop," "get information on health care," "manage personal finances," and "learn about new things" (M = 2.24, S.D. = .77, α = .69).

d. Mean of "used Internet to get online news, weather, or politics information ever" (M = .44, S.D. = .36, α = .59).

e. Mean of "used Internet to get online news, weather, or politics information yesterday" (M = .27, S.D. = .32, α = .59).

*p < .05.

**p < .01.

***p < .001, one-tailed tests.

measures to the outcome measures (see table 11.14). Indeed, some of the usage measures were less influential, and some became nonsignificant. Improved family relations and improved friend relations were both significantly associated (13% and 18% variance explained, respectively) with greater amount of time spent online yesterday, ever engaging in online chat, and ever sending e-mail to family members. The measures of "improved connections to family and friends" and "improved information" were not well predicted (only 3% and 2% of the variance explained), with only ever sending e-mail to family members having much of an influence. Obtaining online news, weather, or politics information ever and yesterday were both predicted (7% and 6% variance explained, respectively). In the first case, being a longer-term use, ever engaging in online chat, and ever sending e-mail to family members were all significant influences. In the case of yesterday's retrieval of this information, spending more time online yesterday was by far the best predictor.

The most plausible explanation of these findings is that experience with the Internet leads to greater sociability or that those who joined earlier were more sociable and remain so. With cross-sectional survey analysis, it is difficult to separate generational and temporal differences —that is, to determine what "causes" what. In any case, the findings do not suggest that the effects, on average (that is, across large samples as opposed to intriguing individual cases), are antisocial as some have asserted. We also find it relevant that checking the weather is one popular use and surpasses gathering political news. This, along with heavy use for interpersonal communication, is what we would predict given our model of the individual-centered motives for Internet use.

Conclusion

Offline Interaction
Users and long-term users were more likely to make more telephone calls in 1995, though this influence disappeared once demographic influences were controlled. In 1995, Internet users knew fewer of their closest 10 neighbors, but this difference disappeared once demographic and other sociability variables were controlled. Users were more likely to be inno-

Table 11.14
Linear Regressions Predicting Selected Outcomes from Usage Measures, Pew Survey, March 2000,

Outcomes	Amount of Time Online Yesterday	Recent User versus Long-Time User	Ever Engaged in Online Chat	Ever Send E-mail to Family Members	Adjusted R^2	F-Ratio	n
Improved family relations	.26***	.08	.14**	.16**	.13	13.5***	328
Improved friend relations	.12*	.07	.29**	.89***	.18	18.8***	336
Improved connections to family and friends	.03	.00	.07*	.15***	.03	5.9***	771
Improved information	.15*	.03	.05	.13*	.02	2.5*	273
Got online news, weather, or politics, information ever[a]	N.A.	.19***	.14***	.15***	.07	16.4***	563
Got online news, weather, or politics, information yesterday	.21***	.06*	.03	.05*	.06	15.3***	956

Note: N.A. = value not available.
a. The responses concerning getting information "ever" were collected from those who said they had not gone online yesterday, so amount of time spent online "yesterday" is inapplicable to these respondents.
*p < .05.
**p < .01.
***p < .001, one-tailed tests.

vative and more likely to have met with friends in the past week, both independently and after controlling for other factors. In 2000, users were more likely to have a greater sense of belonging to a social group, watching less TV, and listening to more radio. The differences persisted for belongingness and radio listening after controlling for demographics. The Pew data showed that users were more satisfied with life in the United States, had more people to turn to for support, and were more likely to have visited family or friends the prior day and have read the newspaper.

Online Interaction

Early users (1995) seemed proportionally more socially active online, with greater percentages reporting contacting family members online and belonging to online communities than users in 2000. The Pew March 2000 data show that over half of all users engage in a wide variety of online activities, especially communicating with friends and family through e-mail. In general, greater usage and more long-term Internet usage were positively, though weakly, correlated with improved relations with family and with friends.

Communicating with family members online was greater for long-term usage and greater expertise (even after demographic controls) in 1995. In both 1995 and 2000, longer-term and more expert users were more likely to belong to at least one online community; while both factors persisted after demographic controls in 1995, only greater expertise did so in 2000. In both 1995 and 2000, over a tenth of users reported they had established friendships with people they had known only online, and this was more likely for those with greater Internet expertise in 2000 (even after demographic controls). Over 10% also met in person some-one they had first met online, and in 2000 85% of these either agreed or strongly agreed that it was a positive experience. In 2000, high belongers were more likely to access the Internet at home or work, like surfing the Internet, like interacting with others on the Internet, and be longer-term users.

The basic issue motivating this chapter was whether Internet usage is associated with decreased or increased social interaction. Using data from our 1995 and 2000 surveys and the Pew March 2000 survey data, the answer is clear. There are many statistically significant, if not very strong, relationships between being an Internet user (and a longer-term Internet user) and greater offline as well as online social interaction. In some cases, having more Internet expertise is also associated with some forms of interaction. The Internet is quite a social environment, inhabited by quite social folks.

Using multivariate statistics we found that Internet use is positively associated with sociability and interaction. This is true even after for controlling for the individual's degree of offline sociability. That is, the Internet seems to produce more, not less, social interaction on average for all users, regardless of existing socializing patterns and regardless of someone's degree of introversion or extroversion. This contradicts the findings of Kraut et al. (1998) and Nie (2000). While Kraut et al. (in press) found that "the rich get richer" in that extroverted people are able to have relatively more social contact via information than introverted people, we find that "the poor get richer" too. That is, even those who tend to be introverted find their social contacts expanded via the information relative to their nonsurfing counterparts.

12

Interaction and Expression: Self, Identity, and Homepages

This chapter continues our exploration of the question of the Internet's social consequences by looking at the Internet and self-expression. How is use of the Internet associated with the individual's sense of self and personal freedom? The Internet can make reality seem quite plastic and moldable, especially when people first go online. Perhaps this experience has led to the frequent speculation by postmodernists about the Internet's potentially radical deconstructive effect on culture and personal identity (Dery, 1996; Haraway, 1991; Hayles, 1998; Poster, 1990; Stone, 1996; Turkle, 1996). Stone says the Internet allows for individual liberation from a "politically imposed" self. Poster (1990, p. 6) claims that in cyberspace "the self is decentered, dispersed, and multiplied in continuous instability." Turkle (1997, p. 148) asserts "we are moving from modernist calculation to postmodernist simulation, where the self is a multiple, distributed system."

Our purpose here is to take issue with the postmodern perspective. We have formulated our own approach, but it has been influenced by Kenneth Gergen's 1991 book, *The Saturated Self: Dilemmas of Identity in Contemporary Life*. Gergen acknowledges the provocative insights generated by the extreme relativity and context sensitivity of postmodernism but says he is inimical to it (pp. 229–330). Gergen does not discuss identity and self-reflexivity on the Internet but presents a more generalized argument about media and human activities. His view is that all these modalities and communication media allow people to populate more fully their identities, becoming "saturated" though perhaps also confused and fragmented. In subsequent work (Gergen, forthcoming), he holds out the prospect that advances in communication technology, especially the mobile phone, might actually contribute to healthier relationships and a better sense of social place. We essentially agree with Gergen's view. New technology can allow people to integrate and explore aspects of their lives and to expand their personal possibilities, freeing themselves from local cultural influences.

Here we explore not Gergen's argument about technology but that of the postmodernists. The postmodern argument is that the Internet allows the expression of separate existences of multiple aspects of the self that would otherwise remain dormant and allows those multiple aspects to remain discrete rather than having to be resolved or integrated into ordinary social participation. These separate existences—disembodiment— also allow the individual to escape the social and political monitoring of repressive commercial and governmental forces.

What Self?

Postmodern writers Turkle and Stone both create a counterpoint between a traditional notion of self using a psychological definition and the postmodern notion of self as nonlocal and not even necessarily embodied (see also Hayles, 1998). Turkle finds "evidence of fundamental shifts in the way we create and experience human identity" (1997, p. 10). Commonly, postmodern commentators on the Internet adopt the constructs of Foucault (1979) and Lacan (1981), asserting that the self is a series of unrelated episodes that connect to society only through disciplinary sanctions that limit the self and dominate it politically.

These views are in contrast to many of those prevalent in the social sciences, where self or identity is not pinned down to a singular presentation but occurs in relationship to others as an organic product of dyads, settings, and groups. Negotiation and coconstruction are central to these definitions of identity or self (Berger & Luckmann, 1967; Schutz, 1970; also, regarding technology as a social artifact, see Bijker, Hughes & Pinch, 1987; Hess, 1994; Katz, 1978; Latour, 1987; Rice, 1999). So too, as the ethnomethodological literature illustrates in painstaking detail, people engage in a constant effort to structure experience together and to establish order in conventions of discourse so that shared meanings are possible (Garfinkel, 1967; Goffman, 1959; Schegloff, forthcoming).

So the idea of self as varied is far from being new but is a feature of mainstream social theory. What we take issue with is the idea that the self is discontinuous and is under the control of that individual or, conversely, is controlled as a political unit. These latter premises underpin the postmodern concept that selfhood can be changed by migrating to an (allegedly) anonymous electronic medium, such as the Internet.

Negotiated and Programmed Orders

Since context is prior to orderly discourse, new contexts do change the way order is constructed and thus can lead to confusion. There is a socially defined difference between the presentations of self that can occur on the Internet if people choose to abandon their everyday attributes and the presentations of self that occur within the boundaries of embodied life. It is also possible to create a persona, at least for a while, on the Internet and for this option to extend to people unlikely to dissimulate in the physical self. While subgroups carry out fantasy lives as Star Trek characters or cross-dressers in the physical social world, they tend to remain marginalized. An axiom at issue, though, is that because the Internet can be more anonymous, more people will take the option to participate in marginalized roles—or even develop these into more centralized roles. This presumes a primacy of fantasy over practical motivations in large numbers of people.

Rather, it appears that most Internet denizens are as aware of status indicators as anyone else. Both Karetnick (2001) and Roper (2001) find that online personae and interactions in the respective MUD and MOO they studied were greatly influenced by preexisting social constructions of gender, by the programmed structures, moves, and forms of discourse, and by the external inspirations, such as a series of fantasy novels. Punday arrives at a similar conclusion: "Conventional social practices shape this new noncorporeal space. When individuals define new identities in an online environment, they frequently rely on stereotypes built up in the real world or learned through mass media" (Punday, 2000, p. 194, cited by Roper, 2001, p. 87). Nuances of conversation are carefully searched for status indicators, certainly according to Correll's (1995) study of an electronic cafe. Wall (1996) also takes issue with the notion that the digital future offers freedom from all boundaries, including social ones. She argues (as have many others) that one responds to e-mail largely by the status indicators they contain. "I have learned the hard way that my .edu address carries more weight than my ⟨aol.com⟩ address. Having an AOL address is akin to living on the wrong side of the tracks" (p. 341).

When Internet users create selves that are distinct from a historical embodied self, these selves are more like programs than they are identities. Turkle (1997, p. 14) argues that this boundary is precisely the point: "In the daily practice of many computer users, windows have become a powerful metaphor for thinking about the self as a multiple, distributed system. The self is no longer playing different roles in different settings at different times." As one informant, a dedicated MUD player and Internet-related content user, said to her: "'Why grant such superior status to the self that has the body when the selves that don't have bodies are able to have different kinds of experiences?'" (Turkle, 1997, p. 14).

Yet this begs the question of how people might invoke an entity that can be called a self if they lack the situated intelligence of historical embodiment (Hayles, 1998). Internet personal exist as artifacts of the being who types them in; therefore, they cannot have equality since the typing being can easily continue without these "selves." They, on the other hand, will discontinue without the person in the body, since, as programs, they lack the situated intelligence to pretend to be "someone." We recognize that the self is always mediated, in some sense. One's self talk, let alone talk to others, is mediated, for instance, by recent food consumption, blood chemistry, and ambient weather. One can communicate only through physically mediated mechanisms, including voice and body movements. All mediated communication is incomplete and, by its very mediation, artificial. But these conditions are different from claiming to have independent multiple selves that can operate in isolation of (and in exclusion of the reality of) the other selves. The possibility of extending these multiple independent selves to a subsequent change of culture is an even more difficult argument to make.

Boundary Renegotiations

Another way to cast the fragmentation that is claimed for Internet activity is to view the Internet as a new social domain where physical-world boundaries or those of prior domains of convention have not yet been worked out. We do expect that media affect the way communication is divided up, directed, received, and interpreted. Some of the most salient features include the ready availability of personal and broadcast text and material, asynchronous distributed dialogue, and real-time transmission. All these have important consequences. But these can be explained using the less radical construct of shifting boundaries for preexisting conventions. There are many ways to look at boundary issues. Three boundaries bear on the present topic—the social and technical boundary, the real and virtual boundary, and the public and private boundary. All of these are embedded in the arguments about the postmodernism of the Internet.

The Social and Technical Boundary Before accepting the premise that technology changes things, we need to consider technology itself as a social construct. Its definition as an artifact is prior to any social effect it can be presumed to have, since it is a social effect itself. The argument posed in the cyberspace literature—that electronic media change culture—would seem tautological since socially situated existence predicates and affects the use of any technology. As Bloomfield and Vurdubakis (1994, p. 10) note: "Any account that takes the 'properties' of a particular technology as its starting point, is from the beginning caught up in those practices that generate and sustain the objectively given quality of those properties. Hence this type of account will, however reluctantly, tend to reinforce the whole notion of a technology as something that develops outside, as it were, the social relations on which it impacts." This is a different point from the seemingly related theme in *Life on the Screen: Identity in the Age of the Internet*, where Turkle (1997, p. 30) says that computers are "experienced as an object on the border between self and not-self. . . . People are able to see themselves in the computer. The machine can seem a second self." Both talk about technology as a constructed "object" in some way. But Bloomfield and Vurdubakis emphasize the priority of social construction and social understanding, while Turkle refers to the individual construction and extension of self as an artifact of technology. This is a critical distinction.

The Real and Virtual Boundary Another boundary issue is between real and virtual. This is a strange boundary to come upon in the postmodernist context because presumably such a boundary does not exist in the underlying philosophy of constructivism (Gergen, 1991). Yet both Stone and Turkle, while asserting that this boundary has been dissolved, continually revert to the premise of that boundary as a backdrop for discussion. Stone (1996, p. 37) says of her *The War of Desire and Technology at the End of the Mechanical Age* that it "is about emergent technologies, shifting boundaries between the living and the non-living, optional embodiment. . . . I am interested in prosthetic communication for what it shows of the 'real' world that might otherwise go unnoticed." Taken to its logical conclusion, Turkle (1997, p. 39) writes, the ultimate result is a disappearance of conventional reality (whatever that might be) from the world outside the computer into the virtual world expressed within the computer: "As the boundaries erode between real and the virtual, the animate and inanimate, the unitary and the multiple self, the question becomes: Are we living life on the screen or in the screen?" Here it is assumed that there has been an agreed upon "reality" in the past, that we are headed toward something virtual, and that a life in text has the ability to compete with the life experienced by the rest of the body. This existence requires a lot of sitting and typing (though with the development of virtual reality and other mediated environments, it may require a lot of gesturing, pacing, and yelling).

The Public and Private Boundary   Certainly there is a contested boundary between the public and private domains of Internet self-presentations. This boundary must be renegotiated both in online text-based discourse and in the "advertisement for oneself" represented by the graphics-based homepage with links to topics that the host feels comprise his or her online surroundings. Speaking to the public and private distinction, postmodernists argue that the Internet is essentially a private domain, an extension of the individual's mind and attributes—in fact, so private and anonymous that social identity is no longer bounded by physical existence attributes. In contrast, we view the Internet as public, as a syntopia or together place. But its illusion of privacy presents a boundary problem. New users or those engaged exclusively in recreational domains probably feel this illusion most strongly. In Internet contexts based in conventional purposes like professional discussion lists, the effort to find satisfactory boundaries between personal and private may be awkward at times, with inadvertent transgressions being both public and recorded (as the case below illustrates).

The Role of Anonymity in the Fragmented Self   An important aspect of the boundary claim is that the fragmented self can be anonymous. While this is true in a local context, we show that true anonymity is probably not attainable on the Internet or even in consciously chosen anonymous group media (see Hayne & Rice, 1997). The appearance of anonymity, though, can have some important (sometimes quite negative) consequences. Even the stories of the postmodern writers illustrate that overindulgence in fragmented selves (to the extent that one pretends to be another biological entity than is the case) and in games without consequence can both induce ennui. In the first example, Stone recounts the story of a male psychotherapist who posed as a disabled woman who then advised women about intimate aspects of their lives. The response was outrage when it was discovered that she was a he. Turkle shows that many users abandon MUDs, seeing them post hoc as "useless and addictive." In all of the stories, new kinds of interactions did became available for the actors, but the substantive outcomes often tend to be either nonproductive (Turkle, 1997, p. 198) or counterproductive outrage over the poses and the disclosures that result from false representation (Stone, 1996, pp. 74–78; Turkle, 1997, pp. 228–229). The anonymity by which the "selves" are achieved in the end seems to be the obstacle to any results that we count as "real" or satisfying. Moreover, anonymity is itself virtual and more and more transparently so.

Counterexamples to the Postmodern Argument

We have taken issue with the postmodern position that the Internet liberates users from physical identity. We have also pointed out the lack of an agreed-on definition of identity of the kind that both Stone and Turkle assume—that is, one person, possibly multiple identities. Finally, we have sketched out the kinds of boundary issues that the case for fragmented identity tacitly depends on—a social and technical boundary, a real and virtual boundary, and a public and private boundary.

This section presents our view of how the Internet works in terms of social processes relative to identity and anonymity. It examines how anonymous and virtual the Internet is and then what political premise underlies the idea of freedom on the Internet. One case presents what happens when someone tries out a persona on a professional discussion list and thus crosses the personal and professional boundary. In closing, it provides an analysis of a few homepages for ideas on how they differ from interactive text communication.

The Internet Is the Panopticon

The postmodern description of the Internet as a playground for the unbounded self fails to take into account the flip side of Foucault's arguments—the premise of the panopticon or constant view of individuals through parasocietal mechanisms that influence behavior simply because of the possibility of being observed (Foucault, 1979; Gandy, 1993). While Internet dialogue may provide a degree of privacy in the moment, it eliminates the ultimate privacy of all communication carried out over it. Box 12.1 provides examples of, and sites concerning, the absence of Internet privacy.

People play at multiplicity at their peril when they experiment with freedom from social constraints and at the same time let down the guards of normal social and political caution that generations have accrued. The anonymity projected by Gumpert (1987) and others onto Internet transactions is far from real (Spears & Lea, 1994). Internet users face prospects of microobservation, and the data collected thereby have no finite end to their existence or availability to inspection at a later time. And what appears to be a technically anonymous identity or discussion may be quite socially identifiable or at least perceived by other participants to be identifiable (Hayne & Rice, 1997). This raises a host of issues such as the extent to which participants are accurate in their determination of supposedly "technically anonymous" others and then the extent to which subsequent attributions about those others are correspondingly correct and appropriate, with consequences for later decision making and assessments. Thus virtual anonymity presents an illusion of privacy and a trap of almost unlimited potential by inducing people to cross critical public and private boundaries.

Box 12.1
Limitations of Privacy on the Internet

• An attempt to violate privacy is an attractive activity to many, and enormous ingenuity is used in its pursuit (Katz & Graveman, 1991).
• Anybody can publish almost anything about anybody else, including their private and personal information (⟨http://chicagotribune.com/news/printedition/article/0,2669,SAV-0106050231,FF.html⟩).
• Various Web sites, software, and Internet service providers track usage and even mouse movements, keystrokes, and clicks through what is often referred to as "spyware."
• General geographic location can be known about many Internet users, and mobile Internet or mobile phone users can yield precise information (Black, 2001).
• Vast archives are being kept of messages, postings, and e-mails, including instant messages (see ⟨http://news.cnet.com/news/0-1005-200-6333967.html?tag=owv⟩).
• Public key encryption methods appear flawed.
• Anonymous remailers and other anonymity-guaranteeing services have been compromised by browser software (⟨http://www.privacytimes.com/NewWebstories/anon_priv_11_16.htm⟩), and some may even be "false flags" to attract and identify precisely those who wish to use such services.
• Information is readily linked across sites (via systems such as ⟨doublclick.com⟩) and back to hidden bugs (⟨www.bugnosis.org/faq.html⟩).
• Internet usage patterns and standard user information required to make the Internet work can reveal personal identities (⟨www.privacytimes.com/NewWebstories/priv_3_7_01_fingerprint.htm⟩).
• Many Internet Web site "privacy policies" do not exist, are fatally weak (such as in the case of ⟨amazon.com⟩, allowing them to reverse policies and begin mining formerly protected data), or are regularly violated (⟨www.ecommercetimes.com/perl/story/10057.html⟩).

Implications of the Illusion of Anonymity: A Listserv Case

The e-mail transcript in box 12.2 illustrates why we find the idea of nonpersonally linked social selves problematical in nonfantasy settings. It is drawn from a business process engineering discussion list (BPR-L) concerning the professional "posing" of a list member.

This account presents a detection of a person using a "naive user" persona to call attention to a product in which he has a proprietary interest but does not label it as such. Note that to F.S. it was the message's "tone" that raised suspicions and led F.S. to take several measures—

Box 12.2
Example of Anonymity on a Listserv

Date: Wed, 21 Aug 19XX, 13:13:13 −0700
From: fs@gg.hh
To: bpr-l@xx.yy
Subject: Deceptive behavior of software vendor message

I feel I need to bring this to the attention of the entire list. Several days ago T.J. posted the following to the BPR-L [business process engineering discussion list]:

⟨Hey everybody, I just found what looks like a great new BPR software package. I think I'm going to pick up a package for my consulting practice. Take a look at it. ⟨http://www.process.model.com⟩. If you know of any other tools that are being used to make BPR easier, please let me know. Thanks.⟩

Then, yesterday, he posted the following:

⟨Is anyone on the list a ProcessModel user? I'd be interested in hearing from you. I looked at their Web site (⟨www.processmodel.com⟩), but I'd like to find someone actually using the software. Thanks T.J.⟩

I suspected from the tone of these posts that Mr. J. was actually employed by the software vendor. I responded once to the list, asking Mr. J. to confirm that he did not work for the software vendor. I also contacted him privately by e-mail. He responded privately to me in an indignant manner, denying that he worked for the software vendor.

However, a phone call to ProModel Corporation asking for T.J. quickly confirmed my suspicion. You may reach him yourself at ProModel Corporation at [work phone] if you want to prove this fact to yourself. Nearly all the software tool vendors that correspond to this list do so in a professional manner with full disclosure of their affiliation. It is sad that Mr. J. cannot follow their example.

The sad part is that the ProcessModel tool that Mr. J. is touting may in fact be an excellent tool. If so, it does not need his deceptive promotion.—F.S.

Note: Names have been modified.

contact the list, locate the real-world location of the product, and check the identity of the person posing as a list member.

The effect of the disclosure brings about a contrite message from T.J., who seems to want to remain a bona fide member of the list (since he publicly humiliates himself and does not simply disappear) or at least not damage his company further (see box 12.3).

T.J.'s apology is elaborate and addresses many implied social codes and contradictions, as well as offers ways for offended parties to mete out retribution. The response also underscores the need to engage in "normal" social behavior by providing an account for one's actions in cyberspace as in any other social domain.

These behaviors are attempts to restore the authenticity of T.J. as a sincere and virtuous person who wants to comply with social codes, is a locatable human, and is willing to learn from others. He places himself at the mercy of the list and through his self-exposure attempts to rehabilitate his reputation. These are the dimensions of his purported authenticity. Although disembodiment can be a departure from physical selfhood, many of the tokens of validity that T.J. offers to the list are historical in nature and indeed led to the location of him as a physical person. Physical and historical revelations—the offer to have a telephone conversation with anyone—are part of the sincerity ritual. Giving out both home and work telephone numbers is a way to add physicality to his electronic person by offering voice interaction, and clues to his home's location are validators.

Attribution issues also arose concerning book reviews posted to an online bookseller. When ⟨amazon.com⟩ discovered that book publishers were posting favorable notices of their products, it promised to indicate authorships of all publisher-posted book reviews.

Our argument about the tension surrounding the boundaries between anonymity and authenticity is supported indirectly by other studies of media choice involving electronic communication (Markus, 1990; Reder & Schwab, 1988; Rice, Kraut, Cool & Fish, 1994) in suggesting that social activity grounded in a purpose employs multiple media (whatever is appropriate) for accomplishing the purpose. It is also supported by research on how linguistic styles are used in an overall communication and social action strategy, how a medium has meaning and effect, and

Box 12.3
Follow-up Example of Anonymity on a Listserv

Date: Wed, 21 Aug 19XX, 15:05:09 −0600
From: T.J. tj@qq.rr
To: bpr-l@xx.yy
Subject: Apologies and thanks

Please accept my apologies to the list. I want to thank Mr. S. for pointing out that my efforts to generate interest in ProcessModel were not acceptable to the list. As soon as I got his voice mail, I ran home to post this message, not knowing that he would also be posting a message to the list about my obviously amateur efforts at Web site promotion.

I must say, in my own defense, that I never denied working for ProModel in any of my e-mail messages to Mr. S. (If you're interested in a copy of them, I'd be happy to forward them to any member of the list.)

I must also make it clear that my own efforts to promote the Process Model Web site was in no way directed or controlled by management at ProModel. I work in Web site development and promotion on the ProcessModel team. I am a novice at this new medium and have obviously followed some very bad advice. In my two previous posts, I put on a persona [emphasis added] designed to generate interest in the Web site. My intention was not to deceive. If that is how Mr. S. perceives it, I'm sure others will as well, and for that I apologize sincerely.

I will gladly accept scathing messages from anyone whom I have offended. I would also appreciate any remarks on how I might better do my job (even snide ones). In fact, if you wish to call me, dial my direct line at [work phone] or call me at home at [home phone]. Had Mr. S. left his number on the voice mail he left me, I would have called him to apologize personally. I would be happy to do the same with anyone else.

Despite my bumbling efforts at promoting the ProcessModel Web site, I think it would be worth your time to check out the product. I appreciate Mr. S.'s allowance that in fact ProcessModel "may be an excellent tool." Please do not judge the product of a company with eight years in the business by the errors of an employee with only months of experience on the Internet. If you want the URL, send me a personal message and I'll be happy to forward it to you. Thanks for your indulgence. Sincerely, T.J.

Note: Names have been modified.

how purpose guides formative context for selection of media (or language strategy) (Gumperz, 1971).

The real difficulty that Internet users face is the effect that boundary ambiguities in the virtual world affect the real world. Daily life and institutionalized forms of communication (such as business letters and publications) have a known intended audience and have tacit ground rules for the conduct of communication in a medium. Their violation, either through malice or ignorance, has long been the gist of office humor.

The Personal Homepage as Presentation of an Integrated Self

The triple boundary issues identified earlier also arise in tens of millions personal homepages. The personal homepage is a more recent phenomenon than MUDs, and despite what should be its compelling interest to communication scholars, it is largely unexplored. (We do not discuss commercial homepages.) The ways personal homepages are constructed —as a presentation of self for what are generally random or unknown viewers—add further evidence for rejecting arguments about the fragmentation of the individual in cyberspace.

These pages typically contain pertinent details that are important to the host and links to other topics. Although there are varying implications of homepages (discussed below), a key feature is that they move in the opposite direction of what the postmodernists would predict. Rather than fragmenting the self, personal homepages are, in general, attempts to integrate the individual, make a personal statement of identity, and show in a stable, replicable way what individuals stand for and deem important. The homepage viewing is the meeting, and most pages are set up as one-sided personal introductions. Homepages are in a sense advertisements for the self or a declaration of identity—a curriculum vitae, personal ad, reflective medium, and art project all rolled into one presentation and more integrative than any conventional medium.

The Ambiguous Boundary between Public and Private: Who Is the Audience?

In 1996, we used Alta Vista to locate arbitrary personal homepages for visiting. We selected 20 pages to examine their uses and meaning (see Wynn & Katz, 1997, for a more detailed analysis).

One striking aspect of these pages is that some homepage creators appear oriented toward the sheltered environment of a peer group, work group, or network of friends—a close community (as discussed in Chapter 6). We detected little that addressed a broader audience. Being unconcerned with the public-private boundary may be an aspect of cyberculture.

Unlike ordinary life, where we can be readily called to account for our behavior and personal histories, standards are ambiguous in the virtual medium. This is partly because there is no physical copresence to make the presenter cognizant of audience, provide the opportunity to mediate and mutually adjust the message, whether verbal or visual, and avoid undesired audiences. Further, the homepage genre is still developing as well as multidimensional: with no copresence or standard audience information, how is an individual to assess what is proper, circumspect, or normal? On the homepage there is no turning away, averting the gaze, or changing the subject as a response to unexpected changes or responses from the audience.

Homepages as a Social Context
To explore the boundary question in more detail, we discuss one homepage that turned up in the Alta Vista search. It belongs to "Ted Kee" (all homepage host names have been changed), who works in a telecommunications research laboratory and has an outrageous but not offensive page, which includes a reference to a romantic poem apparently written to a girlfriend, the "Cuddles" site, sites of his former colleagues at the Massachusetts Institute of Technology, and other interests.

The Public and Private Boundary and the Professional and Personal Boundary   Homepages represent tacit social contexts of the presenters. Presenters have either physical social contexts of real friends and colleagues or virtual social contexts of Net friends and topic groups. Sometimes they have both. Boundary issues become clear when presenters change contexts. Ted Kee's homepage was particularly contemporary in its freewheeling and cheerful self-disclosure and seemed out of context at first because it resided on the site of a telecommunications research lab and telephone companies tend to have a formal corporate cultures regarding to self-expression (Katz, 1995). For instance, the Cuddles site link on Ted's page just touches the boundary between cute affection and too much tickling. This is a selection of Cuddles material:

These are just examples of Tal attacks. Just enjoy them for what they are.... ⟨Pounce out from net onto tim⟩ ⟨Pounce Tim ⟨Bounce Tim⟩ ⟨Flounce Tim ⟨Trounce Tim⟩ ⟨Hug⟩ ⟨hug⟩ ⟨Bouncy hug⟩ ⟨tickling cuddles⟩ ⟨runs away⟩ ⟨moment of silence⟩ ⟨hear hooves trampling down mountain⟩ ⟨Tal on horse, waving fuzzy sword, Charges Tim⟩ ⟨Tickle Tim with fuzzy sword!!!⟩ ⟨chuckles to self⟩ Well you did ask.... ⟨giggles⟩ ⟨cuddle⟩ Tal.

Ted Kee's use of the Cuddles link on his homepage indicates a "softer" interest of his and a "fun" side of himself, but it is a reference to another site and is not his own homepage information. This is something that Ted visits, thinks is fun, but in terms of identity isn't Ted. The boundary situation of the Cuddles site itself is that it is playful, is slightly intrusive in an emotional way, and never transgresses any serious boundaries. It is playful and open but not exhibitionistic. The very fun of Cuddles is that it is safe and yet intimate.

Ted Kee's links, located on his corporate webpage, thus present a context-bending, boundary-confusing situation. Normally the presentation of employees on company media would represent company standards. Yet this homepage represents the individual. It could be inconsistent for a high-tech research lab to censor the innocuous content of its brilliant staff's homepages just as it would be inappropriate to tell employees how to dress, beyond basic shared conventions of propriety. We reviewed other homepages at the lab site and found that they conformed more to our expectation of a telecommunication industry electrical engineering style: personable but restrained—describing family, a few tastes, interests, and pets. The lab director's page focused on research interests. Ted's homepage style may have inspired an Asian manager in the lab to describe liking "hot, spicy food," a disclosure he might have made to try to keep up with the kicky style of his young colleague.

Distributed Contexts and Contextualized Online Selves   To explain the liveliness of Ted's homepage, we looked for another social context for his page. We followed links back to his recent alma mater, MIT, and to the homepages of his friends and colleagues, and what emerged was his milieu. In this new context, Ted's homepage projects a message that the telecommunication company lab has up-to-date young Internet enthusiasts from MIT.

Although his presentation remains an outlier for his new work context, it carries the panache of his alma mater rather than the implication of a person acting out of synch with his environment. This explanation is self-contained in the page itself. Rather than just tell us about himself, which he does, Ted can also illustrate his sources and let them speak for themselves so that we can interpret them as sources of influence on Ted.

Ted's page linked to the page of a colleague at MIT, whose page linked to Tabatha's. Tabatha works for a small software company. Her page is even less constrained than Ted's in its presentation and fosters an authentic-seeming Net identity, which has flooded out into print media discussions of Tabatha as an icon. Tabatha thus becomes a twice-removed social context for Ted. We might think that Ted is slightly outrageous for a telecommunication company lab employee, but his classmates' sites are much more so. This much deeper context for Ted is discovered just by going down one two-step path of his social links. Moreover, the richness of each of the sites on the path tells far more about him than he could express for himself. He is not those people and does not state his membership explicitly (which would tend to cast it into an interpreted one-dimensionality), but he shows that he is part of that milieu.

In this we see a far more powerful social force than the decontextualization of identity described by Stone (1996) and Turkle (1996). While we must consider the possibility that Tabatha is a constructed persona, many clues on her page render this unlikely. The more interesting fact is that the homepage creator (Ted) has the ability to add context to the presentation of self by allowing the visitor to inspect the referenced sites and explore the creator's worldview. The wider social context is displayed more fully and as a form of primary data rather than reconstructed in the individual's explanation of himself or herself. In Gergen's sense of the saturated self, the browser has access to a broad text and thus is in a position to construct an independent interpretation of the page creator. It is also the opposite of the page creator's constructing different and separate selves, which by definition are out of context and which we might expect were the postmodern perspective correct.

The relationship between the virtual and physical reference groups relative to the potential visitors to the homepage is worth noting. Here a distinction appears between those sites that have a work context as a primary reference and those that have a topic context as a primary reference. Some people may derive primary associations from their Web relationships, while others are simply reflecting their primary associations in their links.

Continuing Ambiguity of the Homepage   In contrast to the multiplicity argument posited by postmodern theorists, homepages seem to attempt to construct a unified presentation or at least to pull together diverse aspects of the self so that visitors can follow paths that interest them. They tend to present social context by their location and by the links they establish to other domains and other people. In this way they seem to be inherently social rather than focused on the (fragmented) individualism that is required for anonymous multiple presentations. Because they address an often presumed yet unknowable audience, homepages present unresolved boundary issues, especially in the areas of personal disclosure and privacy and security awareness.

Despite the advice we all received as children ("don't give out your phone number to people you don't know"), our Alta Vista sample revealed a homepage of an eight-year-old village girl in England, replete with family details and home information, a photo, and a voice recording. A single mother in Seattle described her suburb and child. These examples point to a homepage dilemma: to be aware of all the negative possibilities would inhibit most users from entering anything but the most formal information on a homepage. The apparent promise of a wider extension of self—some more essential, less formal, and more fully contextualized self—speaks to social needs, but the medium lacks the differentiators present in social domains, such as screens, gatekeepers, threshold behavior, and discriminating perceptions that tend to avert access by the wrong parties.

Although the homepage is a pulled-together and socially contextualized presentation of self, the self-presentation does not need to be totally consistent. It is less audience-selective than presentation in everyday life, if only because any Internet user has potential access to any publicly posted homepage. In this way, it has the possibility to be a boundary-shifting medium that carries over into physical domains. Alternatively, the homepage may remain a unique venue for the more architectural metaphor of postmodernism—the mixing of styles and features from multiple conventions. However, we see that the efforts at presenting diverse aspects of the persona on a homepage are better understood as attempts to first saturate the self and then juxtapose those multiple identities under a unified architecture of who the "self" is. That is, it allows the individual to differentiate and present specialized aspects of the self and then use the technology as a boundary-spanning mechanism to resolve the differences into an integrated individual. It seems no coincidence that people speak of "my homepage" in the singular.

Conclusion

Despite the claims of postmodernists, the Internet is not (certainly not necessarily) a place in which a physically locatable individual can be abandoned. Nor is it possible to have multiple selves divorced from a physical being. Rather, we find everywhere evidence of the socially grounded nature of identity building and interaction in cyberspace. Hence we see that cyberspace is becoming a syntopia.

While we agree that dimensions of the self can be explored and developed in cyberspace (indeed, that is part of its attraction), these are aspects of a unified individual—albeit one who is richer, more saturated, and more complex as a result of Internet exploration. The Internet makes available newly differentiated aspects of the unitary self as well as opportunities to reconfigure and reorder these newly differentiated aspects via a rich and ever-increasing variety of integrating and linking mechanisms. Thus, this interpretation is more in line with Gergen's argument about the ability to fully reflect one's self through a saturated identity than the fragmented identity of the postmodernists (Gergen, 1991; Gergen, forthcoming). The possibility of separate, disassociated selves exists, but the Internet actually has a tendency to bring these seemingly disassociated selves back into relationship with each other. On the other hand, the individual who ventures in an extreme way into dissociation and assumed anonymity may face potentially embarrassing if not disastrous consequences.

You can dissemble, lie, and cheat on the Internet (just as in the offline world), but you might be traced, tracked, and ultimately held to account, virtuality notwithstanding. The Internet no more (and thus no less) enables identity creation than do conventional communication technologies. These less glamorous communication technologies have largely escaped the attention of postmodernists. The CB radio (Stanley, 2001) and the telephone (Katz, 1999a, ch. 11; Marvin, 1990), for instance, are both frequently used to dissociate oneself from the socially located body and to indulge in created identities.

At the same time, many boundary questions are raised by the ever-novel uses of all these media, and they remain to be resolved as conventions applicable in one domain (physical social contexts) fail to translate to others. However, the resolution of boundary issues is part of the ongoing social process of contextualization and coconstructed self-presentation. It is part of the ever-derivative and ever-innovative choreography of social-based human interaction.

13

Interaction and Expression Examples

Internet-based interaction and expression build personal and social capital and give meaning and identity to people's lives. This self-interest benefits society because it motivates the creation of collective benefits. In this chapter, we examine users' experiences with Web sites to explore how online interactions affect family and friendship ties, and how online creative expression leads to both personal fulfillment and new social relationships.

Interaction to Form Social Ties and Relationships

Making New Friends
The Internet allows people to create and maintain new social relationships (see chapters 9 and 12): it can be used to search for a future spouse, to browse away some hours, to pursue a hobby with people from neighboring towns, or to find new friends in a new locale. Said one student: "In ⟨asianavenue.com⟩, I look for people located in California around my age since I'm planning to move there within the year. I figure it would be good to already have some friends over there.... You can go to sites and type in the gender, age, location, and other information under 'profile,' and it'll list everyone that's registered who fits that description" (Anonymous personal communication, April 13, 2001).

Meeting and Dating Online
Media Metrix says the number of people using online dating services rose between December 1999 and December 2000 from 3.4 to 5 million

Box 13.1
Student Opinions about Online Dating

> "I thought it would be fun to meet people from all over the country and all over the world."
>
> "I didn't take it seriously, but I was definitely curious as to what people talked about."
>
> "I thought only losers met people over the Internet, people who were social outcasts to begin with. But my friends were doing it, so I started to also."
>
> "At first I thought it would actually be boring just sitting there typing away. Then I learned you didn't just sit there. You actually got involved with other people. I found myself really wanting to hear what they had to say."
>
> "I found there were a lot of people on the Internet—not just losers ... successful, smart, funny people."
>
> "It's not such a big deal anymore when a friend tells me about someone they met online."
>
> "I think the stigma associated with online romance is starting to dissolve.... It's becoming more common and acceptable."
>
> *Source:* Anonymous personal communications, April 30, 2001.

(Stone, 2001). According to Trish McDermott of ⟨match.com⟩, "We bring people together who share core values and a lifestyle but who otherwise would never have met" (Stone, 2001). (⟨Match.com⟩ claims that its service has resulted in over 1,100 marriages.) But even without a permanent relationship as its goal, there is social-capital merit in Internet dating services. Another one student said, "I've found lots of dates online. That's what makes me happy. They don't have to last forever" (Anonymous personal communication, March 20, 2001).

Students are meeting and "dating" on the Internet. They have pre-arranged times when they "chat" in real time via keyboards or Internet telephones. They even have monogamous relationships this way, telling others who might ask that they will not go out with them because they are "dating" someone. The quotes in box 13.1 suggest that online dating and matchmaking are becoming normalized and that the stigma that was once attached to the process ("immoral," "for losers," "dangerous") is being lifted.

Box 13.2
The Value of Online Dating, from an Online Journal

> **Ginny:** I agree with Christine that more exposure doesn't mean more dates, but it sure means a lot more opportunities to meet some great folks and not-so-great folks. Ha-ha, it's like trying to find out what you want in your career—sometimes the easiest way is through the process of elimination. So I find the more people I meet, the more I find out what kind of qualities I don't care for in friends and potential partners.
>
> *Source:* Raymond's journal (2001).

Appearance can be important, and a photograph (albeit an atypically attractive one) can be a determining force in a decision to initiate online and offline contact. It is not uncommon for students to say that they corresponded with someone on the Internet because they found the person's picture attractive. "It's just like in real life. If I think you're cute, I'm gonna want to talk to you. Only it's easier for me to approach girls via the Internet because I can get really shy," explained one student (Anonymous personal communication, February 24, 2001). "As you get older, you know fewer and fewer people who aren't married. But go online, and there are hundreds of people who are single. It makes you feel a lot less alone" (Stone, 2001). Box 13.2 suggests one approach to dating online. Ginny's comments reflect that the social interaction search is but one aspect of the larger search one usually participates in throughout one's life—the identity project.

One woman who had been divorced said she felt too old for the bar scene and trying to find a man "sober enough to talk to." She tried online dating, and after two months of activity, she met a man. After a further two months of online chatting, she met him in person halfway between their respective homes in New Jersey. They married and at last report are living happily together (Anonymous personal communication, April 30, 2001).

By way of summary, table 13.1 lists many of the major online dating services. We present it to show the magnitude of the activity as well as to indicate the importance of "community" as an aspect of these Web sites, at least in terms of self-presentation.

Table 13.1
Comparative Attributes of Online Dating Services

Dating Services	Community Claim	Number of Members	Demographics	Forms of Communication	Number of Matches or Marriages	Resources
⟨Lovingyou.com⟩	Yes	N.A.	70% female 64% under age 35 64% single 34% married or involved 33% with household income of over $50,000	E-mail, message boards, public chats, support groups, organized events around the country	N.A.	Advice, love library, dating guide, dining, gift shop, fun and tools, love e-zines, shopping
⟨Udate.com⟩	Yes	3.3 million registered users	People from every category from around the globe	E-mail, private chats, runs events for members to congregate once in a while	N.A.	None
⟨2ofakind.com⟩	No	N.A.	N.A.	E-mail	N.A.	None
⟨Match.com⟩	Yes	Over 5 million registered users	39% female 61% male Average age 30s or 40s Professionals Salaries over $50,000 85% with some college or college degree	E-mail, special organized events, volunteer possibilities	500,000 matches and 1,100 confirmed marriages	MatchScene, dating expertise

⟨Datingclub.com⟩	Yes		80% male 20% female 59% under age 30 61% with incomes between $30,000 and $65,000 31% with high school education	E-mail, forums, public and private chatrooms, interest and demographic communities	N.A.	*Singles Monthly Magazine* (available in English, French, Japanese, Chinese, Spanish, German, Italian, and Hebrew)
⟨Kiss.com⟩	Yes	1.5 million members	Average age 25 to 49 40% female 60% male College educated Professional Single or divorced Single parent	E-mail, relationship expert, private chat	N.A.	Kiss shop, advice
⟨Datingfaces.com⟩	No	N.A.	N.A.	E-mail, private chat	N.A.	None
⟨Lovefinder.clickicc. com⟩	Yes	N.A.	N.A.	Relationship expert, email	N.A.	Advice, travel, sports, news, flower shop, lifestyle guide, things to do

Table 13.1
(continued)

Dating Services	Community Claim	Number of Members	Demographics	Forms of Communication	Number of Matches or Marriages	Resources
⟨Oneandonly.com⟩	No	Over 250,000 profiles	N.A.	E-mail, relationship expert	Average of one marriage every 3 days	Advice, opposite-sex manual
⟨Dreammates.com⟩	Yes	N.A.	N.A.	E-mail, private chat	N.A.	None
⟨Singlessearch.com⟩	No	N.A.	N.A.	E-mail	N.A.	Singles Mall, advice
⟨Matchmaker.com⟩	Yes	N.A.	50% males 50% females	E-mail, public chat, friends list, local-metro communities, special interest communities	N.A.	None
E-mail, public chat, message center	N.A.	None	⟨Matchamerica.com⟩	No	N.A.	N.A.

Source: Courtesy of Maggie Herbasz, personal communication, August 2, 2001.
Note: N.A. = data not available.

Box 13.3
Looking for a Spouse on the Internet

> Sara, 27, is an Indian-born Christian studying in America. After her parents' matchmaking attempts failed, she began her own search by registering with the Internet agency A1 Indian Matrimonials in what began as a search for penpals but quickly developed into a serious quest for a partner. The replies flooded in, and she quickly found a potential husband. "He's a doctor, a real golden boy with a flood of proposals from good families, but his parents have gone nuts trying to get him to accept."
>
> *Source:* Farrell (n.d.).

Finding Marriage Partners

Instead of undermining traditional forms of marriage creation, especially that of arranged marriages, the Internet speeds up and enhances the traditional form; in effect, it makes the tradition all the more viable. The Internet is being adapted to the arranged marriage because it can serve the spirit of that tradition, especially when other modern conditions and technologies seem to undermine tradition. For example, the possibility of emigration and the use of the technologies of modern transportation have led to dramatic flows of people around the world. In 1998 alone, 36,500 Indians and 13,100 Pakistanis moved to the United States (Reena, 2000).

This process of exploiting modern tools to serve ancient traditions is typified in the process of arranged marriages typical of the Indian subcontinent. With the Internet, marriage possibilities, especially for expatriates living in the United States, can be reviewed speedily and inexpensively. Anonymity can be protected, and a wide—indeed global —array of prospective partners can be reviewed. Photos can be exchanged, family backgrounds investigated, and the all-important horoscope can be examined. Today a user can do in a few hours what would have taken weeks or longer in the 1980s. Unlike more typical U.S. dating patterns, families are often involved (though by no means exclusively— see box 13.3) in searching for a partner. Indeed, when reviewing various online ads, we encountered many cases of brothers living in the United States looking for U.S.-based spouses for their sisters still in India.

People can choose to search not only by culture but also by any number of categories, including religion. For instance, Web sites such as ⟨new.catholicsingles.com⟩ and ⟨muslimmarriagejunction.com⟩ expand personal choices in the search for meaningful relationships by aligning core values.

While the Internet can foster traditions, it can also be used to create new opportunities. A growing number of Web sites put marriageable people from around the world in contact with mostly American men, taking the notion of the mail-order bride to new levels. American men who use the Web to search for a wife favor Russian/CIS women, followed by Asian women, particularly Filipina. A March 1998 survey of the reference site ⟨goodwife.com⟩ found a list of 153 Web sites that offer international matchmaking services (Scholes, 1999). Our review in mid-2001 found over 300 sites listed. The founder of a leading Russian contact Web site, ⟨idealmarriage.com⟩, said in late 2000, "There is a very big and growing demand for Russian women. In the past six months, and with almost no advertising except for just being on the Web, we have over 1,000 girls in our database, who are getting a total of about 200 letters a day from American and European men" (Varoli, 2000).

As many as 4,000 to 6,000 of the couples who yearly petition for immigration of the female spouse to the United States use this method. This volume represents about 3% of the direct immigration of female spouses to this country and 0.4% of all immigration to the United States (Scholes, 1999). Anyone interested in seeing more relationships and families being formed should be impressed by these numbers, even though they represent only a tiny fraction of the 2.4 million marriages that occur annually in the United States.

Certainly, online matchmaking presents many opportunities for abuse, just as there are in real life. Tabloid headlines attest to how these meetings can go awry: a cyberarranged date turned into rape, an online relationship led to a marriage in which one partner turned out to have the opposite sex than the one claimed, and a divorce suit claimed that the Internet was a form of alienating affection—that is, the husband spent too much time flirting on the Internet.

On the other hand, the Internet can be used to do some private sleuthing to learn if a potential partner has a criminal record, a stratagem used by at least one online dater. Dyane Roth has met 11 men in person but only "after putting their names into Internet sites that check criminal records, just to be sure" (Stone, 2001).

We do not claim that abuse never takes place online, for surely it does, or even that less abuse takes place online than in real life (we have found no data on the relative rates or intensity of misrepresentation or worse online versus offline). Rather, we see that greater opportunities are created for more people via the Internet and that these opportunities extend the possibilities of ordinary life. We do not find evidence that any of the real-life activities have been hurt. For instance, we see no evidence that the number of singles bars has been decreased or that divorce rates have risen due to the Internet. Instead, people who are not attracted to singles bars now have new and wider choices. The Internet cannot guarantee the trustworthiness or sincerity of people who are met online—no more so than, say, can a college mixer or newspaper personal ad. On the other hand, people's motives are not necessarily fixed. Someone could begin visiting a dating Web site with the intention of duping or tricking others, and in this they may succeed. Yet they may also get involved with someone and find true romance blooming.

Friendship Circles

Instant messaging (IM) technology allows cheap (or free) chatting between people and among groups of family or friends. Subscribers worldwide keep in touch—often on a moment-to-moment basis throughout the day—with those they care about using "buddy lists" of people who have agreed to be included on their instant messaging "rolodex." As of February 2001, the leading services claimed some 60 million subscribers worldwide—America Online Instant Messenger (AIM), 25 million; ICQ ("I seek you"), 9 million; Microsoft Network (MSN), 15 million; and Yahoo!, 12 million) (Hu, 2001). Considering that there is some duplication among lists (since some users belong to more than one group) and that some services do not allow ready interconnection to users of other services (AIM, for example, does not "talk" to people using competing software systems), a conservative estimate of IM users would seem to be at least 40 million. One estimate suggests that 12 billion text messages are sent worldwide each month to personal computers (PCs), personal digital assistants (PDAs), and mobile phones. Another three billion text messages are sent via pagers each month (Gartner Group, 2001).

People can be involved with their friends and family on a remote basis as well. With ICQ and browser-based mail programs, users can be away from their home computers or even mobile and still remain involved (even on a moment-by-moment basis) with others.

This activity leads to a vast outpouring of contact and interactivity. Many people enjoy the ready contact: "It makes me feel plugged in throughout the day. . . . I just like keeping up to date with everybody" (Anonymous personal communication, November 23, 2000). However, too much contact can be excessive, and some users flee the "always on" capability. According to another student, "I have a friend who just is always demanding contact. When I duck out of Instant Messenger, she begins sending me e-mails saying, 'Why aren't you on?'" (Anonymous personal communication, December 7, 2000).

Does instant messaging lead people to long for the physical presence of their friends or to feel overloaded with too many messages? We found no systematic data to answer this question. But on the basis of our discussions with students and colleagues, it appears that most who use the service enjoy it immensely and feel that it keeps their friendship circles alive and fit, even over long distances and long stretches of months and even years. Others turn off or never join an instant-messaging service to avoid the bombardment and remain off despite the occasional pleas from automatic sign-up services or friends who are already enmeshed in the instant-messaging universe. But of the millions of people are voluntarily participating in a system that allows them to update and interact with their friends, few seem to think it is a bad thing.

Trust and Social Relationships Online

Online relationships provide fewer cues about trustworthiness than do offline interactions. This leads to self-protective behavior. In the words of one online dater: "Well, you've got to get a feel for the place first and the people there. Just like in real life, you have to make some sort of judgment call. . . . Can you trust the person you are talking to or not? Of course, that takes time" (Anonymous personal communication, April 1, 2001).

Online daters do not have large emotional investments in their initial forays at social interaction. They report that they "wanted to have fun," "try it out," and "didn't take it too seriously." Hence, they did more lying when they initially started using the Internet. Common lies concerned age, sex, occupation, location, and physical appearance. However, this got "old real fast" (Anonymous personal communication, February 24, 2001). I.G. talks about her online boyfriend: "The longer I talked to him and the more he revealed, the more I revealed. I figured there was no point in consistently talking to someone if all I told were just lies." People sometimes forget their own lies and end up revealing the truth instead. For instance, K.W. states that in trying to impress an older woman, "I forgot that I told her I already graduated from college, and then later on I was complaining about how I had a paper and an exam on the same day.... Well, she noticed it, and when I told her the truth, she didn't know what to believe. She thought I was lying then! She eventually believed me though" (Anonymous personal communication, April 13, 2001; see also Uslaner, 2000, for an analysis of associations between online trust and other behavior on and offline).

Self-Expression: An Underestimated Aspect of the Internet

Self-expression is an important aspect of the "invisible mouse" concept (which we introduce in chapter 1 and discuss further in chapter 14). The motive to find a creative outlet spurs people to enormous effort, and the Internet is impressive in the way that it allows people of many interests and backgrounds to find a creative outlet. This in turn adds to the store of potentially useful and enjoyable material on the Internet and other social capital benefits. This section reviews some examples of Internet self-expression and interaction.

Religious Self-Expression

A Pew survey of churches (retrieved August 3, 2001 from ⟨www. pewinternet.org/reports/toc.asp?Report=28⟩) has highlighted the importance of religious interaction and expression on the Internet. The Pew group polled houses of worship (churches and temples) online and received 1,309 responses from congregations in 49 states. Of the 471 survey respondents, 83% believed that the Internet had helped their congregations in looking for information, researching sermons, and sending and receiving e-mails. Reverend Don Stein, pastor of the Calvary Lutheran Church in Whitewater, Wisconsin, has found that e-mail lowers the barriers to communicating with students. Being close to the University of Wisconsin at Whitewater, Reverend Stein regularly receives e-mails from students concerning religious and other issues. He told the Black Chronicle News Service, "Before e-mail, it was really difficult to talk to students because the dorms would be locked or they [the students] wouldn't be there." While "nothing is as good as talking to them face-to-face," he finds that "students are much more comfortable with e-mail" (Black Chronicle News Services, n.d.).

In terms of the larger U.S. population, Pew surveys show that 21% of Internet users have looked for religious or spiritual information online. This is a higher figure than those who have banked online (18%) or participated in online auctions (15%). Many Web sites and discussion groups are devoted to religious study and practice.

The Internet appears to have had the twin effects of making religious expression easier but also more individualistic. That is, people can express traditional religious practices easily via the Internet, link up with break-away groups, form their own subunits, and recruit new adherents to these heterodox views. In effect, the Internet has repeated the same effect we have seen in other domains: it lowers the barriers to participation and expression and weakens the traditional hold that centralized authorities (the gatekeepers) have over the production of social and intellectual capital.

Prayers ⟨Sourcelife.org⟩ offers real-time prayer and prayer-oriented chat opportunities. Its vision is for its chatrooms "to become a tool for the Lord to lead others to Him and to bless us with fellowship, and on-line live prayer" (retrieved July 27, 2001 from ⟨www.sourcelife.org/chat_rules.html⟩).

A further example is the Web site of the Harrison United Methodist Church in Pineville, North Carolina, which features personal human responses to most prayer requests. In the late 1990s, this 700-person congregation began to invite people to submit online requests for a

Box 13.4
Comments of a Church Webmaster

Early in 1998 our church, Harrison United Methodist, formed a prayer group to pray for congregation members or friends in crisis. Harrison had a Web presence at that time, which was nothing more than a brochure about us. As the founder and webmaster of our site, I was seeking a way to differentiate us and provide a true cyberministry.

I feel that God opened my eyes to this need and opportunity to allow Harrison to have a prayer outreach ministry that could truly be world-wide. I searched for a "cyber prayer group" but soon realized that there were only three established prayer sites. Those sites allowed you to post prayer requests but depended on others to happen upon the site to offer prayer. Our site would have a team of believers dedicated to pray for all requests.

If you notice, we don't offer any scripture or biblical references on our prayer request page. We want this to truly be an outreach to those in need—whether Christian, Jewish, Moslem, or any faith.

We have received requests from all corners of the world. In a typical week, we will receive five to 20 requests. Very few come from this area, but numerous requests come from India and Arab countries. We write a personal reply to most of the requests. Some we offer links to other sites with information on grief or financial aid. Our belief is if we can make a difference for just one person, then all the effort is worth it.

Source: Billy Sample, personal communication, August 3, 2001.

directed prayer or praise of God to be uttered in their name. The church has received local requests, but many come from international locations. The requests use a standardized form on the church's site and are then forwarded to church volunteers, who offer a prayer and respond to submitters with a personal electronic note, often with online references to sites that offer succor or information (box 13.4).

Confessions   It has been said that confessions are good for the soul, and there is significant traffic in online confessions. For instance, ⟨fess-up.com⟩ allows people to recapitulate their blunders (anonymity is said to be preserved, though registration is required). Their submissions are then rated by visitors. Visitors can also send private messages to those who have posted confessions. Veracity is not verifiable, but many confessions seem far too plausible. At ⟨fess-up.com⟩, most confessions seem to be

Box 13.5
A High School Senior's Confession

Category: Personal sins—Annoying habits

High school senior's description: I'm a high school senior ... and a chick. I keep cheeting on my diet, and I know I have to lose 20 more lbs in order for my life to get anywhere, and I tell people I'm working hard to lose it but I eat chocolate almost everyday.

Source: "Annoying Habits" (retrieved August 2, 2001 from ⟨www. fess-up.com/oneconfession.eml?idx=576⟩).

---

of a sexual nature, but other categories are excessive gossip and diet cheating (and, possibly, soon, spending too much time doing Internet research). Box 13.5 presents a representative nonsexual confession.

Self-Expression Leading to Interaction with Others

Art is a form of communication, and creating and posting art on the Internet can lead not only to works that others can appreciate and find interest in but also to social interactions and relationships. Added to this tendency to form a social bond is another human tendency—to use new technology as an innovative medium for self-expression. These characteristics can lead to a "virtuous circle" (unlike a vicious circle, where the feedback loop makes things worse, a virtuous circle has feedback loops that work to the benefit of all concerned). Having at least a potential audience brings forth creative efforts on the part of interested amateurs, which produce aesthetic and social benefits. As with most endeavors, not all products are ultimately deemed worthwhile and of sufficient quality to endure.

Life Experiences as Shared Experiences

Personal Homepages   Chapter 12 discussed how personal homepages are often elaborate forms of self-presentation and as such are a form of self-expression. We also noted how they could result in new relationships. Here we wish to link the personal homepage to the idea of interaction with others. Some of our evidence is drawn from a study by Klein (1997) and reflects the motives of some early Internet users.

Klein's 1997 study used a random method to select nearly 500 home-page addresses from a personal homepage directory listed in the Yahoo! Personal Pages. These addresses were surveyed via e-mail to study the motives and experiences of people who created homepages (Klein, 1997) and yielded a sample of 138 owners of personal homepages (a 27% response rate). The researcher found that one out of eight personal home-page owners had built a page primarily out of a desire to meet other people, and nearly half of the others said this was a secondary reason. An additional 4% volunteered that the primary reason they set up their homepage was to keep in touch with family and friends (this had not been offered as a response category but was written in as "other"). Roughly consistent with Internet usage at the time, 20% of the respondents were women. No statistical differences were found between men's and women's motives for setting up personal homepages, but 65% of the 26 women in the survey had established a homepage within a year of first going online, whereas only 25% of the men had done so (Klein, 1997).

Our 2000 national survey and the Pew March 2000 survey provide some evidence to the contrary, however. In the 2000 survey, of the 99 who indicated they had personal Web pages, there was no statistically significant association between webpage creation and sex, age (below 40 or at least 40), or recency of adoption (less than one year, at least one year). The same was found to be true in the PEW data, except that of the 75 personal Web page owners, 60% were males and 40% were female.

Life Recording, Diaries, and Blogs   Yahoo! has a variety of sites for Weblogs ("blogs") and Webdiaries listed (238 as of June 16, 2001). Blogs, one of the most popular forms, are impressionistic, autobiographical journals of events, and observations in a person's life. Blogs often have multimedia supplements. Probably the most popular blog site, with more than 75,000 registered members, is ⟨blogger.com⟩. A few examples of what is offered at ⟨blogger.com⟩ are shown in box 13.6.

Visually Expressing the Lived Life for Observers   The Webcamera adds an ever-changing visual and often voyeuristic aspect to the Internet by filming live-action events and allowing Internet users to view them.

Box 13.6
Examples of Blog Self-Descriptions

---

mY cRaZy LiFe

Just me ranting and raving about my life, and how weird, confusing, distressing, fun, interesting, and crazy it is.

Most of the Time, Out of Sight*

A weblog for me, Jessica. Mostly keeps me from saying inane things to people who don't really care.

Geek-tastic

Maybe I'm weight-obsessed and man-obsessed, but I'm not shallow.

Brazilian Music Treasure Hunt

Notes from a search for musical treasure from Brazil. A quest for insight and wisdom that has a tendency to lapse into compulsive shopping.

Jenn Powazek

A personal site about the trials of living in New York and trying to get a Broadway show.

Tim's Journal

The thoughts and adventures of a guy trying to get through life. After hours, he's a muay thai fighter and body builder. During the day, he's an ad agency copywriter. Otherwise he spends his time watching loads of movies, tinkering with his dotcom, and trying to appreciate literature.

The Daily Dave

If you have a taste for random esoteric thoughts, or the occasional anecdote—you're not alone! Crawl inside Dave's mind, and be warmed by the constant churn of interesting but useless information.

Source: "Bloggers" (retrieved August 2, 2001 from ⟨www.blogger.com/directory/lastUpdateDirectory_1.pyra⟩).

Box 13.7
Jesse and I Met via My First WebCam Page

Jesse and I met via my first webcam page.... We met in person a short time later, and it was love at first sight. Really! It does exist! Every moment we spent together was special, and FYI our first meeting was in Athens, GA. Not the most romantic place in the world, but my darling Jesse took an 18-hour bus ride to get there! We spent a week together and decided we were destined to be together. Consequently, Jesse moved to Seattle to be with me.... We thought it was only appropriate—with the way we met and the way that we continue to live (on cam)—that we have a webcam wedding.... Please don't stalk us, we don't appreciate it. ;-) We are real people, and as much as we live in the public, there is a limit to how friendly we are with those who watch us.

Source: "My Love" (retrieved August 1, 2001 from ⟨www.users.qwest. net/~jmayes/⟩).

Nearly 8 million WebCams were sold in 2000, and 14% of Internet users have them (retrieved August 7, 2001 from ⟨www.bayinsider.com/ partners/kicu/specialreports/scripts/svb_062901.html⟩).

For some people who turn WebCams on themselves, sharing most aspects of their daily lives is a way to make new acquaintances. For others, life under the casual surveillance of unknown outsiders appears to be a way to heighten their own enjoyment of everyday events. We could not find estimates of the number of people who have WebCams operating from their living quarters, but a casual search found several directories that listed thousands (some may be inactive links). Some were sexually oriented, even to the point of being entirely commercial pornography rather than slices of life. Yet others showed plain life as it is lived. One such site, highlighted in box 13.7, assures visitors that they will encounter no sex or nudity. Most of the content captured by Web-Cams is not necessarily compelling. For instance, Andrew Stein found a WebCam site that consists entirely of the room of an angry teen. The angry teen issues visitors the following invitation: "Wanna watch a lazy stoner listen to the Ron and Fez [radio] Show live on the Net?" (Andrew Stein, personal communication, July 18, 2001).

A good overall index, suggesting the range of WebCam activities, is ⟨earthcam.com⟩ ("where the world watches the world"). Included under its 14 different subject headings and five EarthCam guides are topics (and subtopics) such as Society and People (personal, religion), Computer Cams (labs, personal), and Video Chat Cams (dorm rooms, real life, people). Each day, about 30 new WebCams are added to its listing, and the site itself receives more than 2 million daily visits from people. EarthCam's chief executive and founder, Brian Cury, said, "People are screaming to communicate using this medium. Within hours, they start to create an affinity with the people they're looking at" (Taylor, 2000).

Carla Cole (⟨carlazone.com⟩) has a discussion board, chat, and daily journal on her Web site. Her WebCam is set to update a still image every 30 seconds. Unlike her more famous antecedent, Jennicam (⟨jennicam.com⟩, operated by Jennifer Ringley since 1996), which has occasional and incidental nudity, Carla has never been and never intends to be naked on her WebCam. Carla sees her effort primarily as a way to meet people from around the world and to share with them (Stokley, 2001). WebCams and "real TV" (particularly shows with video feeds of participants, such as *Big Brother*) clearly indicate a changing sensibility about exhibitionism, voyeurism, and socially shared private behavior. (For a more detailed exploration of WebCams in U.S. society, see Calvert, 2000.)

Literary Expression   Literary expressions on the Internet include peotry, short stories, and novels as well as news reporting, journalism, pure opinion pieces, and carefully documented research results. In this section, we look at fan fiction and the "me-zine." (Weblogs, or blogs, could easily fit in this section as well as in the previous section.)

Mary Ellen Curtin estimates that roughly a quarter million stories have been posted for one particular domain of fiction, "fandom" (see table 13.2). Fandom is a genre in which people write stories using popular characters from fiction as central figures. (The word *fandom*, Curtin reminds us, originated more than a century ago to make the analogy between baseball enthusiasts and the words *kingdom* and *Christendom*.) Thus characters such as Captain Kirk and Mr. Spock of Star Trek fame or Harry Potter at Hogwarts might be cast as characters in a fiction story written by an amateur, either in the settings in which they usually figure or mixed in with other characters, eras, and situations. Curtin, who has been following and contributing to this area for an extended time, shares her thoughts in box 13.8. (She also contributed table 13.2.)

Table 13.2
Selected Listing of the Largest Archives of Fan Fiction and Number of Stories, July 2001

Archive	Fandom	Number of Stories Listed
⟨Fanfiction.net⟩ (lists 947 different fandoms)		225,118
	Largest fandom subtopics:	
	Digimon	16,822
	Harry Potter	16,285
	Gundam Wing	13,864
	Dragon Ball Z	8,791
	*N Sync	6,453
	Sailor Moon	6,037
⟨Gossamer.org⟩	*X-Files*	19,403
⟨Trekiverse.org⟩	*Star Trek*	9,500
⟨geocities.com/Hollywood/Academy/5307⟩ and ⟨squidge.org/archive⟩	*The Sentinel*	6,983
⟨slayerfanfic.com⟩ and ⟨dymphna.net/ucsl⟩[a]	*Buffy the Vampire Slayer and Angel*	6,612
Total of largest archives		267,616

Source: Courtesy of Mary Ellen Curtin, personal communication, August 1, 2001.
Note: Data collected in August 2001.
a. This is a pair of archives—one for adult and one for all-ages fiction.

One reason that fan fiction is so popular is that grows out of popular culture. As Jenkins (1992) observes, the characters in popular fiction belong to the entire culture. Thus, just as in earlier times people could make up and alter stories about Paul Bunyon, today's fans feel free to do the same for their characters, many of whom are first encountered in TV or book series. Even after TV shows are cancelled or their characters are changed to suit the show's producers, fans enthusiastically create continuing and alternative lives for the characters.

As in so many other areas of the Internet, online interactions graduate to face-to-face interactions, and individual interests are transformed into

Box 13.8
Creative Fiction on the Internet

The Internet contains a vast jungle of creative work. I'm particularly interested in people using the Internet to share fan fiction—works ranging from novels to haiku based on TV shows, comics, computer games, books, movies, and even music, NASCAR, and WWF stars. Table 13.2 merely suggests the incredible volume and diversity of fan fiction writing. Not even half of the English-language material is covered by these URLs. I collected these statistics in the summer of 2001. I guess that, like everything else on the Internet, fan fiction has been doubling in volume about every 12 to 18 months.

At a science fiction convention, author Theodore Sturgeon once said, "Nine-tenths of science fiction is crud." After a stunned pause, he added, "Nine-tenths of everything is crud." Sturgeon's Law certainly holds for online fan fiction. The majority of writers at ⟨fanfiction.net⟩, for instance, claim to be under 20, and it shows in their writing. But mixed into the ocean of bad or immature writing are some of the best stories being written anywhere, works that do just what fiction is supposed to do—examine the human condition. That they use preexisting lenses from popular culture—Vulcans, vampires, and Amazon women—doesn't make them less powerful but more.

Source: Mary Ellen Curtin.

individual benefits and social capital. A young person who lived in Brooklyn and made innumerable postings to an Internet board named the Bronze flew to Los Angeles to attend the 1998 annual Bronze gathering. Among the approximately 150 attendees, she met a person who helped her get a job as an assistant to a coexecutive producer for an ABC show called *Strange World*. After the short-lived show was canceled, she joined the TV show *Angel* as a script coordinator, submitted a script on speculation, and eventually became a writer for the show (Schulz, 2001).

Fan fiction is only one of many modes of creative literary expression on the Internet. ⟨Poetrysuperhighway.com⟩ lists almost 300 poetry-writing sites (retrieved August 5, 2001). Some sites have computer-generated poetry, including haiku, and others encourage online poetry by offering a forum and a way to provide critical opinions and constructive comments to those who submit efforts. One such site is ⟨exposedbymari.com⟩ (retrieved August 5, 2001 from ⟨http://clubs.

yahoo.com/clubs/exposedbymari⟩). This site has chat and a discussion and comment board; it is run as a free club. The site owner, Mari, greets visitors as follows: "Welcome all. Poetry of all types is welcome here, but please no X-rated or satanic poetry. Feel free to post as much as you like, and do comment, but please be nice and sincere. All poems here are under copywrite [sic] by the poets. Please remember this, and enjoy the poetry and club." The site has 77 members and receives about three to five visits a day. Another site offers "Real time poetry collaboration. You are invited to add a line to a poem in progress and view the finished works" (retrieved August 5, 2001 from ⟨www.csd.net/~cantelow/poem_welcome.html⟩).

Another genre of writing, which also reflects the ability of the Internet to be a form of self-expression, is a growing form of journalism called the *me-zine*, a play on *e-zine* (electronic magazine) (Kuczynski, 2001). Me-zines are usually Web site postings or newsletters created by a journalist working from home. In 1998, Virginia Postrel (⟨www.vpostrel. com⟩) a libertarian, began her site to publicize her latest book. Recently, she has begun making a small profit from her efforts because of an ⟨amazon.com⟩ "tip box" that she attached to her Web site. But far more than making money, she says, "I think this enterprise is about self-expression."

Some me-zines are quite popular, such as the one run by Andrew Sullivan, an editor at the *New York Times*. ⟨Andrewsullivan.com⟩ now gets about 180,000 individual users monthly. Another popular site, begun in 2000, is run by Edward Jay Epstein, the author of *Dossier: The Secret History of Armand Hammer* and *News from Nowhere*. He finds that readers of ⟨edwardjayepstein.com⟩ can sometimes give him valuable news tips for his new book about the business aspects of Hollywood (Kuczynski, 2001).

Collaborative Visual Art On the Internet, many new forms of individual expression in the visual arts are experimental and yield new opportunities for interaction and new relationships. In one experiment, "Life Sharing" (at ⟨www.0100101110101101.org⟩) two Italian artists offer almost complete access to their computer, which they claim represents their lives. This is an internal digital version of a WebCam, or what we

Box 13.9
"Uirapuru" by Eduardo Kac: A Multimedia Webart Performance

Eduardo Kac presented his work "Uirapuru" from October 15 to November 28, 1999, at the InterCommunication Center (ICC) in Tokyo. He describes it as a computer simulation of a flying fish "that hovers above a forest in the gallery, responding to local as well as Web-based commands. Audio and video from its point of view are streamed on the Web. Local and remote participants interact with the avatar of the flying fish in a virtual world. When this happens, the flying fish sings in the gallery. 'Pingbirds' (robotic birds) sing Amazonian bird songs in the gallery in response to the rhythm of Internet traffic. Pingbirds monitor the rhythm of the Internet by sending ping commands to a server in the Amazon. This work unites telepresence, multiuser virtual reality, and networking into a single realm of experience."

Source: "Uirapuru" (retrieved August 5, 2001 from ⟨www.ekac.org/interactive.html⟩).

might call a "computer cam." They post all their e-mail messages and make publicly available most of their computer files. They have financial support from a U.S. art center and are involved in preparing an exhibit for Venice's Biennale art show. In addition to expressing the view, with tongue in cheek, that "we don't have emotions; we have a Hewlett-Packard," the couple has been approached by "people we'd never met that knew everything about us" (Mirapaul, 2001, retrieved August 1, 2001 ⟨www.nytimes.com/2001/04/16/arts/16ARTS.html⟩).

A more systematic attempt at artistic creation jointly produced via the Internet is a piece of performance art in which the performer has his moves choreographed jointly and remotely by Web denizens. Using virtual reality technology, the performer moves according to input from Internet users who can hear and see him and whom he can see (Francalanci, 2001). Another illustration of an artistic production that was jointly produced and enjoyed via the Internet is given in Box 13.9.

The Internet also can be used to uncover and promote hidden talent. The Screenplay Submission site (⟨www.zoetrope.com/join.cgi⟩) is part of Francis Ford Coppola's American Zoetrope virtual studio. (American Zoetrope and associated production companies are owned by Coppola, who directed the Godfather films.) The Web site offers complete motion picture production on the Web, collaborative tools for writers, directors, and producers, and film-related discussion sections and chatrooms. Over 2,000 members have registered at the site, and on a typical day 200 people participate in its reviewing system (some receive as many as 15 critiques during a 30-day term). Screenplays that are evaluated highly are reviewed by Coppola's production company. According to Tom Edgar, the Web developer and sysop of American Zoetrope (and writer-filmmaker, with *Alcatraz Avenue* to his credit), "A screenplay from the site has at least as much chance of being bought or optioned by Zoetrope as one sent by an agent. Perhaps even more, since it comes with rave reviews by a number of disinterested third parties" (Dubelyew, n.d.).

Reviews are provided by anyone who is interested, and aspiring writers must read and review four screenplays (by others) before they can submit a screenplay. For each four screenplays they review, they can upload a screenplay of their own. This intriguing way to create an online information economy results in newly created social capital while screening out free riders. Edgar has said that American Zoetrope's ultimate aim is to "use the Web site workshop to eventually include all of the creative tasks that go into filmmaking; editing, directing, acting, music, design.... entire film projects [will] come together through these sites, where the most talented members of each of these disciplines become the crew to shoot some of the best screenplays" (Dubelyew, n.d.).

Other Forms of Joint Artistic Expression
Social capital is created by artistic self-expression, and much of this self-expression seeks an appreciative audience.

Music Production   Jimmy and Doug's ⟨farmclub.com⟩ is an interactive music site aimed at the contemporary teen audience and has features that encourage both artists and fans. It was founded by two record company executives who said they wanted to "renew and foster the true communal spirit of music" (Flick, 1999, p. 18).

Internet Karaoke   Karaoke singing online is yet another example of how people are able to put new technologies to uses that would probably not have been anticipated by their original designers. Karoke is available from many Internet service sites, such as Yahoo! and Excite. ⟨Paltalk.com⟩, one of the more successful, has found that more than 1,000 karaoke rooms may be active. Said one participant: "There are some absolutely awesome voices out there. When you get on Paltalk, you're hearing people from everyplace—Australia, England, all kinds of foreign countries.... There are operatic rooms in there—just basically whatever kind you want to sing" (Kanaley, 2001).

Creating Games as a Form of Self-Expression   In the 1980s, the available hardware for computer games was simple enough that one person could create, design, program, and market a game. Beginning in the 1990s, though, the rapidly growing complexity of the programming required for computer games has meant that commercial developers have had to work in large, specialized teams. At the same time, the Internet has reduced distance as a factor so that developers no longer need to be colocated. The Internet also reduced another barrier—that of professional employer and amateur enthusiast. Consequently, the talented individual or team can participate again in creating a complex, commercial-level game.

Beginning with the highly successful 1996 Quake, professional developers have begun allowing consumers limited access to the game's code so that they could make modifications (with the resulting games known collectively as "mods"). These mods can range from something as simple as replacing original game characters with celebrities to something as complex as making completely new games. Major publishing houses such as Sierra have realized the potential of these amateur games and have fully supported the amateur mod community with frequent software and documentation updates. Thus, these mod developers have become "farm teams" for the major publishing houses. If the amateurs come up with engaging modifications, these modifications may be commercialized.

The Internet provides an efficient medium for distributing these modifications to a mass audience, allows the formation of new development teams, and provides a channel through which team members may communicate and share workloads. A dramatic example of this new breed of virtual studios is the development team behind the extremely popular modification, Counter-Strike. Despite being a free amateur modification of an already existing game (Half-Life), it is currently the most popular online action game on the Internet. It was an instant success in 1999, and its popularity has skyrocketed. Half-Life's publisher, Sierra, was so impressed that it subsequently bundled the modification in boxed versions of Half-Life and intends to release a single-player version of the game to retail stores.

The designers of the game were two college students who had never met face to face: Minh "Gooseman" Lee of Vancouver, British Columbia, and "Cliffe," of Virginia Polytechnic Institute and State University in Blacksburg, Virginia. All communication and collaboration were handled via the instant messenger service ICQ (personal communication with Cliffe, June 26, 2001). While Minh and Cliffe did the majority of the coding and designing, other chores, such as level design, were delegated to strangers who volunteered their time. Minh and Cliffe "had almost begged [the Half-Life mod community] for maps to get made" (⟨http://csnation.counter-strike.net/features/csy1/⟩).

Although its two main programmers have never met each other and a good portion of the work was done by anonymous volunteers, Counter-Strike is the most popular online action game today, beating out professionally designed games like Quake3 Arena and Unreal Tournament. To give a comparison, ⟨gamespy.com⟩, a Web site that tracks how many people are currently playing various online games, reports that on the evening of June 26, 2001, 36,126 people were playing Counter-Strike online, and 16,623 people were playing the next five most popular games combined (Unreal Tournament, Tribes2, Quake3: Arena, Starsiege: Tribes, and Quake II, respectively) (⟨www.gamespy.com/stats/index.shtm⟩).

Despite the advantages of working in close quarters and sharing instant communication among team members, the Internet conferred advantages not traditionally utilized by traditional development houses, such as the ability to appeal to the fan community online for help. Game development studios probably will not turn into virtual offices where members of the design team telecommute from home. But the Internet allows the workload to be distributed to groups in various locations and does not force all groups to work at a central location.

Software Development as a Form of Creative Expression   The rise of the Linux operating system has been spectacular to the point of challenging Microsoft's Windows system. Working under the same general model of collaborative distributed contributions, Linux has had great impact on the world of computing. In began July 31, 1992, when Finnish computer scientist Linus Benedict Torvalds issued a call for help via Usenet (retrieved July 31, 2001 from ⟨www.li.org/linuxhistory.php⟩). With gathering momentum, developers around the globe responded. An important characteristic of Linux is that it is open source, which allows contributors anywhere to work on it. Developers can add features or correct deficiencies.

Thus, a project of a single developer has turned into a vast collaborative enterprise in which more than 40,000 people around the globe have volunteered their time and expertise. Despite a lack of a formal organization or central authority, Linux has attained immense size. The kernel alone consists of nearly a million lines of code, and the peripheral programs of Linux's commercial distribution are composed of millions more. This achievement is all the more impressive in that writing code for complex software operating systems, a difficult undertaking for even large corporations, is even more impressive given that it is done by part-time hackers scattered across the Internet (Kuwabara, 2000; ⟨www.firstmonday.org/issues/issue5_3/kuwabara/⟩). This may be one of the single largest and most consequential examples of developing social capital through the Internet, motivated largely by individual self-interests.

Political Expression

In this section, we offer examples illustrating political expression through organized political Web sites, school Web sites, political parody and attack Web sites, and hate-group Web sites and also examine questions of privacy of political expression on Web sites.

Organized Political Web Sites

The Internet offers surfers numerous ways to express themselves politically. With a click of a mouse, they can post online opinions, lend their names by signing a petition online, respond to a survey, or launch spamlike e-mails to lists of elected officials (especially members of the Congress) and all top federal executive departments and agencies.

For instance, at ⟨speakout.com⟩, petitions are available concerning the death penalty, power regulation, handgun lockout devices, and universal health care. Even more petitions are available at ⟨e-thepeople.com⟩, where visitors are invited to start their own. Among the hundreds of petitions at this site are ones to make English the official language of the United States, require "plant facts" labeling on household plants to reduce accidental poisoning by ingestion, and "Stop cops from killing friendly dogs and puppies in Maryland" (retrieved August 12, 2001 from ⟨www.e-thepeople.com/affiliates/national/index.cfm?PC= PETFV1&PETID=522882⟩).

Web site postings can be created at no cost and can espouse any point of view or claim. Sites can attack anyone for anything (as long as writers are careful to avoid libel laws). They can propagate any rumor, assertion, or babble no matter how ludicrous, irrational, stupid, or hurtful. Any lie can be presented as truth. (On the other hand, people are allowed to post any truth or helpful comment as well. The playing field is not level, by any means, but the full range of opinion and dissenting opinion can be expressed, with only a few exceptions, such as threats of violence.

School Web Sites and E-mail
Freedom can play itself out in ugly ways, especially in a school setting during an era of high concern about violence. Schools have special responsibility for the welfare and education of their students, and attempts to meet these responsibilities can run directly into constitutional protections of free speech. When one school did not allow its students to express certain views in a student-run newspaper, the students organized an online newspaper that was written, produced, and published electronically beyond school control. The authorities tried to challenge it but were unsuccessful. Similar off-campus student endeavors, including a site that allows students (and visitors) to vote on the "best" rumors, are protected by free-speech and freedom-of-expression considerations, and the subjects of the rumors are largely without direct recourse.

According to the Student Press Law Center (SPLC), the First Amendment to the U.S. Constitution protects off-campus expressions from the control of government (including public schools): "Public school officials cannot legally censor or punish a student for posting a personal home-page, publishing a Web-based 'zine,' or using a personal account to send e-mail outside of school from a home computer, even if the subject mat-ter of the site is school-related or offensive." Since the First Amendment limits only government restrictions on speech, private school admin-istrators may have more latitude in punishing students or censoring their off-campus speech (retrieved August 11, 2001 from ⟨www.splc.org/resources/cyberlawguide1.html⟩). This limit has resulted in some pro-tracted court cases in which students seek relief for having been punished for "jokingly" using the Internet to seek money for a hit man to kill a teacher or to make disparaging remarks about the genitalia of their teachers (Illinois Association of School Boards, 2001, summarizes these cases).

Parody and Attack Web Sites

Humor and satire also abounds on the Web. Early in the 2000 election campaign, the owner of a parody Web site, ⟨www.gwbush.com⟩, was harassed by workers for the George W. Bush campaign who petitioned the Federal Election Commission to force him to "cease and desist" his satire of Governor Bush's Web site. The 2000 election was unusual in the rich humorous material that satirized the protracted and puzzling resolution in Florida. Satirical news stories, for example, reported on the "nationwide riots" and "National Guard responses" as partisans fought throughout the country burning cities. One site reprised in parody form the election-night mobile phone call that Vice President Al Gore made to Governor George W. Bush retracting Gore's first concession. After the election, another site parodied the Bush-Cheney transition Web site by offering its own mimicry. "Welcome to the Bush-Cheney Transition Site!" headline greeted visitors. Then visitors were told, "Putsch your money where your mouth is." It also includes the painful pun claiming that its goal is "Parody for Parity" (retrieved August 11, 2001 from ⟨http://bush-cheneytransition.com/sys-tmpl/homepage2/⟩).

Attack Web sites also proved popular in the 2000 election. These included ⟨www.hillaryno.com⟩, which was supported by Friends of Guiliani, a committee that backed Hillary Clinton's opponent, New

York Mayor Rudolph Guiliani, for U.S. Senator. The Republican National Committee built a Web site attacking Vice President Gore titled ⟨www.gorewillsayanything.com⟩. But parody and satire are by no means limited to political candidates. So many satirical Web sites are aimed at conservative commentator Rush Limbaugh that a Web site has been dedicated to listing sites (negative and positive) about him.

Even more broadly, the Internet also allows political dissent and critical free speech in the form of parody or insulting Web sites that attack corporations. Wal-Mart and McDonald's have been frequent victims. One of the most vigorous critics of a corporation has been ⟨untied.com⟩, which encourages, publicizes, and archives complaints against United Airlines. At many complaint Web sites, consumers can register complaints and even get a response from the target organization. Seattle Washington's Office of Consumer Affairs is one example (⟨www.ci.seattle.wa.us/finance/consumer/complaintform.htm⟩).

Hate Groups

Hate groups also propagate their messages on the Internet. These include the Imperial Klans of America (⟨www.k-k-k.com⟩) and ⟨stormfront.org⟩. ⟨Stormfront.org⟩ is apparently the first, and certainly the most popular, hate Web site. It boasts more than 5,000 daily visitors and several hundred daily visitors to its "children's pages." The children's page, run by the teen son of the Web site owner, offers puzzles and games, animated Confederate flags, and sound files of white-pride songs (McKelvey, 2001). The latest edition of *Intelligence Report* notes that "Internet-based 'radio' shows stream racist music around the world at all hours of the day. In the U.S., racist music from 123 domestic bands and 229 foreign ones is available online from more than 40 distributors" (⟨www.nytimes.com/2001/08/20/opinion/20HERB.html⟩).

The information revolution is global, and freedom of expression in the United States affects other countries. Because the United States has among the world's most protective policies toward free expression, due to its Bill of Rights, U.S. freedoms conflict with the laws of other governments that limit harmful and incendiary propaganda. This is especially pertinent for Germany, which has been particularly vigilant in restricting inflammatory speech since World War II. In 2001, the German government reported that the number of far-right hate sites available in Germany had doubled in one year. About 90% of these 800 German-language Web sites were based in the United States and thus beyond the reach of German police, according to an official from the German federal Office for the Protection of the Constitution. This U.S. presence allows the sites to avoid Germany's strict laws barring racist propaganda (Agence France-Presse, 2001a). The Internet's potential for harm has been addressed by Mary Robinson, the United Nations commissioner for human rights. At the 2001 International Forum on Combating Intolerance, she said that the Internet "becomes, in the hands of some, a weapon of racism" disseminating "messages of hate and prejudice.... We must be alert to the corrupting effect of such messages" (Agence France-Presse, 2001b).

Privacy of Political Expressions

Internet users can collect information on individual users by tracking visits to Web sites. The information provided at or surreptitiously collected from sites may result in lifelong profiling that can affect the ads, e-mails, and solicitations sent to individuals and also influence future opportunities.

⟨Aristotle.com⟩ is an online consultancy that collects enormous amounts of personal data. It claims to have a list of more than 150 million registered voters. Among its armamentarium are tools that identify large contributors and frequent voters (dubbed "fatcats" and "super-voters") and that track who casts absentee ballots and online banner ads directed at specific voter groups (Johnson, 2000; Zeller, 2000).

Many campaign Web sites ask for a visitor's e-mail address, and some will not relate information until the e-mail address is surrendered. Data collected can include survey responses to opinion polls covering everything from abortion to taxes, and visitors are often asked for mailing addresses and especially zip codes. Ultimately, detailed geographic maps can be drawn overlaying individual traits, such as income, with U.S. Census demographic data. This information is used directly in political campaigns and also is a potential profit source for some political news and chat Web sites, such as ⟨vote.com⟩ and ⟨speakout.com⟩. These sites do not sell their databases but will serve as a conduit for campaigns or groups seeking to target a particular group.

E-mail and databases are part of a larger movement toward micromarketing, which has been affecting every sector of the economy. With data collection via Web sites, highly personal and individual data can be collected to determine voters' interests, and campaigns can begin interacting with precise voter information rather than coarse (and potentially misleading) demographic indicators. By merging formerly separate databases, Internet political consultants (and other interested parties) can learn about magazines subscriptions, mortgage amounts, credit histories, group memberships, and car purchases. Some programs even predict ethnicity based on family name and street address. This micromapping of individuals was reflected by a comment from a spokesperson for North Carolina attorney general candidate Mike Easley during his 2000 reelection campaign. According to Jay Rieff, "We can team [voter registration] up with other information about their neighborhood, where they live. We can pull census data. There's information that is increasingly available to make sure you target your message in an appropriate form. A campaign could target people who subscribe to a fishing magazine" (Zeller, 2000).

Self-Expression, Self-Identity, and Human Memory

We see the Internet as an important technology in the human identity project. The technology allows millions of people to explore their persona, origins, and destiny. If the past is father to the present, and if those who control the past control the future, then the Internet is our largest memory lost-and-found center. Internet users are persistently searching the Web for lost friends and relatives—people who have shared memories or can contribute to understanding users' life experiences. One example, plucked from a military history Web site, is presented in box 13.10.

Perhaps the process of the search for and recovery of memory reaches its ultimate expression in the relationship that people have with those who have died. This relationship can be carried on, at least by the living, through the Internet. Nowhere is this more clearly seen than in the online

Box 13.10
Joe Arluck

My name is Joe Arluck. My brother, Robert, served on the U.S. Navy ship *Rupertus* in the time frame 1965 to 1966, returning with the ship to Long Beach. I have sent for his service records to get the exact dates. Bob suffered a head injury about five years ago that left him confined in Laguna Honda Hospital in San Francisco. He lost some recent memories but still retains pretty good long-term memory, which makes his memories of his service time very valuable. He continues to have physical problems but is fun to talk to and enjoys company. I know it's a long shot, but could you see if any of his shipmates remember him and have memories to share. (Someone from the Bay Area would be too much to hope for.)

Source: "Contact" (retrieved August 2, 2001 from ⟨www.multied.com/ navy/stories/Rupertus.html⟩).

memorial Web pages (briefly discussed in an earlier chapter). Cerulo and Ruane (1997, p. 460) have argued that technologies of communication have reduced the barriers between life and death, taking "much of the grimness out of the reaping." In the context of self-expression and the Internet, "online memory gardens" are a popular extension of this commingling. Geiser's (1998) analysis of personal memorial Web sites identifies several trends that contribute to their popularity and proliferation. These include the increased individualization of lifestyles and the replacement of professional services by informal self-help groups. The Internet, unlike any other media or social institution, allows heterogeneous and unpredictable forms of grief and mourning and accessibility without limits of distance and synchronicity.

Boxes 13.11 and 13.12 provide examples of this mourning process. Special words and views are expressed that are meaningful to a few visitors who understand the secrets. The Internet provides an opportunity for people to verbalize feelings that might not otherwise be expressed. Virtual personal memorials can also be a catalyst for the expressions of others and for learning from the experiences described by others.

Another remarkable aspect of these created life memories is that they can be interactive: a life can be viewed as a work in transition, rather than a life completed. Geiser describes one individual whose memorial

Box 13.11
Memorial Web Pages as Catalysts for Expressions of Grief

Apr 28 1997, 1:29:04—Melissa Arnold ⟨mailman@citcom.net⟩
What a beautiful page. I cried when I went through it. I accidentily found it, and I am glad I did! The pictures, the music, they are all beautiful!! Just like your little girl. I lost my baby boy very recently, the day after he was born. I know how it hurts, but I also know how much of a blessing she was to you.
Source: Geiser (1998).

Box 13.12
An Online Memorial as an Outlet for Grief and Tribute

Daddy, it is fathers day, and I decied to do an online tribute to you. I want everyone to know how wonderful of a father you were, and how greatlly you are missed, not a day goes by when I don't think of you. Kristen looked up at me yesterday, and she looked just like you. I wish you could have been around to see her born.
Source: "Tributes" (retrieved on July 9, 2001 from ⟨http://catless.ncl. ac.uk/vmg/K/Ki.html⟩).

Web site serves as both a repository of oral histories and a way to become part of the dynamic history of the individual as well (see box 13.13).

Conclusion

The evidence strongly suggests that the Internet has already been used to powerfully enhance self-expression and interaction. The uses reviewed in this chapter celebrate the individual, yet the consequences are social, enriching the stock of human creative achievements and creating both individual-level and collective-level social capital. A rich store of data is also being accumulated for future research into society and the Internet. At the same time, some might question the worth of many of these expressive and creative acts and ask whether the vast outpouring of words, sounds, and images is actually clogging up the senses and sensibilities— that much of what is said is full of sound and fury, signifying nothing.

Box 13.13
A Garden of Memories as an Interactive Work-in-Transition

A Collection of Oral Histories

Grammy Mirk died when I was eight years old. Growing up, I have come to know her through the recollections of older family members. Because she was extremely judgmental, she showed different parts of herself to different people. In turn, they became polarized in how they viewed her. Since a grain of truth exists in everybody's perspective, I have attempted to create a composite sketch of her as seen from many different perspectives. This website is a collection of oral histories of those who have survived her.

A Living History

The site is interactive.

Not only can you read about Grammy Mirk; you can e-mail questions about her life.

Maybe you want to direct questions to a family member about a specific story.

Maybe there are aspects of her life you want to know more about.

Your questions and their answers will be posted and become part of this dynamic and evolving history.

Source: Geiser (1998).

The primary motive for producing works of self-expression on the Internet is to create meaning for an individual (even though many, if not most, of those who are contributing their creative efforts to the Internet would like fame and recognition). The intrinsic reward of the activity is that the inner creative voice is given expression. The Internet provides alternative channels of expression (exciting, bland, creative, and tasteless) in an era when the media are increasingly dominated by a few self-serving corporate interests and by bland entertainment that panders to base interests. Despite initial fears that the Internet would reinforce the dominant cultural canon, it instead has provided an outlet for millions of creative people.

IV

Integration and Conclusion

14

Access, Involvement, Interaction, and Social Capital on the Internet: Digital Divides and Digital Bridges

In chapters 1 through 13, we analyze extensive research done by us and others on the social consequences of the Internet for access, civic and community involvement, and social interaction. We present and discuss our survey results and those of the Pew Internet and American Life Project. In this chapter, we extend our findings and put forth conclusions concerning the syntopian view of the Internet. But before going forward, we recapitulate our major findings.

Summary of Basic Issues and Survey Results

Access
Basic Issues The digital divide—demographic differences in access to and usage of the Internet—is an important policy, social, and ethical concern. Internet access equates with access to the information and interactions leading to both individual and collective social capital. There are legitimate fears that a denial of civil rights to information will produce an information underclass or "digital balkanization."

Others downplay the access problem. For Compaine (2001), the fact that some groups do not use the Internet equally is not necessarily problematical. According to this argument, it is an injustice to launch programs, especially ones paid for by public monies collected from people at every level of society, that are based on sentiment and bias rather than on facts. It might be a problem no greater than (nor less than), say, the fact that European Americans tend to be "adoption laggards" in terms of mobile phones relative to African Americans, Hispanic Americans, and Asian Americans (Katz & Aakhus, 2002).

A dystopian access argument is that Internet users are beneficiaries of a multidimensional and possibly increasing digital divide. This fragments society and reduces the contributions and access to social capital by the information have-nots. A utopian access argument holds that these differences will naturally decline, that simply accessing the Internet's huge database of information will reduce knowledge gaps and social differences, and that, as with any innovation, initial disparities will soon disappear.

Our Primary Results   Adoption of the Internet has grown quickly from less than 10% of the U.S. population online in 1995 to almost 60% of the population online in 2000. The digital divide based on usage is shrinking. Those who were less well educated, less affluent, female, or older were less likely to be Internet users. However, the divide is narrowing on all the dimensions we have considered—age, household income, education, and population density. Further, when we consider the actual year of adoption, as opposed to the year of the survey, the gender and racial divide disappeared by 2000. Nevertheless, for some dimensions of the digital divide—especially income and age—there is still a long way to go before the digital divide disappears. Users are also more likely to have children, be full-time workers or students, own as oppose to rent their homes, live in their homes for fewer years, and be more satisfied with life and communication.

Our research on access to the Internet has identified a second digital divide beyond the usage divide—awareness. A substantial proportion of the population—in 2000, around 8.3%—was still unaware of the Internet, though the percentage dropped from 15.2% in 1995. By 2000, those who were older, female, and African American and had lower incomes were less likely to be aware of the Internet. One important result is that we found no racial or ethnic effect relating to usage: once awareness is achieved, digital divides on the basis of race or ethnicity virtually disappear.

Regarding motivations for Internet use, two points stand out. Users as compared to nonusers rate more highly Internet activities such as people interaction and information access. We identified three key barriers to

Internet usage—cost, access, and complexity. Two of these—cost and access—were more strongly felt by nonusers, perhaps reflecting their lower incomes (ability to pay for the Internet) and educational achievements (ability to navigate the Internet). Most significantly, both users and nonusers were equally concerned about Internet complexity. Without improvements here, frustration levels will remain high, and potential user benefits will in many cases go unrealized.

Internet experience makes little difference in perceptions of motivations and barriers. Long-term users (those having used the Internet for more than a year) were more likely to rate sending and receiving e-mail and "it's a good thing to do" as good reasons for being an Internet user and were slightly less likely to feel that complexity was a barrier. Thus we identified yet another digital divide, based on the cohort when people first began using the Internet.

Internet dropouts are usually overlooked in discussions about communication technologies in general and the Internet in particular. We suggest this is a fourth important kind of digital divide. We find a fairly constant level over the years (about 10% of all respondents) and a very large proportion of users (from 50% to 15%) between 1995 and 2000. Dropouts have less expertise than users and are significantly younger, less affluent, less well educated, and less likely to have been married. The main reasons offered by dropouts for ceasing to use the Internet were lost access to the Internet, not sufficiently interesting, problems with use, took too much time, and bills too high.

The digital divide is currently primarily one of income and education rather than of race or gender. This fits with the notion that the Internet has become an extension of everyday life and is useful according to one's interests and social location. The fact that there is a digital divide based on income rather than race does not mean the problem does not have a racial component. It is clearly the case that large income inequities exist across racial divides. Aspects of low-income cultures might dissuade people from adopting the technology. For example, we review research showing that some members of various subcultures view the Internet as "not our thing" due to local social influences, media patterns, and social relationships. However, income rather than race is the driver of Internet use; hence possible solutions to the digital divide should presumably emphasize relevance on the basis of income and education issues. It is misleading to lay the blame or responsibility for unequal Internet access and use on racial (or, for that matter, gender) factors.

Civic and Community Involvement
Basic Issues: Civic, Political, and Community Involvement   Some researchers theorize that the Internet may narrow the range of participants, limit the number and privacy of participants, constrict the kinds of discourse available, and not really have much potential for transforming politics. Others hold that the Internet has already been applied to the political process, has provided greater involvement, is associated with greater tolerance for diversity, and provides more opportunities for participation in political activities.

Some say that online communities are secondary and often quite controlled types of relationships, that involvement in mediated communities detracts from the kinds of social capital built up through local offline communities, and that online communities generally consist of homogeneous members sharing one narrow interest. However, research and theory also indicate that online communities can overcome physical and temporal constraints, be vibrant and supportive, allow diverse voices to create shared information, spur both local and global activism, generally complement offline communities, and foster otherwise suppressed dialogue.

Thus a dystopian civic and community involvement argument is that users spend time by themselves seeking narrowly self-interested information and likeminded enclaves or identity categories, avoiding exposure to diverse or even accurate information, reducing their use of traditional mass media, and retreating from becoming physically involved in community or political activities. Here, both individual and collective interests erode civic involvement and thus broader social capital, including democratic principles. A utopian involvement argument proposes that increased access to many other people and reduced constraints of time and distance will allow communities of those with shared norms and interests to form and thrive while physical communities are stringently limited in the types of actors and action possible.

Our Primary Results: Similar Offline Political Involvement, Expanding Online Political Involvement, and Expanding Community Involvement
Internet use was positively associated with political involvement in the 1996 general election. Internet users were no more or less likely than nonusers to engage in traditional political activities such as voting, attending political rallies, giving money to a political cause, and controlling for demographic differences. Nor did they differ in their perception of the importance of traditional media (print and television). Further, we found no evidence that heavy and light users or long-term and short-term users differed in terms of offline political activity, including voting. The Internet did provide between a tenth and a fifth of users a platform for two general forms of online political activity—browsing (following the election news) and interaction (exchanging e-mail and engaging in online discussion about politics). And Internet users who engaged in more frequent online political activities were more likely to report greater political awareness and have more political information.

Contrary to pessimistic predictions, our research revealed no support for the hypothesis that Internet participation is diminishing community participation and social integration, which help create social capital. Indeed, by some measures, cyberspace denizens report that they are even more involved in social activities than their non-Internet-using counterparts. In general, Internet users were more likely to belong to leisure organizations in 1995 and to community organizations in 2000. There was no difference in membership in religious organizations in either year, although more frequent users in 2000 were very slightly more likely to belong to at least one religious organization. The 2000 relationship between Internet usage and membership in community organizations held even when controlling for a variety of demographic and attitudinal variables.

Social Interaction and Expression
Basic Issues: Isolation Versus Communication   There are strong claims that interaction via the Internet is too impersonal and isolating to constitute real social interaction, that students who use the Internet too frequently have lower academic performance and feel more lonely, that people can present and get caught up in misleading and illusory identities,

and that these situations lead to many negative uses and consequences such as stalking, pornography, hate groups, and sexist language. However, other theory and research emphasize that online interaction is highly social. The Internet complements and even strengthens offline interactions, provides frequent and diverse uses for social interaction, and extends communication with family and friends. Further, a new generation has grown up with the Internet, experiencing greater communication with family and friends, developing their social identities, and watching TV less. Finally, Internet users are not less trusting, not more isolated or depressed, not less diverse, and not less tolerant than nonusers; indeed, usage tends to be negatively related to all these indicators of low social interaction.

Thus a dystopian social interaction argument is that the Internet attracts or creates socially isolated individuals who will replace their strong direct and interpersonal face-to-face ties with weak and secondary mediated relationships. This lowers trust, reduces the extent to which norms are developed and reinforced, and distances friends and family. A utopian interaction argument is that the Internet overcomes many obstacles to regular interaction with others so that those who like to communicate more in any medium can now do so even more.

Our Primary Results: Offline Interaction, Online Interaction, Friendship Creation, and Social Identity We found no significant differences between users and nonusers in letter writing. Although simple relationships could be found between being an Internet user, being a long-term user, and making more phone calls, these disappeared when controlling for demographic variables. So in general, Internet usage is not associated with use of traditional interpersonal communication media; alternatively, Internet users are no less sociable than nonusers.

In 1995, users were slightly more likely to know more of their 10 closest neighbors, but this difference disappeared when demographic differences were controlled. Users were also more likely to be innovative and were more likely to have met with friends in the past week, even when controlling for demographic influences. In 2000, users were more likely than nonusers to report a greater sense of belonging and to like radio more, even controlling for other factors.

Our data and that of the Pew studies show that people intensively use e-mail to keep in touch with family and friends. From 10% to 25% of users reported being a member of an online community.

More than a tenth of Internet users in our surveys had established friendships via the Internet. Those with greater Internet experience or skills appeared more likely to make friends via the Internet. There appeared to be only weak or in most cases nonexistent statistical relationships with demographic variables, measures of traditional forms of interaction, and measures of personality attributes. Again, over 10% of those who indicated they had met someone online went on to meet that other user in person, and the vast majority (85%) indicated that it was a positive experience. Online relationships seem to come about in two ways—through sites and services designed to help people meet others and as a by-product of interaction in other online venues.

In 1995, the extent to which Internet users engaged in online interaction was not predicted by measures of offline sociability. In 2000, those with a greater sense of belonging did like surfing the Internet (and interacting with others on the Internet) more and were more likely to be long-term users. As in 1995, this measure of offline sociability was not associated with various forms of online interaction. Thus different measures from different years indicate that being an Internet user is itself a source of online sociability.

There has been much speculation that Internet communication alters cultural processes by changing the basis of social identity. Despite these adverse speculations, we have found evidence that socially grounded interaction exists everywhere in cyberspace. We researched several examples (such as listserv discourse) that illustrate the importance of authentic identity in Internet professional groups and also explored cases of homepage self-presentation mediated through socially defined links.

The Internet: Access, Involvement, Interaction, and Social Capital

As noted in earlier chapters, sharp intellectual controversies are swirling around the Internet's effect on social involvement. These are not simply abstract academic questions; their answers have important ramifications for how millions of people spend their time and money, society allocates scarce resources for social objectives, and power is exercised in American society. A central issue involves social capital.

Evidence and argument are important since they affect the course of these debates and spill over to affect the behavior of individuals who are exposed to them. For example, the HomeNet study (Kraut et al., 1998) described in chapter 10 led some people to believe that spending significant amounts of time on the Internet would cause people to become depressed and lonely. Even more poignant, people who had been downsized and were unemployed avoided using the Internet as a job-search tool because they feared it would make them still more depressed and lonely (Lorber, 2000; Stephen Lerit, personal communication, September 21, 2000).

The following eight propositions about the Internet relate to our three primary themes and the concept of social capital.

1. The Internet Contributes to Social Capital

Our first and most important conclusion is that our evidence (see chapters 8 and 11) indicates that the Internet does not reduce social capital. The pessimistic macro-level predictions that the Internet would reduce social involvement seem to be mistaken. As we show in chapter 8, online users in 1995 and 2000 were no less, and in some cases were more, involved than nonusers in community, religious, and recreational events. We realize, of course, that self-selection takes place in terms of who elects to go on the Internet. We tried to minimize this potential effect by statistically controlling for demographic variables, but some self-selection bias probably remains. The critical social-capital perspective would say that people who had been engaging in certain levels of social participation would decrease those levels after spending time online. Therefore, unless especially energetic community-involved citizens were recruited to the Internet and then became less active after being on the Internet, there would be little reason to believe that the Internet cuts into social capital at the macro level. The evidence clearly suggests that the effects are either neutral or positive.

Chapters 9 and 13 use circumstantial data to make the case that the Internet provides rich resources that enable people to pursue their own goals and interests. We note that in the process they create both individual-level and collective-level social capital (intentionally or not). Although this social capital can be harmful to some groups and individuals, we found that much of it seemed positive. These findings bring us into opposition with the pessimistic, or dystopian, interpretation of the social consequences of the Internet, reviewed in chapters 2 and 6.

2. The Internet Creates Traditional Forms of Social Capital

The Internet does not supplant prior communication forms but rather supplements them. Some users appear to send more e-mail and watch less television, but we found no reduction in overall communication levels. Further, there was no evidence that Internet usage diminishes friendship or kinship networks; Internet users are slightly more sociable and communicate more with friends and family. These data, along with the confirmation of them by other studies such as those presented in a special issue of the *American Behavioral Scientist* (Wellman & Haythornthwaite, 2002), suggest that the findings of HomeNet (Kraut et al., 1998) are anomalous.

We also note in chapters 7, 8, and 11 that the Internet makes it easier to participate in all the traditional forms of social capital that Putnam (2000) has identified. These include keeping up with neighborhood and family relationships, voluntary community civic, social, and religious organizations, and political activities. The barriers to finding a group that shares a user's interests and to finding ways to participate in the group are generally lowered due to the Internet's existence.

A two-pronged argument can be put forward in opposition to our view. The first prong operates at the individual-interaction level. Some hold that the Internet replaces authentic interaction with fake or less valuable interaction (see the review in chapter 10). This means that interactions will develop neither the trust nor the emotional commitment that creates a sound basis for social capital to arise. This certainly occurs in some cases, but for vast numbers of activities people can find the virtual interaction offered by the Internet to be equal and in some cases superior to that of face-to-face interaction. Moreover, the Internet is but one of several communication modes and interaction opportunities, so looking at the Internet in isolation can be misleading. Finally, as we point out in chapter 11, virtual relationships often gravitate to face-to-face ones. Uslaner's analysis (2000) highlights the important role of trust and the consequences of its absence in the online world.

The second prong of the opposing argument operates at the level of the group. Some argue that virtual participation is so easy that participants will have a lower commitment to the group and that concomitantly the group will have fewer gains. Members can come and go at will without loss of psychic and temporal investments. Hence, online organizations cannot achieve the same positive levels or effects from collective social capital as do physically operating ones. Less is put in, so less can come out. Though we found no direct evidence of this, the argument makes sense. On the other hand, it also seems that if many new organizations do many things with many people (partially because of the ability of Internet groups to use the Internet to overcome previously existing time, distance, and cost obstacles), their gains could theoretically counterbalance the lower achievements that any particular online group might make.

In sum, our evidence has shown many ways in which the Internet builds traditional forms of social capital, including new relationships, access to and cocreation of practical information and theoretical understandings, and networks of friendship, purposive community, and political organizations. The social support that can be obtained in turn yields richer ways to link with those who share interests and to benefit from the knowledge and networks created by users. Thus, the Internet provides more opportunities to activate resources and create new knowledge for oneself and others.

Earlier technologies of interpersonal communication, such as the car (Flink, 1970) and telephone (Fischer, 1992; Katz, 1999a), had parallel effects of making it easier to participate in groups, find others of similar interests, and restore and maintain ties. (They also had the effects of weakening parental authority over children and increasing shopping opportunities, which also seems to be the case with the Internet.) Both the telephone and car also allowed innovative forms of social capital to be created. For example, the telephone enabled donation and membership solicitations and "get out the vote" calling chains. The car allowed people to drive significant distances to participate in meetings, meet with kin and friends, and participate in political activities.

3. The Internet Builds New Forms of Social Capital

The Limits and Paradoxes of Social-Capital Conceptualizations   While our research finds that traditional social capital is increased rather than diminished by the Internet, we also uncovered some difficulties with the way the social-capital model operates. Specifically, in most of the measures we have seen, computer-mediated communication is not included in definitions of the social-capital processes of community, interaction, or participation. Indeed, the Internet is often seen as more of an obstacle than a solution, at least in terms of taking away time that might otherwise be spent enjoying immediate friends and family (Nie, 2000).

In terms of the Internet's effect on social capital, Putnam (2000) approaches the subject gingerly. In his book *Bowling Alone: The Collapse and Revival of American Community*, he expresses some positive sentiments but notes heavily conflicting, often negative evidence (pp. 174–179) and concludes that no evidence shows that the Internet's impact has been positive (pp. 170–171). Despite his theoretical ambivalence about the Internet, however, he strongly advocates using the Internet to promote his own ideas. At his ⟨bowlingalone.com⟩ site, visitors are encouraged to buy the book from ⟨amazon.com⟩ (via a hotlink) and not from their local bookstores, a traditional community resource. And rather than recommend that readers meet with people face to face (to have book-reading parties, for instance), the Web site provides another hotlink to "E-mail your friends and colleagues to let them know about the book." (Clicking this link will initiate an e-mail program.) Indeed, the Internet appears to be an important medium through which the very message of social capital itself should be propagated, as site visitors are told to "Mention the book and this Web site in Internet discussions, bulletin boards, and newsletters." Putnam's Web site seems to be an implicit endorsement of the idea that the Internet is the answer, if social capital is the question (retrieved July 13, 2001, from ⟨www.bowlingalone.com⟩).

New Online Forms of Social Capital   Our data do not tend to support the so-called Internet paradox (Kraut et al., 1998; Nie, 2000), which says that using the Internet (or using it more) makes us lonely and isolated. The global measures that Kraut and Nie use miss the innovative forms that are the special province of the Internet, discussed below.

The Internet offers new forms of building social capital that are in many ways different and more powerful than the local, physical means of earlier eras. Fantasy games, for instance, have led to ongoing bonds among supposedly isolated male sports fans, the self-organizing clans (teams), and even marriages. International matchmaking has created families. Personal Web sites have created meaningful environments of personal knowledge and family history. These and other novel forms, as well as expansions of traditional ones, are discussed in chapters 9 and 13. In essence, the new forms of social capital are insufficiently accounted for in social-capital theory. Thus, if social capital is measured by dinner parties, as it often is (Putnam, 2000), the Internet may appear to be a negative. At the New York Echo site (⟨www.echonyc.com⟩), people meet online and then offline in a blended community. If social capital is measured by meeting and forming meaningful relationships with people who would otherwise be impossible to know about much less meet, then the Internet appears to be a positive force in social-capital formation.

4. Although Potentially Influential, the Internet Is Not Politically Transformative

A Complement to Traditional Politics   Our analyses show that Internet users are as politically active offline as are nonusers but of course participate in a variety of online activities that are not available to nonusers. The Internet is a great source for breaking political news and news of all sorts and can influence people's opinions somewhat.

This online activity is influential, but it is not likely to be politically decisive: no immediate and revolutionary transformation is occurring in political expression or representation. Instead, the Internet is gradually playing an increasingly important role in extending and enriching people's ability to learn about news and topics of interest to them. Because the kinds of involvement online are similar in type and intensity as those offline, they represent an extension of offline interests, which is not surprising since each new technology tends to reproduce the elements of its predecessors (Carey, 1988). Our view is largely in line with that of Davis, who feels that the Internet "will not lead to the social and political revolution so widely predicted" (Davis, 2000, p. 168). He has noticed that existing power structures, traditional media, and powerful groups are adapting to the Internet and will use it to extend "politics as usual" to a new turf.

Thus the Internet does not appear capable of being either the elites' hobnailed jackboot of political suppression or the workers' callused fist of popular revolutionary fury. Although the technology appears at first blush to have the power to fulfill these dystopian or utopian expectations, the record of accomplishments to date has proved them to be misguided. Certainly, the Internet can inspire fear, and repressive governmental policies can reduce or eliminate the free flow of ideas for which the Internet is so well known. Thus, for instance, the People's Republic of China has built a firewall to keep unwanted Internet ideas away from its people, and the Taliban rulers in Afghanistan outlawed the use of the Internet entirely (Reuters, 2001). But the Internet can also help raise awareness of popular revolutionary groups or those who are fighting for social justice. Antigovernment groups in Mexico, such as the Zapatistas, have been particularly effective in publicizing news and views on the Internet.

The Limits of Online Politics Based on an analysis by *PC Data* (MacPherson, 2000), in the first week of September 2000, an estimated 191,000 users visited Governor George W. Bush's Web site (⟨www.georgewbush.com⟩), while 146,000 visited that of Vice President Al Gore's (⟨www.gore2000.org⟩). The popular political Web sites ⟨voter.com⟩ and ⟨election.com⟩ were visited respectively by 146,000 and 91,000 surfers. By contrast, 6.3 million people visited ⟨luckysurf.com⟩, a sweepstakes and lottery Web site (MacPherson, 2000). Clearly, the election was less satisfying than the sweepstakes. The Pew Internet study conducted during the 2000 campaign found that 18% of Americans—nearly one out of five—went online for election news during some point of the election year campaign. As impressive as this figure is, it is a mere 4% greater than the number that sought online news about the 1996 national elections—during a period in which the percentage of people online grew from 18.8% to 59.7%. The Pew researchers also found that the preferences of Internet users were largely those of the offline world: consumers were gravitating to the online sites of major news organizations rather than seeking out specialized political sites or the candidates' own sites (Pew Internet and American Life Project, 2000). These data suggest not that the Internet has had no impact but rather that its impact is incremental and modest rather than transformative and revolutionary.

Some critics see low involvement in political Web sites as a moral failure of American society. For them, it represents the triumph of privatization and isolation over the interests of society, of individual (destructive) interests over group solidarity. For others, however, this tendency points to a preference for personal autonomy over collective control and influence. Political scientist Robert Dahl (2000) makes the point that a citizen who refrains from engaging in political discussions with other people or even from voting, does not necessarily not value these rights. The differences between valuing and acting have been rarely investigated, he asserts. The bulk of social science research has gone to measuring and analyzing various forms of political participation, such as voting and canvassing. Much less attention has been given to understanding what people value politically, so society has a blindspot in this regard. He argues that valuing a right and exercising that right are two quite different dimensions and that confusing them spawns misguided efforts that may ultimately erode the legitimacy of major political institutions (Dahl, 2000).

Despite these modest increases in the audience for online political Web sites, the Internet has helped activists coordinate internally as well as propagate interest and recruit adherents from the outside. Progress toward an international treaty to ban landmines, for instance, can be partly attributable to the tireless Internet-based efforts of Vermonter Jody Williams. But Williams, who was awarded a Nobel Prize for peace for her work, conducted her efforts in various physical venues as well as on the Internet (which reinforces our point that the Internet is part of a continuum of people's lives generally and communication processes in particular and should not be viewed in isolation). And yet for every landmine treaty that succeeds, large numbers of online policy projects have failed. Moreover, early successes can become Pyrrhic victories when they teach the other side what tactics will be deployed and how to react better next time. Thus, using the Internet as a tactic of the less powerful can easily lead opponents to prepare effective countermeasures, feeding a cycle of diminishing returns for the online activists' investment.

However, the Jody Williams model of intense personal involvement is rarely pursued. Most people simply do not wish to be politically engaged and find the right to privacy—the right to be let alone—very appealing. Low or moderate political participation may not necessarily be bad. Indeed, places with the highest participation in public voting are precisely those places where there is the most compulsion over the individual: the totalitarian states routinely turn out 99.8% of the vote. Democracies that penalize citizens for not voting, such as Australia, obtain high turnouts as well, but at the cost of criminalizing a desire not to get involved.

Policy-Specific Information: More of It But with Less Credibility   A line of research in political science suggests that many people are poorly informed about political choices and processes and do not have the knowledge base to agree or disagree with particular choices (Converse, 1962; Zaler, 1992). Many Americans therefore hold political views that they would not hold if they had policy-specific information: ignorance is bliss. Moreover, a body of research shows that giving policy-specific information to people leads them to change their positions. This effect is strongest for those with the highest levels of general political knowledge (Gilens, 2001). This suggests that as people use the Internet increasingly as a source for news and information, the quality of news they find will be more specific for their interests and will encourage them to change their policy views. Thus, in this sense, the Internet is likely to have substantial impact over time on the public policies of the United States: as voters learn more about issues that matter to them, there is likely to be a better alignment between the interests of the voters and public policy.

There is no shortage of online news services or online newspapers. Many otherwise small outlets are commanding a larger audience. But the editorial function, embedded in the structured sites (portals), is still not only important but vital. The notion of some Web sites was to have the people be the reporters to overcome the editorial biases of mass circulation outlets. A successful example of this style of Web site is a site operated by Matt Drudge (⟨www.drudgereport.com⟩). But even he relies on tips and information from others and decides what appears on his page, which thus becomes an online version of a gossip sheet. This is far from the notion that each person will be a reporter and a reader. Further, while the Internet provides much more total and diverse information, people can post whatever they want without a guarantee that information is accurate or unbiased. So greater usage may not necessarily lead to better-informed users and thus more aligned political activity.

A Teledemocracy?   Finally, we have said little about online voting. Little needs to be said. The year 2000 was supposed to be the year of the Internet in terms of the national election, but the ludicrously narrow margin in the presidential victory makes the prospect of Internet voting vanish into the future. The process would have to be both anonymous and secure, but these two forces work in opposition (Katz, 1990b). So while Internet elections might be possible for primaries controlled by parties and for local positions such as school boards, the stakes in a national election are simply too high and the vulnerabilities too great for the foreseeable future.

5.   Social-Capital Theory: An Integration of Individual and Collective Conceptualizations

Levels of Social Capital   Social-capital theories often disagree about whether the locus of social-capital formation is at the individual level or at the group (collective) level. Sociologist James Coleman (1988) sees social capital as a function of the ambient social structure that can be turned to advantage by an individual. He does not see it ontologically— that is, as an identifiable "thing," such as the total number of memberships in organizations, frequency of dinner parties, or number of hours volunteered for charity. For Coleman, social capital is the value of aspects of social structure "to actors as resources that they can use to achieve their interests" (p. S101).

Although some (Portes & Landold, 1996) endorse this view, we find it problematical. Since the focus is on the individual, it minimizes an appreciation of the public goods, shared resources, and collective benefits that may be used—in the future and by others—and that would not have been created or used if kept at the individual level. Another sociologist,

Pierre Bourdieu (1986), defines social capital as including both current and potentially accessible resources, based on group membership. In other words, one's membership in a group "provides each of its members with the backing of the collectively owned capital" (p. 249). This richer concept of social capital defines it as a process—what it can do for members of a social system and not just for specific individuals.

A third perspective is offered by Robert Putnam (2000), who emphasizes the normative aspects of social interaction that produce collective benefits. He highlights the collective benefits of all forms of face-to-face social interaction. We like the analogy with physical capital. Education, paid for by tax dollars, better prepares an entire society to handle the subtleties and complexities of environmental and social challenges. Canals can be built by one generation, and their towpaths can be enjoyed by a later generation of bicyclists. The Internet memorial sites mentioned in chapter 13 also reflect this process. Table 14.1 contrasts these three perspectives (plus our own) on how social capital is defined, why it is used, who possesses it, and where it resides.

The Internet as an Indicator of Social Capital   Rather than a technology of isolation and loneliness, the Internet is a technology through which social capital can be created. Its capability may be entirely potential and not used. But in many cases, it draws people into contact with others to create shared resources and communal concerns. In chapters 7, 8, 9, 11, and 13, we present data and examples that support this position. Here we build on the correlational arguments of Putnam (2000). His wide-ranging roundup of data suggests that participation in a vast array of social activities yields positive individual, community, and even national benefits. (Correlation, of course, does not necessarily mean causation.)

We can show that both Internet penetration and overall measures of social capital work in a similar fashion. We demonstrate this by taking a detailed look at one of the relationships that Putnam highlights as a particular benefit of social capital—suppressing crime. He shows a strong statistical relationship between high social-capital rates and low crime rates on a state-by-state level (figure 14.1). In this context, Putnam also says that murder rates are "generally the most reliable index of the incidence of crime" (p. 309). Using his social-capital index (of more than

Table 14.1
Definition, Rationale, and Action Environment of Competing Theories of Social Capital

Authors	Definition	Rationale for Use	Locus of Power	Action Environment
Coleman (1988)	Aspects of ambient social structure that actors leverage for own interests	To influence other social actors for individual gain	The individual in a social network	Kin and community settings that benefit the individual
Bourdieu (1993)	Social, economic, and cultural resources that allow actors to command group goods	To expand and increase the economic resources of the group	The social class of the member, leveraged and limited by class characteristics	Social classes that compete with other social classes for resources
Putnam (2000)	Trust, norms, and networks that lead to mutually beneficial cooperation	To create political participation and social well-being that benefits society and the individual	A social relationship among actors	Communities and states in a national and international context, primarily in a positive mode
Katz & Rice	Personal and knowledge resources that can be drawn on to advance the interests of the individual or collectivity	To advance individual interests but create collective benefits as well	The individual activating a social relationship or a knowledge base	A digital and networked Internet that enables positive and negative network externalities through connected areas of life

Source: Modified from Winter (2000).

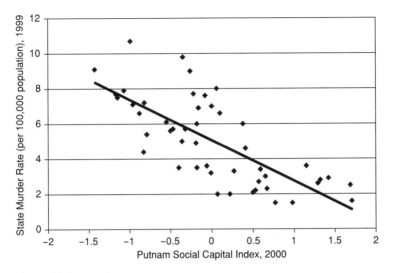

Figure 14.1
1999 State Murder Rate by 2000 Putnam Social Capital Index
Source: Compiled from Department of Justice statistics and the Putnam Social
Capital Index (retrieved July 21, 2001 from ⟨http://www.bowlingalone.com/
data.php3⟩).
Note: Adjusted $R^2 = .52$.

120 items, such as voting turnout in presidential elections and frequency
of attending club meetings), there is indeed a high negative correlation
between social capital and violent crime, though the specific statistical
results are not provided. (In fact, our recalculation of his numbers yields
a correlation of $-.73$, with an adjusted R-square of .53—that is, about
half the variance in violent crime is explained by the social-capital index.)

Putnam (2000) does not include computer ownership or Internet use
among his social-capital variables. We suggest that Internet technology
reflects the same positive environment in which other social capital
accumulates. At least in terms of this example of murder rates, the
Internet is associated (that is conceptually as a correlate, not as a pre-
cursor or cause) of social capital and its benefits.

By using just one variable—household penetration of the Internet
in a U.S. state—we arrive at roughly the same slope and a respectable
correlation of $-.49$ (with an adjusted R-square of .24, or 24% of the

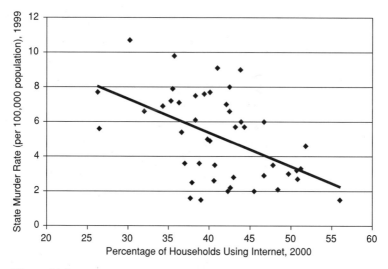

Figure 14.2
1999 State Murder Rate by 2000 Household Internet Use
Source: Compiled from Department of Justice and U.S. Census Bureau statistics (retrieved August 18, 2001 from ⟨http://www.census.gov/statab/www/⟩).
Note: Adjusted R^2 = .24

variation in murder rates, as figure 14.2 shows). Thus, rather than using 120 or so variables, we can statistically "explain" by just one variable (household Internet penetration) a quarter of the variation in murder rates.

We do not think household penetration of Internet use cuts murder rates. Rather, social capital and Internet penetration are co-correlates of a positive social environment that brings many social benefits into being. However, we also recognize that social capital is an embedded concept and cannot be pulled out piecemeal. Internet awareness and use depend on cognitive skills, general knowledge, economic and educational resources, and stages in users' lifecycles and social settings. The opportunity structure dictates the choices that individuals make and affects the consequences of those choices. Despite the causal murkiness, these correlations strongly suggest that the Internet does not gravely harm the quality of life. Moreover, it does seem related to many things that help make life good.

6. The Internet Fosters Involvement and Interaction, Resulting in New Forms of Social Organization

Like some theorists, Manuel Castells foresees that the Internet will serve as a "reinforcement of the culturally dominant social networks" (Castells, quoted in Putnam 2000, p. 175). Other observers predict that the "technologies of freedom," in the phrase of Ithiel de Sola Pool (1984), support personal liberation and free people to pursue their interests. Political liberation frees people to participate or not to participate in politics. To many who have lived under political dictatorships, such as Bulgaria when it was a Communist cult state, the requirement to be politically mobilized was often one of life's most repugnant aspects.

Personal Freedom and Self-Realization   Beyond building social capital, another dimension may be even more meaningful to participants—personal involvement via the Internet to pursue an identity project. Although people are interested in maintaining social contacts and conducting their personal business on the Internet, a new form of self-organizing activity is also arising that has great sociocultural significance. This new form is the search for personal meaning. People are using the Internet to seek their roots, reinforce their cultural identity, find sustenance for and propagate their beliefs, and give themselves and their loved ones a form of enduring meaning and presence.

In this sense, the Internet becomes interesting as a technology not only of communication but also of personal freedom and self-realization. It fulfills what seems to be the next step in the evolution of human rights. Throughout history, kings could build a cathedral, pyramid, or statue to themselves, impressing the living and guaranteeing themselves immortality (and often taking with them servants to wait on them in the afterlife). But the people who worked the land and produced goods and services were chattel who had few or no civil rights. As the rights to which people are entitled have increased, so have the categories of people eligible for those rights. This expansion in human rights has never been smooth or without setbacks and has at times even collapsed with catastrophic effects, and yet the overall trend of tens of thousands of years seems clear.

We can stretch the analogy too far, certainly. Yet intriguing parallels can be drawn between the coins, statues, and proclamations that memorialize the achievements of royalty and today's Internet homepages, which display photos, documents, sounds, and other creative works for all to admire.

Extensions of the Realm of Social Capital   The concern of the social capitalists is valid: the Internet may threaten some kinds of social capital. But this might not occur in the way that the critics and policy wonks have predicted. Rather than turning people into unhappy morbid, and apolitical isolates, it has allowed those who were already interested in politics to aggressively pursue those interests in a new and powerful venue. Those who have little interest in politics find not a wasteland for the pursuit of loneliness but rather a rich ground for individual self-expression and self-exploration, whether through individual Web sites, collaborative newsgroups, online fantasy games, or commercial and informational resources. So rather than building communities only at the neighborhood level, which was the domain of unmediated community involvement, Internet users extend their personae in novel and creative ways across counties, states, and national boundaries. In some cases, this may not have strengthened mainline organizations, but it has created new hybrid and virtual communities of interest with far-flung communication networks of personal contacts.

7.   The Internet Also Has Negative Aspects

We have emphasized the positive aspects of the Internet to balance the intensely negative scholarly and journalistic criticisms of how the Internet is affecting U.S. society. But like any technology—and indeed human actions generally—the Internet can be used for destructive and harmful purposes. There are dark sides to the Internet, and threats exist at every level. In addition to cases of unfair denial of access to the Internet, destructive actions have harmed communities, and twisted forms of personal expression have injured individuals.

The negative perspective on the Internet has some validity. Throughout this book we have cited critics who have documented negative effects in various segments of the Internet. Although these negative aspects are unfortunate, the Internet is a reflection or more precisely an extension and elaboration of ordinary life. Legitimate concerns are often the subject of governmental and other efforts to improve the situation. Further, there are still considerable digital divides in terms of both awareness and use of the Internet. Attempts to improve the situation that are based on incorrect assumptions about the nature and impact of the Internet, however, are likely to be ineffective or worse.

8. Individual Motivations, the Nature of Information, and Internet Features Interact in a Syntopian Approach

In general, evidence shows that the Internet can foster civic and community involvement and social interaction and expression, which may maintain and create traditional and new forms of social capital at both individual and collective levels. Evidence for a phenomenon, though, and understanding the reasons for a phenomenon are two different things. Indeed, many plausible competing explanations have been put forth for why the Internet creates (and, some argue would argue, destroys) social capital. We review some of these in chapters 2, 6, and 10 and explicitly discuss their relation to social capital in earlier sections of this chapter.

Our view of why the Internet fosters involvement and expression is based on three general factors—(1) the individual situated in a social-opportunity structure, (2) the nature of digitized information, and (3) the network of networks that has been created and is now known as the Internet. Some of these factors may be familiar to those who have studied the information society, the economics of information, telecommunications policy, and the social consequences of communication technologies (see, for example, Negroponte, 1995). However, for those who find these concepts to be abstract and confusing, we briefly explicate them. The primary role of the following discussion, however, is to show how these three general factors interact to facilitate the process of individual self-interest and involvement leading to the formation of collective social capital through the Internet. People's motivations and social interests, the nature of information and communication, the wide range of processes made possible by the digitization of information, and the networked nature of the Internet converge to create a special information and communication environment that no other unmediated or mediated situation can approximate.

The Individual Is Socially Situated   The variables faced by the socially situated individual have been discussed in chapters 10 and 12. The main ones are self-interest, the search for identity and meaning, the desire for social interaction, and normative pressures. Self-interest motivates people to do things that inadvertently benefit others. Their motivations may be both heightened and suppressed by demographic and resource factors, such as education, age, sex, income, and race. The Internet allows others to capture benefit from the residuals of these actions in a way unprecedented by other communication technologies. Of course, Internet denizens also act altruistically out of a sense of moral commitment and community, and these actions can contribute mightily to online collective social capital.

Information Differs from Material Goods   The nature of information, and especially digitized information, can be quite different from that of material goods. (For a good general review of the social and economic implications of digitization, see Negroponte, 1995; for a wide-ranging and highly visual explanation of digital representations of data, see Oettinger, 1999; for a comparison of media on the basis of various attributes, see Rice, 1987a.)

The computers, keyboards, mice, and transmission media required to connect people and databases to the Internet all require and are manifested in physical materials, but the fundamental resource of the Internet—content—is not material. The form of communication and information is symbols, which traditionally have been physically carried on, in, or by physical materials—such as people, books, newspapers, and letters. Note that each of these material carriers involves considerable potential constraints (such as temporal, geographical, and social) and costs (production, distribution, and marketing).

Electronic media encode symbols into electromagnetic waves, freeing them (to a large extent) from the physical constraints and costs of material carriers:

• Marginal costs of additional copies, after the first costs of production, are low (as in print media) or negligible (as in electronic media);

• Diverse information creates unpredictable interactions, leading to new knowledge;

• The value of particular information is highly contextual so that it may vary widely across different users;

• This value can be determined largely only by actually using the information, which means that the information has already been shared;

• It is difficult to prevent additional users from accessing information (so, for example, electronic media like radio and television provide the content free and charge advertisers for access to the users);

• It's easy to provide to a wide range of unknown audience members (a letter has to be addressed to a specific person, while a television show is broadcast to anyone with a television);

• The benefits from information are very difficult to fully—often even partially—appropriate by the original creators.

This means that information, in many situations, is a public good, which all potentially may use. Another result is that various entities will try to control the distribution of information. These efforts include international regimes for copyright protection and trade secrets and other systems to restrict access to information.

Particular forms of information that have the potential to contribute to the greater public good—such as governmental information, public education, and innovative research and development—are heavily subsidized by society precisely because private firms cannot control, appropriate, or even predict the benefits of information and because many collective benefits are derived from providing the information. However, many of the intriguing aspects of information apply equally well to traditional media, both print and mass media, as well as to more interpersonal media such as the telephone, to the extent that the main product of these media is providing a means for exchanging information, the preliminary basis of communication. The main points here are that communication is essentially symbolic (where symbols in language represent possibilities for meaning for other symbol-processing actors) and that the forms in which these symbols are conveyed are symbolic as well. In material transactions, the form is physical, even if there is abundant symbolic value as well (consider the giving of a gift).

Digitized Information Differs from Material Goods and Analog Information   Digitization—that is, converting continuous analog waveforms into patterns of on-off signals (popularly represented as zeroes and ones)—heightens some of these intriguing characteristics of information. Traditional transmission of information, such as through sound or electromagnetic waves, uses analog signals, which are physical analogies to the initially created sounds or images. But without digitization, the content of the signals cannot be indexed for easy storage, retrieval, and associations with other content (for example, readers must rely on section and front-page content indexes to know where to find newspaper stories, but the content of each story is not indexed, and it's pretty difficult to know which stories might be covering related issues); the messages are typically limited to one particular medium (for example, television programs cannot be portrayed in newspapers), to only a few access points (such as a radio or television program schedule, or to a subject/author/ title index or Dewey decimal numbers for books); and the content cannot easily be further reprocessed (either through editing, such as revising a videotaped television show or audiotaped radio show, or redirecting, such as sending an interesting audiotaped radio show to one's friends).

Transforming content from analog form into digital form enables three significant possibilities:

• Convergence happens when content from any source is combined with content from any other source (such as video with text) and made available through a variety of output devices (for example, cell phones, personal digital assistants, pagers, and hand-held computers can all provide each other's services). Content received can easily be resent to one or more others using one or more kinds of devices.

• Processing happens when content is treated like any other kind of data. The text in e-mail messages can be stored, searched, edited, grouped (such as by the same or similar content), linked, and analyzed. That text (whether in a message subject header or in the body of the e-mail message) can also be used as input for other processes, such as sending an e-mail message to a listserv program to subscribe or to change one's preferences. The structure of communication processes can be programmed, allowing users to retrieve all messages that have been posted that relate to an initial posting (threaded conversations), allowing only subscribed members to access posted contributions to a newsgroup or Web site, providing systemwide administrative control of a MOO to the "wizard" or systems operator, or sending out a copy of every message posted to a discussion list to all members of that list.

• Metadata—data about the data, or information about the process and the content—can be created, extracted, and analyzed. We can easily obtain the number of all messages posted to particular Usenet groups, a list of which other books have also been selected by others interested in a particular book from an online bookseller's catalog, or a listing of all listservs devoted to a particular topic.

Convergence, processing, and metadata make computer-mediated communication, especially the multimedia and multisystem Internet, extremely different from unmediated interpersonal communication and from both print-based and electronic, broadcast traditional mass media.

The Internet Is a Technological and Social Network The Internet is networked. An assumption underlying the issues of information and digitization is that the Internet allows communication among users: the Internet connects providers and users of information. In this simple sense of a channel connecting people with information (and thus allowing communication between people), the Internet is no different from interpersonal media and print and electronic mass media. However, it is crucially different from all of those other channels in that its fundamental network form is neither the one-to-one (or in some cases one-to-few) communication among pairs of people communicating face to face, by letter, or by telephone nor the one-to-many (or in some cases one-to-few) communication between a mass-medium broadcaster and its audiences. Rather, it supports any network form involving from one-few-many to one-few-many.

Thus, it can provide not only different forms and scale of communication but also different kinds of benefits than do traditional communication channels. Each member or the pair of a dyad can benefit directly from interaction, but others can benefit only indirectly, at some additional cost. For example, more than two people can engage in a conversation, talk on the telephone, listen to a radio, or watch television together. But this joint experience is by the nature of the media limited to those few participants. There is little major network externality from this small group. Individual audience members can benefit individually from having access to information through broadcast media (such as news or entertainment) and possibly collectively if every one is better informed (such as about the health consequences of various behaviors), but they cannot create content and programming or interact with each other about it. In these cases, the actual flow of communication is limited in form, scope, and direct access to benefits. From the other perspective, a broadcaster can benefit economically from many users through advertising and subscription revenues and through economies of scale by having large and diverse audiences and multiple media creators and media outlets.

One major difference between networked, interactive communication media and traditional interpersonal or broadcast media is that this advantage of allowing interaction among a large number of participants is also a requirement. For the value of a network to become sufficiently greater than the costs of accessing, maintaining, learning, and contributing to it, a critical mass of users and of valuable content (including computer programs, postings, jokes, emotional support, and links to other pages) must exist early enough to interest current and subsequent users to join. Otherwise, the system (or particular online community) will die out (see Katz, 1998; Markus, 1990; Rice, 1982, 1990).

Social Factors, Information Attributes, and Internet Features Interact
This confluence of attributes of social situatedness, information, digitalization, and Internet network features has important implications for the creation of social capital via the Internet in a way that links individuals and groups. Specifically, once individuals have cognitive, physical, and economic access to the Internet, the exchange of information and communication and the interaction among participants begin to take on special characteristics that are not available in other media. In addition,

a normative framework can be readily established that confers benefits at the group level and influences behavior at the individual level. This process is the justification for our conceptualization of the Internet as syntopia.

1. *Transparency of Association, People, Information, Ideas, Action* Internet users can connect with others on the basis of simple or complex indicators of content (such as shared interests found through keyword searches, conversational threads, named newsgroups or Web sites, or associated Web page links), thus increasing the likely relevance of the shared information. However, the Internet is becoming increasingly multimedia in its content and communication forms. Voice, other forms of audio, and video are supplementing and even replacing text input and processing. This change in the content of the Internet may paradoxically erode the rate at which social capital is produced on the Internet. This is because these new "richer" forms of expression are not as scannable or as easy to classify or search as is text. Consequently, the ability to avail oneself of created benefits of information, expression, and interaction may be reduced. It may be that progress in voice-to-text and audio translation may be able to compensate for some of this transition. But it is unlikely that much can be done in the near future in the way of automatic photo or picture interpretation. The results of this change are likely to be reduced accumulation of social capital. This is an ironic outcome in that the richer the media, the less collateral value it might have.

2. *Great Potential for Connectivity without Much Intention or Social Cost* The networking and associative attributes of the Internet allow people to reestablish broken social ties. The Internet also allows people to more easily maintain ties as they move through their lives and maintain their memories of those who are deceased. Chapter 13 demonstrates these aspects of connectivity through various examples. The immediate value and potential benefit of information can be filtered by others whose reputations are respected, which avoids time-consuming or costly usage and assessment efforts. Online community identities can be used to quickly introduce, assist, and socialize new participants, as well as sustain participation over time.

New information sources such as Web sites and discussion groups are highly "trialable" at low risk. It is as easy to create and distribute content (information, ideas, opinions, emotional support) to many people as it is to do so to one individual. Information sharing and use and communicating with others can be performed at little additional financial or social cost compared to the traditional brokering and status recognition needed in unmediated personal relationships. Information can be received from or provided to others without knowing who or where they are. On the other hand, users can engage in rich subnetworks of "private" interaction that do not distract the group interaction, that may develop shared understandings before being shared with the group, and that allow dyadic discussion away from group scrutiny. Thus, there are low entry and transaction costs involved in collective communication.

3. *Critical Mass Leads to Positive Network Externalities and Collective Benefits* As more people share information in any particular venue, the ratio of potentially valuable information to the number of participants rises much faster than the number of participants—even if many participants do not actually contribute any particular content—as long as a critical mass of participants generates enough collective social capital to provide reusable individual social capital to the other participants. Consequently, collective benefits (public goods) can be created without (typically) any more cost than that involved in obtaining individual benefits.

4. *Interaction Is Voluntary* On the other hand, one can more easily ignore, discard, or avoid communication and information that is either irrelevant, is of poor or negative value, or challenges one's current beliefs. This is demonstrated by the ease by which users may leave an online community. This is a benefit in the sense that the risk of heavy up-front investment in becoming a member of a social group does not become a chain or anchor that keeps people in unsatisfying, harmful, or even just boring communities. It is also a disadvantage in that true discourse between opposing positions may be difficult as supporters of each side retreat to their self-reinforcing online newsgroup or community.

5. *Content Can Be Process and Processed; Process Can Be Content and Self-Organizing* With networked digital information, one can retrieve, reuse, adapt, enhance, link, and recontribute content to the same or other collectivities (such as posting on multiple newsgroups or forwarding annotated messages to others in a group). These can be done at

lower (and thus more feasible) costs than through traditional communication media but also in ways that are simply not possible through traditional media. This process of making shared values still more visible—including the value of sharing itself—reinforces those shared values and fosters more contributions by others.

The Internet thus enables continuous iterative possibilities. This allows complex questions to be addressed and allows the questions themselves to be improved and refined. It is thus consequential in terms of its size and scope as a repository of information, with a wide range of tools being developed to organize, search, retrieve, and display contents (see Rice et al., 2001). It also is a stimulus for ongoing creation of information, communication, and knowledge. Thus one can access and use the public goods created on the Internet without reducing the stock or the value to others. This avoids the "tragedy of the commons" where "free riders" use publicly available resources at such a rate that the common resource disappears (such as traffic jams that clog highways or private polluters who contaminate public wilderness). There are, of course, forms of the tragedy of the Internet commons—massive information overload, spam, viruses and worms, and network congestion resulting from intensively focused usage (such as millions of people downloading pictures of Princess Diana's funeral or copies of the Starr report on President Clinton's impeachment trial). Hence the Internet can help ensure that communication efforts will be relevant to, or even create, a particular group without generating costs for or conflict with other groups. Because of the nature of information, online interaction is not a zero-sum game: benefits to some do not have to come at costs to others. Again, this is a characteristic of syntopia, a synthesis of individual actions and contributions in a "together place."

6. *Collective Benefit Is a By-Product of Individual Self-Interest, Identity, and Involvement but Can Also Be an Intentional Goal* Individuals using the Internet can readily engage in activities that generate individual social capital while also creating collective social capital, often as a by-product that is neither intended nor even known. The interaction of digitized information, characteristics of users, and the networked Internet yields easy, valuable, and extensive connectivity among networked users. The by-product of this connectivity, when used by self-interested

individuals in hot pursuit of information, entertainment, self-expression, and communication is a rapid proliferation of interconnected self-organizing systems. The Internet has an important property of emergence. Like the telephone and the mobile phone that has evolved beside it, this interpersonal communication technology creates unique and unexpected benefits. These benefits grow from the interaction and innovativeness of users and result in a richer medium for participants, whose activities may yield positive outcomes that exceed significantly the original intent of Internet user. No individual can control the nature or flow of Internet content, which means that groups (even highly transient and nonidentifiable ones) can create, maintain, adapt, and terminate multiple communities as they wish. They can do this while simultaneously creating sufficient social capital for the communities to generate benefits and opportunities for individual exploration of identity.

Conclusion

Although the Internet has not led to any political revolutions, it has supported and encouraged them (as have—and do—the phone and fax). This finding is in keeping with our view that the Internet is a part of syntopia, a together place that allows people to pursue their interests but that is also a continuity with other aspects of their lives, including their technology of communication, such as the mobile phone. At the same time, the Internet is not only a political phenomenon but an expressive one as well. The same processes that draw people onto the Internet and into social relationships can, in many cases, create new intellectual and artistic terrain for themselves and others to enjoy. We have argued that syntopia includes both individual and collective levels and that by looking at the total communication picture, not just one modality called the Internet, we can understand more accurately the social processes involving and revolving around the Internet. Despite the heavy Internet focus of this book, we have included collateral communication technology and modes in our analysis and have compared users and nonusers, including former users. By considering what we term the "invisible mouse," the ways in which social capital accumulates can be more accurately examined.

Our evidence has demonstrated that (1) the Internet does not reduce social capital but rather contributes to social capital, (2) innovative uses of the Internet build what is commonly thought of as social capital, and (3) new forms of social capital are enabled by the Internet. However, we also point out that (4) the Internet has not (yet) transformed politics or the nature of government. We argue that (5) an integration of both individual-level and collective-level social-capital theories seems best suited for understanding the relation of Internet usage and social capital.

We also put forth the idea that (6) the Internet draws people who are interested in advancing their personal interests and not necessarily in promoting community per se. This does not mean that community benefits will not be forthcoming, only that motives are individually centered. Thus the pursuit of individual interests leads to new and unexpected forms of social interaction and group activity. However, throughout our analyses, (7) our view is not celebratory because we recognize both the limitations and fearsome abuses of the technology. Indeed, like the atomic bomb, automobiles, electricity, and antibiotics, the Internet contains catastrophic potentials for humankind. Finally, we argue that (8) the interaction of social values and context, the nature of information (especially digitized information), and the features of the networked Internet all interact to foster the satisfaction of individual identity projects while also creating collective social capital.

We can identify a cycle regarding individual use of the Internet, social interaction, and collective social capital. Individuals follow their self-interest, which leads them to interact with others. This interaction leads to the creation of new information and forms of organization. This creativity in turn alters individuals' views of themselves and their relationships with others. This then enlarges what Merton (1957) has called an "opportunity structure."

An expanding opportunity structure allows people to have what feels like (and is) increased personal freedom. This increased personal freedom allows individuals to remake themselves to fulfill their existing desires (Gergen, 1991). It also gives rise to previously unidentified "needs and desires" or, perhaps more accurately, allows them to be coconstructed within the person and between the ego and the other. These include psychological, social, biological or sexual, cultural, and material needs.

When these areas are intermixed, the process moves the individual into new areas. One person may be brought together with another due to their mutual interest in topic A and through that new relationship may be led to a new area of activity and interest and a new online community of participants.

The Internet is not a substitute for ordinary life off the screen. Rather, it is part of a continuum that allows people to meet their individual needs and develop new interests, often while creating collective social capital—for good and for bad.

Given the tools, which for the Internet we have symbolized by the "invisible mouse," people use their natural inclinations to communicate to create self-organizing and self-serving social systems throughout the multimedia domain we call syntopia. Syntopia is a synergistic "together place" that integrates people's ideas and actions. It can foster both virtue and sin even while it synthesizes dystopian and utopian impulses. Syntopia brings together the offline and online realms of action, local and global concerns, and individual and collective pursuits.

Appendixes

A

Methodology

This appendix briefly summarizes the sources of the data that we analyze and discuss throughout the book and provides some comments on methodology. Appendix B provides the question wording, response choices, and summary statistics from the two primary data sources—the combined dataset from our surveys and from the Pew Internet and American Life Project March 2000 survey.

National Telephone Surveys

All surveys asked about social and personality attributes and about demographic and occupational characteristics.

Surveys

• *October 1995 General Survey* The October 1995 national random telephone sample was conducted under contract by a commercial firm. The survey yielded 2,500 respondents and did not specify where users used the Internet, so our results should encompass usage at work, in the home, or at school.

• *November 1996 General Survey* The second national random telephone survey, carried out in November 1996 by a commercial firm just after the general election, yielded 557 respondents.

• *November 1996 Internet User Survey* The 1996 sample of Internet users was augmented by a national random telephone survey of 450 Internet users, making a total of about 550 Internet users.

• *November 1997 General Survey*   The November 1997 survey questioned a national random telephone sample and was conducted by a commercial firm working under our direction. The survey yielded 2,148 respondents.

• *November 1997 Internet User Survey*   Once again, the sample of users was augmented by a second national sample of 153 users, making a total of 800 users.

• *February 2000 Pilot General Survey*   This survey included primary questions from the 1995, 1996, and 1997 surveys. It also included questions relating to community participation, social isolation, and information overload. We used this survey to pretest the measures by providing the survey to 125 undergraduate students and then analyzing the responses and relationships among the variables. Measures were revised or dropped based on these results. Because of the small and biased sample, we do not report any results from this data but mention it to indicate the nature of some of our pilot testing.

• *June 2000 General Survey*   The resulting revised survey was pretested again on a national telephone survey of 200 respondents. A few measures were dropped based on these results. The final survey was then administered nationally by a commercial survey company. Because U.S. Internet usage was near 50% at the time of this survey, we set a quota goal of 1,000 Internet users, resulting in a total sample of approximately 1,800. Therefore, we did not need an additional follow-up survey for Internet users only, as was the case in the prior national telephone surveys.

Initial and Augmented Samples

As noted above, the 1996 and 1997 samples were augmented with a sample of additional Internet users. Whenever we report for those two years any population estimates of usage, they will be from the initial, unaugmented samples. This way our extrapolations to the underlying population will be not biased (at least due to improper weighting). But whenever we compare relative distributions of variables, we use the combined samples since this gives us more accuracy in terms of making statistical estimates.

The Pew Internet and American Life Project

(The following description is based on the description found on the Pew Foundation Web site at ⟨www.pewinternet.org⟩). The Pew Internet and American Life Project is a noncommercial, nonpartisan attempt to survey public opinion to produce timely and topical reports on the social role of Internet use. It is administered by the Tides Center, a nonprofit organization, and is directed by Lee Rainie, who can be contacted at Pew Internet and American Life Project, 1100 Connecticut Avenue, Suite 710, Washington, D.C. 20036-4116, (202) 296 0019.

The project's collection of data is built around a system of tracking polls, beginning with the findings of a telephone poll that was conducted every day in March 2000 by Princeton Survey Research Associates among a sample of 3,533 adults who were 18 years of age or older and living in the continental United States during the period March 1 to 31, 2000. The survey was conducted using a rolling daily sample, with a target of completing 100 interviews each day throughout the month. Many questions in the March survey were asked only of 1,690 adults who were Internet users.

Each sample is a random-digit sample of telephone numbers selected from telephone exchanges in the continental United States. The random-digit aspect of the sample is used to avoid listing bias and provides representation of both listed and unlisted numbers (including not-yet-listed numbers). The design of the sample achieves this representation by random generation of the last two digits of telephone numbers selected on the basis of their area code, telephone exchange, and bank number.

A new sample was released daily and was kept in the field for at least five days. This ensured that the complete call procedures were followed for the entire sample. At least 10 attempts were made to complete an interview at every household in the sample. The calls were staggered over times of day and days of the week to maximize the chances of making contact with a potential respondent. Interview refusals were recontacted at least once to try again to complete an interview. All interviews completed on any given day were considered to be the final sample for that day.

Survey Limitations

Representativeness   As with any survey (or any form of measurement), measurement errors occur. There are well-known biases in respondents, even when using a random-digit dialing approach as we did. (See Katz et al., 1997, and Keeter, 1995, for more information about possible response biases.) A particularly critical point is that the approximately 5% of households without telephones cannot be included in the survey. It is probable that this 5% would be drawn from the lowest socioeconomic strata (Schement, 1995), be likely not to have heard of the Internet, and be extremely unlikely to have Internet service in their home.

As Tables A.1 and A.2 show, the 1995 and 1996 survey distributions are similar to the U.S. Census data, but those with somewhat more education are overrepresented while those with the lowest incomes are underrepresented. Based on comparisons with 1990 and 1991 U.S. Census data, respondents in the 1995 and 1996 samples are similar to the national average in sex, ethnic mix, and age composition. Table 3.7 provided comparative data from the 1999 and 2000 census data.

Some, but by no means all, public opinion surveys use weighting post hoc to compensate for nonresponse bias or ineffective sampling frames. Lansing and Morgan (1971, p. 233) recommend this technique. However, many other statisticians express deep concern about applying weighting procedures to correct problems of this nature. They view weighting as highly susceptible to serious (and difficult to detect) errors. These statisticians include Kalton (1983, p. 74), Zieschang (1990, p. 987), and the enormously influential sampling expert, Leslie Kish (Kish, 1967, p. 403). We have not weighted our data because we share these concerns and believe that the "cure" of weighting raises more problems than it resolves. Further, most of our analyses test for any significant effects of a wide set of demographic variables, so some biases are controlled for statistically.

The survey company had interviewers who spoke Spanish so that speakers of that language could be included in our sample. On the other hand, there may be some underestimation of who is online because people who use a modem may not be reachable via phone for extended periods since they are already "on the line."

Table A.1
Sample 1995 Demographics versus U.S. Census Data

Demographic Categories	Study (percentage)	U.S. Census (percentage)
Age[a]		
18–24	11.9%	14.2%
25–29	12.4	11.1
30–34	12.1	11.9
35–39	11.3	10.9
40–44	11.6	10.0
45–49	8.8	7.6
50–54	7.8	6.2
55–59	5.8	5.5
60–64	5.5	5.7
At least 65	12.8	17.0
Sex[a]		
Male	44.3	48.0
Female	55.7	52.0
Education[a]		
Kindergarten to 11th grade	11.3	22.5
Graduated from high school	30.1	36.6
Vocational or technical school graduate	5.4	2.1
Some college	27.0	17.6
College graduate	17.8	16.1
Graduate-level work	8.4	5.0
Marital status[a]		
Married living with spouse	54.5	61.4
Widowed	5.5	7.5
Divorced or separated	13.1	8.6
Never married (single)	26.9	22.6

Table A.1
(continued)

Demographic Categories	Study (percentage)	U.S. Census (percentage)
Race[a]		
White	80.9	80.3
Black	8.8	12.1
Asian	1.6	2.9
Hispanic	4.8	0.8
Native American	N.A.	3.9
Other	3.8	—
Children under 18 present[a]	48.5	51.0
Household income[b]		
Below $15,000	16.0	24.1
$15,000 to $24,000	18.4	16.8
$25,000 to $34,000	22.2	14.8
$35,000 to $49,000	17.1	17.1
$50,000 to $74,000	15.0	16.1
At least $75,000	11.2	11.0

Note: N.A. = data not available.
a. U.S. Department of Commerce (1992). Where possible, census percentages are with respect to the over age 18 population, not the total population. Age data are from 1991.
b. U.S. Department of Commerce (1992, *Money Income of Households, Families and Persons in the United States: 1992*, Table 5, Total Money Income of Households in 1992, All races).

Perceptions and Recall   Despite their best attempts to be conscientious, people may have given distorted answers to our questions. These may be due to memory telescoping and a strain toward providing socially desirable answers. While we tried to mitigate these problems via careful wording, modification after pretesting, and timely sampling, problems remain. In addition to the above problems of cognition, there may be some confusion about what the questions mean and how they are operationally applied to ambiguous cases. In particular, we have no independent way of establishing which respondents actually went on the Internet and for how long. Also, participation in an organized community, social, or religious group may be open to a variety of interpreta-

Table A.2
Sample November 1996 Demographics versus U.S. Census Data

Demographic Categories	Study (percentage)	U.S. Census (percentage)
Age[a]		
18–24	14.4	14.2
25–29	9.8	11.1
30–34	9.8	11.9
35–39	12.6	10.9
40–44	10.8	10.0
45–49	8.8	7.6
50–54	8.8	6.2
55–59	5.8	5.5
60–64	4.8	5.7
At least 65	14.2	17.0
Sex[a]		
Male	45.7	48.0
Female	54.3	52.0
Education[a]		
Kindergarten to 11th grade	14.3	22.5
Graduated from high school	30.3	36.6
Vocational or technical school graduate	4.4	2.1
Some college	26.1	17.6
College graduate	14.5	16.1
Graduate level work	10.4	5.0
Marital status[a]		
Married living with spouse	55.7	61.4
Widowed	6.1	7.5
Divorced or separated	9.7	8.6
Never married (single)	29.0	22.6

Table A.2
(continued)

Demographic Categories	Study (percentage)	U.S. Census (percentage)
Race[a]		
White	83.0	80.3
Black	9.7	12.1
Asian	2.3	2.9
Hispanic	3.4	0.8
Native American	N.A.	3.9
Other	1.6	—
Children under 18 present[a]	48.7	51.0
Household income[b]		
Below $15,000	15.4	24.1
$15,000 to $24,000	20.5	16.8
$25,000 to $34,000	18.4	14.8
$35,000 to $49,000	19.6	17.1
$50,000 to $74,000	17.2	16.1
At least $75,000	8.8	11.0

Note: N.A. = data not available.
a. U.S. Department of Commerce (1992). Where possible, census percentages are with respect to the over age 18 population, not the total population. Age data are from 1991.
b. U.S. Department of Commerce (1992, *Money Income of Households, Families and Persons in the United States: 1992*, Table 5, Total Money Income of Households in 1992, All races).

tions. Fully resolving these problems was not possible given the limited resources we had for this study. To some extent, though, a saving grace is that we were looking not for absolute measurements of participation but rather relative differences among groups. For the purposes of this study, we accept the working assumption that to whatever extent misinterpretation or misrecollection occurred, it probably varied approximately equally across all groups. Thus, if differences occur among groups, we tentatively attribute them to social forces rather than to measurement error. Further, as mentioned above in the context of possible sampling bias, the survey agency used Spanish-speaking interviewers for any Hispanic respondents, reducing problems of cross-language interpretations.

Statistical Analyses

Recoding Measures

These various survey datasets contain a large number of variables. As each of them was used for specific purposes and some by different participants over time, the surveys contain both common as well as unique measures, and many of the common measures are operationalized differently. So there were three main issues guiding our analyses to make the various analyses as consistent, straightforward, and comparable for the reader as possible.

First, all common variables were recoded into similar categories. This involved checking the distributions and frequencies of all the responses to establish comparable cut-points—treating missing, nonresponse, and zero answers in consistent ways and making all the variables point in the same direction (that is, typically, higher values mean "more").

Second, almost all the variables were dichotomized. This conversion makes what might be highly complex and differing measures much easier to interpret and summarize. That is, almost all variables were converted into either "high/low" or "yes/no." While most of the variables were in fact categorical or ordinal, so that such a recoding is easily justified, some of the variables were interval or even ratio. Recoding such data into ranked (ordinal) categories or collapsing them into binary categories throws away much data, reduces variance, and reduces possible variance explained and thus statistical significance. However, as noted below, logistic regressions require binary independent variables. So the trade-off for making the many and complex analyses simpler to present and interpret is a conservative set of results. That is, such dichotomizing reduces the strength and significance of relationships, working against finding supportive results. However, given the nature, breadth, and complexity of the various data sources and measures, we felt this was a worthwhile tradeoff. Further, most policy and social questions are typically discussed in terms of such basic categories (consider the very term *digital divide*), and so this approach is probably most useful and understandable.

Third, to make the various results as consistent, straightforward, and comparable for the reader as possible, we relied on essentially three forms of analysis—simple frequencies, cross-tabulations with statistical tests of association, and combined multivariate regressions (almost exclusively logistic regressions because most of the variables were dichotomized) with statistical tests of overall model and individual predictor variables. Again, many other kinds of analyses might be as, or even more, appropriate (such as analysis of variance tests of differences in mean scores across categories) but would, again, increase the complexity of presentation, interpretation, and understanding. So throughout, we opted for minimal complexity, maximal comparability, and some cost in analytical rigor and sophistication.

Logistic Regressions

Logistic regression is the appropriate statistical method for analyzing dependent variables that are dichotomous (binary). Unlike the assumption in linear (multiple) regression of a continuous and normal distribution of values of the dependent variable around a mean, here the dependent variable can take only one of two values (0 or 1). So predicting a generally continuous value for a binary variable is statistically invalid. Doing this will likely create a heteroscedastic distribution of residual error and invalidate the standard error estimates. However, some argue that as long as the dichotomous dependent variable is not too heavily weighted toward one outcome or the other (say, if 95% of all the cases have a value of 1 and only 5% have a value of 0), then linear regression is a fairly robust and good approximation. Nonetheless, we have opted to use (binary) logistic regression to conform to good methodology and to emphasize that many (though not all) of our dependent variables are conceptually dichotomous (that is, users versus nonusers). As noted above, though, in some cases we have created dichotomous dependent variables from essentially continuous ones (such as recent versus long-term user) for analytical and reporting parsimony.

All logistic regression tables include B values, which are unstandardized beta coefficients. The B statistic represents the partial correlation, in unstandardized units, of the dependent variable and each independent variable. When B is negative, the presence of that variable indicates that the event is less likely to occur, but if B is positive, the event is more likely to occur. The Exp(B) values are odds ratios. The Nagelkerke

R-square is roughly analogous to the R-square of multiple regression. The term *odds ratio* is used here to mean the ratio of the probability that the event will occur to the probability that it will not occur; we do not mean it in the sense of informal probability of occurrence. Also when we speak of changes in odds for one variable, it is a change that the presence (or absence) of that dichotomous variable makes assuming all the values of the other variables remain the same. The Exp(B) values are the odds ratios.

The following explanation refers to columns 1 and 2 of table 4.2 from chapter 4 and is an example of how to read the results in the logistic regression tables. For the overall model depicted in columns 1 and 2, the log odds and odds ratios of someone being a dropout change significantly by their age and education. Race and marital status are not significant predictors. The log odds ratio of being a dropout are decreased for those in the "at least 40" age group compared to those in the "under 40" age group by .51; the odds ratio (the change in odds of a respondent being a dropout relative to a change from the "at least 40" to the "under 40" category, with all other variables held statistically constant) is .60 that Is, "at least 40s" are only about two-thirds as likely to be dropouts. For education, the log odds are cut by .63 for college graduates compared to the log odds for those who did not graduate college. The odds ratio is .53, or being a dropout is about half as likely in the graduate group as in the nongraduate group.

Small Percentages of Variance Explained in Most Analyses

Overall, little of the statistical variance has been explained by the models reported in this book. While every researcher likes to find powerful explanatory models, it is not at all surprising that little of the variation in some of the dependent variables is explained by a few independent variables. In something as complex as life—involving knowing neighbors, deciding to vote, or joining an organization—it is unrealistic to expect that the mere fact of being online would be a decisive factor. When we look at the large number of people involved in a behavior that numbers in the millions and accounts for 8.1% of the population in 1995 or 59.7% in 2000, we cannot expect that one individual characteristic variable would account for huge variation in people's behavior. That is, the Internet should not prove to be an overwhelmingly decisive factor. In a different context, we approached this point when we referred to the equivalence (in statistical terms) of Putnam's multiple indicator of "quality of life" and the single measure of Internet household penetration in the formation of social capital (or more specifically, social capital as measured by the per capita murder rate in states). The same point could be made here—namely, that the Internet can be but one factor in people's opportunity matrix. At the same time, even a small percentage of variance explained translates into huge actual numbers. Even if cigarettes cause cancer in only 1% of smokers (though the percentage is presumably much higher), this means that cigarettes will kill by cancer a million Americans living today. This may be a small percentage, but in numerical terms it is more than the combined number of Americans killed in all the wars the United States has ever fought.

Large Sample Sizes and Small Probability Levels

Conversely, our samples are larger than most in social science research. They were not large enough to do the detailed analysis we might have liked, certainly, and that is one reason we relied heavily on logistic regression. But the sample size also affects significance levels, so as our sample sizes increase, the significance levels diminish, all other things being equal. Hence, we suggest that readers direct their attention to effect sizes (etas, beta coefficients, odds ratios) rather than depend on the traditional .05 or other p levels as a guide to interpretation about the strength of associations.

Combination of Quantitative and Qualitative Approaches

We have combined qualitative and quantitative data in an attempt to strengthen and broaden our understanding. By drawing on the tradition of quantitative statistical analysis, we are able to give both the solid backdrop of how the Internet is (and is not) changing life in America, controlling for a variety of demographic and individual variables. Drawing on the tradition of qualitative analysis, we were able to depict the variety and human meaning of the Internet and reflect on the folk stories of interpretation that people apply to their experiences of the Internet.

User Interviews and Site Samples

A word is in order about the methodology used in those chapters where we present qualitative findings and comments concerning user experiences and perceptions. We have used this descriptive material to complement our national statistical sample data. Our rationale was that the survey data alone would be insufficient context for our results given the importance and breadth of the topic. True, the survey data had the virtue of being representative, within known parameters, of the U.S. population and thus could address with strong evidence many of the incompletely tested assertions about the social consequences of the Internet. But they could not give us the rich, nuanced understanding of what this technology means in terms of normative behavior and social perception in dynamic situations. For this, we would need qualitative insights that might reveal what people do and say relative to the Internet. In other words, we wanted a context for our statistical data that would help advance our understanding of the uses and meaning of the Internet.

To extend our sources of reports beyond those of our own powers of observation, we relied on our own network of contacts. Some thoughts by various subject-matter experts are shown in the chapter boxes. Other comments stem from students who as part of their regular assignments do research on Internet-related topics. Thus, we were getting comments and observations from a wider reach of people than we would have by relying on our own experiences alone. We found value in this approach because of its projective nature. That is, we were not trying to get a comprehensive report of everything that was going on but wanted guides to what topics and issues were salient to others. Thus, we created something of a contour map of the issues as seen by young people at an eastern U.S. university. Our aim was to illustrate and enrich descriptions of the Internet in daily life. The reports from these students cannot be extended beyond the group they represent, which is also the case with other studies of the Internet (e.g., Kraut et al., 1998). This nonrandom sample speaks only for them. Yet what they say and what they experience we believe has inherent interest. Not the least reason is that they help provide if not "thick description" then at least "thicker description." Their comments increase local knowledge of what is happening from the perspective of the informant and the participant (Geertz, 1985). Hence, it helps us understand the context and import of our national surveys.

We readily admit that this method of gathering reports is affected by saliency and recency effects. But this has some benefits since we are trying to identify the social and dialogic qualities of the Internet, and these can, at one level, be provided by examining the topical choices of rhetorical expression about a phenomenon. This in turn means that we can see some of the manifest effects and concerns, which is what we are after with the qualitative analysis.

B

Descriptive Statistics from Surveys

Space limitations preclude providing the question wordings, response choices, frequencies, and means for all variables from each of the 1995, 1996, 1997, and 2000 national telephone surveys, the 2000 student pilot survey, the common variables combined across all the years, the common variables broken out by year, and the Pew Internet and American Life Project March 2000 survey. Instead, this appendix provides only the question wording, response choices, and frequencies and means of all items that occurred in more than one of our national surveys broken out by survey year (table B.1) and the frequencies from selected measures of the Pew March 2000 survey. Of these we include only those reported in this book and recode them to match the coding of the other surveys (table B.2).

Table B.1
Measures Occurring in at Least Two Surveys, by Survey Year

Variable	N	Percentage/ Mean	S.D.
Usage			
1995Q2 Have you ever used a computer?			
Yes	1785	71.1	
No	724	28.9	
		1.29	.45
1996Q19 Ever use computer			
Yes	851	84.4	
No	157	15.6	
		1.16	.36
1995Q3 Do you currently use a personal computer in your home?			
Yes	833	46.7	
No	952	53.3	
		1.53	.50
1996Q20 Currently use computer at home			
Yes	584	68.6	
No	267	31.4	
		1.31	.46
1995Q5S Do you use a computer at school?			
Yes	376	44.5	
No	468	55.5	
		1.55	.5
1995Q5W Do you use a computer at work?			
Yes	942	91.1	
No	92	8.9	
		1.09	.28
1996Q21 Currently use computer at work			
Yes	546	64.2	
No	305	35.8	
		1.36	.48
1996Q22 Currently use computer at school			
Yes	267	31.4	
No	584	68.6	
		1.69	.46

Table B.1
(continued)

Variable	N	Percentage/Mean	S.D.
1996Q23 Currently use computer at friends'/relatives'			
Yes	326	38.3	
No	525	61.7	
		1.62	.49
1995Q13 Have you heard of the Internet (the information superhighway or electronic superhighway)?			
Yes	2130	84.9	
No	378	15.1	
		1.15	.36
1996Q24 Ever heard of Internet			
Yes	952	94.4	
No	56	5.6	
		1.06	.23
1997Q25 Have you ever heard of the Internet (also known as the information or electronic superhighway)?			
Yes	2088	90.7	
No	213	9.3	
		1.09	.29
2000pAWAREI01 Have you heard of the Internet?			
Yes	124	99.2	
No	1	.8	
		1.01	.09
2000Q25 Have you ever heard of the Internet (also known as the information or electronic superhighway)?			
Yes	1307	91.7	
No	118	8.3	

Table B.1
(continued)

Variable	N	Percentage/ Mean	S.D.
1995Q14 Which statement best describes your use of the Internet?			
Have not used the Internet	1715	81.5	
Presently not an Internet user	190	9.0	
Presently a Internet user	200	9.5	
		1.28	.63
1996Q25 Describe use of internet			
Not used	333	35.0	
Past user	64	6.7	
User	554	58.3	
		2.23	.94
1997Q27 Which of the following best describes your use of the Internet or online service?			
You have NOT used	1078	51.6	
You have used in the past but not currently using	210	10.1	
You're presently a user	800	38.3	
2000pUSE02 Which of the following best describes your use of the Internet or online services?			
No longer	2	1.6	
User	123	98.4	
2000Q32 Which of the following best describes your use of the Internet or online service?			
You have NOT used	305	23.4	
You have used it in the past but not currently	150	11.5	
You're presently a user	850	65.1	
1995Q23 What year did you start using the Internet?	200	1993.82	2.26
1995Q24 What month did you start using the Internet?	129	6.14	3.02
1996Q30m When start using Internet (month)	613	7.47	2.50
1996Q30y When start using Internet (year)	513	1994.55	2.07
1997Q32m Month in which you started using Internet?	998	7.72	3.30

Table B.1
(continued)

Variable	N	Percentage/ Mean	S.D.
1997Q32y Year in which you started using Internet?	998	1995.52	1.60
2000pFRSTUS05Y When did you first start using the Internet?	123	1996.5	.97
2000Q36 When did you first start using the Internet or going online?	1000	1996.67	2.67
1995Q18m When stop using Internet (month)	165	6.96	2.38
1995Q18y When stop using Internet (year)	165	1994.73	.63
1996Q32m When stop using Internet (month)	57	7.39	2.48
1996Q32y When stop using Internet (year)	57	1995.53	.59
1997Q29m Month in which you stopped using Internet?	195	7.81	2.87
1997Q29y Year in which you stopped using Internet?	195	1996.74	.57
2000Q34 When did you stop using the Internet?	152	1999.16	1.06
1995Q27 In the last month, how often did you use the Internet?	193	13.90	14.87
1996Q113C How many hours online in last seven days			
<1	61	11.1	
1–2	179	32.6	
3–5	125	13.7	
6–10	75	13.7	
>10	109	19.9	
		2.99	1.31
1997Q30C In last seven days how many hours online?			
<1	84	10.9	
1–2	283	36.8	
3–5	177	23.0	
6–10	110	14.3	
>10	116	15.1	
		2.86	1.24

Table B.1
(continued)

Variable	N	Percentage/ Mean	S.D.
2000pHRSWK04 In the last seven days, about how many hours would you guess you've spent online?			
<1	17	13.8	
1–2	35	28.5	
2–5	37	30.1	
5–10	21	17.1	
>10	13	10.6	
		2.82	1.19
200035C In the last seven days, how many hours would you guess you spent online:			
<1	90	10.6	
1–2	180	21.2	
3–5	187	22.1	
6–10	106	19.6	
>10	225	26.5	
		3.30	1.34
1995Q30 Compared to other Internet users, how do you rate your expertise?			
Novice	95	47.5	
Average	70	35.0	
Above average	20	10.0	
Excellent	15	7.5	
		1.78	.91
1997Q33 What would you say is your Internet skill level?			
Novice	206	25.8	
Average	368	46.0	
Above average	151	18.9	
Excellent	75	9.4	
		2.12	.90

Table B.1

(continued)

Variable	N	Percentage/ Mean	S.D.
2000pSKILL06 What would you say is your Internet skill level?			
Novice	8	6.4	
Average	52	41.6	
Above average	48	38.4	
Excellent	15	12.0	
		2.57	.79
2000Q37 What would you say is your Internet skill level?			
Novice	209	20.9	
Average	482	48.2	
Above average	213	21.3	
Excellent	96	9.6	
Reasons for starting or stopping			
1995Q21 Why did you stop using the Internet?			
Cost: Monthly bills were too high	10	6.7	
Access: Lost access from work or school	35	23.4	
Time: No time	22	14.7	
Interest: Lost interest	4	2.7	
Hard: Too hard	3	2.0	
Other: Specify	75	50.3	
1997Q80C What is the main reason you stopped using the internet? (coded from open-ended comments)			
Cost	10	16.4	
Access	31	50.8	
Time	10	16.4	
Interest	7	11.5	
Hard	2	3.3	
Other	1	1.6	

Table B.1
(continued)

Variable	N	Percentage/ Mean	S.D.
I am going to read a list of reasons why a person might be interested in becoming an Internet user:			
1995Q40a Send and receive electronic mail or e-mail			
Very good reason	323	35.1	
Good reason	397	43.2	
Not a good reason	200	21.7	
		1.87	.74
1995Q40b Have contact with new people			
Very good reason	138	15.0	
Good reason	363	39.5	
Not a good reason	419	45.5	
		2.31	.72
1995Q40d Find out information about your special interests			
Very good reason	339	36.8	
Good reason	438	47.6	
Not a good reason	143	15.5	
		1.79	.69
1995Q40e Nowadays it is just a good thing to do			
Very good reason	107	11.6	
Good reason	400	43.5	
Not a good reason	413	44.9	
		2.33	.67
I am going to read a list of reasons why a person might be interested in becoming an Internet user. For each one, please tell me how important that item is to you—1 Very important, 2 Important, 3 Not important.			
2000Q26 Send and receive electronic mail	1307	1.88	.78
2000Q26a Have contact with new people	1307	2.52	.66
2000Q26b Find out information about your special interests	1307	1.77	.69

Table B.1

(continued)

Variable	N	Percentage/ Mean	S.D.
2000Q26c Nowadays it is just a good thing to do	1307	2.42	.68
2000Q26d Get in contact with people who share your special interests	1307	2.31	.68
I am going to read a list of obstacles for people interested in becoming an Internet user:			
1995Q41 No idea about how to do it			
Very much an obstacle	121	13.9	
An obstacle	314	36.0	
Not an obstacle at all	438	50.2	
		2.36	.71
1995Q41a Costs too much			
Very much an obstacle	187	22.3	
An obstacle	361	43.1	
Not an obstacle at all	289	34.5	
		2.12	.74
1995Q41b No way to get access			
Very much an obstacle	140	15.2	
An obstacle	282	30.7	
Not an obstacle at all	449	48.8	
		2.35	.74
1995Q41c Too complicated			
Very much an obstacle	75	8.2	
An obstacle	294	32.0	
Not an obstacle at all	503	54.7	
		2.49	.65
How important were the following as reasons for stopping using the Internet (1 Extremely important to 5 Not at all important)?			
2000Q112 Not interesting	110	2.67	1.53
2000Q112b Too expensive	110	2.40	1.51
2000Q112c Too complicated	110	2.06	1.34
2000Q112d Because you lost access	110	2.84	1.77
2000Q112e Wasted my time	104	2.16	1.41

Table B.1
(continued)

Variable	N	Percentage/ Mean	S.D.
Online contact			
1995Q55 Do you know people only through the Internet that you consider to be your friends?			
Yes	23	11.5	
No	177	88.5	
		1.89	.32
2000pFREND10 Do you know people only through Internet that you consider friends?			
Yes	21	16.8	
No	104	83.2	
		1.83	.38
2000Q43 Do you know people only through the Internet that you consider your friends?			
Yes	122	13.6	
No	775	86.4	
1995Q57 Have you ever met any of these people in person?			
Yes	34	17.0	
No	166	83.0	
		1.83	.38
2000pFRENDM12C Have you ever met someone online and gone on to meet them in person?			
Yes	25	20.0	
No	100	80.0	
		1.80	.40
2000Q45 Have you ever met someone online only and then gone on to meet them in person?			
Yes	92	9.2	
No	908	90.8	
		1.91	.29

Table B.1
(continued)

Variable	N	Percentage/ Mean	S.D.
1995Q59 Do you consider yourself to be a member of an Internet community or communities?			
Yes	51	25.5	
No	149	74.5	
		1.74	.44
2000pCMMUN13C Do you consider yourself a member of an online community?			
Yes	52	41.9	
No	72	58.1	
		1.58	.50
2000Q48C Do you consider yourself a member of an online community?			
Yes	93	100	
1995Q62 Have you ever contacted family members over the Internet?			
0	116	58.0	
Once or twice	16	8.0	
Several times a year	18	9.0	
Several times a month	29	14.5	
Several times a week or more	21	10.5	
		2.12	1.48
2000pCONFM14C Have you ever contacted family members over the Internet?			
0	24	19.2	
Several times a year	50	40.0	
Several times a month	25	20.0	
Several times a week	26	20.8	
		3.23	1.33
2000Q50C How many times have you contacted family members over the Internet in the past month?			
Several times a year	27	14.1	
Several times a month	46	24.0	
Several times a week or more	119	62.0	
		4.48	.73

Table B.1
(continued)

Variable	N	Percentage/ Mean	S.D.
1996Q89 Online participation has been important personal growth			
Strong agree	147	27.3	
Somewhat agree	135	25.1	
Somewhat disagree	99	18.4	
Strong disagree	157	29.2	
		2.49	1.18
2000pPARTGR15 Online participation has been important to my personal growth.			
Strong agree	17	15.3	
Somewhat agree	46	41.4	
Somewhat disagree	23	20.7	
Strong disagree	25	22.5	
		2.50	1.01
Community participation			
1995Q131N How many religious organizations do you belong to (e.g., church or synagogue member)?			
0	824	35.8	
1–4	1460	63.5	
5–9	14	.6	
10–19	1	.0	
		1.65	.49
2000pGRELIG16 How many religious organizations do you belong to?			
0	54	43.5	
1–4	69	55.6	
5–9	1	.8	
		1.57	.51
2000Q78bN Religious (e.g., church or synagogue)			
0	648	45.5	
1–4	773	54.2	
5–9	4	.3	
		1.55	.50

Table B.1
(continued)

Variable	N	Percentage/ Mean	S.D.
1995Q131aN How many leisure organizations do you belong to (e.g., hiking, biking, bowling, or tennis club)?			
0	1329	60.8	
1–4	814	37.2	
5–9	36	1.6	
10–19	8	.4	
		1.42	.55
2000pGLEIS17 How many leisure (hiking, biking, bowling, tennis) organizations do you belong to?			
0	59	47.2	
1–4	57	45.6	
5–9	8	6.4	
10–19	1	.8	
		1.61	.65
2000Q78N How many leisure (e.g., hiking, biking, bowling, or tennis club) organizations do you belong to?			
0	1341	94.1	
1–4	81	5.7	
5–9	3	.2	
		1.06	.25
1995Q131bN How many community organizations do you belong to (e.g., Lions Club or volunteer for political cause)?			
0	1397	64.0	
1–4	748	34.3	
5–9	30	1.4	
10–19	8	.4	
		1.38	.53

Table B.1
(continued)

Variable	N	Percentage/Mean	S.D.
2000pGCMNT18 How many community (Lions Club, volunteer) organizations do you belong to?			
0	77	61.6	
1–4	44	35.2	
5–9	3	2.4	
More than 20	1	.8	
		1.43	.63
2000Q78aN How many community (e.g., Lions Club or volunteer for political causes) organizations do you belong to?			
0	1096	70.9	
1–4	313	22.0	
5–9	16	1.1	
		1.24	.45
Overload, satisfaction			
1995Q110 How often do you feel rushed to do the things you have to do?			
Always	478	36.6	
Sometimes	581	44.5	
Almost never	247	18.9	
	1306	2.46	1.17
2000pRUSH29 How often do you feel rushed to do the things you have to do?			
Always	34	27.2	
Most of time	59	47.2	
Sometimes	28	22.4	
Seldom	4	3.2	
		2.02	.79

Table B.1

(continued)

Variable	N	Percentage/ Mean	S.D.
2000Q55 How often do you feel rushed to do the things you have to do?			
Always	296	22.3	
Most of the time	343	25.8	
Sometimes	482	36.3	
Seldom	146	11.0	
Never	62	4.7	
		2.5	1.09
1995Q140 You feel you have more to do than you can comfortably handle.			
Strongly agree	438	17.5	
Agree	694	27.7	
Neutral	369	14.7	
Disagree	862	34.4	
Strongly disagree	143	5.7	
		2.83	1.23
2000pDOMORE30 You feel you have more to do than you can comfortably handle.			
Strongly agree	17	13.6	
Agree	46	36.8	
Neutral	41	32.8	
Disagree	19	15.2	
Strongly disagree	2	1.6	
		2.54	.96
2000Q56 You feel you have more to do than you can comfortably handle.			
Strongly agree	225	16.9	
Agree	334	25.1	
Neutral	294	22.1	
Disagree	379	28.5	
Strongly disagree	97	7.3	
		2.84	1.22

Table B.1
(continued)

Variable	N	Percentage/Mean	S.D.
1995Q111 Overall how satisfied are you with the way your life is going?			
Very satisfied	407	31.2	
Satisfied	657	50.3	
Neutral	170	13.0	
Dissatisfied	49	3.8	
Very dissatisfied	23	1.8	
		1.95	.86
2000pLIFESA31 Overall, how satisfied are you with the way your life is going?			
Very satisfied	19	15.2	
Satisfied	67	53.6	
Neutral	28	22.4	
Dissatisfied	9	7.2	
Very dissatisfied	2	1.6	
		2.26	.86
2000Q57 Overall, how satisfied are you with the way your life is going?			
Very satisfied	515	38.8	
Satisfied	613	46.1	
Neutral	138	10.4	
Dissatisfied	45	3.4	
Very dissatisfied	18	1.4	
		1.82	.85
1995Q112 How satisfied are you with your level of communication with friends and family and work colleagues?			
Very satisfied	515	39.4	
Satisfied	660	50.5	
Neutral	89	6.8	
Dissatisfied	31	2.4	
Very dissatisfied	11	.8	
		1.75	.75

Table B.1

(continued)

Variable	N	Percentage/ Mean	S.D.
2000pCOMSA32 How satisfied are you with your level of communication with friends and family and work colleagues?			
Very satisfied	24	19.2	
Satisfied	66	52.8	
Neutral	22	17.6	
Dissatisfied	12	9.6	
Very dissatisfied	1	.8	
		2.20	.89
2000Q58 How satisfied are you with your level of communication with friends and family and work colleagues?			
Very satisfied	563	42.4	
Satisfied	596	44.8	
Neutral	117	8.8	
Dissatisfied	44	3.3	
Very dissatisfied	9	.7	
		1.75	.80
Demographics			
1995Q148 Which describes your current work status? Check all that apply.			
Full-time	1404	56.1	
Part-time	303	12.1	
Retired	352	14.1	
Not working for pay or unemployed	270	10.8	
Student	172	6.9	
1996Q97 Work status			
Full-time	556	55.8	
Part-time	120	12.0	
Retired	111	11.1	
Not working for pay or unemployed	76	7.6	
Student	134	13.4	

Table B.1
(continued)

Variable	N	Percentage/ Mean	S.D.
1997Q55 Which best describes your current employment status?			
Full-time	1260	56.8	
Part-time	221	10.0	
Retired	328	14.8	
Not working for pay or unemployed	219	9.9	
Student	191	8.6	
2000pWRKST19 Which best describes your current work status?			
Full	11	8.9	
Part	57	46	
Not working	4	3.2	
Student	52	41.9	
2000Q79 Which best describes your current work status?			
Full-time	806	56.6	
Part-time	181	12.7	
Retired	207	14.5	
Not working for pay or unemployed	137	9.6	
Student	94	6.6	
1995Q149 What is your current marital status			
Never married	667	26.6	
Married	1345	53.7	
Divorced/separated	316	12.6	
Widowed	149	5.9	
Living with a partner	12	.5	
Other	17	.7	
1996Q98 Current marital status			
Never married	335	33.2	
Married	546	54.2	
Divorced/separated	80	7.9	
Widow	37	3.7	
Living with a partner	7	.7	
Other	3	.3	

Table B.1
(continued)

Variable	N	Percentage/ Mean	S.D.
1997Q56 What is your current marital status?			
Never married	667	29.0	
Married	1173	51.0	
Divorced/separated	248	10.8	
Widowed	125	5.4	
Living with a partner	13	.6	
Other	75	3.3	
2000pMARIT21 What is your current marital status?			
Never married	115	92.0	
Married	4	3.2	
Living with a partner	6	4.8	
2000Q27 What is your current marital status?			
Never married	460	32.3	
Married, living with spouse	687	48.2	
Divorced/separated	174	12.2	
Widowed	78	5.5	
Living with a partner	26	1.8	
1995Q151 Number of children in household	2441	1.41	.69
1996Q100 How many children	993	1.06	1.44
2000pCHILDN22 How many children under 18 years old are living in your household?	124	1.35	.63
2000Q81 How many children under 18 years old are living in your household?	1425	.78	1.1
1995Q154 Sex			
Male	1402	55.9	
Female	1104	44.1	
		1.44	.50
1996Q103 Sex			
Male	496	49.2	
Female	512	50.8	
		1.51	.50

Table B.1
(continued)

Variable	N	Percentage/ Mean	S.D.
1997Q62 Sex			
Male	1113	48.4	
Female	1188	51.6	
		1.52	.50
2000p Sex			
Male	39	31.2	
Female	86	68.8	
		1.69	.47
2000Q28 Sex			
Male	656	46.0	
Female	769	54.0	
		1.54	.54
1996Q114 Age (combining q102, q113 midpoint)	991	38.80	16.29
1997Q60 Age (with midpoints of those who responded by categories added in)	2301	41.21	16.96
2000pAGE23 Age (using midpoints)	125	21.7	3.22
2000Q82 Age	1425	43.15	19.79
1995Q155 Highest education completed			
Less than high school diploma	277	11.1	
High school diploma or GED	767	30.6	
Some college	669	26.7	
Technical school	133	5.3	
Bachelor's degree	382	15.2	
Some graduate school	278	11.1	
1996Q104 Highest level of education			
Less than high school	106	10.6	
High school diploma or GED	210	21.0	
Some college	291	29.2	
Tech school	36	3.6	
Bachelor's degree	182	18.2	
Some graduate school	173	17.3	

Table B.1
(continued)

Variable	N	Percentage/ Mean	S.D.
1997Q63 Highest level of education you have completed?			
Less than high school	246	11.3	
High school diploma or GED	576	26.6	
Some college	559	25.8	
Technical school	94	4.3	
Bachelor's degree	408	18.8	
Some graduate school	286	13.2	
2000pEDUC25C Highest level of education you have completed?			
Some college	125	100.0	
2000Q83 Highest level of education you have completed?			
Less than high school	159	11.2	
High school diploma or GED	365	25.6	
Some college	378	26.5	
Technical/vocational school	46	3.2	
College graduate	321	22.5	
Attended graduate school	156	10.9	
1995Q156C Annual household income range (personal income if respondent is not in family)			
Less than $35,000	1125	55.8	
$35,000 to $50,000	360	17.9	
More than $50,000	530	26.3	
		1.70	.86
1996Q105C Annual household income			
Less than $35,000	294	46.1	
$35,000 to $50,000	118	18.5	
More than $50,000	226	35.4	
		1.89	.90

Table B.1
(continued)

Variable	N	Percentage/ Mean	S.D.
1997Q64 Annual household income			
Less than $35,000	717	39.0	
$35,000 to $50,000	490	26.7	
More than $50,000	631	34.3	
		1.95	.86
2000pINCOME26 Annual household income			
Less than $35,000	31	25.0	
$35,000 to 50,000	25	20.2	
More than $50,000	68	54.8	
		2.30	.85
2000Q84C Annual household income			
Less than $35,000	411	35.4	
$35,000 to $50,000	262	22.5	
More than $50,000	489	42.1	
		2.07	.88
1995Q157 Do you			
Own your own home	1597	63.7	
Rent	742	29.6	
Trailer/mobile	61	2.4	
Other	105	4.2	
1996Q106 Do you			
Own home	625	62.0	
Rent	313	31.1	
Trailer/mobile	15	1.5	
Other	55	5.5	
1995Q158 How long have you been living at your current address?	2479	9.79	10.97
1996Q108Y How long at current address (less than 1 year = 0)	1008	4.2	8.7
2000pOCCUP27Y How long have you lived at your current address? (less than 1 year = 0)	125	4.26	3.4
2000Q85 How long have you lived at your current address? (less than 1 year = 0)	1400	10.32	11.89

Table B.1
(continued)

Variable	N	Percentage/ Mean	S.D.
1995Q159 Which category best describes you?			
White non-Hispanic	2023	80.7	
African American or black	232	9.3	
Asian	42	1.7	
Hispanic	113	4.5	
Other	96	3.8	
1996Q111 Which category best describes you?			
White	866	85.9	
Black	75	7.4	
Asian	20	2.0	
Hispanic	32	3.2	
Other	15	1.5	
1997Q69 Which category best describes you?			
White non-Hispanic	1802	78.3	
African American or black	251	10.9	
Asian	51	2.2	
Hispanic	111	4.8	
Other	86	3.7	
2000p Which category best describes you?			
White non-Hispanic	78	62.4	
African American	10	8	
Asian	23	18.4	
Hispanic	7	5.6	
Other	7	5.6	
2000Q86 Which category best describes you?			
White non-Hispanic	1103	77.4	
African American or black	160	11.2	
Asian	44	3.1	
Hispanic	69	4.8	
Other (Specify)	49	3.4	

Table B.1
(continued)

Variable	N	Percentage/ Mean	S.D.
Communication			
In the last week, how many times did you contact people using the following forms of communication, outside of work (that is, sending, not receiving)?			
2000pLETT#34 How many times in last week did you contact people via letters?			
0	95	76.0	
1–4	25	20.0	
5–9	4	3.2	
10–19	1	.8	
		1.29	.57
2000Q59L Letters			
0	667	66.7	
1–4	263	26.3	
5–9	39	3.9	
10–19	20	2.0	
At least 20	11	1.1	
		1.45	.76
2000pPHONE#35 How many times in last week did you contact people via phone calls?			
0	1	.8	
1–4	16	12.8	
5–9	28	22.4	
10–19	40	32.0	
At least 20	40	32.0	
		3.82	1.05
2000Q59aL Phone calls			
0	35	3.5	
1–4	151	15.1	
5–9	207	20.7	
10–19	263	26.3	
At least 20	344	34.4	
		3.73	1.18

Table B.1

(continued)

Variable	N	Percentage/ Mean	S.D.
2000pVOICE #37 How many times in week did you contact people via voice mail or answering machine?			
0	3	2.4	
1–4	54	43.2	
5–9	47	37.6	
10–19	15	12.0	
At least 20	6	4.8	
		2.74	.88
2000Q59bL Leave a message by voice mail or answering machine			
0	216	21.6	
1–4	340	34.0	
5–9	206	20.6	
10–19	155	15.5	
At least 20	83	8.3	
		2.55	1.22
2000pEMAIL #38 How many times in last week did you contact people via e-mail?			
0	10	8.2	
1–4	42	34.4	
5–9	25	20.5	
10–19	25	20.5	
At least 20	20	16.4	
2000Q59cL Electronic mail (e-mail)			
0	360	36.0	
1–4	183	18.3	
5–9	142	14.2	
10–19	149	14.9	
At least 20	166	16.6	
		2.58	1.50

Table B.2
Descriptive Statistics for Variables Used from the Pew March 2000 Survey ($n = 3533$)

Variable and Values	Frequency	Percent
Users and Nonusers		
Sex		
Male	1654	46.8
Female	1879	53.2
Ageb		
Under 40 (0)	1538	44.7
At least 40 (1)	1902	55.3
educb		
Less than college (0)	2551	73.0
College or more (1)	943	27.0
Raceb		
AA (0)	388	13.0
WnH (1)	2597	87.0
D7b (maritalb)		
All other	1599	46.8
Married	1816	53.2
D8b (work)		
Full-time	1969	56.3
Other	1531	43.7
D11b (income binary)		
Under $40,000	1399	39.6
At least $40,000	2134	60.4
d2 Parental status		
No	2287	64.9
Yes	1239	35.1
q1 Satisfaction with way things are going in US		
Dissatisfied	1450	44.8
Satisfied	1783	55.2
q2 Read newspaper yesterday		
No	2078	58.8
Yes	1454	41.2

Table B.2

(continued)

Variable and Values	Frequency	Percent
q3 Watch news on TV yesterday		
No	1487	42.2
Yes	2034	57.8
q25 Can turn to people for help		
None, hardly any people	460	13.3
Just a few people	1469	42.4
Many people	1535	44.3
q26a Visited with family or friends yesterday		
No	1164	33.0
Yes	2360	67.0
q26b Called a friend or relative yesterday		
No	1401	39.8
Yes	2115	60.2
Users Only		
curruse		
No (0)	548	24.5
Yes (1)	1690	75.5
q10 Amount of time spent online yesterday		
Less than 15 minutes	95	.5
15 minutes to less than a half hour	150	5.0
Half hour to less than 1 hour	183	8.3
About an hour	185	8.5
More than one hour but less than 2	107	0.7
2 hours to less than 3 hours	117	1.7
3 hours to less than 4 hours	56	.6
4 hours or more	105	0.5
q12b		
Recent (under 1 year)	635	37.7
Long-term (at least 2 years)	1050	62.3
q17a Ever send or read e-mail		
No, have never done	118	17.3
Yes, have done this	565	82.7

Table B.2
(continued)

Variable and Values	Frequency	Percent
q17b Ever get news online		
No, have never done	341	49.9
Yes, have done this	342	50.1
q17c Ever get financial information online		
No, have never done	446	65.3
Yes, have done this	237	34.7
q17d Ever look for information about product online		
No, have never done	216	31.7
Yes, have done this	466	68.3
q17e Ever get information about travel online		
No, have never done	282	41.3
Yes, have done this	401	58.7
q17f Ever do research for school or training online		
No, have never done	303	44.4
Yes, have done this	379	55.6
q17g Ever look for health or medical information online		
No, have never done	341	50.0
Yes, have done this	341	50.0
q17h Ever check weather information online		
No, have never done	326	47.7
Yes, have done this	357	52.3
q17i Ever check sports information online		
No, have never done	462	67.7
Yes, have done this	220	32.3
q17j Ever do research for job online besides e-mail		
No, have never done	389	57.0
Yes, have done this	294	43.0
q17k Ever look for news about politics online		
No, have never done	484	70.9
Yes, have done this	199	29.1

Table B.2

(continued)

Variable and Values	Frequency	Percent
q17bhk (mn: news, weather, politics; alpha = .59; M = .44, sd = .36)		
.00	206	30.2
.33	173	25.3
.67	187	27.4
1.00	117	17.1
q17l Ever look for information about a hobby online		
No, have never done	195	28.6
Yes, have done this	488	71.4
q17m Ever go online just for fun or to pass time		
No, have never done	275	40.3
Yes, have done this	408	59.7
q17n Ever send instant messages		
No, have never done	408	59.7
Yes, have done this	275	40.3
q17o Ever buy a product online		
No, have never done	443	65.0
Yes, have done this	239	35.0
q18a Sent or read e-mail yesterday		
No, have never done	127	12.6
Yes, have done this	880	87.4
q18b Got news online yesterday		
No, have never done	624	62.0
Yes, have done this	382	38.0
q18c Got financial information online yesterday		
No, have never done	743	73.9
Yes, have done this	263	26.1
q18d Looked for information about product online yesterday		
No, have never done	772	76.7
Yes, have done this	234	23.3

Table B.2
(continued)

Variable and Values	Frequency	Percent
q18e Got information about travel online yesterday		
No, have never done	896	89.0
Yes, have done this	111	11.0
q18f Did research for school or training online yesterday		
No, have never done	823	82.0
Yes, have done this	181	18.0
q18g Looked for health or medical information online yesterday		
No, have never done	896	89.1
Yes, have done this	110	10.9
q18h Checked weather information online yesterday		
No, have never done	745	74.0
Yes, have done this	262	26.0
q18i Checked sports information online yesterday		
No, have never done	871	86.5
Yes, have done this	136	13.5
q18j Did research for job online besides e-mail yesterday		
No, have never done	738	73.3
Yes, have done this	269	26.7
q18k Looked for news about politics online yesterday		
No, have never done	840	83.6
Yes, have done this	165	16.4
q18bhk (mn: news, weather, politics; alpha = .57; M = .27, sd = .32)		
.00	509	50.7
.33	248	24.7
.67	181	18.0
1.00	66	6.6
q18l Looked for information about a hobby online yesterday		
No, have never done	689	68.8
Yes, have done this	313	31.2

Table B.2

(continued)

Variable and Values	Frequency	Percent
q18m Went online just for fun or to pass time yesterday		
No, have never done	657	65.2
Yes, have done this	350	34.8
q18n Sent instant messages yesterday		
No, have never done	799	79.4
Yes, have done this	207	20.6
q18o Bought a product online yesterday		
No, have never done	934	92.8
Yes, have done this	73	7.2
q23b Ever take part in chatrooms		
Yes, have done this	176	25.8
No, have never done	507	74.2
q23c Ever download or listen to music online		
Yes, have done this	237	34.7
No, have never done	446	65.3
q23d Ever look for information about a job online		
Yes, have done this	245	35.9
No, have never done	438	64.1
q23e Ever look for information about place to live online		
Yes, have done this	162	23.8
No, have never done	520	76.2
q23f Ever do any banking online		
Yes, have done this	84	12.3
No, have never done	599	87.7
q23g Ever watch a video clip or listen to audio clip online		
Yes, have done this	302	54.2
No, have never done	381	55.8
q23h Ever play a lottery or gamble online		
Yes, have done this	22	3.2
No, have never done	661	96.8

Table B.2
(continued)

Variable and Values	Frequency	Percent
q23i Ever buy or sell stock online		
Yes, have done this	50	6.3
No, have never done	633	92.7
q23j Ever play a game online		
Yes, have done this	248	6.3
No, have never done	435	63.7
q23k Ever look for information about leisure activities online		
Yes, have done this	400	58.6
No, have never done	283	41.4
q23l Ever look for information from government Web sites		
Yes, have done this	253	37.2
No, have never done	428	62.8
q23m Ever look for religious or spiritual information online		
Yes, have done this	135	21.4
No, have never done	495	78.6
q23n Ever participate in online auction		
Yes, have done this	29	7.5
No, have never done	357	92.5
q24a Made reservation for travel service online yesterday		
Yes, did this yesterday	23	2.3
Yes, have done but not yesterday	388	38.6
No, have never done	595	59.1
q24b Took part in chatroom yesterday		
Yes, did this yesterday	82	8.1
Yes, have done but not yesterday	215	21.4
No, have never done	710	70.5
q2324b Chat (ever, yesterday)		
Never	1217	72.0
Ever, yesterday	473	28.0

Table B.2
(continued)

Variable and Values	Frequency	Percent
q24d Look for information about a job		
Yes, did this yesterday	82	8.1
Yes, have done but not yesterday	317	31.5
No, have never done	608	60.4
q24e Looked for information about place to live online yesterday		
Yes, did this yesterday	41	4.1
Yes, have done but not yesterday	256	25.4
No, have never done	709	70.4
q24l Looked for information from government web sites yesterday		
Yes, did this yesterday	121	12.0
Yes, have done but not yesterday	427	42.5
No, have never done	457	45.5
q24m Looked for religious or spiritual information online yesterday		
Yes, did this yesterday	42	4.6
Yes, have done but not yesterday	158	17.2
No, have never done	718	78.2
q27 Ever send e-mail to family members		
No	357	23.3
Yes	1176	76.7
q28 Usefulness of e-mail for communicating with family		
Not at all useful	30	2.6
Not too useful	111	9.5
Somewhat useful	430	36.6
Very useful	603	51.4
q34 Communicate more with person now that use e-mail		
Less often	16	1.5
Hasn't made any difference	435	40.1
More often	634	58.4

Table B.2
(continued)

Variable and Values	Frequency	Percent
q38 Ever send e-mail to friends		
No	317	20.6
Yes	1219	79.4
q39 Usefulness of e-mail for communicating with friends		
Not at all useful	19	1.6
Not too useful	103	8.5
Somewhat useful	439	36.0
Very useful	657	53.9
q45 Communicate more with friend now that you use e-mail		
Less often	442	37.7
Hasn't made any difference	25	2.1
More often	705	60.2
q49 Have an e-mail group list for friends and family		
No	706	46.2
Yes	821	53.8
q53 Person last e-mail was sent to		
Family member	410	27.8
Friend	503	34.1
Someone related to your work	419	28.4
Someone else	144	9.8
q54 Now keep in touch with family member you didn't before		
Hasn't happened	836	67.1
Started communicating with family member	410	32.9
q50i webpage: respondent (me and both)		
No, or family member	1638	95.6
Yes	75	4.4
q50f webpage: family (them and both)		
No, or respondent	1467	85.6
Yes	246	14.4

Table B.2
(continued)

Variable and Values	Frequency	Percent
q59a Ever send e-mail to parent or grandparent		
No, do not	476	73.0
Yes, e-mail	176	27.0
q59b Ever send e-mail to brother or sister		
No, do not	335	51.4
Yes, e-mail	317	48.6
q59c Ever send e-mail to child not living at home		
No, do not	504	77.4
Yes, e-mail	147	22.6
q59d Ever send e-mail to extended family		
No, do not	369	56.6
Yes, e-mail	283	43.4
q59e Ever send e-mail to spouse or partner you live with		
No, do not	520	79.8
Yes, e-mail	132	20.2
q59f Ever send e-mail to roommate		
No, do not	603	92.5
Yes, e-mail	49	7.5
q59g Ever send e-mail to child who lives at home		
No, do not	590	90.4
Yes, e-mail	63	9.6
q59h Ever send e-mail to friends who live close by		
No, do not	284	43.6
Yes, e-mail	368	56.4
q59i Ever send e-mail to friends who live far away		
No, do not	235	36.0
Yes, e-mail	418	64.0
q59j Ever send e-mail to romantic partner don't live with		
No, do not	584	89.4
Yes, e-mail	69	10.6

Table B.2
(continued)

Variable and Values	Frequency	Percent
q59k Ever send e-mail to people you work with		
No, do not	351	53.8
Yes, e-mail	301	46.2
q60a Sent e-mail to parent or grandparent yesterday		
No, do not	567	65.2
Yes, yesterday or before	303	34.8
q60b Sent e-mail to brother or sister yesterday		
No, do not	351	40.3
Yes, yesterday or before	521	59.7
q60c Sent e-mail to child not living at home yesterday		
No, do not	691	79.3
Yes, yesterday or before	180	20.7
q60d Sent e-mail to extended family yesterday		
No, do not	410	47.1
Yes, yesterday or before	461	52.9
q60e Sent e-mail to spouse or partner you live with yesterday		
No, do not	633	72.6
Yes, yesterday or before	239	27.4
q60f Sent e-mail to roommate yesterday		
No, do not	817	93.6
Yes, yesterday or before	56	6.4
q60g Sent e-mail to child who lives at home yesterday		
No, do not	790	90.5
Yes, yesterday or before	83	9.5
q60h Sent e-mail to friends who live close by yesterday		
No, do not	296	33.9
Yes, yesterday or before	576	66.1
q60i Sent e-mail to friends who live far away yesterday		
No, do not	224	25.7
Yes, yesterday or before	649	74.3

Table B.2
(continued)

Variable and Values	Frequency	Percent
q60j Sent e-mail to romantic partner don't live with yesterday		
No, do not	731	83.7
Yes, yesterday or before	142	16.3
q60k Sent e-mail to people you work with yesterday		
No, do not	361	41.4
Yes, yesterday or before	510	58.6
q61a Email brought me closer to family		
Not true	737	59.7
True	498	40.3
q61b Easier for family to say frank things in e-mail		
Not true	815	67.9
True	386	32.1
q61c Email is too impersonal for talking with family		
Not true	982	79.7
True	250	20.3
q61d Email keeps touch with family without spending time talking		
Not true	456	37.1
True	773	62.9
q61e Have learned more about family since using e-mail		
Not true	934	75.0
True	311	25.0
q61f Email has improved relationships in family		
Not true	756	61.7
True	469	38.3
q61g Email has added to stress in family		
Not true	1175	94.5
True	69	5.5

Table B.2
(continued)

Variable and Values	Frequency	Percent
q61aef (mn: family relations; alph = .78; M = .35, sd = .39)		
.00	602	49.7
.33	182	15.0
.67	207	17.1
1.00	220	18.2
q63a Email brought me closer to friends		
Not true	207	48.3
True	222	51.7
q63b Easier for friends to say frank things in e-mail		
Not true	278	65.4
True	147	34.6
q63c Email keeps touch with friends without spending time talking		
Not true	112	26.3
True	314	73.7
q63d Have learned more about friends since using e-mail		
Not true	266	61.0
True	170	39.0
q63e Email has improved relationships with friends		
Not true	222	51.5
True	209	48.5
q63f Email has added to stress with friends		
Not true	416	95.6
True	19	4.4
q63ade (mn: friend relations; alpha = .82; M = .46, sd = .43)		
.00	161	37.8
.33	71	16.7
.67	60	14.1
1.00	134	31.5

Table B.2

(continued)

Variable and Values	Frequency	Percent
k1a Internet improved ability to shop		
Not at all	250	43.3
Only a little	120	20.8
Some	114	19.8
A lot	93	16.1
k1b Internet improved getting information on health care		
Not at all	291	50.3
Only a little	102	17.6
Some	106	18.3
A lot	79	13.7
k1c Internet improved managing personal finances		
Not at all	363	62.5
Only a little	72	12.4
Some	69	11.9
A lot	77	13.3
k1d Internet improved connections to family members		
Not at all	170	29.1
Only a little	91	15.6
Some	142	24.3
A lot	182	31.1
k1e Internet improved connections to friends		
Not at all	104	17.8
Only a little	90	15.4
Some	173	29.6
A lot	218	37.3
k1f Internet improved ability to learn about new things		
Not at all	65	11.1
Only a little	57	9.8
Some	174	29.8
A lot	287	49.2

Table B.2
(continued)

Variable and Values	Frequency	Percent
kinfo (mn k1a,b,c,f alph = .66; M = 2.24, sd = .77)		
1.00	48	8.5
1.25	28	4.9
1.50	63	11.1
1.75	67	11.8
2.00	52	9.2
2.25	65	11.5
2.50	69	12.2
2.75	54	9.5
3.00	36	6.3
3.25	38	6.7
3.50	22	3.9
3.75	17	3.0
4.00	8	1.4
kcomm (mn k1d,e alph = .69; M = 2.72, sd = 1.0)		
1.00	75	12.9
1.50	36	6.2
2.00	89	15.3
2.50	77	13.2
3.00	104	17.8
3.50	68	11.7
4.00	134	23.0

Note: Some sets of questions were asked only of subsets of respondents, so total sample size is smaller for those.

References

Abramson, R. (2000, November 10). Election special: Internet used in campaign for Florida re-vote. The Industry Standard. Retrieved January 10, 2002 from ⟨http://www.infoworld.com/articles/hn/xml/00/11/10/001110hnmobilize.xml⟩.

Agence France-Presse. (2001a, January 14). German official says hate Web sites doubled last year. Agence France-Presse. Retrieved August 11, 2001 from ⟨http://archive.nandotimes.com/global/story/0,1024,500299538-500478312-503272064-0,00.html⟩.

Agence France-Presse. (2001b, August 11). Internet, globalisation spreading racism and intolerance: U.N. official. Agence France-Presse. Retrieved August 11, 2001 from ⟨http://www.wiesenthal.com/social/press/pr_item.cfm?itemID=119⟩.

America Online (2000). American Online/Roper Starch Cyberstudy 2000. Roper #CNT375.

Anonymous. (1998). Retrieved July 13, 2001 from ⟨http://www.tloma.on.ca/events/educonf98_speakers.html⟩.

Anonymous. (n.d.). Retrieved July 11, 2001 from ⟨http://www.internet-xchange.ch/conc_pub_an.htm⟩.

Aonline. (2001). Greetings page. Retrieved June 22, 2001 from ⟨http://www.aonline.com/top.shtml⟩.

Aspden, P., & Katz, J. E. (2001). Assessments of quality of health care information and referrals to physicians: A nationwide survey. In R. E. Rice & J. Katz (Eds.), The Internet and health communication (pp. 107–119). Thousand Oaks, CA: Sage.

Associated Press. (2000, December 23). Survey: Churches are embracing the Internet, new technologies. Retrieved June 19, 2001 from ⟨http://www.thehollandsentinel.net/stories/122300/rel_38.html⟩.

Associated Press. (2001, August 18). Survey: Convention coverage sought on Web. Retrieved January 10, 2002 from ⟨http://quest.cjonline.com/stories/081800/dem_0818005652.shtml⟩.

Bakardjieva, M., & Smith, R. (2001). The Internet in everyday life. New Media and Society, 3(1), 67–83.

Bannan, K. (2000, March 30). Getting hooked on an online game and hitched to a fellow gamer. *New York Times*. Retrieved June 25, 2001 from ⟨http://www.nytimes.com/library/tech/00/03/circuits/articles/30wedd.html⟩.

Barney, D. (2000). *Prometheus wired: The hope for democracy in the age of network technology*. Chicago: University of Chicago Press.

Baron, N. S. (1984). Computer-mediated communication as a force in language change. *Visible Language, 18*(2), 118–141.

Batt, C., & Katz, J. E. (1998, January). Consumer spending behavior and telecommunications services: A multi-method inquiry. *Telecommunications Policy*, 23–26.

Baudrillard, J. (1983). *Simulations*. P. Foss, P. Patton, & P. Beitchman, Trans. New York: Semiotext(e).

Baym, N. K. (1995). The emergence of community in computer-mediated communication. In S. G. Jones (Ed.), *Cybersociety: Computer-mediated communication and community* (pp. 138–163). Thousand Oaks, CA: Sage.

Becker, L. (1979). Measurement of gratifications. *Communication Research, 6*, 54–73.

Beniger, J. (1987). The personalization of mass media and the growth of pseudocommunity. *Communication Research, 14*(3), 352–371.

Berentson, B. (2000, September 11). Steinbrenner wannabes. *Forbes.com*. Retrieved June 25, 2001 from ⟨http://www.forbesbest.com/0911/038.html⟩.

Berger, P., & Luckmann, T. (1967). *The social construction of reality*. New York: Doubleday.

Bijker, W. E., Hughes, T., & Pinch, T. (1987). *The social construction of technological systems*. Cambridge, MA: MIT Press.

Bikson, T., & Panis, C. (1999). *Citizens, computers, and connectivity*. Santa Monica, CA: RAND.

Bimber, B. (1999). The Internet and citizen communication with government: Does the medium matter? *Political Communication, 19*, 409–428.

Black Chronicle News Services. (n.d.). Click, point, pray: Congregations putting their faith in the Net. *Black Chronicle News Services*. Retrieved August 3, 2001 from ⟨http://www.blackchronicle.com/Chronicle/Religion/Religion_1/religion_1.html⟩.

Black, J. (1999). Losing ground bit by bit. BBC News Online, November 1. Retrieved July 26, 2001 from ⟨http://cgi.apnic.net/mailing-lists/s-asia-it/9910/msg00037.html⟩.

Black, J. (2001, June 21). No hiding from a cell phone. *Business Week Online*. Retrieved July 1, 2001 from ⟨http://www.businessweek.com/bwdaily/dnflash/jun2001/nf20010621_803.htm⟩.

Bloomfield, B. P., & Vurdubakis, T. (1994). Boundary disputes: Negotiating the boundary between the technical and the social in the development of IT systems. Information *Technology and People, 7*(1), 9–24.

Blumler, J., & Katz, E. (Eds.) (1974). *The uses of mass communication.* Beverly Hills, CA: Sage.

Bollier, D. (Ed.) (1995). *The future of community and personal identity in the coming electronic culture.* Washington, D.C.: The Aspen Institute.

Bonisteel, S. (2001, June 14). Billions have no need for the Internet, survey says. *Newbytes.* Retrieved August 17, 2001 from ⟨http://www.newsbytes.com/news/01/166875.html⟩.

Borchert, M. (1998). The challenge of cyberspace: Internet access and persons with disabilities. In B. Ebo (Ed.) *Cyberghetto or cybertopia; Race, class, and gender on the Internet* (pp. 45–64). Westport, CT: Praeger.

Bourdieu, P. (1986). The forms of capital (R. Nice, Trans.). In John G. Richardson (Ed.), *Handbook of theory and research for the sociology of education* (pp. 241–258). New York: Greenwood.

Bourdieu, P. (1990). *The logic of practice.* (R. Nice, Trans.). Stanford, CA: Stanford University Press.

Bourdieu, P. (1993). *Sociology in question.* London: Sage.

Bourque, S. C., & Warren, K. B. (1987). Technology, gender, and development. *Daedalus, 116*(4), 173–198.

Browning, G., & Weitzner, D. (1996). *Electronic democracy: Using the Internet to influence American politics.* White Plains, NY: Information Today.

Brundage, S. (2001, February). Playing with death. *Computer Gaming World,* 29–31.

Buchanan, L. (1996). The virtual campaign. *CIO, 7,* 66.

Bunn, A. (2000, August). Rise of the teen guru. *Brill's Content.* Retrieved July 13, 2001 from ⟨http://www.brillscontent.com/2000aug/features/teen_guru2.shtml⟩.

Calhoun, C. (1986). Computer technology, large-scale societal integration and the local community. *Urban Affairs Quarterly, 22,* 329–349.

Calhoun, C. (1998). Community without propinquity revisited: Communications technology and the transformation of the urban public sphere. *Sociological Inquiry, 68*(3), 373–397.

Calvert, C. (2000). *Voyeur nation.* New York: Westview Press.

Calvo, D. (2000, November 9). America waits: Vote turnout is low despite tight race. *Los Angeles Times,* pt. A, p. 44.

Canary, D., & Spitzberg, B. (1993, December). Loneliness and Media Gratifications. *Communication Research, 20*(6), 800–821.

Carey, J. (1988). *Communication as culture: Essays on media and society.* New York: Routledge.

Carey, J., & Pavlik, J. (1993). Videotex: The sword in the stone. In J. Pavlik & E. Dennis (Eds.), *Demystifying media technology* (pp. 163–168). Mountainview, CA: Mayfield.

Carpini, M. X. D. (1996). Voters, candidates, and campaigns in the new information age: An overview and assessment. *Harvard International Journal of Press/Politics*, 1, 36–56.

Carr, C. (2001, January 8). Information poisoning. *Salon.com*. Retrieved August 16, 2001 from ⟨http://www.salon.com/books/feature/2001/01/08/carr/index.html⟩.

Carrier, R. (1998). Training the information-poor in an age of unequal access. In B. Ebo (Ed.) *Cyberghetto or cybertopia: Race, class, and gender on the Internet* (pp. 153–168). Westport, CT: Praeger.

Case, S. (1998). Steve Case: AOL Community Update for January, 1998. Retrieved July 9, 2001 from ⟨http://stevecase.aol.com/community_update/steve_case_community_update_jan61998.html⟩.

Cerulo, K. (1997). Reframing sociological concepts for a brave new (virtual?) world. *Sociological Inquiry*, 67(1), 48–58.

Cerulo, K., & Ruane, J. (1997). Death becomes alive: Technology and the reconceptualization of death. *Science as Culture*, 6(28), pt. 3, 444–466.

Chen, K., Chen, I., & Paul, H. (2001, Spring). Explaining online behavioral differences: An Internet dependency perspective. *Journal of Computer Information Systems*, 59–64.

Cherny, L. (1999). *Conversation and community: Discourse in a social MUD*. London: Cambridge University Press.

Civin, M. (1999). *Male, female, e-mail: The struggle for relatedness in a paranoid society*. New York: Other Press.

Clines, F. (2001, May 24). Wariness yields to motivation in Baltimore free-computer experiment. *New York Times*. Retrieved August 6, 2001 from ⟨http://www.nytimes.com/2001/05/24/technology/24BALT.html⟩.

Cobb, J. (1998). *Cybergrace: The search for God in cyberspace*. New York: Crown.

Coffey, S., & Stipp, H. (1997). The interactions between computer and television usage. *Journal of Advertising Research*, 37(2), 61–67.

Cole, J. (1999, June 22). Press release from the director of the UCLA Center for Communication Policy. Retrieved June 2, 2000 from ⟨www.cc.ucla.edu/press_releast.htm⟩.

Coleman, J. (1988). Social capital in the creation of human capital. *American Journal of Sociology*, 94, 95–120.

Compaine, B. (2001). *The digital divide: Facing a crisis or creating a myth?* Cambridge, MA: MIT Press.

Congress Online Project (2001). Reuters/Cnet. Retrieved March 18 from ⟨http://news.cnet.com/news/0-1005-200-5173083.html?tag=lh⟩.

Connolly, T., & Thorn, B. (1990). Discretionary databases: Theory, data, and implications. In J. Fulk & C. Steinfield (Eds.) *Organizations and communication technology* (pp. 219–234). Newbury Park, CA: Sage.

Converse, P. (1962, Winter). Information flow and the stability of partisan attitudes. *Public Opinion Quarterly, 26,* 578–599.

Cooper, M., & Kimmelman, G. (1999). *The digital divide confronts the Telecommunications Act of 1996: Economic reality versus public policy.* Washington, DC: Consumer Union. Retrieved Summer 2001 from ⟨http://www.consunion. org/other/telecom2-0299.htm⟩.

Cooper, M., & Shah, D. (2000). *Disconnected, disadvantaged, and disenfranchised: Exploration in the digital divide.* Consumer Federation of America/ Consumer's Union Report. Retrieved July 16, 2001 from ⟨http://www. consumersunion.org/pdf/disconnect.pdf⟩.

Cornwell, B., & Lundgren, D. C. (2001). Love on the Internet: Involvement and misrepresentation in romantic relationships in cyberspace versus realspace. *Computers in Human Behavior, 17,* 197–211.

Corrado, A. (2000). *Campaigns in cyberspace: Toward a new regulatory approach.* Queenstown, MD: The Aspen Institute.

Correll, S. (1995, October). The ethnography of an electronic bar: The Lesbian Cafe. *Journal of Contemporary Ethnography, 24,* 270–298.

Crispell, D. (1997). The Internet on TV. *American Demographics, 19*(5), 32–33.

Cultural Access Group. (2001). *Ethnicity in the electronic age: Looking at the Internet through multicultural lens.* Los Angeles: Access Worldwide Communications.

Cunneen, C., & Stubbs, J. (2000). Male violence, male fantasy and the commodification of women through the Internet. *Interactive Review of Victimology, 7,* 5–28.

Dahl, R. (2000). A democratic paradox? *Political Science Quarterly, 115*(1), 35–40.

Dahlberg, L. (2001). Democracy via cyberspace: Mapping the rhetorics and practices of three prominent camps. *New Media and Society, 3*(2), 157–177.

Darin, B. (2000). *Prometheus wired: The hope for democracy in the age of network technology.* Chicago: University of Chicago Press.

Davis, R. (2000). *The Web of politics: The Internet's impact on American political system.* New York: Oxford University Press.

Davison, P., Pennebaker, J., & Dickerson, S. (2000). Who talks? The social psychology of illness support groups. *American Psychologist, 55*(2), 205–217. Retrieved from ⟨http://www.ahealthyme.com/article/iac/100535083⟩.

Dear, M. J., Schockman, H., & Hise, G. (Eds.). (1996). *Rethinking Los Angeles.* Thousand Oaks, CA: Sage.

Deetz, S. (1989a, May 30). Communication technology policy and interest representation: Habermas' theory of communicative action. Paper presented at the annual meeting of the International Communication Association, San Francisco.

Deetz, S. (1989b). Representation of interests and communication technologies Issues in democracy and policy. In S. Deetz (Ed.), *Introduction to Communica-*

tion, 2nd ed. (pp. 128–145). Needham Heights, MA: Ginn. Reprinted from S. Deetz (1980) *Communication and the culture of technology.* Pullman, WA: Washington State University Press.

Deetz, S. (1990, June). Suppressed conflict, consent, and inequitable interest representation. Paper presented at the annual meeting of the International Communication Association, Dublin, Ireland.

Deirmenjian, J. M. (1999). Stalking in cyberspace. *Journal American Academic Psychiatry Law, 27*, 407–413.

Dervin, B., & Shields, P. (1990, August). Users: The missing link in technology research. Paper presented at the annual meeting of the International Association for Mass Communication Research, Communication Technology Section Meeting, Lake Bled, Yugoslavia.

Dery, M. (1996). *Escape velocity.* Cambridge, MA: MIT Press.

Dimmick, J., Sikand, J., & Patterson, S. (1994). The gratifications of the household telephone: Sociability, instrumentality, and reassurance. *Communication Research, 21*(5), 643–663.

Dines, J. (1998). Quoted in "Is it the Canadian dollar's turn to crash?" Retrieved January 7, 2002 from ⟨http://www.gold-eagle.com/gold_digest_98/dines081998.html⟩.

Dingle, D. (1999, April). Smart market moves. Lou Holland of Holland Growth Fund. *Black Enterprise.* Retrieved July 12, 2001 from ⟨http://www.findarticles.com/cf_0/m1365/9_29/54680948/print.jhtml⟩.

Doheny-Farina, S. (1998). *The wired neighborhood.* New Haven: Yale University Press.

Donath, J. S. (1999). Identity and deception in the virtual community. In P. Kollock & A. S. Smith (Eds.), *Communities in cyberspace* (pp. 29–59). London: Routledge.

Douglas, A. (n.d.). Adoption in the computer age. Retrieved June 22, 2001 from ⟨http://www.ecst.csuchico.edu/~progman/adoption/#intro⟩.

Downing, J. D. H. (1989). Computers for political change: PeaceNet and public data access. *Journal of Communication, 39*(3), 154–162.

Dubelyew, D. (n.d.) How to collaborate on the Internet. Retrieved August 1, 2001 from ⟨http://www.wga.org/tools/webcollaboration.html⟩.

Dutton, W., Rogers, E., & Jun, S.-H. (1987). The diffusion and impact of information technology in households. *Oxford surveys in information technology, 4*, 133–193.

Edgar, P. (1977). Families without television. *Journal of Communication, 27*(3), 73–77.

Edlund, M. (2000, November 28). Online politics: A post-mortem. *The New Republic Online.* Retrieved August 10, 2000 from ⟨www.thenewrepublic.com/cyberspace/edlund112800.html⟩.

Egan, J. (2000, December 16). Lonely gay teen seeking same. *New York Times Magazine*, 110–117.

Eisenberg, A. (2000, December 28). Cutting the cost of e-mail for the blind. *New York Times*. Retrieved from ⟨www.nytimes.com/2000/12/28/technology/28NEXT.html⟩.

Electronic Commerce Research Laboratory (ECRL). (1999). The evolution of the digital divide: Examining the relationship of race to Internet access and usage over time. Tennessee: Vanderbilt University, Owen Graduate School of Management. ⟨http://www.ecommerce.vanderbilt.edu⟩.

Elliott, P. (1974). Uses and gratifications research: A critique and a sociological alternative. In J. Blumler & E. Katz (Eds.), *The uses of mass communication*. Beverly Hills, CA: Sage.

Eppright, T., Allwood, M., Stern, B., & Theiss, T. (1999). Internet addiction: A new type of addiction? *Missouri Medicine*, 96(4), 133–136.

Evans, R. D. (2001). Examining the informal sanctioning of deviance in a chat room culture. *Deviant Behavior: An Interdisciplinary Journal*, 22, 195–210.

Fallows, J. (2000, November 16). Internet illusions. *New York Times Book Review*, 28–31.

Farrell, S. (n.d.) Star-crossed Asian lovers click with net matchmaker. *Clarion News*. Retrieved June 25, 2001 from ⟨http://www.clarionnews.com/tradmusrootf.html⟩.

Feldman, M. D. (2000). Munchausen by Internet: Detecting factitious illness and crisis on the Internet. *Southern Medical Journal*, 93, 669–672.

Ferguson, D., & Perse, E. (2000). The World Wide Web as a functional alternative to television. *Journal of Broadcasting and Electronic Media*, 44(2), 155–174.

Figallo, C. (1995). The WELL: A regionally based on-line community on the Internet. In B. Kahin & J. Keller (Eds.), *Public access to the Internet* (pp. 49–61). Cambridge, MA: MIT Press.

Finn, J., & Banach, M. (2000). Victimization online: The downside of seeking human services for women on the Internet. *CyberPsychology and Behavior*, 3, 785–796.

Fischer, C. (1992). *America calling: A social history of the telephone to 1940*. Berkeley: University of California Press.

Fischer, C. (1997). Technology and community: Historical complexities. *Sociological Inquiry*, 67(1), 113–118.

Fisher, R. J., & Katz, J. E. (2000). Social desirability bias of the validity of self-reported values. *Psychology and Marketing*, 17(2), 105–120.

Flanagin, A., & Metzger, M. (2001). Internet use in the contemporary media environment. *Human Communication Research*, 27(1), 153–181.

Flick, L. (1999, November 5). Farmclub sprouts on Web. *Billboard*, 47, 18.

Flink, J. (1970). *America adopts the automobile, 1895–1910*. Cambridge, MA: MIT Press.

Forrester Reports. (1996). *People and technology: Unlocking PC potential*. Cambridge, MA: Forrester Research.

Foucault, M. (1979). *Discipline and punish*. London: Penguin.

Francalanci, G. (2001, January 19). Il corpo celibe e Pangello della matazione: Perché il futuro non ha piu bigogno di noi? (The single body an angel of mutation: Why it is that the future will not need us). Paper presented at the converence on Umano e corpo, Milan.

Franzen, A. (2000). Does the Internet make us lonely? *European Sociological Review, 16*(4), 427–438.

Freire, P. (1969). *Pedagogy of the oppressed*. New York: Continuum.

Furlong, M. S. (1989). An electronic community for older adults: The SeniorNet network. *Journal of Communication, 39*(3), 145–153.

Gackenbach, J. (Ed.). (1998). *Psychology and the Internet: Intrapersonal, interpersonal, and transpersonal implications*. San Diego, CA: Academic.

Gandy, O., Jr. (1993). *The Panoptic sort*. Boulder, CO: Westview.

Gandy, O., Jr. (2002). The real digital divide: Citizens versus consumers. In L. Lievrouw & S. Livingstone (Eds.), *The handbook of new media*. London: Sage.

Garfinkel, H. (1967). *Studies in ethnomethodology*. Englewood Cliffs, NJ: Prentice-Hall.

Garson, B. (1988). *The electronic sweatshop: How computers are transforming the office of the future into the factory of the past*. New York: Simon and Schuster.

Gartner Group. (2001, February 15). Gartner pegs instant messaging at 15 billion per month worldwide. Press release. Gartner Group, New York.

Geertz, C. (1985). *Local knowledge: Further essays in interpretive anthropology*. New York: Basic Books.

Geiser, H. (1998). "Yours virtually forever: Death memorials and remembrance sites in the WWW. Towards cybersociety and "vireal" social relations. *Sociology in Switzerland. Online Publications*. Retrieved July 9, 2001 from ⟨http://socio.ch/intcom/t_hgeser07.htm⟩.

Gergen, K. (1991). *The saturated self: Dilemmas of identity in contemporary life*. New York: Harper Collins.

Gergen, K. (forthcoming). The challenge of absent presence. In J. Katz & M. Aakhus (Eds.), *Perpetual contact: Mobile communication, private talk, public performance*. New York: Cambridge University Press.

Gilens, M. (2001). Political ignorance and collective policy preferences. *American Political Science Review, 95*(2), 379–396.

Gillespie, A., & Robins, K. (1989). Geographical inequalities: The spatial bias of the new communications technologies. *Journal of Communication, 39*(3), 7–19.

Glass, A. (2000, August 3). Online broadcasts add new dimension to politics. Cox News Service. Retrieved August 11, 2001 from ⟨http://www.coxnews.com/2000/news/cox/080300_skybox.html⟩.

Goffman, E. (1959). *Presentation of self in everyday life.* New York: Anchor Books.

Goldsmith, S. (2000). First Breaux Symposium features leading national journalists. Louisiana University Relations. Retrieved July 11, 2001 from ⟨http://www.lsu.edu/university_relations/lsutoday/000421/pageone.html#page1⟩.

Goslee, S. (1998). Losing ground bit by bit: Low-income communities in the Information Age. Washington, DC: Benton Foundation. Retrieved July 26, 2001 from ⟨http://www.benton.org/Library/Low-Income/intro.html⟩.

Graphics, Visualization and Usabilities Center (GVU). (1997). *GVU's seventh WWW user survey.* Retrieved Summer 2001 from ⟨http://www.gvu.gatech.edu/user_surveys/survey-1997-04⟩.

Greenberg, J. L., Lewis, S. E., & Dodd, D. K. (1999). Overlapping addictions and self-esteem among college men and women. *Addictive Behaviors, 24,* 565–571.

Greenberger, M., & Puffer, J. C. (1989). Telemedecine: Toward better health care for the elderly. *Journal of Communication, 39*(3), 137–144.

Greenfield, D. N. (1999). *Virtual addiction.* Oakland, CA: New Harbinger.

Greenman, C. (2000, October 12). E-mail mentoring. *New York Times.* Retrieved June 17, 2001 from ⟨http://www.nyt.com⟩.

Griffiths, M. (1998). Internet addiction: Does it really exist? In J. Gackenbach (Ed.), *Psychology and the Internet, intrapersonal, interpersonal, and transpersonal implications* (pp. 61–75). San Diego: Academic.

Griffiths, M. (2000). Does Internet and computer "addiction" exist? Some case study evidence. *CyberPsychology and Behavior, 3,* 211–218.

Griffiths, M., & Wood, R. T. A. (2000). Risk factors in adolescence: The case of gambling, videogame playing, and the Internet. *Journal of Gambling Studies, 16,* 199–225.

Grossman, L. (2001, June). Play nation. www.onmagazine.com (print magazine and online), 26–31. Retrieved Summer 2001 from ⟨http://www.onmagazine.com/on-mag/magazine/article/0,9985,108096,00.html⟩.

Gumpert, G. (1987). *Talking tombstone and other tales of the media age.* New York: Oxford University Press.

Gumperz, J. (1971). *Language in social groups.* Stanford: Stanford University Press.

Gurak, L. (1997). *Persuasion and privacy in cyberspace: The online protests over Lotus Marketplace and the Clipper Chip.* New Haven: Yale University Press.

Gurstein, M. (Ed.) (2000). *Community informatics: Enabling communities with information and communications technologies.* Hershey, PA: Idea Group.

Haddam, J. (1999). Jane Haddam interview. Mystery One Bookstore. Retrieved July 11, 2001 from ⟨http://www.mysteryone.com/JaneHaddam.htm⟩.

Haddon, L. (2001). Social exclusion and information and communication technologies. *New Media and Society, 2*(4), 387–406.

Hamburger, Y. A., & Ben Artzi, E. (2000). The relationships between extraversion and neuroticism and the different uses of the Internet. *Computers in Human Behavior, 16,* 441–449.

Hamman, R. (1999). Computer networks linking communities: A study of the effects of computer network use upon pre-existing communities. In U. Thiedke (Ed.), *Virtual groups: Characteristics and problematic dimensions* [in German]. Wiesbaden, Germany: Westdeutshcer Verlag. Retrieved Summer 2001 from ⟨http://www.socio.demon.co.uk/mphil/short.html⟩.

Hampton, K. (2000, October). *Grieving for a lost network: Collective action in a wired suburb.* Cambridge, MA: MIT Department of Urban Studies and Planning.

Hampton, K., & Wellman, B. (2000). Examining community in the digital neighborhood: Early results from Canada's wired suburb. In T. Ishida & K. Isbister (Eds.), *Digital cities.* (pp. 475–492). Heidelberg: Springer-Verlag.

Haraway, D. (1991). *Simians, cyborgs and women.* New York: Routledge.

Harcourt, W. (1999). *Women@Internet: Creating new cultures in cyberspace.* New York: Zed Books.

Hayles, N. K. (1998). *How we became posthuman.* Chicago: University of Chicago Press.

Hayne, S., & Rice, R. (1997). Accuracy of attribution in small groups using anonymity in group support systems. *International Journal of Human Computer Studies, 47,* 429–452.

Heim, M. (1993). *The metaphysics of virtual reality.* Oxford: Oxford University Press.

Hennig, W. (1999, August). Don't byte the baby. *Diablo Magazine.* Retrieved July 12, 2001 from ⟨http://www.diablomag.com/archives/DM9908/Behind.html⟩.

Herring, S. (1994). Keynote talk at panel on Making the Net*Work*: Is there a Z39.50 in gender communication?, American Library Association annual convention, Miami, June 27. Retrieved Summer 2001 from ⟨http://cpsr.org/cpsr/gender/herring.txt⟩.

Hess, David J. (1994), *Science and technology in a multicultural world: The cultural politics of facts and artifacts.* New York: Columbia University Press.

Hill, K. A., & Hughes, J. (1997). Computer-mediated political communication: The USENET and political communication. *Political Communication, 14,* 3–27.

Hill, K. A., & Hughes, J. (1998). *Cyberpolitics: Citizen activism in the age of the Internet.* New York: Rowman and Littlefield.

Hiltz, S. R., & Turoff, M. (1995). *Network nation* (rev. ed.). Cambridge, MA: MIT Press.

Hoffman, D., Kalsbeek, W., & Novak, T. (1996). Internet and Web use in the U.S. *Communications of the ACM, 39*(12), 36–46.

Hoffman, D., & Novak, T. (1998). Information access: Bridging the racial divide on the Internet. *Science, 280*(5362), 390–391.

Horn, S. (1998). *Cyberville: Clicks, culture, and the creation of an online town.* New York: Warner Books.

Howard, P., Rainie, L., & Jones, S. (2001). Days and nights on the Internet: The impact of a diffusing technology. *American Behavioral Scientist, 45*(3), 383–404.

Hu, J. (2001, April 5). Did AOL shoot the messenger? Decision to cut off rivals may backfire in Microsoft battle. CNET News.com. Retrieved June 13, 2001 from ⟨http://news.cnet.com/news/0-1005-201-5464191-0.html⟩.

Hudson, H. E. (1988). Ending the tyranny of distance: The impact of new communications technologies in rural North America. In J. R. Schement & L. A. Lievrouw (Eds.), *Competing visions, complex realities: Social aspects of the Information Society* (pp. 91–104). Norwood, NJ: Ablex.

Huff, W. S., & Syrcek, B. (1997). Town government in cyberspace. In A. M. Cohill & A. Kavanaugh (Eds.), *Community networks: Lessons from Blacksburg, Virginia* (pp. 73–87). Washington, DC: Artech House.

Hundt, R. (2000). *You say you want a revolution: A story of information age politics.* New Haven: Yale University Press.

Igor. (2001). Welcome. Retrieved February 26, 2001 from ⟨http://www.voyeurweb.com/main/Main.html⟩.

Illinois Association of School Boards. (2001, June). *School Board News Bulletin.* Retrieved August 11, 2001 from ⟨http://www.iasb.com/files/nb0601.htm⟩.

Internetnews. (2000, August 31). Internet is gaining ground on TV watching. ⟨http://www.internews.com/intl-news/article/0,,6_450071,00.html⟩.

James, M., Wotring, C., & Forrest, E. (1995). An exploratory study of the perceived benefits of electronic bulletin board use and their impact on other communication activities. *Journal of Broadcasting and Electronic Media, 39*, 30–50.

Jansen, S. C. (1989). Gender and the information society: A socially structured silence. *Journal of Communication, 39*(3), 196–215.

Jenkins, H. (1992). *Textual poachers: Television fans and participatory culture.* New York: Routledge, Chapman and Hall.

Jensen, J. (1999). Interactivity. In P. Mayer (Ed.), *Computer media and communication* (pp. 160–187). New York: Oxford University Press.

Jessel, M. (1995). Internet begins to cut into TV viewing. *Broadcasting & Cable, 40*, 318–330.

Johnson, L. (2000, March 25). Point, click, politics. *Charlotte Observer.* Retrieved August 11, 2001 from ⟨http://www.aristotle.com/article.asp?id=032500&d=3/25/00&bc=ff6600⟩.

Johnson, S. (1997). *Interface culture: How new technology transforms the way we create and communicate.* New York: Harper Edge.

Jones, S. (Ed.). (1997). *Virtual culture: Identity and communication in cybersociety.* Thousand Oaks, CA: Sage.

Jones, S. (1999). Understanding community in the information age. In P. Mayer (Ed.), *Computer media and communication* (pp. 219–240). New York: Oxford University Press.

Jonscher, C. (1999). *The evolution of wired life: From the alphabet to the soulcatcher chip-how information technologies change our world.* New York: Wiley.

Jordan, T. (1999) *Cyberpower: The culture and politics of cyberspace and the Internet.* New York: Routledge.

Jung, J.-J., Qiu, J., & Kim, Y. (2001, August). Internet connectedness and inequality: Beyond the "divide." *Communication Research, 28*(4), 507–535.

Jupiter Communications. (2000). Assessing the digital divide. Press release. New York: Jupiter Communications. Retrieved June 15 from ⟨http://www.jup.com/company/pressrelease.jsp?doc=pr000615⟩.

Kahin, B., & Keller, J. (Eds.). (1995). *Public access to the Internet.* Cambridge, MA: MIT Press.

Kalton, G. (1983). *Introduction to survey sampling.* Beverly Hills, CA: Sage.

Kamarck, E., & Nye, J. (Eds.) (2000). *Democracy.com?: Governance in a networked world,* Runnels Hill, NH: Hollis.

Kanaley, R. (2001, January 15). Internet gives karaoke crooners anonymity, stage. Knight Ridder News Service. Retrieved July 13, 2001 from ⟨http://www.spokesmanreview.com⟩.

Kapor, M. (1993). Where is the digital highway really heading? The case for a Jeffersonian information policy. *Wired, 1.03,* 53–59, 94.

Karetnick, R. (2001). Identity in cyberspace: An ethnographic and microanalytic study of participation in a virtual community. Dissertation, Information and Library Studies, Rutgers University School of Communication, New Brunswick, NJ.

Katz, J. E. (1978). *Presidential politics and science policy.* New York: Praeger.

Katz, J. E. (1983). The uses of scientific evidence in congressional policymaking: The Clinch River Breeder Reactor. *Science, Technology, and Human Values, 9*(1), 51–62.

Katz, J. E. (1990a). Caller-ID, privacy, and social processes. *Telecommunications Policy,* 372–411.

Katz, J. E. (1990b). Social aspects of telecommunications security policy. *IEEE Technology and Society, 9*(2), 16–24.

Katz, J. E. (1995, Spring). Transforming corporate culture in the US telecommunications industry: Notes on social engineering. *Human Systems Management, 14,* 21–38.

Katz, J. E. (1998, November). Struggle in cyberspace: Fact and fiction on the world wide Web. *Annals of the American Academy of Political and Social Science, 560,* 194–199.

Katz, J. E. (1999a). *Connections: Social and cultural studies of the telephone in American life.* New Brunswick, NJ: Transaction.

Katz, J. E. (1999b, October 23). New Jersey votes. WNJO Television.

Katz, J. E., & Aakhus, M. (Eds.). (2002). *Perpetual contact: Mobile communication, private talk and public performance.* New York: Cambridge University Press.

Katz, J. E., & Aspden, P. (1997a). Motivations for and barriers to Internet usage: Results of a national public opinion survey. *Internet Research: Electronic Networking Applications and Policy, 7*(3), 170–188.

Katz, J. E., & Aspden, P. (1997b). Motives, hurdles, and dropouts: Who is on and off the Internet and why. *Communications of the ACM, 40*(4), 97–102.

Katz, J. E., & Aspden, P. (1997c). A nation of strangers? Friendship patterns and community involvement of Internet users. *Communications of the ACM, 40*(12), 81–86.

Katz, J. E., & Aspden, P. (1998a). Internet dropouts in the USA. *Telecommunications Policy, 22*(4,5), 327–339.

Katz, J. E., & Aspden, P. (1998b). Social and attitudinal correlates of mobile communications ownership. *Technological Forecasting and Social Change, 57,* 133–156.

Katz, J. E., Aspden, P., & Reich, W. (1997). Elections and electrons: A national opinion survey on the role of cyberspace and mass media in political opinion formation during the 1996 general election. Paper presented at the Twenty-fifth Annual Conference on Telecommunications Policy Research, Arlington, VA.

Katz, J. E., & Graveman, R. (1991). Privacy issues in a national research and education network. *Telematics and Informatics, 8*(1), 71–120.

Katz, J. E., Rice, R. E., & Aspden, P. (2001). The Internet, 1995–2000: Access, civic involvement, and social interaction. *American Behavioral Scientist, 45*(3), 405–419.

Katz, J. E., & Wynn, E. (1997, June). *Civic action on the Internet: Case studies of voluntary organizations.* Report prepared for the Markle Foundation. Morristown, NJ: Bellcore.

Kayany, J., & Yelsma, P. (2000). Displacement effects of online media in the socio-technical contexts of households. *Journal of Broadcasting and Electronic Media, 44*(2), 215–229.

Keeter, S. (1995). Estimating telephone noncoverage bias with a telephone survey. *Public Opinion Quarterly, 59*(2), 196–217.

Keller, J. (1995). Public access issues: An introduction. In B. Kahin & J. Keller (Eds.), *Public access to the Internet* (pp. 34–45). Cambridge, MA: MIT Press.

Kellner, D. (1992). Popular culture and the construction of post-modern identities. In S. Lash & J. Friedman (Eds.), *Modernity and identity* (pp. 141–177). Oxford: Basil Blackwell.

Kiesler, S., Siegel, H., & McGuire, T. W. (1984). Social psychological aspects of computer-mediated communication. *American Psychologist, 39*(10), 1123–1134.

Kilborn, L. (2000, October 31). Any woman's fantasy: Female players make up 25 percent of rotisserie-league competitors. *Denver Post*, p. D-10.

King, S. A. (1999). Internet gambling and pornography: Illustrative examples of the psychological consequences of communication anarchy. *CyberPsychology and Behavior, 2*, 175–193.

King, S. A., & Barak, A. (1999). Compulsive Internet gambling: A new form of an old clinical pathology. *CyberPsychology and Behavior, 2*, 441–456.

Kish, L. (1967). *Survey sampling*. New York: Wiley.

Klein, P. (1997, December 11). Student homepages. Department of Communication, Rutgers University, New Brunswick, NJ.

Kolko, B., Nakamura, L., & Rodman, G. (Eds.). (1999). *Race in cyberspace*. London: Routledge.

Kollock, P. (1999). The economies of online cooperation: Gifts and public goods in cyberspace. In M. A. Smith & P. Kollock (Eds.) *Communities in cyberspace* (pp. 220–239). London: Routledge.

Kraut, R. E. (1989). Telecommuting: The trade-offs of home work. *Journal of Communication, 39*(3), 19–47.

Kraut, R. E., Kiesler, S., Boneva, B., Cummings, J., Helgeson, V., & Crawford, A. (in press). Internet paradox revisited. *Journal of Social Issues*.

Kraut, R. E., Lundmark, V., Patterson, M., Kiesler, S., Mukhopadhyay, T., & Scherlis, M. (1998). Internet paradox: A social technology that reduces social involvement and psychological well-being? *American Psychologist, 53*(9), 1017–1031.

Kraut, R. E., Mukhopadhyay, T., Szczypula, J., Kiesler, S., & Sherlis, B. (1999). Information and communication: Alternative uses of the Internet in households. *Information Systems Research, 10*, 287–303.

Krendl, K. A., Broihier, M. C., & Fleetwood, C. (1989). Children and computers: Do sex-related differences persist? *Journal of Communication, 39*(3), 85–93.

Krim, J. (2001, July 10). Survey shows support for Internet rules. *Washington Post*, p. A10. Retrieved Summer 2001 from ⟨http://washingtonpost.com/wp-dyn/articles/A38828-2001Jul9.html⟩.

Kroker, A., & Weinstein, M. (1994). *Data trash: The theory of the virtual class*. New York: St. Martin's.

Kubey, R., Lavin, J., & Burrows, J. (2001). Internet use and collegiate academic performance decrements: Early findings. *Journal of Communication, 51*(2), 366–382.

Kuczynski, A. (2001, July 9). Me-zine journalism for fun and (sometimes) profit. *New York Times*. Retrieved August 1, 2001 from ⟨www.nytimes.com/2001/07/09/business/09ZINE.html⟩.

Kuwabara, K. (2000, March). Linux: A bazaar at the edge of chaos. *First Monday*, *5*(3). Retrieved August 1, 2001 from ⟨http://firstmonday.org/issues/issue5_3/kuwabara⟩.

Lacan, J. (1981). *The language of the self: The function of language in psychoanalysis*. (A. Wilden, Trans., notes, and commentary). Baltimore: Johns Hopkins University Press.

Lansing, J., & Morgan, J. (1971). *Economic Survey Methods*. Ann Arbor, MI: Institute for Social Research.

LaRose, R., Eastin, M., & Gregg, J. (2001). Reformulating the Internet paradox: Social cognitive explanations of Internet use and depression. *Journal of Online Behavior*, *1*(2). Retrieved July 7, 2001 from ⟨http://www.behavior.net/JOB/v1n1/paradox.html⟩.

LaRose, R., & Mettler, J. (1989). Who uses information technologies in rural America? *Journal of Communication*, *39*(3), 48–60.

Lavin, M., Marvin, K., McLarney, A., Nola, V., & Scott, L. (1999). Sensation seeking and collegiate vulnerability to Internet dependence. *CyberPsychology and Behavior*, *2*, 425–430.

Leets, L. (2001). Responses to Internet hate sites: Is speech too free in cyberspace? *Communication Law and Policy*, *6*, 287–317.

Leibenstein, H. (1950). Bandwagon, snob, and Veblen effects in the theory of consumer's demand. *Quarterly Journal of Economics*, *64*, 183–207.

Leibowitz, E. (2001). The Hollywood forever way of death. *Atlantic Monthly*, *287*(3), 21–22.

Leibowitz, S., & Margolis, S. (1998). Network externality. *The New Palgraves Dictionary of Economics and the Law*. New York: MacMillan.

Leon, D. T., & Rotunda, R. J. (2000). Contrasting case studies of frequent Internet use: Is it pathological or adaptive? *Journal of College Student Psychotherapy*, *14*(4), 9–18.

Levy, P. (1997). *Collective intelligence: Mankind's emerging world in cyberspace*. (R. Bononno, Trans.). New York: Plenum Press.

Levy, P. (1998). *Becoming virtual: Reality in the digital age*. (R. Bononno, Trans.). New York: Plenum Press.

Lievrouw, L. A. (1994). Information resources and democracy: Understanding the paradox. *Journal of the American Society for Information Science*, *45*(6), 350–357.

Lindlof, T., & Shatzer, M. (1998). Media ethnography in virtual space: Strategies, limits and possibilities. *Journal of Broadcasting and Electronic Media*, *42*(2), 170–189.

Lipschultz, J. (1999). *Free expression in the age of the Internet: Social and legal boundaries.* Boulder, CO: Westview Press.

Loader, B. (Ed.). (1997). *The governance of cyberspace: Politics, technology and global restructuring.* New York: Routledge.

Lorber, L. (2000). Time management is key when job hunting online. *National Business Employment Weekly.* Retrieved July 17, 2001 from ⟨http://www.ctrc.com/html/help/help29.html⟩.

MacPherson, K. (2000, October 3). Need another political fix? Try the Web. *Post-Gazette.* Retrieved July 21, 2001 from ⟨www.post-gazette.com/election2000/20001003netguide1.asp⟩.

Mann, W. P. (1995). *Politics on the net.* Indianapolis: Que.

Margolis, M., & Resnick, D. (2000). *Politics as usual: The cyberspace "revolution".* Thousand Oaks, CA: Sage.

Markus, M. L. (1990). Toward a critical mass theory of interactive media: Universal access, interdependence and diffusion. In J. Fulk & C. Steinfield (Eds.), *Organizations and communication technology* (pp. 194–218). Newbury Park, CA: Sage.

Marvin, C. (1990). *When old technologies were new: Thinking about electric communication in the late nineteenth century.* New York: Oxford University Press.

McCabe, K. (2000). Child pornography and the Internet. *Social Science Computer Review, 18,* 73–76.

McChesney, R. (2000). *Rich media, poor democracy: Communication politics in dubious times* (rev. ed.). New York: New Press.

McConnaughey, J. (2001, June). Taking the measure of the digital divide: Net effects of research and policy. Summary of U.S. Department of Commerce (2000), *Falling through the net* (see reference), presented at the Web Workshop, Department of Sociology, University of Maryland.

McConnaughey, J., & Lader, W. (1998). *Falling through the Net II: New data on the digital divide.* Washington, DC: U.S. Department of Commerce. Retrieved Summer 2001 from ⟨http://www.ntia.doc.gov/ntiahome/net2/falling.html⟩.

McCreadie, M., & Rice, R. E. (1999a). Trends in analyzing access to information, Part I: Cross-disciplinary conceptualizations. *Information Processing and Management, 35*(1), 45–76.

McCreadie, M., & Rice, R. E. (1999b). Trends in analyzing access to information, Part II: Unique and integrating conceptualizations. *Information Processing and Management, 35*(1), 77–99.

McDonald, D. G., & Glynn, C. J. (1980). The stability of media gratifications. *Journalism Quarterly, 61,* 542–549, 741.

McKelvey, T. (2001, August 10). Father and son team on hate site. *USAToday.com.* Retrieved August 11, 2001 from ⟨http://www.usatoday.com/life/2001-07-16-kid-hate-sites.htm⟩.

McKenna, K. Y. A., & Bargh, J. A. (1998). Coming out in the age of the Internet: Identity "demarginalization" through virtual group participation. *Journal of Personality and Social Psychology, 75*, 681–694.

McKenna, K., & Bargh, J. (2000). Plan 9 from cyberspace: The implications of the Internet for personality. *Personality and Social Psychology Review, 4*(1), 57–75.

McNutt, J. (1998). Ensuring social justice for the new underclass: Community interventions to meet the needs of the new poor. In B. Ebo (Ed.), *Cyberghetto or cybertopia; Race, class, and gender on the Internet* (pp. 33–44). Westport, CT: Praeger.

Meckler, L. (2000, August 13). Democrats promise to use Internet to its fullest. Cable News Network. Retrieved January 10, 2002 from ⟨http://www.cnn.com/2000/ALLPOLITICS/stories/08/13/dem.internet.ap⟩.

Media Metrix. (1997). Press release. Retrieved Summer 2001 from ⟨http://www.mediametric.com/pcmpr33.htm⟩.

Mele, C. (1999). Cyberspace and disadvantaged communities: the Internet as a tool for collective action. In M. A. Smith & P. Kollock (Eds.), *Communities in cyberspace* (pp. 290–310). London: Routledge.

Merton, R. (1957). *Social theory and social structure* (3rd ed.) New York: Free Press.

Microsoft-Europe. (2001). Technology a change agent for democracy. Retrieved July 21, 2001 from ⟨http://www.microsoft.com/europe/public_sector/Gov_Politicians/68.htm⟩.

Miller, J. D. (2001). Who is using the Web for science and health information? *Science Communication, 22*(3), 256–273.

Miller, T., & Clemente, P. (1997). 1997 American Internet user survey. New York: FIND/SVP Emerging Technologies Research Group. Retrieved Summer 2001 from ⟨http://etrg.findsvp.com/internet/findf.html⟩.

Mirapaul, M. (2001, April 16). Artists share their files and lives on the Web. *New York Times*. Retrieved August 1, 2001 from ⟨http://www.nytimes.com/2001/04/16/arts/16ARTS.html⟩.

Mitchell, P. (2000). Internet addiction: Genuine diagnosis or not? *The Lancet, 355*, 632–633.

Mitra, A. (2001). Marginal voices in cyberspace. *New Media and Society, 3*(1), 29–48.

Moody, E. J. (2001). Internet usage and its relationship to loneliness. *Cyber-Psychology and Behavior, 4*, 393–401.

Morris, D. (2000). *Vote.com*. Los Angeles: Renaissance Books.

Moses, T. (1996, August 1). From the windowseat. *Boston Book Review*. Retrieved July 19, 2001 from ⟨http://www.bookwire.bowker.com/bookinfo/review.aspx?3492⟩.

Mueller, M. (2001). Universal service policies as wealth redistribution. In B. Compaine (Ed.), *The digital divide: Facing a crisis or creating a myth?* (pp. 179–187). Cambridge, MA: MIT Press.

Mukerji, C., & Simon, B. (1998). Out of the limelight: Discredited communities and informal communication on the Internet. *Sociological Inquiry, 68*(2), 258–273.

Mulgan, G. J. (1991). *Communication and control: Networks and the new economies of communication.* New York: Guilford Press.

Murdock, G., & Golding, P. (1989). Information poverty and political inequality: Citizenship in the age of privatized communications. *Journal of Communication, 39*(3), 180–195.

National Telecommunications and Information Administration (NTIA). (1999). *Falling through the Net: A report on telecommunications and the information technology gap in America.* Washington, D.C.: NTIA. Retrieved Summer 2001 from ⟨http://www.ntia.doc.gov/ntiahome/digitaldivide⟩.

Negroponte, N. (1995). *Being digital.* New York: Knopf.

Net users mirror nation's gender breakdown. (2001, June 15). *USA Today.* Retrieved Summer 2001 from ⟨http://www.usatoday.com/life/cyber/nb/nb5.htm⟩.

Netelection.org. (2001). Congressional candidate Web sites in campaign 2000. Retrieved July 21, 2001 from ⟨http://netelection.org/research/jan10report.pdf⟩.

Neu, C. R., Anderson, R. H., & Bikson, T. K. (1999). *Sending your government a message: E-mail communication between citizens and government.* Santa Monica, CA: RAND.

Neuman, R. (2001, June). Internet politique: The evolution of American politics, public discourse and the Web. Paper presented at the Web workshop, Department of Sociology, University of Maryland.

Nie, N. (2000, February 16). Internet disconnect. Interview on *PBS NewsHour.* Retrieved July 9, 2001 from ⟨http://www.pbs.org/newshour/bb/cyberspace/jan-june00/disconnect_2-16.html⟩.

Nie, N., & Erbring, L. (2000). *Internet and society.* Retrieved Summer 2001 from ⟨http://www.stanford.edu/group/siqss/Press_Release/Preliminary_Report.pdf⟩.

Nielsen/NetRatings. (2001). *Three out of five Americans on the Web.* Retrieved Summer 2001 from ⟨http://news.excite.com/news/r/010214/14/net-interaccess-dc⟩.

Noll, A. M. (1992). Anatomy of a failure: Picturephone revisited. *Telecommunications Policy, 16*(4), 307–316.

Noll, A. M. (1997). *Highway of dreams: A critical view along the information superhighway.* Mahwah, NJ: Erlbaum.

Noll, A. M., & Woods, J. (1979, March). The use of picturephone service in a hospital. *Telecommunications Policy,* 29–36.

Norris, P. (1998, July 19–22). Who surfs? New technology, old voters, and virtual democracy in America. Paper for the Third Annual Meeting of the John F.

Kennedy *Visions of Governance for the Twenty-first Century* Project, Bretton Woods. Retrieved August 10, 2001 from 〈http://ksghome.harvard.edu/~. pnorris.shorenstein.ksg/acrobat/whosurfs.pdf〉.

Numes, M. (1995). Jean Baudrillard in cyberspace: Internet, virtuality, and postmodernity. *Style, 29*(2), 31–27.

Odzer, C. (1997). *Virtual spaces: Sex and the cyber citizen.* New York: Berkeley.

Oettinger, A. (1999). Understanding digital. In B. Compaine & W. Read (Eds.), *The information resources policy handbook: Research for the information age.* (pp. 111–194). Cambridge, MA: MIT Press.

Olson, E. (1997, November 24). Nations struggle with how to control hate on the Web. *New York Times.* Retrieved August 11, 2001 from 〈http://www.pili. org/lists/piln/archives/msg00107.html〉.

O'Neill, J. (2001, January 12). As voters log on, so must politicians: Most campaigns didn't use the Web effectively, but they'll need to get Web-savvy for the next election, experts say. *Medill News Service.* Retrieved July 21, 2001 from 〈http://www.pcworld.com/resource/printable/article/0,aid,38662,00.asp〉.

On Line. (1996, April 26). *Chronicle of Higher Education, 42*(33), A21.

Papacharissi, Z., & Rubin, A. (2000). Predictors of Internet use. *Journal of Broadcasting and Electronic Media, 44*(2), 175–196.

Parks, M., & Floyd, K. (1996). Making friends in cyberspace. *Journal of Communication, 46,* 80–97.

Parks, M., & Roberts, L. (1998). "Making MOOsic": The development of personal relationships online and a comparison to their off-line counterparts. *Journal of Social and Personal Relationships, 15,* 519–537.

Patterson, S. J. (1997). Evaluating the Blacksburg Electronic Village. In A. M. Cohill, & A. Kavanaugh (Eds.), *Community networks: Lessons from Blacksburg, Virginia.* (pp. 55–71). Washington, DC: Artech House.

PC Gamer (2001). The age of clans. *PC Gamer, 9*(9), 43.

Perkins, M. (1996, March 1). Mining the Internet gold rush. *Red Herring Magazine.* Retrieved July 16, 2001 from 〈http://www.redherring.com/index. asp?layout=story&channel=70000007&doc_id=260016026〉.

Perse, E., & Dunn, D. (1998). The utility of home computers: Implications of multimedia and connectivity. *Journal of Broadcasting and Electronic Media, 42,* 435–456.

Pew Internet and American Life Project (2000, December 3). Internet election news audience seeks convenience, familiar names: Youth vote influenced by on-line information. A joint release from the Pew Research Center for People and the Press and the Pew Internet and American Life Project. Retrieved July 21, 2001 from 〈http://www.pewinternet.org/reports/toc.asp?Report=27〉.

Pew Reports. (2001). Online reports on the October and November 2000 surveys of online election information. Retrieved Summer 2001 from 〈http:// www.people-press.org/online00mor.htm〉 and 〈http://www.pewinternet.org/

reports/reports.asp?Report=27&Section=ReportLevel2&Field=Level2ID&ID= 135#navigate⟩.

Pew Research Center. (1997). *TV news viewership declines*. Retrieved Summer 2001 from ⟨http://www.people-press.org/mediaque.htm⟩.

Pew Research Center. (2000). *Tracking online life: How women use the Internet to cultivate relationships with family and friends*. Retrieved Summer 2001 from ⟨http://www.pewinternet.org/reports/toc.asp?Report=11⟩.

Pfaffenberger, B. (1990). *Democratizing information: Online databases and the rise of end-user searching*. Boston: Hall.

Podlas, K. (2000). Mistresses of their domain: How female entrepreneurs in cyberporn are initiating a gender power shift. *CyberPsychology and Behavior*, *3*, 847–854.

Pool, I. de Sola. (1983). *Technologies of freedom*. Cambridge, MA: Belknap Press.

Porter, D. (Ed.). (1997). *Internet culture*. New York: Routledge.

Portes, A., & Landolt, P. (1996). The downside of social capital. *The American Prospect*, *26*(May–June), 18–21, 94.

Poster, M. (1990). The mode of information: *Post-structuralism and social context*. Chicago: University of Chicago Press.

Pratarelli, M. E., Browne, B. L., & Johnson, K. (1999). The bits and bytes of computer/Internet addiction: A factor analytic approach. *Behavior Research Methods, Instruments and Computers*, *31*, 305–314.

Pryor, L. (1994). The videotex debacle. *American Journalism Review*, *16*(9), 41–42.

Punday, D. (2000). The narrative construction of cyberspace: Reading Neuromancer, reading cyberspace debates. *College English*, *63*(2), 194–213.

Putnam, R. (1995). Bowling alone: America's declining social capital. *Journal of Democracy*, *6*(1), 65–78.

Putnam, R. (1996). The strange disappearance of civic life in America. *The American Prospect*, *24*, 34–46.

Putnam, R. (2000). *Bowling alone: The collapse and revival of American community*. New York: Simon & Schuster.

Rakow, L. (1992). *Gender on the line: Women, the telephone, and community life*. Urbana: University of Illinois Press.

Rash, W. (1997). *Politics on the nets: Wiring the political process*. New York: Freeman.

Raymond's journal (2001, May 26). Retrieved July 5, 2001 from ⟨http://alumni.eecs.berkeley.edu/~rayning/2001_05_20_log.html⟩.

Reagan, J. (1987). Classifying adopters and nonadopters of four technologies using political activity, media use and demographic variables. *Telematics and Informatics*, *4*, 3–16.

Reder, S., & Schwab, R. (1988). The communicative economy of the workgroup. *Office: Technology and People*, 4(3), 177–196.

Reena, J. (2000, August 17). Arranged marriages, minus the parents. *New York Times*. Retrieved June 25, 2001 from ⟨http://www.nytimes.com/library/tech/00/08/circuits/articles/17matr.html⟩.

Reuters. (2001, July 13). Afghanistan's Taliban bans Internet. Retrieved July 15, 2001 from ⟨http://dailynews.yahoo.com/h/nm/20010713/wr/tech_afghan_internet_dc_1.html⟩.

Reuters Health. (2001, August 10). The Internet may encourage risky sexual behavior. Reuters. Retrieved August 11, 2001 from ⟨http://dailynews.yahoo.com/h/nm/20010810/hl/netsex_1.html⟩.

Rheingold, H. (1993). *The virtual community: Homesteading on the electronic frontier*. Reading, MA: Addison Wesley.

Rice, R. E. (1982). Communication networking in computer conferencing systems: A longitudinal study of group roles and system structure. In M. Burgoon (Ed.), *Communication Yearbook* (vol. 6, pp. 925–944). Newbury Park, CA: Sage.

Rice, R. E. (1987a). Computer-mediated communication and organizational innovation. *Journal of Communication*, 37, 65–94.

Rice, R. E. (1987b). New patterns of social structure in an information society. In J. Schement & L. Lievrouw (Eds.), *Competing visions, complex realities: Social aspects of the information society* (pp. 107–120). Norwood, NJ: Ablex.

Rice, R. E. (1990). Computer-mediated communication system network data: Theoretical concerns and empirical examples. *International Journal of Man-Machine Studies*, 32(6), 627–647.

Rice, R. E. (1999). What's new about new media? Artifacts and paradoxes. *New Media and Society*, 1(1), 24–32.

Rice, R. E. (2001a). The Internet and health communication: A framework of experiences. In R. E. Rice & J. E. Katz (Eds.), *The Internet and health communication: Experiences and expectations* (pp. 5–46). Thousand Oaks, CA: Sage.

Rice, R. E. (2001b). Primary issues in Internet use: Access, civic and community involvement, and social interaction and expression. In L. Lievrouw & S. Livingstone (Eds.), *Handbook of new media* (pp. 105–129). London: Sage.

Rice, R. E., & Katz, J. E. (Eds.). (2001). *The Internet and health communication: Experiences and expectations*. Thousand Oaks, CA: Sage.

Rice, R. E., Kraut, R., Cool, C., & Fish, R. (1994). Individual, structural and social influences on use of a new communication medium. In D. Moore (Ed.), *Academy of management best papers proceedings* (pp. 285–289). Madison, WI: Omni Press.

Rice, R. E., McCreadie, M., & Chang, S.-J. (2001). *Accessing and browsing information and communication: A multidisciplinary approach*. Cambridge, MA: MIT Press.

Rierdan, J. (1999). Internet-depression link? *American Psychologist, 54,* 781–782.

Riphagen, J., & Kanfer, A. (1997). How does e-mail affect our lives? National Center for Supercomputing Applications. Retrieved Summer 2001 from ⟨http://www.ncsa.uiuc.edu/edu/trg/e-mail/index.html⟩.

Robertson, D. (1998). *The new renaissance: Computers and the next level of civilization.* New York: Oxford University Press.

Robinson, J. (2001, June). The digital divide: Recent results. Paper presented at the WebShop Summer Institute, University of Maryland.

Robinson, J., Barth, K., & Kohut, A. (1997). Social impact research: Personal computers, mass media and use of time. *Social Science Computer Review, 15*(1), 65–82.

Rojas, V., Roychowdhury, D., Okur, O., Straubhaar, J., & Estrada-Ortiz, Y. (in press). Beyond access: Cultural capital and the roots of the digital divide. In E. Bucy & J. Newhagen (Eds.), *Media access: Social and psychological dimensions of new technology use.* Hillsdale, NJ: Erlbaum.

Roper, S. (2001). *Muddying identity: The construction of gendered personae in an online role-playing environment.* Dissertation, School of Communication, Information, and Library Studies, Rutgers University, New Brunswick, NJ.

Rosen, L., & Weil, M. (1995). Adult and teenage use of consumer, business, and entertainment technology: Potholes on the information superhighway? *Journal of Consumer Affairs, 29*(1), 55–84.

Rubinyi, R. M. (1989). Computers and community: The organizational impact. *Journal of Communication, 39*(3), 110–123.

Sanders, C. E., Field, T. M., Diego, M., & Kaplan, M. (2000). The relationship of Internet use to depression and social isolation among adolescents. *Adolescence, 35*(138), 237–242.

Sarder, Z. (Ed.). (1996). *Cyberfutures: Culture and politics on the information superhighway.* New York: New York University Press.

Schegloff, E. (forthcoming). Opening sequencing. In J. Katz & M. Aakhus (Eds.), *Perpetual contact: Mobile communication, private talk, public performance.* New York: Cambridge University Press.

Schement, J. (1995). Beyond universal service: Characteristics of American without telephones. *Telecommunications Policy, 19*(6), 477–485.

Scherer, K. (1997). College life online: Healthy and unhealthy Internet use. *Journal of College Student Development, 38*(6), 655–665.

Schiller, H. (1996). *Information inequality: The deepening social crisis in America.* London: Routledge.

Scholes, Robert J. (1999, March 4). The "Mail-order bride" industry and its impact on U.S. immigration. *International match-making services: a report to Congress.* United States Immigration and Naturalization Service. Retrieved July 10, 2001 from ⟨http://www.clas.ufl.edu/users/rscholes/writeup.htm⟩.

Schon, D., Sanyal, B., & Mitchell, W. (Eds.). (1999). *High technology and low-income communities*. Cambridge, MA: MIT Press.

Schroeder, K., & Ledger, J. (1998). *Life and death on the Internet*. Menasha, WI: Supple.

Schuler, D. (1996). *New community networks: Wired for change*. New York: ACM.

Schulz, N. (2001, April 29). The e-files. *The Washington Post*. Online edition, p. G-1. Retrieved May 17, 2001 from ⟨http://www.washingtonpost.com⟩.

Schutz, A. (1970). *On phenomenology and social relations*. Chicago: University of Chicago Press.

Selnow, G. W. (1994). *High-tech campaigns: Computer technology in political communication*. New York: Praeger.

Senft, T. (2001, June 14). Debating reality: An online hoax is not a pox. *New York Times*. Retrieved July 14, 2001 from ⟨http://www.nytimes.com/2001/06/14/technology/14REAL.html⟩.

Shaffer, H. J., Hall, M. N., & Vander Bilt, J. (2000). "Computer addiction": A critical consideration. *American Journal of Orthopsychiatry, 70*, 162–168.

Shapira, N. A., Goldsmith, T. D., Keck, P. E., Khosla, U. M., & McElroy, S. L. (2000). Psychiatric features of individuals with problematic Internet use. *Journal of Affective Disorders, 57*, 267–272.

Shapiro, A., & Leone, R. (1999). *The control revolution: How the Internet is putting individuals in charge and changing the world we know*. New York: Public Affairs/Century Foundation.

Shapiro, J. S. (1999). Loneliness: Paradox or artifact? *American Psychologist, 54*, 782–783.

Sink, M. (2000a, December 28). Going online to build a family. *New York Times*. Retrieved July 13, 2001 from ⟨http://www.nytimes.com/2000/12/28/technology/28ADOP.html⟩.

Sink, M. (2000b, August 17). The Web helps military "brats" find long-lost friends. *New York Times*. Retrieved July 14, 2001 from ⟨http://www.nytimes.com/library/tech/00/08/circuits/articles/17brat.html⟩.

Skocpol, T. (2000). *The missing middle: Working families and the future of American social policy*. New York: Norton.

Skog, B. (forthcoming). Mobiles and the Norwegian teen: Identity, gender and class. In J. Katz & M. Aakhus (Eds.), *Perpetual contact: Personal communication, private talk, and public performance*. Cambridge, MA: Cambridge University Press.

Slack, R. S., & Williams, R. A. (2000). The dialectics of place and space: On community in the "information age." *New Media and Society, 2*(3), 313–334.

Smith, M., & Kollock, P. (Eds.). (1998). *Communities in cyberspace*. New York: Routledge.

Smith, T. (1999). *The emerging twenty-first century American family*. Chicago: Report to National Opinion Research Center.

Sobchack, V. (1996). Democratic franchise and the electronic frontier. In Z. Sardar & J. Ravetz (Eds.), *Cyberfutures: Culture and politics on the information superhighway* (pp. 77–88). New York: New York University Press.

Spears, R., & Lea, M. (1994). Panacea or panopticon? The hidden power in computer-mediated communication. *Communication Research, 21*(4), 427–459.

Spooner, T., & Rainie, L. (2001). *Hispanics and the Internet*. Washington, DC: Pew Internet and American Life Project. Retrieved Summer 2001 from ⟨http://www.pewinternet.org⟩.

Sproull, L., & Faraj, S. (1995) Atheism, sex, and databases: The Net as a social technology. In B. Kahin & J. Keller (Eds.), *Public access to the Internet* (pp. 62–80). Cambridge, MA: MIT Press.

Stafford, L., Kline, S., & Dimmick, J. (1999). Home e-mail: Relational maintenance and gratification opportunities. *Journal of Broadcasting and Electronic Media, 43*(4), 659–669.

Stanley, J. (2001, July 1). Talk radio. *New York Times*, sec. 14, p. 1.

Starobin, P. (1996, June 25). On the square. *National Journal*, 1145–1149.

Stebbins, R. (2001, May/June). Serious leisure. *Society, 38*(4), 53–57.

Stefik, M. (1999). *The Internet edge: Social, legal, and technological challenges for a networked world*. Cambridge, MA: MIT Press.

Sterling, B. (2000). Ideological freeware: Distribute at will. Tom's Casa on the Net. Retrieved July 11, 2001 from ⟨http://www-atdp.berkeley.edu/9932/fletcher/casa/index.html⟩.

Stern, S. E. (1999). Addiction to technologies: A social psychological perspective of Internet addiction. *CyberPsychology and Behavior, 2*, 419–424.

Stokley, N. (2001). Women, Webcams, and the Web. Retrieved August 6, 2001 from ⟨http://camden-www.rutgers.edu/~wood/445/stokley.html⟩.

Stoll, C. (1995). *Silicon snake oil: Second thoughts on the information highway*. New York: Doubleday.

Stoll, C. (1999). *High tech heretic*. New York: Doubleday.

Stone, A. (1991). Will the real body please stand up? Boundary stories about virtual cultures. In M. Benedikt (Ed.), *Cyberspace: First steps* (pp. 81–119). Cambridge, MA: MIT Press.

Stone, A. (1996). *The war of desire and technology at the end of the mechanical age*. Cambridge, MA: MIT Press.

Stone, B. (2001, February 19). Love online. *Newsweek*. Retrieved June 24, 2001 from ⟨http://www.courses.psu.edu/hd_fs/hd_fs315_rxj9/love_on_line.pdf⟩.

Straus, S. (1997). Technology, group processes, and group outcomes: Testing the connections in performance in computer-mediated and face-to-face groups. *Human-Computer Interaction, 12*, 227–266.

Stringer, H. (2000, November 13). The games people play. *TechWeek*. Retrieved August 5, 2001 from ⟨http://www.techweek.com⟩.

Study shows four hundred twenty-nine million net users in twenty-seven countries. (2001). Nielsen/NetRatings Global Internet Trends, June 12, ⟨http://www.newsbytes.com/news/01/166705.html⟩.

Sudweeks, F., McLaughlin, M., & Rafaeli, S. (Eds.). (1998). *Network and netplay: Virtual groups on the Internet*. Cambridge, MA: MIT Press.

Suler, J. R., & Phillips, W. L. (2000). The bad boys of cyberspace: Deviant behavior in a multimedia chat community. *CyberPsychology and Behavior, 1*, 275–294.

Sunstein, C. (2001). *Republic.com*. Princeton, NJ: Princeton University Press.

Surratt, C. (1998). *Netlife: Internet citizens and their communities*. Commack, NY: Nova Science.

Symposium (1995). Emerging media technology and the First Amendment. *Yale Law Journal, 104*, 1613–1850.

Tapscott, D. (1997). *Growing up digital: The rise of the net generation*. New York: McGraw-Hill.

Taylor, C. (2000, June 26). Looking online. *Time Canada, 155*(26). Retrieved August 7, 2001 from ⟨http://www.canoe.com/TimeCanada0006/26_time25.html⟩.

Terry, J., & Calvert, M. (Eds.). (1997). *Processed lives: Gender and technology in everyday life*. New York: Routledge.

Times Mirror (1995, October 16). *Technology in the American household: Americans going online—explosive growth, uncertain destinations*. Washington, DC: Times Mirror Center for the People and the Press.

TR Daily (1997, August 18). *Telecom Reports*, p. 1.

Tsagarousianou, R., Tambini, D., & Bryan, C. (Eds.). (1998). *Cyberdemocracy: Technology, cities and civic networks*. New York: Routledge.

Tsai, C., & Lin, S. S. J. (2001). Analysis of attitudes toward computer networks and Internet addiction of Taiwanese adolescents. *CyberPsychology and Behavior, 4*, 373–376.

Tufekcioglu, Z. (2001). Rethinking the theory behind the digital divide initiatives: It's not all good all the time in the age of deskilled, low-paying "hi-tech" jobs. Department of Communication, University of Texas, Austin. Paper presented at the International Communication Association Conference, Washington, DC.

Turkle, S. (1985). *The second self*. New York: Simon & Schuster.

Turkle, S. (1996). Virtuality and its discontents: Searching for community in cyberspace. *American Prospect, 24*, 50–57.

Turkle, S. (1997). *Life on the screen: Identity in the age of the Internet*. New York: Simon & Schuster.

Turner, J., Grube, J., & Meyers, J. (2001). Developing an optimal match within online communities: An exploration of CMC support communities and traditional support. *Journal of Communication*, 51(2), 231–251.

Umble, D. Z. (1996). *Holding the line: The telephone in Old Order Mennonite and Amish life*. Baltimore: Johns Hopkins University Press.

Uncapher, W. (1999). Electronic homesteading on the rural frontier: Big Sky Telegraph and its community. In M. A. Smith & P. Kollock (Eds.), *Communities in cyberspace* (pp. 264–289). London: Routledge.

United States Congress, Office of Technology Assessment. (1987). *The electronic supervisor: New technology, new tensions*. OTA Publication No. OTA-CIT-333. Washington, DC: U.S. Government Printing Office.

United States Congress, Office of Technology Assessment. (1990). *Critical connections: Communication for the future*. OTA Publication No. OTA-CIT-407. Washington, DC: U.S. Government Printing Office.

United States Department of Commerce, Bureau of the Census. (1992). *Statistical Abstracts for the United States*. Washington, DC: U.S. Government Printing Office.

United States Department of Commerce. (2000). *Falling through the Net: Toward digital inclusion*. Washington, D.C.: Government Printing Office.

University of California–Los Angeles (UCLA) Center for Communication Policy. (2000). *The UCLA Internet report: Surveying the digital future*. Retrieved Summer 2001 from ⟨http://www.ccp.ucal.edu⟩.

Uslaner, E. (2000, April). Trust, civic engagement, and the Internet. Paper presented at the Joint Sessions of the European Consortium for Political Research, Switzerland, University of Grenoble. Retrieved Summer 2001 from ⟨http://www.pewinternet.org/papers/paper.asp?paper=5⟩.

Valovic, T. (2000). *Digital mythologies: The hidden complexities of the Internet*. New Brunswick, NJ: Rutgers University Press.

Van Alstyne, W. W. (1995). *First Amendment: Cases and materials* (2nd ed.). Westbury, NY: Foundation Press.

Van Dijk, J. (1999). *The network society: Social aspects of new media*. (L. Spoorenberg, Trans.). Thousand Oaks, CA: Sage.

Varoli, J. (2000, December 17). American lion seeks Russian lioness. *New York Times*. Retrieved July 10, 2001 from ⟨http://www.nytimes.com/2000/12/17/living/17OUT.html?pagewanted=1⟩.

Virnoche, M., & Marx, G. (1997). "Only connect"—E. M. Forster in an age of electronic communication: Computer-mediated association and community networks. *Sociological Inquiry*, 67(1), 85–100.

Wall, L. (1996). Review of *City of bits: Space, place, and the Infobahn*, by William Mitchell. *The Information Society*, 112(3), 332.

Wallace, P. (1999). *The psychology of the Internet*. New York: Cambridge University Press.

Walsh, E., Gazala, M., & Ham, C. (2001). The truth about the digital divide. In B. Compaine (Ed.), *The digital divide: Facing a crisis or creating a myth?* (pp. 279–284). Cambridge, MA: MIT Press.

Walther, J. (1996). Computer-mediated communication: Impersonal, interpersonal, and hyperpersonal interaction. *Communication Research, 23*, 3–43.

Wastlund, E., Norlander, T., & Archer, T. (2001). Internet blues revisited: Replication and extension for an Internet paradox study. *CyberPsychology and Behavior, 4*, 385–391.

Webster, F. (1995). *Theories of the information society.* New York: Routledge.

Weinberg, S. (1987). Expanding access to technology: Computer equity for women. In B. D. Wright, M. M. Ferree, G. O. Mellow, L. H. Lewis, M.-L. D. Samper, R. Asher & K. Claspell (Eds.), *Women, work, and technology: Transformations* (pp. 281–290). Ann Arbor: University of Michigan Press.

Wellman, B. (2001). Physical place and cyberspace: The rise of networked individualism. *International Journal of Urban and Regional Research, 25*(2), 227–252.

Wellman, B., & Gulia, M. (1999a). Net surfers don't ride alone. In B. Wellman (Ed.), *Networks in the global village* (pp. 331–366). Boulder, CO: Westview Press.

Wellman, B., & Gulia, M. (1999b). Virtual communities as communities: Net surfers don't ride alone. In M. A. Smith & P. Kollock (Eds.), *Communities in cyberspace* (pp. 167–194). New York: Routledge.

Wellman, B., Haase, A. Q., Witte, I., & Hampton, K. (2001). "Does the Internet increase, decrease, or supplement social capital? *American Behavioral Scientist, 45*(3), 436–455.

White, C. S. (1997). Citizen participation and the Internet: Prospects for civic deliberation in the information age. *Social Studies, 88*, 23–28.

Winner, L. (1999). Who will be in cyberspace? In P. Mayer (Ed.), *Computer media and communication* (pp. 207–218). New York: Oxford University Press.

Winter, I. (2000). Towards a theorised understanding of family life and social capital. Working paper 21. *Australian Institute of Family Studies.* Retrieved July 17, 2001 from ⟨http://www.aifs.org.au/institute/pubs/WP21.html⟩.

Wolf, A. (1998). Exposing the great equalizer: Demythologizing Internet equity. In B. Ebo (Ed.), *Cyberghetto or cybertopia; Race, class, and gender on the Internet* (pp. 15–31). Westport, CT: Praeger.

Wresch, W. (1996). *Disconnected: Haves and have-nots in the information age.* New Brunswick, NJ: Rutgers University Press.

Wright, C. (1975). *Mass communication: A sociological perspective.* New York: Random House.

Wyatt, S. (2001). Fleeing the dot com era. *UNESCO Courier*, February. Retrieved July 18, 2001 from ⟨http://www.unesco.org/courier/2001_02/uk/medias.htm⟩.

Wynn, E., & Katz, J. E. (1997). Hyperbole over cyberspace: Self-presentation and social boundaries in Internet home pages and discourse. *The Information Society*, *13*(4), 297–329.

Yahoo!News. (2001, February 19). *Hispanics, blacks and women surfing the Internet in greater numbers*. Retrieved Summer 2001 from ⟨http://dailynews. hayoo.com/h/ll/20010219/co/hispanics_blacks_and_women_surfing_the_internet_ ingreater_numbers⟩.

Young, J. (2001, June 15). A study finds that Web users are more tolerant than non-users. *Chronicle of Higher Education*. Retrieved Summer 2001 from ⟨http:// chronicle.com/free/2001/06/2001061501t.htm⟩.

Young, K. (1996). Internet addiction: The emergence of a new clinical disorder. Retrieved Summer 2001 from ⟨http://www.pitt.edu/~ksy/apa.html⟩.

Zaler, J. (1992). *The nature and origins of mass opinion*. New York: Cambridge University Press.

Zeller, S. (2000, October 14). Campaign finance: Clicking on e-dollars. *National Journal*. Retrieved August 11, 2001 from ⟨http://www.aristotle.com/article. asp?id=101400&d=10/14/00&bc=700018⟩.

Zieschang, K. (1990). Sample weighting methods and estimation of totals in the Consumer Expenditure Survey. *Journal of the American Statistical Association*, *85*(12), 986–1001.

Zuboff, S. (1988). *In the age of the smart machine: The future of work and power*. New York: Basic Books.

Index

References to drawings and tables are printed in italic type.

Abramson, R., 182
Access creation, 85–86, 98–99
Access programs, 86, 94, 95, 96
  public access, 19, 34, 88, 95
Access to the Internet, 1(ch. 1), 4–5,
  15, 17, 18, 88, 323. *See also*
  Barriers or limitation to access;
  Demographic factors and Internet
  access
  dystopian perspective of, 6, 7, 8, 19–
  20, 83–84, 104, 322 (*see also*
  Digital divide)
  as a human right, 84, 86
  and Internet technology, 33, 34, 96
  levels and types of connectivity, 22–
  23, 28–29, *38*, 112–113, *250*
  syntopian perspective of, 13, 34, 65,
  99, 322–324
  utopian perspective of, 30
Addiction (Internet), 7, 193, 207,
  271
Adolescence. *See* Youth and the
  Internet
Afghanistan, 333
African Americans and the Internet
  levels and types of access, 26, 28, 33,
  62, *63*, *64*, 65, 321
  online communities, 123, 184
Age cohort influences, 322, *390*, *396*.
  See also Older persons and the
  Internet

community involvement and, *156–*
  157
  and the digital divide, 25–26, 27–28,
  32
  media use and, *232–233*, *245*
  and political involvement, 147
  social interaction and, *232–233*, *245*
  of U.S. Census vs. survey sample,
  361, 363
  of users vs. nonusers across survey
  years, *40*, *43*, *44–45*, 48, *49–50*,
  50, *51*, *52–53*, *53–54*, *54*, *62*, *64*
Agence France-Presse, 314
Alpha-1 Foundation/Alphanet, 96, 97,
  97–98
Alta Vista, 277, 281
Altruism and charity, 195–196, 198
American Behavioral Scientist, 329
American Conservative Union (ACU),
  176
American Internet user survey, 217
Americans with Disabilities Act, 34
American Zoetrope virtual studio,
  306–307
America Online (AOL) survey, 17,
  30–31, 111
Anonymity. *See also* Privacy
  and the fragmented self perspective,
  271
  limitations to on the Internet, 272,
  273, 273, 274, 275, 276, 277

Antigovernment groups, 122, 125, 333
AOL survey, 17, 30–31, 111
Archives of Internet usage, 273
Arnold, David, 90
Arpanet, 121, 203. *See also* Internet technology
Art on the Internet. *See also* Music on the Internet
artists' outreach, 11, 89
literature and poetry Web sites, 302, 304–305
screenplay review and submission Web site, 306–307
virtual studios, 306–307, 307–309
visual art and multimedia Web sites, 305–308
WebCam Web sites, 301–302
Asian Americans and the Internet, 21, 28, 33
Web sites serving, 185
Aspden, P., and J. Katz, 208
Asynchronous distributed dialogue feature, 269
Audio technology, 130–131
Authenticity issues, 7, 104, 105–106, 275
Authority or hierarchy, Internet challenges to, 108, 213, 214
Automobile, 330
Awareness of the Internet, 48, *51*, 94, 322, *373*
demographic and social factors influencing, 35, 48, *49–50*, 50
and Internet usage (combined factors), 35, *49–50*, 50, *51*, *52–53*, *54*, *54–55*

Bakardjieva, M., and R. Smith, 123
Bannan, K., 193
Banning of the Internet, 333
Barlow, John Perry, 1–2
Barney, D., 108
Baron, N. S., 203
Barriers or limitations to access, 23–24, *57*, 58, 322–323. *See also*

Access to the Internet; Disabled persons access
cultural and social rather than technological, 34, 36, 96–99
political barriers, 86
Battle games Web sites, 191–192
Baudrillard, Jean, 10, 114, 204
Baym, N. K., 208–209
Belonging (sense of), *244*, 249, *250–251*
Beniger, James, 10, 115, 120
Benton Foundation Report, "Losing Ground Bit by Bit," 11
Berger, P., and T. Luckmann, 266
Bikson, T., and C. Panis, *Current Population Survey*, 19, 20, 21
Bimber, B., 112–113
Black, J., 208
Blacksburg, Virginia, 127
Blind access to the Internet, 86, 87
Blogs, 299, 300
Bloomfield, B. P., and T. Vurdubakis, 269
Blumler, J., and E. Katz, 36
Bollier, D., 119, 222
Bonisteel, S., 29, 34, 91
Books. *See* Print media consumption
Borchert, M., 34
Boundaries
the Internet as a boundary-shifting medium, 282
personal and professional boundary, 272, 278–279
postmodern concept of fragmentation and, 268, 269–270
public and private boundary, 270, 271, 272, 277–278
real and virtual boundary, 269–270, 271
Bourdieu, Pierre, 337, *338*
Bourque, S. C., and K. B. Warren, 18
Brown, John Seely, 115
Buddy lists, 212, 293
Bunn, A., 221
Burmese dissidents, 125
Bush, George W., 182–183, 312

Calhoun, C., 106, 107, 114, 115
Calvert, C., 302
Canary, D., and B. Spitzberg, 36
Cancer research on the Internet, 197
Carey, J., 103, 332
Carnegie-Mellon Study, xviii
Carr, Caleb, 6
Carrier, R., 19
CB radio, 283
Cellular phone, 36–37, 252, 254, 294,
   352. *See also* Telephone
Censorship, 86, 333
Census Bureau (U.S.), 20, 314
  demographic data compared to
  study, *361–362*
Cerulo, K., 120
Charity and altruism, 195–196, 198
Chatrooms, *250, 252, 253, 293, 401,
   402. See also* Discourse on the
   Internet
  political, 104
  prayer-oriented, 296–297
  social-interactive benefits claimed for,
   208
Cheating, 197
Cherny, L., 125, 213
Child pornography, 7
Children in household, *46, 47*
  community involvement and, *156–
   157*
  and the digital divide, 27, *63, 63, 64*
  of Internet users vs. nonusers, 46–47,
   53, 54, 227
  and level of Internet access, 37–38,
   46–47
  media use and online interaction
   and, *233*
  of U.S. Census vs. survey sample,
   361
China, People's Republic of, 333
Chong, Curtis, "How the Blind Access
   the Internet," 87
Chron X game, 191
Cinema, 130
Citizen-government contact, 31, 107–
   108, 178–179, *403. See also*

Political involvement of older
   persons, 20
Civic involvement. *See* Community;
   Neighborhood; Political
   involvement
Class reunion Web sites, 170
Cliffe, 309
Clines, F., 95
Clinton, Hillary, 312–314
Clinton, William (Bill), 113
Clipper Chip protest, 36, 109–110
CMC. *See* Computer-mediated
   communication (CMC)
Coffey, S., and H. Stipp, 216
Cold fusion, 121
Cole, Carla, 302
Cole, Jeffrey, xviii, 2
Coleman, James, 336, *338*
Collective benefit of the Internet
  the "invisible mouse" effect, 13, 161,
   162, 295, 351–352, 354
  public-goods aspect, 224, 345
Commercialization of the Internet,
   24–25, 106, 315. *See also*
   Economic activity and the Internet
Communication. *See also* Communication technologies; E-mail;
   Information over the Internet
  asynchronous distributed dialogue,
   269
  by letter, 228, *229, 232, 235, 394*
  by phone, 228, 235, *394–395*
  by voice mail, *395*
  interpersonal, 36–37, 93–94, 99
  symbolic communication, 345–346
Communication technologies, 18, 36–
   37, 116–117, 225, 283. *See also*
   Computer-mediated communication
   (CMC); Internet as a social
   technology; *and by specific
   technology*
  assessment of, 131
  impact of, 129–131, 133, 330, 344
Communitarianism, 113–114
Communities online. *See* Virtual
   communities

Community. *See also* Community involvement and Internet use; Community networks; Neighborhood; Social capital; Virtual communities
decline in, 130, 131, 153
the nature of community, 117–119, 132
physical or organic vs. virtual, 115–116, 117
traditional communities, 117–118, 131
Community involvement and Internet use, 1(ch. 1), 4, 53, *54*, 85–86, 103(ch.6), 153(ch.8), *154*, *159*, 162–163. *See also* Community networks; Virtual communities
demographic factors and, 154–155, *156–157*, 158–160
dystopian view on, 105, 114–117, 152, 153, 155, 158
extent of contact with neighbors, 235, *236–237*
offline efforts to create community Internet access, 85–86, 98–99
syntopian perspective on, 132–133, 199–200, 325
utopian perspective on, 119–120, 324
Community networks, 85–86, 119, 125–128, *126*
Compaine, B., 33–34, 94, 321
Complexity
as a barrier to access, 57, 58, *60*, 61
skill-level and Internet usage, *233*, *251*, 376–377
Computer-mediated communication (CMC), 3, 115, 116–117, 209, 331. *See also* Information over the Internet
other media use and, 216
Computer technology, 269
Computer use, 293, 372–373
Confessions over the Internet, 297–298, *298*

Congress Online Project, 106
Connectivity, 349–350
Consequences of the Internet. *See* Social impact of the Internet
Conservative or right wing Web sites, 176, 177–178
Constructionism, 266, 269, 270
Consumer class, 24–25
Consumer Federation of America study, 22, 112
Consumer's Union survey, 91–92
Contact lists, 212, 293
Content of the Internet, 349, 350–351
Convention coverage. *See under* Election campaigns
Converse, P., 335
Cooper, M., and G. Kimmelman, 8, 19
Cooper, M., and D. Shah, 22, 92, 92–93
Coppola, Francis Ford, 306–307
Cornwell, B., and D. C. Lundgren, 207
Corporate complaint Web sites, 313
Corporate control issue, 7, 24
Corporate parody Web sites, 313
Corrado, A., 26
Correll, S., 267–268
Cost as an access factor, 57, 58, *60*, 91, 204–205, 323
Counter-hegemonic movements, 122, 125, 333
"Counter-Inaugural Oath," 183
Counter-Strike, 309
CPS research study, 30
Craigmillar Community Information Service, 125–126
Crime prevention, 337, *339*, 339–340, *340*
Crispell, D., 216
Crosscultural communication, 11
Cultural Access Group (2001) study, 26, 123
Cultural barriers to Internet access, 96

Cultural capital notion, 28. *See also*
Art on the Internet; Social capital
Cultural resources. *See* Art on the
Internet; Music on the Internet
Curtin, Mary Ellen, 302, 304
Cury, Brian, 302
Cyberbalkanization, 7, 8
Cybersociety. *See* Social interaction
online; Virtual communities
Cyberspace
as nonmaterial space, 119–120, 121,
191, 223, 269–270, 344

Dahl, R., 334
Dahlberg, L., 113
Dating
online dating services, 208, 285–286,
288–290
online efforts, 286–287
Davis, Doug, 129, 182, 193, 332–333
Davis, R., 107
Davison, P., J. Pennebaker, and S.
Dickerson, 163, 164
Day of Defeat, 192
Death and dying support groups, 172
Death. *See* Memorial Web sites
Decontextualized identity in
postmodern theory, 265–266, 267,
269, 271, 280
Deetz, S., 18
Deliberative democracy, 114
Democracy, 107, 113–114. *See also*
Election campaigns; Political
involvement
Democratic campaign Web sites, 175–
176, 333
Demographic data, *387–393*
of study compared to Census Bureau
statistics, *361–362*
Demographic factors and Internet
access, 41, *64*, 322
age cohort differences, 37–38, *40*
by start year, *44–45*
by survey year, *41*
the digital divide and, 22, 23–24,
25–26, 27–28, 30–32, 35, 50

family-related factors and, 37–38
of users vs. nonusers, *38*, 38–40, *40*,
44–45, 48, *49–50*, 50, *51*, *52–53*,
53–55, *54*
Depersonalization concern, 10
Depression
assertion that Internet use is related
to, 204–205, 220, 221, 328
findings challenged, 205, 220–222,
329
Dery, M., 265
Digital divide, 20–21, 33–34,
35(ch. 3), 65, 83(ch. 5). *See also*
Access to the Internet; Gender;
Internet usage; Race or ethnicity
awareness of or interest in the
Internet and, 23, 35
decline in, 30–32, 39, 41, *42*, *43*, *49*,
55, 62, *63*, *64*, 65, 322
demographic factors influencing, 22,
23–24, 25–26, 27–28, 30–32, 35,
50 (*see also* Demographic factors
and Internet use)
international-level digital divide, 29–
30, 34, 91
rural vs. urban, 21
subtle conceptions of, 28–29
syntopian perspective on, 321–322
Digital highway, 24, *373*
"Digital jukebox," 90–91
Digitized information, 343, 344–
347
Dimmick, J., J. Sikand, and S.
Patterson, 36
Disabled persons' access, 30, 34, 86,
88, 96–98
blind access, 86, 87
Web sites and online communities,
184, 222
Discourse on the Internet, 105–108,
206–207. *See also* Chatrooms
Disease-related support networks, 97–
98, 123, 128, 163–164, 172, 222
Disembodiment, 266
Diversity. *See* Tolerance for diversity
Doheny-Farina, S., 114

Dropouts, xviii, 1, 18, 23, 67(ch. 4),
99, *377*
compared to users by demographic
variables, *70–75, 77, 79*
factors influencing, 68, 80, 81, 323
Drudge, Matt, 335–336
Dubelyew, D., 307
Dystopian perspective, xviii–xix, 6–
10, 7, 20
access to the Internet is unequal, 6,
7, 8, 19–20, 83–84, 104, 322 (*see
also* Digital divide)
community involvement reduced/
virtual communities are pseudo
communities, 115–116, 105, 114–
117, 152, 153, 155, 158, 324
political involvement superficial and
encouraging inaction, 104–108
social isolation and Internet use/
Internet interactions superficial,
115–116, 204–207, 224, 324

Earthcam.com, 301–302
Echo (New York), 120, 125
Economic activity and the Internet, 4,
19
commercialization, 24–25, 106, 315
corporate control issue, 7, 24
illegal or destructive commercial
uses, 167, 200, 274, 275
Internet as a "gift economy," 128–
129
micromarketing and commercial
profiling, 315
pyramid marketing, 200
Edlund, M., 109, 178
Educational level, *391, 396*
community involvement and, *156–
157*
and the digital divide, 22, 23–24,
25–26, 32
media use and online interaction by,
232–233
political involvement and, 140, *141*
sociability indicators and, *237*

of U.S. Census respondents vs.
survey sample, 361(app.A.1),
363(app.A.2)
of users vs. nonusers across survey
years, *40, 43, 44–45, 49–50, 51,
52–53, 54, 54, 62, 64*
Egan, J., 88–89
Eisenberg, A., 86
Elderly. *See* Older persons and the
Internet
Election campaigns, 108–109, 111,
148, 151, 325. *See also* Political
involvement
convention coverage, *136*, 180–181
Democratic campaign Web sites,
175–176, 333
donation solicitations, 109
Presidential campaign 2000 and
post-election fallout, 182–183, 312
Republican campaign Web sites, 178,
179, 180–181, 333
Electronic cafes, 267, 332
Electronic democracy
electronic town meetings, 113
electronic voting, 105, 336
online focus groups, 109
Electronic graffiti, 207
Electronic magazines (*e-zines* and *me-
zines*), 305
Electronic stalking, 207, 223
Electronic voting, 105, 336
Elliott, P., 36
E-mail. *See also* Communication;
Social interaction online
buddy lists, 212, 293
communication and interaction with,
33, *258–259, 257, 395, 399, 403–
408*
as a motivation for using the
Internet, *56, 58, 59*
number of messages sent, 293–294
political, *137*
scientific, 121
studies or personal of benefit of,
209–210, 222

Emotional support, 187. *See also* Family; Friendship; Social interaction
Emphysema-related Web site, 97–98
Employment. *See also* Workplace information-based, 30
job-seeking online, 31, *398*
Employment-related factors, *233*, *387–388*
of Internet users vs. nonusers, 43, *46–47*, 227–228
Encryption methods, 273
Entertainment seeking, 217, *253. See also* Leisure involvement online
Equifax/Lotus Marketplace— Household CD ROM protest, 36, 109–110
Ethnic virtual communities, 123, 184, 185
European survey of Internet use, 216–217
Expert vs. novice. *See* Skill-level on the Internet
Expression. *See* Art on the Internet; Self-presentation; Social interaction online

Family. *See also* Children in household; Low-income families; Marital status
Internet viewed as beneficial to, 214
online communication with, 210, 211–213, *229*, 232, *239*, 245, 247, 252, *253*, 258, 258–259, 263, *381*, *404–408*
single-parent families, 27
Family resources on the Internet
adoption and reunion Web sites, 166–167
genealogy resources, 168
reuniting birth families via internet research, 167
virtual baby shower, 188
Family Web sites, 169

Fandom (fan fiction), 138, 302–303, *303*, 304
Fantasy, 267
Fantasy games, 191–193, 332
Fantasy Sports Players Association, 190
Fantasy sports teams Web sites, 189–190
Federally funded access program(s), 95
Feeling overloaded
Internet users vs. nonusers, 43, *48*
Feminist networking, 222–223
Ferguson, D., and E. Perse, 217
Figallo, C., 120
Film, 130
Filtering programs, 106, 115, 122
Firestone, Charles M., 119
First Amendment (Freedom of Speech), 105–106, 311–312, 313
Fischer, Claude, 116, 129, 131, 330
Fisher, R. J., and J. E. Katz, 149
Flanagin, A., and M. Metzger, 217–218
Flink, J., 330
Florida Presidential re-vote, 182–183
Forbes, Malcolm Steve, 151, 178
Forrester Reports, 33, 37
Foucault, Michel, 272
Fragmented self in postmodern theory, 265–266, 267, 269, 271, 280
Francalanci, G., 306
Franzen, A., 221–222
Freedom, 105, 106, 272
of speech (First Amendment), 105–106, 311–312, 313
Friendship
communication with friends via the Internet, 209, 247, *258*, 258–259, *404–408*
Internet viewed as beneficial to, 215
online friendships, 13, 165, 211, *229*, 230, 232–233, 242, 246–247, 248, 252, *253*, 285, *380* (*see also* Virtual relationship)

Friendship (cont.)
offline friendships, *236–237*, 238–239, *248*
reunions online, 211

Gambling online, 333, *401*
Games on the Internet. *See also* Leisure involvement online
fantasy gaming Web sites, 191–193, 332
game creation online, 308–309
online gamers, 214
online/offline (blended) interactions, 192–193, 194, 195
real-time interactive games, *250*
Gandy, O., Jr., 24, 25, 272
Garfinkel, H., 266
Garrett Rural Information Cooperative (GRIC), 85–86
Garson, B., 18
Gartner Group, 294
Gatekeeping intermediaries, 108, 115, 335
Gay Internet venues, 88–89, 172, 184
Geertz, Clifford, 370
GenConnect, *169*
Gender, 30–31, 111–113, *389–390, 396. See also* Women and the Internet
developers predominantly male, 25–26, 36
information seeking behavior, 31, 147
media use and online interaction by, 232
and personal homepages, 299
political involvement and, 147, 148, 223
predicting Internet use, *52–53, 54, 54*
of U.S. Census respondents vs. survey sample, 361(app.A.1)
of users vs. nonusers across survey years, *40*, 41, *44–45, 49–50, 51,* 53

Gender gap
decline in, 21, 29, *55, 62, 63, 64, 65,* 322
Genealogy resources, 168, *169*
General Social Survey, 112, 124
Gergen, Kenneth, *The Saturated Self,* 265–266, 270, 280, 282, 353
Gilens, M., 335
Gillespie, A., and K. Robins, 19
Global aspect. *See* International aspects of the Internet
Goffman, E., 266
Goldsmith, S., 2
Government. *See* Citizen-government contact; United States government
Greenfield, David N., 193
Greenman, C., 165
Griffith, Jeremiah, 95
Group isolation (overcoming), 86
Guiliani, Rudolph, 313
Gumpert, G., 272, 277
Gurak, L., 109–110
Gurstein, M., 127
Guzman, Debra, 177
Gyaw, Htun Aung, 125

"Habitus," 28
Haddam, J., 2
Haddon, L., 27
Half-Life mod community, 309
Hampton, K., 126
Handicapped. *See* Disabled persons
Harassment, 199
Harcourt, W., 222–223
Hate groups or online hatred, 107, 177–178, 207, 313–314
Hayne, S., and R. Rice, 271, 272
Health-related use of the Internet, *398, 400*
disease-related support networks, 97–98, 123, 128, 163–164, 172, 222
information Web sites and searching, 31, 33, 208
listservs, 121–122
Hennig, Wanda, 2

Herring, S., 36
Hill, K. A., and J. Hughes, 104, 105, 107–108, 111, 176, 223
Hiltz, S. R., and M. Turoff, 103
Hispanics and the Internet. *See also* Race or ethnicity
Hispanic community Web sites, 123, 185
levels and types of access, 26, 32–33, 321, 364
personal reports of benefits, 222
Hoaxes, 121, 187. *See also* Legitimacy or authenticity issues
Hobbies and Internet use, 186, *400*
Hoffman, Donna, 221
Holland, Lou, 2
Homeless peoples' shelters, 88
HomeNet study, 204–205, 220–222, 328, 329
Homosexual Internet venues, 88–89, 172, 184
Howard, P., L. Rainie, and S. Jones, xviii, 31–32, 32
Human identity project, 315–317, 341–342. *See also* Self-identity
Human memory, 315–317
Human Rights Information Network, 177
Hundt, R., 108

Identity project, 315–317, 341–342. *See also* Self-identity
Illusory or false identities, 187, 206–207, 223
Image transmission
photos of family and friends, 210
Income (household), *391–392, 396*
and the digital divide, 22, 23–24, 32, 322, 323–324
low-income families, 88, 95
media use and, *245*
media use and online interaction by, *232*
and political involvement, 147
sociability indicators and, *237*
social interaction and, *245*

of U.S. Census respondents vs. survey sample, 361(app.A.1), 363(app.A.2)
of users vs. nonusers across survey years, *40*, 43, *44–45*, 48, *49–50*, *51*, *52–53*, 53, *54*, 54, 62, *64*
Indiana University survey, 190
Indian diasporic Web sites, 123
Individual. *See also* Personal interests; Self-expression; Self-identity; Self-presentation
as socially situated, 278–279, 298–299
Information over the Internet. *See also* Political information over the Internet
diversity of, 345
filtering programs, 106, 115, 122
information surplus, 105
metadata and classification utilities, 347
profiling programs, 273, 314, 315
self-organizing potential of, 349, 350–351, 354
sharing of, 122–123, 129, 224
Information seeking and retrieval, 214, 215, 217, *257*, 398–340, 417–418. *See also* Political information over the Internet
access to, 84, 86
genealogy resources, 168, 168, *169*
health-related, 31, 33, 208 (*see also* Health-related use of the Internet)
historical archives, 189
job-seeking online, 31, *398*
as a motive for using the Internet, *55, 56, 58, 59*
news groups, 122
type of and demographic factors, 31, 32
vs. active involvement, 180
Information superhighway, 24, *373*
Innovativeness, *236–237*, 238
sociability indicators and, *237, 248*
Instant messaging (IM) services, 309

Instant messaging (IM) technology, 205, 208, 211, 212, 269, 293. *See also* Chatrooms
Intel-United Devices Cancer Research Project, 197
Interaction. *See* Social interaction
Interactive media, 116
Intermittent community, 119
International aspects of the Internet access differences and the digital divide, 29–30, 34, 91
inflammatory speech concerns, 313–314
transnational activism, 125–126, 223
International treaty to ban landmines, 334
Internet connectedness index (ICI), 28–29
Internet dropouts. *See* Dropouts
Internetnews (2000), 217
Internet paradox, 331
Internet persona, 223, 267
Internet service providers (ISTs), 211 for remote areas, 85–86
Internet as a social technology, 337, 339–340, 343, 344–347. *See also* Boundaries; Communication; Information over the Internet
connectivity with little cost, 349–350
enabling public image trialability, 120–121, 207, 349–350
a normative framework for assessing, 348–353
overcoming physical boundaries, 120, 125–126, 129 (*see also* Cyberspace)
social construction approach to assessing, 266, 269, 270
sociocultural traits of designers, 25–26
Internet technology features, 132, 161–163, 345
asynchronous distributed dialogue, 269

convergence and processing, 346–347
critical mass and positive network externalities, 83, 350
filtering capability, 106, 115, 122
interactivity, 116
instant transmission, 205, 208, 211, 212, 269, 293
metadata and classification utilities, 347
personal broadcasting capability, 269, 270–271
Internet usage. *See also* access; Long-term vs. short-term users; Motivations for using the Internet; Users vs. nonusers of the Internet
awareness of the Internet and, 35, 49–50, 50, 51, 52–53, 54, 54–55
by type of use. *See* Information seeking; Information-seeking; Self-presentation; Social interaction online
"Falling Through the Net" surveys, 3
growth in, 38, 38–39, 39
household use and murder rate, 339–340, 340
household use in U.S., 17–18, 21–22, 27
international access differences, 29–30, 34, 91
predictors of, 35, 52–53, 53, 54, 54–55
studies of, xvii–xviii, 17, 26, 28, 30–34 (*see also* National study of the Internet; *and by study*)
time spent online, 61, 375–376, 397
Investigation services online, 292–293
"Invisible mouse" effect, 13, 161, 162, 295, 351–352, 354
Ipsos-Reid study, 29
Irving, Larry, 208
Isolated areas, Internet access efforts of, 85–86
Isolation. *See* Social isolation
Issues in assessing the Internet's consequences, 1–6

a normative framework for assessing the technology, 348–353

James, M., C. Wotring, and E. Forrest, 216
Jenkins, H., 303
Jensen, J., 116
Jobs. *See* Employment; Workplace
Joe Arluck, 316
John Birch Society, 176–177
Johnson, L., 178, 314
Johnson, S., 122, 207, 224
Jones, S., 115, 122
Jordan, T., 208
Jung, J.-J., Qiu, J., and Kim, Y., 28–29
Jupiter Communications study (2000), 30, 193, 218

Kac, Eduardo, "Uirapuru," 306
Kalton, G., 360
Kamarck, E., and J. Nye, 180
Kanaley, R., 308
Kapor, M., 108
Kareau, Steve, 86, 88
Katz, James E., 93, 116, 131, 151, 182, 279, 330, 336
Katz, James E., and M. Aakhus, 34, 321
Katz, James E., and P. Aspden, 18, 36
Katz, James E., P. Aspden, and W. Reich, 174, 360
Katz, James E., and Ronald E. Rice, xx–xxii, *338*. *See also* National study of the Internet
Katz, James E., Ronald E. Rice, and P. Aspden, 23, 30, 210
Katz, James E., and E. Wynn, 97
Kayany, J., and P. Yelsma, 216
Keeter, S., 360
Kellner, D., 13
KidsCom Company study, 218
KinderView, 169–170
Kish, Leslie, 360
Klein, P., 298–299
Knowledge networks, 99

Kollock, P., 128–129
Kraut, Robert E., 28, 193, 220
Kraut, Robert E., et al., xvii, 10, 155, 331, 369
HomeNet study, 204–205, 220–222, 328, 329
Krim, J., 206
Kubey, R., J. Lavin, and J. Burrows, 206
Kuwabara, K., 310

Lansing, J., and J. Morgan, 360
LaRose, R., M. Eastin, and J. Gregg, 220–221
Lee, Minh ("Gooseman"), 309
Left-wing or liberal Web sites, 174–175, 177
Legitimacy or authenticity issues, 7, 104, 105–106, 206–207, 275, 311
Leibowitz, S., and S. Margolis, 83
Leisure involvement offline
of Internet users vs. nonusers, *156–157*, *158*, 158–159, *159*, 160
Leisure involvement online, 186, *383*. *See also* Games on the Internet
entertainment seeking, 217, *253*
fantasy sports teams Web sites, 189–190
hobbies, 186, *400*
Levy, P., 223–225
Liberal individualism, 113–114
Liberal or leftist Web sites, 174–175, 177
Lievrouw, L. A., 18
Limbaugh, Rush, 313
Linux, 310
Listservs, 114
health-related, 121–122
Literature and poetry Web sites, 302, 304–305
Loader, B., 113
Local community involvement. *See* Community involvement
London, neighborhood network in, 127

Loneliness or isolation, 86, 206, 220–
    221, 325, 331
Long-term vs. short-term users, 323,
    374–375, 397
  demographic differences of, 28–29,
    58, 63
  motivations for using the Internet,
    58, 59–60, 61
  overall media use by, 230
  political involvement of, 142, 147
  sociability indicators and, 235, 236–
    237, 247, 251
Lorber, L., 328
Low-income cultures, 323
Low-income families, 88, 95
Low income neighborhoods
  public housing access, 88, 95, 127

Magazines. See Print media
    consumption
Majestic game, 193, 194, 195
Margolis, M., and D. Resnick, 108,
    113
Mari, 305
Marital status, 63, 64
  political activity and, 140, 141
  of users vs. nonusers, 46, 47
  of U.S. Census respondents vs.
    survey sample, 361(app.A.1),
    363(app.A.2)
Markle Foundation survey, 206
Markus, M. L., 275
Marriage partners. See also Dating
  arranged marriages via the Internet,
    291–293
  mail-order bride services online,
    292
Martian Craters research, 197–198
Marvin, C., 283
Mass media. See Media
Match.com, 286, 288
McChesney, R., 108
McConnaughey, J., 19, 21, 30
McDermott, Trish, 286
McKenna, K., and J. Bargh, 204
McNutt, J., 19, 20

Media, 25. See also Communication
    technologies; Media use
  disintermediation, 115
  gatekeeping intermediaries, 108, 115,
    335
  interactive media, 116 (see also
    Communication technologies)
  Internet impacts on traditional, 105–
    106, 108, 150
  mediated communication, 224, 268–
    269
  mediated identity, 268
  mediated relationship, 116–117,
    120
  media uses and gratifications
    approach, 36–37, 217
Media Metrix, 216
Media system dependency approach,
    28
Media use, 216. See also Television
    viewing
  demographic data and, 230–234,
    396–397
  overall use by long-term vs. short-
    term Internet users, 230
  political use of, 136, 136–137, 138–
    139, 138–139
  print media consumption, 150, 216–
    217, 255
  radio listening, 216
  sociability differences and, 242–243,
    256–257
  type of and level of Internet use,
    216–219, 230–231, 230–234
Medical information. See Health-
    related use of the Internet
Mele, C., 127
Memorial Web sites and mourning on
    the Internet, 315–316, 317
Mentoring and tutoring Web sites,
    164–165
Merton, R., 353
Metadata, 347
Methodology, 357(app.A). See also
    National study of the Internet
  national telephone surveys, 357

Quantitative and qualitative
approaches, 368
random samples, 358, 368
site samples (non-random), 369–371
statistical analyses, 365–368
survey limitations, 360, 362, 364
telephone surveys, 357–358
Microsoft-Europe, 108
Miller, T., and P. Clemente, 217
Minitel, 170
Minnesota E-Democracy Project, 114
Mitra, A., 123
Mobile phone, 36–37, 252, 254, 294, 352
"Mods" (games created online), 308–309
MOOs (object-oriented MUDS), 124, 208, 267
Moral economy, 131
Morino Institute Report, 96
Moses, T., 2
Motivations for using the Internet, 55
e-mail, 56, 58, 59
of long-term vs. short-term users, 58, 59–60, 61
nonusers and users describing, 55, 56–57, 58, 343–344
perceived uses, 91–94, 92
perceptions of usefulness, 91–94, 92
of recent vs. long-term users, 55, 59–60, 61
social contact, 55, 56, 58, 59, 322
to gain information on personal interests, 55, 56, 58, 59, 322
MUDs (multiuser domains), 124, 125, 208, 267, 271, 305
Mueller, M., 33
Mukerji, C., and B. Simon, 120, 121
Multimedia trend of the Internet, 305–308, 349
Music on the Internet. *See also* Art on the Internet
fan clubs, 189
Karaoke singing online, 307–308
musicians' sites and downloading, 32, 89–91, *401*

music production Web sites, 307
Mystery games (online/offline), 192–193, 194, 195

National Aeronautics and Space Administration (NASA), 197–198
National Geographic Society Web site, 212
National Mentoring Partnership, 165
National Science Board, 17, 21
National study of the Internet, xvii–xxii. *See also* Katz, James E., and Ronald E. Rice
demographic data and descriptive statistics, 372(app.B.1)
demographics compared to U.S. Census data, *363–364*
methods. *See* Methodology
survey limitations, 360, 362, 364
Negroponte, N., 343, 344
Neighborhood
contact with neighbors, 235, *236–237*
motivations for choosing, 120, 132
Net generation (N-Gen), 213, 215
Netville, 126
Networks, 121, 221–222. *See also* Community networks; Disabled persons' access
critical mass and positive externalities of, 83, 350
feminist networking, 222–223
health or disease-related support networks, 97–98, 123, 128, 163–164, 172, 222
Internet as the network of networks, 343, 347–348
personal social networks, 170–171
SeniorNet Web network, 124, 222
support networks, 97–98, 163–164, 184
for youth, 184
Neu, C. R., R. H. Anderson, and T. K. Bikson, 20, 25, 107
Neuman, W. Russell, 106, 150
News groups online, 122

Newspapers. *See* Print media
consumption
New technologies. *See* Communica-
tion technologies
New York Echo, 120, 125
N-Gen (Net generation), 213, 215
Nielsen/NetRatings reports, 17, 29–
30, 31
Nie, Norman, 10, 155, 331
Nie, Norman and Erbring, L., 205
Noah Group, 95
Noll, A. M., *Highway of Dreams*, 9
Nonusers, 21–23, 38. *See also*
Dropouts; Users vs. nonusers of the
Internet
Norris, P., 179–180
Novice vs. expert. *See* Skill-level on
the Internet

Obstacles to use of the Internet, *379*
of recent vs. long-term users, *59–60*
Odyssey study, 218–219
Oettinger, A., 344
Offline social interaction. *See* Social
interaction offline
Older persons and the Internet, 27–
28, 171. *See also* Age cohort
influences
citizen-government contact, 20
SeniorNet Web network, 222
OnLine (1996), 205
Online communities. *See* Virtual
communities
Online games. *See* Games on the
Internet
Online interaction. *See* Social
interaction online
Online/offline (blended) interactions
community networks, 119, 125–
128
community networks (online/offline
networks), 119, 125–128
creating Internet access, 85–86, 98–
99
family online communication, 210,
211–213, 229, *232*, 239, 245, 247,

252, *253, 258*, 258–259, 263, *381,
404–408*
Internet complementing offline
interactions, 132–133, 209–210,
326
Internet gaming and, 192–193, 194,
195
online communication with friends,
247, *258*, 258–259, *404–408*
political activities, 135–136, *136–
137*, 138, *138–139*
reunions online, 211
virtual relationships becoming face-
to-face, 329 (*see also* Dating)
Online voting, 105, 336
Opportunity structure, 343–344,
353–354
Oral histories, 316, 317, 318
Overloaded (feeling), *232–233, 384–
385*
users vs. nonusers, *48, 55*, 228
Overpersonalization danger
filtering programs, 106, 115, 122
profiling, 273, 314, 315
selective exposure to information,
106
Oxford University, 197

Pacific Islanders, 21
Parks, M., and K. Floyd, 204
Parks, M., and L. Roberts, 209
Party politics. *See also* Election
campaigns
Democratic campaign Web sites,
175–176, 333
Republican campaign Web sites, 178,
179, 180–181, 333
People with disabilities. *See* Disabled
persons
Perceived usefulness of the Internet
and access interest, 91
Perse, E., and D. Dunn, 216
Personal broadcasting feature of the
Internet, 269
public image experimentation and
trialability, 120–121, 207, 349–350

Personal digital assistants (PDAs), 294
Personal homepages, *247, 250,*
  265(ch. 12), 277
  gender and, 299
  integrated self-presentation through,
  277–278, 281–282
  motives for, 299
  social contexts and shared
  experiences in, 278–279, 298–299
Personal interests, 55, 56, 58, *59*
  and Internet access, 88
  pursuit of as a motive for Internet
  use, 55, 56, 58, *59*
  personal communities, 119
Personalization of news, 106
Personal and professional boundary,
  272, 278–279
Pew Internet and American Life
  Project
research, xviii, 31–32, 153, 216, 327,
  359
  survey of religious information, 295–
  296
Pew Research Center (2000) data, *396*
  analyses of, 219–220, 330
  demographic factors and Internet
  use, 30–31, 62, 64, *396*
  types of Internet use, 32, *63*
Pew Research Center (2000) study
  findings, 17, 61, 180, 254, 333–334
  on benefits of e-mail, 209
  on family contact online, 211–212
  on media use overall and Internet
  use, 254, *256–257, 255, 256–259,
  260,* 261
  on offline friendships and Internet
  use, 254, *256–257*
  on political involvement and Internet
  use, 146–149, 150
  on sociability on Internet use, 254,
  256–257, 255, 256–259, 260, 261
  on social interaction and Internet
  use, 254, *256–257, 255, 256–259,
  260,* 261
  users vs. nonusers, 61–62, *63*
Phonographs, 130–131

Pidgeon, Billy, 193
Plagiarism, 7
Poetry and literature Web sites, 302,
  304–305
Political activity or expression online,
  106–108, 109, 136, 148, 310, 325.
  See also Election campaigns
  demographic factors and, 104
  antigovernment efforts, 122, 125,
  333
  chatrooms, 104, 107, 148
  regarding Internet issues, 36, 109–
  110
Political activity offline
  demographic factors and, *131, 143*
  general media use, 136, *136–137,*
  138–139, *138–139*
  of users and nonusers, 112–113,
  131, 143
Political information over the Internet,
  144, 145, 146, *147,* 147–148
  electronic town meetings, 113
  policy-specific information, 335
  public conferencing, 120
  vs. other media, *400*
Political involvement and Internet use,
  103, 182, 310
  demographic factors influencing,
  111, 147–148
  dystopian perspective on, 104–108
  extent of political awareness, 142,
  144, 145, 146, *147*
  Internet complementing traditional
  politics, 332–333
  of Internet users vs. nonusers, 139–
  140, *141,* 142
  limits of Internet mobilization, 178–
  183, 333–335
  long-term vs. short-term users, 142,
  147
  online/offline (blended) interactions,
  135–136, *136–137,* 138, *138–139*
  Pew 2000 findings on, 146–149,
  150
  syntopian perspective, 149–151
  utopian perspective on, 108–110

Political parties. *See* Election campaigns
Political profiling and databases, 314–315
Political use of media, 136, *136–137*, 138–139, *138–139*
Political values, 334
Political Web sites, 113, 114, 151, 174, 175, 181, 333, 334
  Democratic campaign Web sites, 175–176
  left-wing or liberal Web sites, 174–175, 177
  online petitions, 310–311
  parody and attack sites, 312–313
  political game sites, 191
  Republican campaign Web sites, 178, 179, 180–181
  right-wing sites, 104, 111, 176–178, 313, 313–314
Pool, I. de Sola, 121
Pornography
  child pornography, 7
  on the Internet, 207
Porter, D., Ed., 209
Portes, A., and P. Landolt, 336
Postal mail survey, 33
Poster, M., 265
Postmodernism. *See also by author*
  boundaries and, 268–270
  the fragmented self, 265–266, 267, 269, 271, 280
  issues involved and counter examples, 271–272 (*see also* Anonymity; Privacy; Self-presentation)
Postrel, Virginia, 305
Praying over the Internet, 296–297
Presidential election (2000), 312
  Florida re-vote, 182–183
Presidential Town Hall Meeting, 113
Print media consumption *See also* Anonymity
  Internet use and, 150, 216–217, *255*
Privacy, 7, 103–105, 115, *145*, 146
  privacy policies of Web sites, 273

Profiling, 273, 314, 315
Protein folding research, 196
Protest events network, 174, 175
Pseudocommunity, 115–116, 120, 324
Pseudoreality, 10
Public access, 19, 34, 88, 95
Public conferencing, 120
Public-goods aspect of the Internet, 224, 345
Public housing access, 88, 95, 127
Public image experimentation and trialability, 120–121, 207, 349–350
Public and private boundary, 270, 271, 272, 277–278
Punday, D., 267
Putnam, Robert, 331
  Bowling Alone, 9, 116–117, 331
  on the Internet and social capital, 153, 155, 158
  social-capital index, 337, *339*, 339
  social capital model of, 132, 162, 329, 331–332, 337, *338*t
Pyramid marketing, 200

Quake, 308

Race or ethnicity, 21, 112, *393*, *396*.
  See also African Americans and the Internet; Asian Americans and the Internet; Hispanics and the Internet
  awareness of the Internet and, 55
  community involvement and, *156–157*
  digital divide persistent but declining, 25, 26–27, 62, *63*, *64*, *65*, 206–207, 322
  Indian diasporic Web sites, 123
  media use and online interaction by, *232*
  political involvement, 148
  racism, 314
  types of Internet use and, 32–33
  of U.S. Census respondents vs. survey sample, 361(app.A.1), 362(app.A.1), 363(app.A.2)

of users vs. nonusers across survey
years, *40*, 43, *44–45*, *49–50*, *51*,
52–53, *53*, *54*
Radio listening and Internet use,
216
Rakow, L., 36
Rash, W., 109
Reagan, J., 216
Real-time transmission feature of the
Internet, 205, 208, 211, 212, 269
Real and virtual boundary, 269–270,
271
Recreation. *See* Leisure involvement
online
Reid, Ipsos, 91
Relationship
hyperpersonal relations, 121–122
mediated relationships, 116–117,
120, 132–133
online friendships, 13, 165, 211,
229, *230*, *232–233*, *242*, 246–247,
248, 252, *253*, 285, *380*
trust and online relationships, 294–
295
virtual relationships becoming face-
to-face, 329
virtual relationships as secondary,
124–125, 324
virtual relationships as secondary or
inauthentic (assertion and
response), 124–125, 204, 206, 324,
329
Relationship. *See* Sociability
Religious community organizational
involvement
of users vs. nonusers, *156–157*, *158*,
158–159, *159*, 160
Religious involvement online
online religious interaction, 31, 223,
382, *402*
religious Web sites, 183, 185, 186,
223, 295–296, 297
Religious self-expression, 296–298
confessions over the Internet, 297–
298
praying over the Internet, 296–297

Republican campaign Web sites, 178,
179, 180–181, 333
Resch, Mark, 1
Residency factors, *392*
home ownership or rental, 43, *46–
47*, *49–50*, *53*, *54*
rural vs. urban residency, 21
Reuters, 333
health study, 172–174
Rheingold, Howard, 8, 114
Rice, Ronald E., 115, 120, 207, 208.
See also National study of the
Internet
Rice, Ronald E., M. McCreadie, and
S.-J. Chang, 86, 351
Right-wing sites, 104, 111, 176–178,
313, 313–314
Riphagen, J., and A. Kanfer, 209–210
Robinson, John, 112, 124
Robinson, John, K. Barth, and A.
Kohut, 216
Robinson, Mary, 314
Rojas, V., et al., 27
Role-playing games (RPG), 192–193
Romance, 301. *See also* Dating
online communication with partners,
258
Romances online, 301
Roper Starch Cyberstudy, 170
Rosen, L., and M. Weil, 36
Rural areas
Internet access efforts of, 84, 85–86
vs. urban residency and the digital
divide, 21
Rwanda violence, 183

San Francisco Bay Area network
(WELL), 120, 125, 222
Satisfaction ratings, *386–387*, *396*
media use and online interaction
and, *232–233*, 254
of users vs. nonusers, 43, *48*, 53–54,
54, 55, 228
Schegloff, E., 266
Schement, Jorge, 114
Scherer, K., 205–206

Scholes, Robert J., 292
School Web sites, 311–312. *See also*
   Student Internet users
Schroeder, K., and J. Ledger, 205, 206
Schutz, A., 266
Screen-access technologies, 87
Search for Extraterrestrial Intelligence
   (SETI), 196
Selective exposure to information
   filtering, 106, 115, 122
   profiling, 273, 314, 315
Self-efficacy, 221
Self-expression, 265, 295, 317–318
   blogs, 299, 300
   leading to social interaction, 298
   religious, 296–298
Self-identity, 13, 266, 271, 282, 315,
   317
   distributed identity, 268
   embodied vs. virtual domains of,
      268, 282–283
   the fragmented self perspective, 265–
      266, 267, 269, 271, 280
   historical, 268
   the saturated self perspective, 265–
      266, 270, 280, 282
   youth identity development, 215
Self-presentation. *See also* Personal
   homepages
   experimentation with and trialability,
      120–121, 207, 349–350
   as the expression of identity, 1(ch. 1),
      4, 265(ch. 12), 285, 295, 315, 317
   integration of through distributed
      contexts, 277–278, 279–281
   Internet persona, 223, 267
   misrepresentations in, 187, 206–207,
      223
Senft, T., 88
SeniorNet Web network, 124, 222
Seniors. *See* Older persons and the
   Internet
Settlement houses, 88
Sex. *See* Gender
Sexuality and the Internet. *See also*
   Dating; Marriage partners

gay Internet venues, 88–89, 172,
   184
online eroticism, 223 (*see also*
   Pornography)
sexual encounters, 88–89, 172
Shapiro, A., and R. Leone, 106, 115,
   127, 205
Single parent households study, 27
Sink, M., 170
Skill-level on the Internet, *233, 251,*
   376–377
   media use by level of, *230–231,*
      230–234
Skog, B., 13
Slack, R. S., and R. A. Williams, 125
Smith, Adam, 13, 162
Smith, M., and P. Kollock, 116
Sociability. *See also* Community
   involvement; Friendship; Social
   interaction
   indicators of, 227–228, *229, 235,*
      236–237, 237–239, 240–243, 263–
      264, 265(ch. 12)
   of long-term vs. short-term users,
      235, 236–237, 247, *251*
   sense of belonging, *244,* 249, *250–*
      251
   social skills, 222
Social capital, 183, 199–200, 342. *See*
   also Internet as a social technology;
   Social impact of the Internet
   creation of, 191, 224, 310, 331–332
   Internet as an indicator of, 337,
      339–340
   Internet contributing to, 319(ch. 14),
      321, 327, 328–329, 343, 352, 353
   network advantages, 83
   Putnam's model of, 153, 155, 158
   theory of, 162, 336, *338,* 353
   traditional forms of supplemented by
      the Internet, 329–330
Social-capital index (Putnam), 337,
   339, 339
Social class. *See* Educational level;
   Income (household); Race or
   ethnicity; Residency factors

Social construction approach, 266, 269, 270

Social context, Internet as a, 278–279, 298–299

Social creativity, 208, 341
creation of social capital, 191, 224, 310, 331–332

Social desirability bias in survey responses, 136, 149

Social exclusion, 27

Social impact of the Internet, *40*, 326–328, 353–354. *See also* Dystopian perspective; Internet as a social technology; Social capital; Syntopian perspective; Utopian perspective
impact on traditional media, 105–106, 108, 150
issues basic to assessing, 1–6
negative aspects, 342–343
personal assessments of, *144, 259, 260–261, 261, 262, 382, 407–409*
transformation potential, 223–225

Social interaction, 203(ch.10), 227(ch.11), 236–237. *See also* Online/offline (blended) inter-actions; Sociability
demographic factors influencing Internet uses for, 210
the dystopian perspective of Internet impact on, 204–207, 224, 325–326
the syntopian perspective, 225
types and levels of use of the Internet for, 210–211
the utopian perspective of Internet impact on, 207–210, 326

Social interaction offline, 261, 263, *397*
Internet use and, 219–220
organizational involvement, 53, *54, 156–157, 158, 159*, 162–163
of users vs. nonusers, 112, *244, 245*

Social interaction online, 221–222, 239, 247, *248, 249, 253*, 261. *See also* Chatrooms; E-mail; Networks; Virtual communities

communication with friends, 209, 247, *258, 258–259, 404–408* (*see also* Friendship)
emotional support, 187
length and type of Internet use and, 263–264
as a motive for using the Internet, 55, *56*, 58, *59*
as parasocial interaction, 116
and sociability, 247, *248*, 249, *250–251*
unusual interests served by, 186, 196, 197–198

Social isolation, 86, 206, 220–221, 325, 331

Social-opportunity structure, 343–344, 353–354

Social skills, 222

Social technology, xix. *See also* Internet as a social technology

Software development, 310

Spam, 200

Spears, R., and M. Lea, 272

Special needs. *See* Disabled persons access

Spillovers. *See* Online/offline (blended) interactions

Spirituality, 223, 344. *See also* Religious self-expression

Spooner, T., and L. Rainie, 32

Sproull, L., and S. Faraj, 203

Spyware, 273

Stafford, L., S. Kline, and J. Dimmick, 210

Stalking, 198–199
electronic stalking, 207, 223

Standards for the Internet, 348–353

Stanford University online research program on proteins, 196

Stanley, J., 283

Starobin, P., 105

Statistical analyses, 365–368

Status indicators, 267, 268

Stefik, M., 130

Stein, Andrew, 301

Stokley, N., 166, 302

Stoll, C., *Silicon Snake Oil*, 9–10, 204
Stone, A., *The War of Desire and Technology*, 122, 265, 271, 280
Stone, B., 286, 287, 293
Storck, Don, 86
Straus, S., 209
Stress, 221
  feeling overloaded, *232–233, 384–385*
  feeling overloaded and Internet use, *48, 55*, 228
  feeling worn out, *244*
  friendships stressed, *408*
Stringer, H., 193
Student Internet users, 213–214, 227, 228. *See also* School Web sites
  academic performance and, 205–206
  online dating, 286, *286*
Student Press Law Center (SPLC), 311–312
Sullivan, Andrew, 305
Sunstein, C., 24, 124
Support networks, 164, *165*
  disability-related, 184, 222
  health or disease-related, 97–98, 123, 128, 163–164, 172, 222
Surfing. *See* Entertainment seeking; Information seeking and retrieval
Surveys of Internet use. *See* National study of the Internet; *and by study*
Survey response biases, 136, 149
Symposium on emerging media and the First Amendment, 105
Syntopian perspective
  community involvement and Internet use, 132–133, 199–200, 325
  on the impact of the Internet, 13–14, 186, 282, 321(ch.14), 323–324, 354
  on political involvement and Internet use, 149–151
  regarding access to the Internet, 13, 34, 65, 99, 322–324
  on social interaction and Internet use, 225

the Syntopian project, xx–xxii (*see also* National study of the Internet)

Taliban, banning of the Internet, 333
TalktoGov Web site, 178–179
Tapscott, D., 23–24, 213–214, 218
Taylor, C., 302
Technologies of connection. *See* Communication technologies; Internet as a social technology
Teens. *See* Youth and the Internet
Telecommunications Act, 34
Telecommunications services. *See* Cellular phone; Telephone
Telecommuting, 130, 309
Teledemocracy. *See* Electronic democracy
Telephone, 33, 116, 129, 283, 330, 352. *See also* Communication technologies
  cellular phone, 36–37, 252, 254, 294, 352
Television viewing. *See also* Media use
  and Internet use, 205, 216–217, 218, *245*, 326
  social impact of, 130
Terry, J., and M. Calvert, 222
Tiananmen Square violence, 183
Times Mirror survey, 111–112, 211
Tolerance for diversity, 107, 111–112, 223
  intolerance, 313–314 (*see also* Hate groups)
Toronto
  Netville community network, 126
Torvalds, Linus Benedict, 310
Town meetings over the Internet, 113
Tracking of Internet use, 273, 314, 315
Transparency of association, 349
Trialability and image experimentation, 120–121, 207, 349–350
Trust
  Internet use and, 219–220
  and online relationships, 294–295

Tufekcioglu, Z., 30
Turkle, Sherry, 9, 124–125, 207, 265, 266, 268, 269, 270, 271, 280
ethnographic study of a computer community, 208–209
Turner, J., J. Grube, and J. Meyers, 121
TV. *See* Television viewing; Web TV

UCLA Center for Community Policy Study (2000), 17, 21–22, 23, 112, 212–213
"Uirapuru" (Kac), 306
Ultima Online, 192
Uncapher, W., 127
Unequal access argument, 6, 7, 8, 19–20, 20, 83–84, 104, 322. *See also* Digital divide
United Nations, 314
United States government. *See also* Census Bureau (U.S.)
Department of Commerce, 19, 208
Department of Defense employees' battle clan, 192
Department of Housing and Urban Development (HUD), 95
University of California
UCLA Center for Community Policy Study (2000), 17, 21–22, 23, 112, 212–213
University of Minnesota Web site, 168
Unusual interests, 186, 196, 197–198
Use of the Internet. *See* Internet usage
Usenet, 114, 122–123, 310
Users vs. nonusers of the Internet, *374*
contact with neighbors, 235, *236–237*
demographic factors and, *38, 38, 39, 40, 40, 44–45*, 48, *49–50, 50, 51, 52–53, 53–55, 54, 63*
family-related factors and, *46, 47*
media use by, *244*
print media exposure of, *255*
social interaction of, 112, *244, 245*
Uses and gratifications approach, 36–37, 217. *See also* Media

Uses of the Internet. *See* Motivations for using the Internet
Uslaner, E., 219, 330
Utopian perspective, xix
Utopian perspective, 2, 11–12, *12*, 30
access to the Internet is improving, 30 (*see also* Digital Divide; Gender; Race or ethnicity)
community enhanced/new social forms created, 119–120, 324 (*see also* Social creativity; Virtual community)
political involvement enhanced, 108–110
online social interaction extending sociability, 207–210, 223–224, 326 (*see also* Networks; Online/offline interactions)

Van Dijk, J., 24, 25, 105, 117, 209
Varoli, J., 292
Veterans online networks, 171–172
Victimization, 207
Vinroot, Richard, campaign Web site, 179
Virnoche, M., and G. Marx, 119, 126
Virtual communities, 114–115, 117, 222, 252, *253*, 320–330, 342, *381*. *See also* Games on the Internet; MUDs (multiuser domains); Networks
affirmation groups, 171–172
clans and tournaments between, 192–193
ethnic virtual communities, 123, 184, 185
long term Internet use and, *230*
percent of users in, *232–234, 245–246*
as pseudocommunities, 115–116, 120, 124–125, 324
Virtual-issue constituencies, 108
Virtual reality, 224, 270
Virtual relationship. *See also* Friendship
as secondary or inauthentic, 124–125, 204, 206, 324, 329

Virtual social space, 109–110
Virtual town meetings, 113
Voluntary interaction, 350
Voting behavior
  by demographics, *131, 143*
  of users and nonusers, *131, 143*

Wallace, P., 222
Wall, L., 267–268
Walsh, E., M. Gazala, and C. Ham, 33
Walther, J., 121
WebCams, 169–170, 298–302
  WebCam Web sites, 301–302
Webdiaries, 299
Web TV, 205
Well-being. *See* Feeling overloaded; Satisfaction ratings
Wellman, B., 29, 117, 119, 121
Wellman, B., and M. Gulia, 119, 129
WELL (Whole Earth Lectronic Link), 120, 125, 222
White, C. S., 104
Williams, Jody, 334, 335
Winner, L., 131
Women and the Internet. *See also* Gender
  all-women battle clans, 192
  international networks and empowerment, 223
  online communities, 129, 184
Working Assets, 182
Workplace. *See also* Employment
  coworker communication, 19–20, 279
  distributed workplace potential, 309
  productivity costs issue, 9
  telecommuting, 130, 309
Wright, C., 38
Wynn, E., and J. E. Katz, 277

Yahoo!News, 30
Year Two Thousand (2000) survey
  additional variables, *240–243*
Young, J., 205
Youth and the Internet

AOL study of, 111
identity development and the Internet, 215
information seeking, 218–219
Internet use and, 206, 215
the Net generation (N-Gen), 213, 215
online friendships, 212
online networks for, 184

Zaler, J., *335*
Zapatistas, 333
Zeller, S., 175
Zieschang, K., 360